Theraplay

Second Edition

Ann M. Jernberg

Phyllis B. Booth

Theraplay
Second Edition

Helping Parents and Children Build
Better Relationships Through
Attachment-Based Play

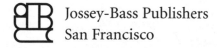
Jossey-Bass Publishers
San Francisco

Published by

JOSSEY-BASS
A Wiley Company
350 Sansome St.
San Francisco, CA 94104

www.josseybass.com

Copyright © 2001 by John Wiley & Sons, Inc.

Jossey-Bass is a registered trademark of John Wiley & Sons, Inc.

Jossey-Bass books and products are available through most bookstores. To contact Jossey-Bass directly, call (888) 378-2537, fax to (800) 605-2665, or visit our website at www.josseybass.com.

Substantial discounts on bulk quantities of Jossey-Bass books are available to corporations, professional associations, and other organizations. For details and discount information, contact the special sales department at Jossey-Bass.

We at Jossey-Bass strive to use the most environmentally sensitive paper stocks available to us. Our publications are printed on acid-free recycled stock whenever possible, and our paper always meets or exceeds minimum GPO and EPA requirements.

Library of Congress Cataloging-in-Publication Data

Jernberg, Ann Marshak, date
    Theraplay: helping parents and children build better relationships through attachment-
    based play / Ann M. Jernberg, Phyllis B. Booth. — 2nd ed.
    p. cm.
    Includes bibliography references (p. 407) and index.
    ISBN 0-7879-4302-9
    1. Play therapy. 2. Family psychotherapy. I. Booth, Phyllis B.,
    date. II. Title.
    RJ505.P6 J47 1998
    618.92'891653—ddc21

                               98-25303

SECOND EDITION
PB Printing   10 9 8 7 6 5 4

Contents

To my mother,

who provided my model for nurturing children.

To my father,

who taught me how to play.

To my children,

Kathie, Richie, and Alison,

who taught me what I needed to know about

being a good parent.

And to my husband,

Wayne Booth,

whose love and support have sustained

me for over fifty years.

—P. B. B.

Preface to the Second Edition

When this book was first published, in 1979, Theraplay was a ten-year-old, innovative, highly successful short-term treatment method. Because of our confidence in it, we had been eager to introduce it to a wider group of people than could be reached through word of mouth, personal observation, or our local training courses. Ann Jernberg had written the book, with contributions, case studies, and research help from the small group of trained Theraplay therapists working in the Chicago area. Over the next two decades the book sold well, generating increasing interest in this exciting treatment method.

As a challenging (and for some, still controversial) approach to treatment, Theraplay has gained increasing acceptance. Its appeal stems from its success in working with attachment and relationship problems, its inclusion of parents in the treatment process, and its ability to transform relationships in a remarkably short time.

From the beginning the book was well received. It was translated into Japanese in 1986 and German in 1987. People continue to come in increasing numbers from all over the world, including Australia, Finland, Germany, Israel, Japan, Korea, and South Africa, for training in the Theraplay approach to helping children with attachment and relationship problems.

This second edition responds to the many changes that have taken place since the first edition was published—changes in our understanding of child development and the nature of attachment and changes in the treatment method itself. The following are just a few of the developments we address throughout:

- Although attachment was an important concept in the original book, our knowledge about the nature of attachment and interest in the treatment of attachment problems have expanded greatly. With the increase in adoptions of children from foreign orphanages, the problem of forming an attachment to older adopted children has become especially pressing.

- Theraplay began with a special interest in autism. Our understanding of the nature of autism has evolved, and with this evolution our optimism about the possibility of successful treatment for children with autism has grown.

xi

- Our knowledge about regulatory disorders and sensory integration problems, all of which contribute to the relationship problems that Theraplay treats, has expanded.

- The issue of touching children has become increasingly controversial. Because a secure attachment relationship depends on appropriate, nurturing touch, Theraplay has always considered touch as essential to effective treatment. In this new edition we reaffirm the importance of touch in order to counteract the fear that prevails in many child-care settings of litigation that could result from accusations of inappropriate touch. This fear is so pervasive that children are in danger of suffering a reverse kind of abuse—abuse resulting from the absence of essential, nurturing touch.

- Our greater awareness of the importance of early experience to healthy development has led to an increased emphasis on early intervention. At the same time, many therapists are unprepared to treat young children. Because it is designed to meet early emotional needs, Theraplay is an ideal model for early intervention.

- Finally, this second edition reflects the changes that have occurred in Theraplay treatment as we have applied it to a wider range of problems and an increasing number of settings. As we demonstrate here, the method is vibrant and effective today.

ACKNOWLEDGMENTS

Like the first edition, this book is the culmination of the dedicated efforts of many valued friends and colleagues. I am grateful to those who made the first edition possible by developing Theraplay: Ernestine Thomas, whose exuberant spirit and intuitive wisdom, together with her concern for excellence, have led all of us to pursue the search for Theraplay perfection; Charles West, whose enthusiasm and compassion have guided his coworkers as much as they helped the children he treated; Terrence Koller, whose contributions to Theraplay stem from his humor, perspective, flexibility, and keen empathy; and Theodore Hurst, president of Worthington, Hurst, and Associates, whose interest and support have been steady over the years. I also thank others who contributed in a variety of ways to the first edition:

Carol Adamitis, Martha Fowler, Margaret Nezezon, James Thomas, Tony Vitiello, and Brenda Winslow. Some of the original group are still actively involved with the Theraplay Institute in Chicago and have contributed to the second edition; others have carried the idea and spirit of Theraplay to a wider audience.

I give special thanks for this new edition to the following colleagues:

Sandra Lindaman, executive director of the Theraplay Institute, whose calm support and wise guidance have been available at all stages of the writing, and who wrote the chapter on adoption and foster care

Margery Rieff, clinical coordinator of the Theraplay Institute, who contributed immensely to our knowledge of how to treat very young children with physical disabilities, autism, and pervasive developmental disorders (PDD), and who provided the basic outline and crucial information for the chapters on autism, PDD, and regulatory problems

Phyllis Rubin, psychotherapist and speech and language pathologist at Therapeutic InterActions, LaGrange, Illinois, who adapted the Theraplay concept to working with groups and who wrote the chapter on Group Theraplay

Terrence Koller, executive director of the Illinois Psychological Association, who provided material for the chapter on adolescents

Amy Zier, pediatric occupational therapist, who contributed material on sensory integration for the chapter on regulatory disorders

Charles West, of Worthington, Hurst, and Associates in Chicago, who prepared a computerized version of the original book and who continues to provide insights into Theraplay with older children.

Finally, my thanks to the many friends and colleagues throughout the United States, Canada, and England who have contributed to the book by reading the manuscript at various stages, by providing case examples, and by sharing insights and helpful suggestions: Annie Aubrey, Chicago; Susan Bundy-Myrow, Buffalo, New York; Jean Crume,

Centers for Youth and Families, Little Rock, Arkansas; Lark Eshelman, Life Management Associates, Lancaster, Pennsylvania; Laverne Fesperman, Dr. Carlton G. Watkins Center, Charlotte, North Carolina; Normal Finnell, Children's Home Society of South Dakota; William Fuller, College of Nursing, University of Arkansas Medical Sciences, Little Rock, Arkansas; Susan Garofolo, Toronto, Ontario, Canada; Leigh Gibby, Chicago; Beverly James, Hawaii; Emily Jernberg, Ann Arbor, Michigan; Margo Kelly, Therapeutic Play Services, New Castle, Ontario, Canada; Doris Landry, Davis Counseling Center, Farmington Hills, Michigan; Heather Lawrence, Family Theraplay, Brampton, Ontario, Canada; Paula Mercer, Treatment Home, Inc., Little Rock, Arkansas; Peggy Miller, Integrative Learning Services, Highland Park, Illinois; Janet Mullen, Provena-St. Joseph Medical Center, Joliet, Illinois; Evangeline Munns, Blue Hills Child and Family Services, Aurora, Ontario, Canada; David L. Myrow, Buffalo, New York; Kathie Booth Stevens, Oxford, England; Juan Valbuena, Chicago; Cheryl Walters, Life Management Associates, Lancaster, Pennsylvania. Margo Wickersham Bouer, Laguna California.

Leslie Keith Hulsizer typed transcripts of videotaped Theraplay sessions and did helpful library research. Adam Kissel provided invaluable research and editorial help. I want to give special thanks to Karen Sharpe for her insightful editing of the manuscript. And finally I thank Wayne Booth both for his constant loving support and for his editorial help, which I would have to say was beyond the call of duty had I not provided similar help to him throughout the years.

Our special and warmest thanks go to the many children and families from whom we have all learned so much.

Although Ann Jernberg had long considered a revision of the first edition, she died in 1993 before she was able to begin the task. When we learned in the fall of 1996 that Jossey-Bass wanted to publish a revised paperback edition, we at the Theraplay Institute were delighted with the opportunity to bring the book up to date with current theory, research, and practice and to introduce Theraplay to an even wider audience.

When the question arose as to who should do the revision, the task fell to me. I was among the small group of Theraplay therapists who had been involved with the development of the Theraplay method from the beginning. As director of training for many years, I had thought a great deal about how to present Theraplay ideas to others. I have completed the revision with the generous help from many of the people associated with the Theraplay Institute.

This second edition is offered as a tribute to Theraplay's pioneering genius, Ann Jernberg, and to all the Theraplay therapists who, through the years, have contributed to its development and vitality.

Chicago, Illinois   PHYLLIS B. BOOTH
August 1998

The Authors

Phyllis B. Booth is director of training at the Theraplay Institute in Chicago. She collaborated with Ann Jernberg in the development of the Theraplay method from its inception.

Booth was awarded a B.A. in music from Brigham Young University in 1947 and an M.A. in human development and clinical psychology from the University of Chicago in 1966. She completed an internship in clinical psychology at the University of Chicago Hospitals Department of Psychiatry in child and adult treatment. She is a licensed marriage and family therapist, a licensed clinical professional counselor, and a registered play therapist and supervisor.

In 1969–70 she was an associate at the Tavistock Clinic in London, England, where she studied under John Bowlby, D. W. Winnicott, and Joyce and James Robertson. In 1981 she completed a two-year training program in family therapy at the Family Institute of Chicago. She spent a year (1992–1993) at the Anna Freud Centre, London, England, attending classes, lectures, and case conferences.

Booth began her career of working with children and their parents as a nursery school teacher. She and Ann Jernberg were teachers together at the University of Chicago Nursery School from 1949 to 1950. In 1967 she was among the first group of psychological consultants to the Head Start program in Chicago, where she began her long collaboration with Jernberg in developing the Theraplay method. She was a clinical therapist at the Southeast Community Mental Health Center in Chicago from 1982 to 1987, where she worked with children and adults, conducted parent support groups, and supervised interns.

In addition to providing Theraplay to children and families, Booth has a private practice in adult and marital therapy. She has been a consultant to Head Start programs, state pre-kindergarten programs, and special programs for autistic children. A major commitment in recent years has been to the training and supervision of Theraplay therapists. She has presented training seminars throughout the United States and Canada, and most recently in Finland.

Ann M. Jernberg was clinical director of the Theraplay Institute in Chicago from its inception in 1969 until her death in 1993.

Born in Germany, she came to the United States in 1939. Jernberg was awarded a Ph.B. in liberal arts in 1948 and a Ph.D. in human development in 1960 from the University of Chicago. She began her clinical work in the department of psychiatry there (1955–1960) and was research associate in the School of Social Service Administration for a special project to study emotionally disturbed preschoolers and their parents (1959–60). From 1960 to 1967 she was senior staff psychologist at Michael Reese Hospital in Chicago. For many years, beginning in 1967, she developed and supervised psychological services to the Chicago Head Start, Title XX Day Care, and Parent-Child Center programs encompassing some 5,000 children annually. She also served as chief psychologist at the LaPorte County Comprehensive Mental Health Center in Indiana. She made presentations and conducted training in the Theraplay method throughout the United States and Canada.

Jernberg's writings include numerous articles and papers on a variety of topics, including parent-child relationships, psychosomatic medicine, anorexia nervosa, the psychologist as consultant, adoption, the role of the paraprofessional, and Theraplay techniques. She directed three films: "It Can Be Done," "There He Goes," and the award-winning "Here I Am."

THE CONTRIBUTORS

Sandra Lindaman, executive director of the Theraplay Institute in Chicago, is a certified Theraplay therapist and trainer. She holds an M.A. in speech pathology from Northwestern University and an M.S.W. in social work from Loyola University. She also completed a one-year externship in family systems therapy at the Institute for Juvenile Research at the University of Illinois. She joined the Theraplay staff in 1990 and became executive director in 1993. Her responsibilities include the administration of the institute, the assessment and treatment of emotional, behavioral, and developmental problems of children and their families, and the training and supervision of professionals in the Theraplay approach. Her special interests are working with children who are adopted or in foster care, young children with pervasive developmental disorders, and teen mothers and their infants. She is the editor of *The Theraplay Institute Newsletter* and the author of several articles about Theraplay.

Phyllis B. Rubin, an affiliate of the Theraplay Institute in Chicago, is a Certified Theraplay Therapist and Group Theraplay Trainer. She is also a licensed speech and language pathologist and holds a doctorate in clinical psychology from the Illinois School of Professional Psychology. She is on the staff of Therapeutic InterActions, LaGrange, Illinois, where she provides psychotherapy and speech-language services to children and their families. She specializes in the "hard-to-reach" child, including children with attachment problems, foster and older adopted children, and children within the autistic spectrum. For a number of years she worked for Proviso Area for Exceptional Children, Maywood, Illinois, where she developed and implemented the present framework for group Theraplay. She is coauthor of *Play with Them: Theraplay Groups in the Classroom* and has presented programs on Theraplay and Group Theraplay both nationally and internationally.

Introduction

Theraplay is a lively, engaging, playful treatment method that produces remarkable changes in the lives of children and their families in a short time. It achieves its success by aggressively addressing four serious problems that face too many children and parents in our society today and that prevent the development of the secure attachment relationship that is essential to healthy development: inadequate *structure* in daily experience; too little personal *engagement*; insufficient empathic, *nurturing* touch; and failure to provide the right kinds of *challenge*. Each problem is manifested in many forms, but the success of Theraplay therapists springs from how they use attachment-based play to meet the treatment needs of children whose relationship with their parents suffers from problems in the four dimensions.

The following vignettes illustrate the problems and briefly describe the focus of successful treatment for each.

Structure: Who Is in Charge?

Lisa, three and a half years old, stands beside her mother as a woman Lisa has never seen before reaches out to greet her, saying "Hello. What a pretty girl you are." Lisa slaps at her hand and screams, "Don't talk to me!" Her mother, embarrassed, says pleadingly, "Please Lisa, be nice. The lady just wanted to say 'Hello.'"

Lisa struggles to be in control of all interactions: with her parents, with her teachers, and with her peers. If she cannot be in control, she cries, screams, and withdraws. At home, her parents "walk on eggshells" around her in order to avoid an outburst of temper. In her preschool, she tries to control everyone. As a hypersensitive infant, she was unable to be soothed and comforted, and she quickly developed a belief that she alone could keep life safe and predictable. She became the family tyrant.

Theraplay treatment for this family focused on modulating the level of sensory input so that Lisa could feel comfortable, finding ways to draw her into playful activities, and helping her accept having her parents take charge of making her world safe and comfortable. After only a few sessions, her parents were delighted to have a much more relaxed and happy relationship.

Engagement: When Should You Intrude?

Kolya, a tiny, dark-haired boy looking more like a three-year-old than his actual age of five, sits quietly rocking back and forth in the corner of the consulting room. When I move toward him, he ducks his head and scoots away. He doesn't speak, and his body is soft and floppy. If it weren't for his moving away when I approach, I would think that he was not even aware of my presence.

When they first brought him home from the orphanage, where he had been since birth, his adoptive parents were advised by their pediatrician to follow his lead. It was assumed that because his life had been so understimulating and because his movement had been so restricted, he needed free exploration and movement before he would be ready for more structured learning experiences. Following this advice, his parents watched as Kolya wandered aimlessly and often withdrew into endless rocking. After two years he still had no language and seemed uninterested in communicating even through gestures. Perhaps most disturbing to his parents was his total lack of relationship with them. "He doesn't seem to care whether we are here or not."

Rather than freedom to explore, Kolya needed someone to entice him out of his isolation into a genuine relationship. Within a few Theraplay sessions in which his therapist used simple engaging baby games such as peek-a-boo and push-me-over, Kolya became much more focused and responsive. Although he still has many problems to overcome, his parents report a great change in his ability to relate.

We do not have to look to such an extreme case to find families with relatively little of the engagement and interaction that is so essential to development. Consider the plight of many families today in which both mother and father work long hours at highly responsible jobs, children are in care outside of the home from early morning to late afternoon, and family members all arrive home tired and in need of rest and nurturing care. Where do they turn? Who has the energy to care for the children? Often the families welcome the TV or computer games or newspaper or evening cocktail, which allow all of them to unwind in isolation.

Nurturing Touch: When Is It Safe to Touch Children?

LaShawn, four years old, is enrolled in a Head Start preschool. She does not speak at school, and her angry, provocative behavior disrupts the classroom. When a teacher approaches, she throws a toy at her and threatens, through gesture, to toss her full cereal bowl. Some days LaShawn runs around the room pushing children or breaking toys. Her teacher's words do not seem to reach her, and her behavior escalates until she wears herself out.

LaShawn's parents are recovering addicts. From the psychosocial assessment interview, it is clear that they are concerned about her development but also that they provide very little nurturing care or appropriate stimulation. During one meeting, LaShawn, her mother, and her sister sit on a couch. The ten-year-old sister sucks her thumb; the mother appears tired and edgy. LaShawn swings her legs anxiously and the mother says sharply, "Stop swinging those legs." LaShawn responds, "I got a rock in my shoe." Mother threatens, "You're gonna have rocks in your head if you don't stop your legs."

LaShawn's preschool is orderly and offers many opportunities for appropriate cognitive stimulation. Many of the children are well cared for, happy, and confident. But a substantial number, like LaShawn, come to school tired, hungry, dirty, and miserable. In order to protect the school from accusations of inappropriate physical contact with children, the school policy prohibits all touching. Teachers are frustrated by this rule, since it makes it impossible to offer precisely what the unhappy child needs—a comforting hug. The best interests of the caretaking agency have taken precedence over the best interests of the children.

Young children like LaShawn are incapable of making use of the merely verbal comforting that teachers now see as the only substitute for the physical care children need. They are especially vulnerable if their parents also are unable to provide them comforting, soothing touch. LaShawn's situation highlights the importance of consistent, empathic caretaking and the role of nurturing touch in that caregiving.

Theraplay treatment for LaShawn included a great deal of comforting, nurturing touch, which to everyone's surprise she accepted eagerly. Her parents gradually learned to respond in a more empathic nurturing manner. After only four sessions, LaShawn's teachers reported a difference in her behavior. By carefully spelling out what kind of touch LaShawn needed and obtaining permission for her teacher to give it to her, we were even able to negotiate a modification in the school's policy about touch.

Challenge: How Much Challenge Is Too Much?

Paul was adopted at the age of four after being in two foster homes. Now eight, he is entering third grade. He seems alert and bright, but his academic performance is scattered. He has difficulty focusing his attention on any task, and he is unable to follow through unless his teacher stays right by his side. He never asks for help and often dangerously violates safety rules. At home he sneaks food and hoards it in his room until it spoils. He is always hungry and claims that his adoptive mother never feeds him enough. When he is tired he cannot handle any criticism and becomes angry and defiant. His mother confesses that she doesn't really like him. "When he goes all cold and distant and defies me, I feel like sending him back where he came from." What hurts his parents the most is that he doesn't seem attached to them at all.

Paul's parents are busy, energetic people who expect mature, grown-up behavior from their children. Parenting their adopted son is important to them and they often plan outings together, hoping that the outings will be stimulating and educational. Since Paul is capable of responding to their educational efforts when he is feeling good and well connected to them, they find it very difficult to accept that when he is tired, he becomes babyish and seems to forget what he has learned. They find themselves saying often, "If only you would try harder."

As an adopted child, Paul has the emotional needs of a much younger child. There is often a divergence between his adoptive parents' challenging expectations and his capacity to respond. Paul can respond to challenges if they are accompanied by his parents' positive support and if they readily lead to success. Activities in which he and his parents interact in a playful, mildly challenging manner would help Paul feel more connected to his parents and build the bond they long for.

Paul's treatment focused on helping his parents understand that, like most children adopted after infancy, his emotional needs are those of a much younger child. Once his needs are met, he can respond to appropriate challenges. His Theraplay therapist demonstrated how to meet those needs while also providing challenges that he could master and feel good about. We describe Paul's successful treatment in Chapter Nine.

These four examples represent the range of problems that we all face today. We are surrounded by children who cannot accept adult authority and by parents who have given up too much authority. We are hesitant about how much to intrude on children. We are worried about the implications of touching and cuddling children. We can't decide whether to push children harder or let them move forward at their own pace.

These problems are reinforced by the almost overwhelming stress and violence in our society. More and more children are violent and out of control. Teenagers who have not experienced good parenting are having babies yet know nothing about how to parent them well. Theraplay addresses the challenge of how we can hope to raise emotionally healthy children.

WHAT THERAPLAY HAS TO OFFER

Theraplay's intuitively natural approach produces its impressively rapid results by replicating healthy parent-child interaction; it is structured, engaging in a lively way, nurturing, and playfully challenging. We teach parents

- How to take charge without humiliating or hurting their children
- How to stay with them when they are angry and upset
- How to engage children in a more loving relationship
- How to use appropriate touch as part of tender nurturing care
- How to use challenge to build competence and self-esteem
- How to infuse all their interactions with the sheer fun of joyful play

How Theraplay Began

In 1967, when the Head Start program began, Ann Jernberg accepted the daunting task of becoming director of psychological services for the entire Chicago Head Start program. The federal mandate at that time was to locate children in need of psychological services and refer them to existing treatment centers. During that first year, several hundred children in Head Start were identified as in need of help. When we looked for treatment resources in the Chicago area, we discovered that finding effective treatment for even a few children, much less several hundred, was impossible. Child therapy, when available, was long-term and expensive, and the few existing treatment centers were far from the families who needed them.

We faced a crisis. We had been mandated to find treatment for these children, but none was available. It was immediately apparent that we would have to create a program of our own, one that would take treatment directly to the child and would be effective quickly. Furthermore, it had to be an approach that could be used by relatively inexperienced mental health workers.

Ever resourceful, Jernberg used the model of healthy parent-infant interaction and borrowed elements from the work of Austin Des Lauriers (1962, 1969) and Viola Brody (1978, 1993) to develop the new approach. Des Lauriers emphasized vigorous intrusiveness and intimacy between child and therapist through direct body and eye contact, while focusing on the here-and-now and ignoring fantasy. Viola Brody focused on the nurturing relationship between therapist and child, including touch, rocking and singing, and physical holding. As the work developed, Ernestine Thomas, an early student of Viola Brody, contributed one of the most important aspects of Theraplay: a strongly affirmative and hopeful emphasis on the child's health, potential, and strength.

With this model in mind, we then gathered everyone we could find who had experience working with children, including Head Start mothers, college students, and professionals in the field of child therapy. We looked for people with a lively, playful ability to engage children and a strong commitment to helping them realize their full potential. In a relatively short time, we began training and supervising a group of mental health workers to go into the schools to work individually and intensively (two or three times a week) with the children who needed help.

When we ran into resistance to our unorthodox ways of working—from principals, teachers, social workers, and other Head Start staff—we made films to demonstrate the effectiveness of our work: *Here I Am* (Jernberg, Hurst, and Lyman, 1969) and *There He Goes* (Jernberg,

Hurst, and Lyman, 1975). Using these films we presented our new method throughout the Head Start system, gradually gaining acceptance and, finally, full recognition of our work.

In 1970, while we were searching for a name for this playful and therapeutic treatment method—so unlike traditional play therapy—Charles Lyman, filmmaker of *Here I Am,* suggested the name *Theraplay.* Theraplay classes were first taught in 1971, and it was written into a Health, Education, and Welfare (HEW) proposal in March 1972. The Theraplay Institute was established in 1971.

Observing our success with Head Start children, teachers, parents, and social workers began referring children to us for private treatment. Soon Theraplay sessions were conducted not only in Head Start classrooms but in a specially constructed Theraplay treatment room in Chicago as well. Unfortunately, we then learned that a few individuals around the country, having heard something of Theraplay, were treating children in ways we found questionable and were calling these treatment methods "Theraplay." It was for this reason that in 1976 we registered Theraplay as a service mark (the equivalent of a copyright or trademark).

Since its beginnings in the Chicago Head Start program, the Theraplay Institute has developed into a not-for-profit treatment, training, and consulting center. We treat children who have emotional, behavioral, and relationship problems as well as children with regulatory problems, autism and pervasive developmental disorders, and physical handicaps. Because of our focus on building better relationships between parents and children, we have a special interest in working with children who have been adopted or are in foster care.

In the 1980s we began training people at other centers in the United States and Canada, including the Centers for Youth and Families in Little Rock, Arkansas, Children's Home Society of South Dakota, and Blue Hills Child and Family Services in Aurora, Ontario, Canada. Trained Theraplay therapists have carried the ideas back to their various centers not only throughout the United States and Canada but in Australia, Finland, Germany, Israel, Korea, and South Africa.

In addition to our long-term involvement as consultants through Worthington, Hurst, and Associates to the Head Start Programs in Chicago, we have consulted to early intervention programs; day-care and preschools; and to agencies that provide foster and adoption services; support, training, and care for teen mothers; and day care for the elderly. The settings have included hospitals, day treatment centers, and home-based treatment. In this book we describe a few of these many applications.

The Innovative Aspects of Theraplay

With its roots in interactional theories of development, attachment theory, developmental psychology, and good preschool practice, the Theraplay approach is not so much a break with tradition as a fruitful extension of work from a number of fields. When Theraplay was first developed, however, many of the techniques were in striking contrast to the then-popular ways of working with children. The following innovations distinguish Theraplay from most other treatment methods:

- The Theraplay therapist takes charge, carefully planning and structuring the sessions to meet the child's needs rather than waiting for the child to lead the way.
- The therapist does all in her power to entice the child into a relationship, including, if necessary, intruding on the child in order to begin the engagement. Treatment emphasizes the interactional relationship between the therapist and the child rather than focusing on conflicts within the child's psyche.
- Nurturing touch is an integral part of the interaction.
- The therapist remains firm in the face of resistance, whether passive or active. If the child responds with anger, the therapist stays with the child throughout the duration of the angry outburst.
- Treatment involves active, physical, interactive play. There is no symbolic play with toys and very little talk about problems.
- Treatment is geared to the child's emotional level and therefore often includes "babyish" activities that many people would consider appropriate for a younger child.
- Parents are actively involved in the treatment to enable them to take home the new ways of interacting with their child.
- The therapist initially steps into the parental role in order to model, for the watching parents, a new way of relating to their child.

THE AUDIENCE FOR THIS BOOK

This book is addressed to those who directly provide services to children and families with attachment and relationship problems: child therapists (including psychiatrists, psychologists, social workers, counselors, and family therapists), pediatric nurses, child-care workers, special educators, and speech and physical therapists. Those in the field of primary prevention and early intervention, and especially those in education for parenthood programs, will find it a useful approach for preventing later problems and reducing mental illness. Administrators of mental health or special education programs and agencies will also find it useful. Because Theraplay is not just a set of techniques but a whole way of relating to children that is positive, playful, and enriching, the book will prove helpful to parents, grandparents, teachers, and a wider reading public as well.

No doubt, some psychotherapists will take issue with some parts of the Theraplay theory and practice. Some may be shocked by its emphasis on the adult's structuring role. Others will be put off by its insistence that the therapist neither engage in discussion of intrapsychic issues nor attend to what the others define as inappropriate behavior. But we have learned from experience that few indeed will quarrel with the sheer fun and joy that Theraplay provides.

Although we intend the guidelines for Theraplay treatment to be easily understood and are certain that some of the ideas can be usefully incorporated into any trained therapist's repertoire, we do not expect anyone to become a fully trained Theraplay therapist without going through our regular training process. In spite of its apparent simplicity and naturalness, Theraplay is not an easy method to learn. There are many subtleties involved in responding appropriately to each child's needs. The training process takes time and involves intensive training courses and supervision, which are available at the Theraplay Institute in Chicago and at a few other centers. Appendix A outlines the requirements for becoming a Certified Theraplay Therapist.

HOW THE BOOK IS ORGANIZED

Part One provides an overview of the Theraplay method. Chapter One outlines the structure of treatment; describes how we use the four Theraplay dimensions of *structure, engagement, nurture,* and *challenge* to tailor treatment to each child's needs; identifies the sources of the attachment or relationship problems that bring children into Theraplay treatment; and addresses the issue of when Theraplay should be modified or not be used at all. Chapter Two describes research, theory, and practice that support the importance of the many facets of Theraplay treatment, including the role of healthy parenting in fostering secure attachment.

Part Two gives comprehensive instructions about how to practice Theraplay. Chapter Three describes how to structure Theraplay treatment, how to plan the sequence within a Theraplay session, and how sessions are organized around each child's particular need for structure, engagement, nurture, and challenge. Chapter Four addresses issues that the Theraplay therapist faces in working with any child: how treatment evolves over time and how it must be tailored to the individual needs of the child and family, how to handle a child's resistance and difficult behavior, and how to recognize and avoid countertransference acting out. Chapter Four concludes with a list of practical guidelines for the therapist. Chapter Five describes how we work with parents, including helping them become more responsive to their children's needs and teaching them to carry on the Theraplay approach with their children at home.

Part Three shows how we adapt treatment to the needs of children with a variety of behavioral, emotional, and relationship problems. Chapter Six deals with problems in regulation: sensory integration, regulatory disorders, and hyperactivity. Chapter Seven describes treatment of children with autism and pervasive developmental disorders. Chapter Eight addresses the special needs of children with physical disabilities using the examples of two specific disabilities: children with hearing impairment and children with cerebral palsy. Chapter Nine describes how Theraplay must be adapted to meet the needs of children who have been traumatized. Chapter Ten gives the basic principles of successful treatment with children who have been separated from their biological parents and placed either in foster care or in institutions. Chapter Eleven describes how to adapt Theraplay in working with adolescents. Chapter Twelve moves beyond individual treatment to describe how Theraplay's positive, playful ways of relating can be applied to groups.

To preserve the confidentiality of the families represented in case examples throughout this book, all names have been changed and the details of their lives disguised.

An Overview of the Theraplay Method

In the first chapter of Part One we present an overview of the Theraplay method. We discuss the kinds of problems Theraplay is designed to address and why these problems might develop. In the second chapter we explain why Theraplay treatment is effective. To answer this question, we first discuss the various elements involved in treatment and then outline the theory and research that supports the importance or value of each element.

CHAPTER ONE

Learning the Basics of the Theraplay Method

~~~

heraplay is a playful, engaging, short-term treatment method that is intimate, physical, personal, focused, and fun. It is modeled on the natural, healthy parent-infant relationship. Treatment actively involves parents, first as observers and later as cotherapists. The focus of Theraplay treatment is on the underlying disturbance in the relationship between the child and her caretakers. The goal of treatment is to enhance attachment, self-esteem, trust, and joyful engagement and to empower parents to continue on their own the health-promoting interactions learned during the treatment sessions.

In this chapter we introduce you to the Theraplay method, beginning with a brief description of the overall process, including a transcript of a Theraplay session. We then describe how Theraplay is modeled on the healthy parent-infant relationship. To explain the kinds of problems that Theraplay is best suited to address, we first discuss the experiences in the child's early life that might cause problems to develop, and then describe the kinds of behaviors that signal an attachment problem that Theraplay can treat. Finally, we discuss situations for which Theraplay would not be the treatment of choice.

GETTING A PICTURE OF THE PROCESS

Theraplay is practiced in a variety of settings: in schools, outpatient mental health clinics, hospitals, residential treatment centers, private practices, and homes. Throughout this book, especially in Part Three, you will find examples of the use of Theraplay in a variety of settings. Theraplay has been used for people of all ages, from infancy through adolescence to old age, but it is most frequently practiced with children from eighteen months to twelve years of age. Chapter Eleven describes how it can be adapted for use with adolescents. Theraplay is effective with a variety of behavior problems ranging from withdrawal, depression, and passivity to aggressiveness and hyperactivity. The severity of problems ranges from mild anxiety and classroom misbehavior to autism and pervasive developmental disorder (PDD). Later in this chapter we discuss why such disturbances in the attachment relationship might develop and how an understanding of these reasons can help the Theraplay therapist adapt treatment to the child's specific needs.

The goal of Theraplay treatment for all children is three-fold: to help the child replace inappropriate solutions and behaviors with healthy, creative, and age-appropriate ones; to increase the child's self-esteem; and to enhance the relationship between the child and her caretakers. Theraplay therapists do this by being vigorous and engaging, all the while working to establish a *real* relationship between the child and the adult, by ignoring fantasy, and focusing on what is going on in the present between them. In short, we do everything possible to enhance the intimacy and engagement between the child and the adult.

The Theraplay therapist, like the "good enough" parent,[1] takes charge while remaining carefully attuned and responsive to the child's needs. Whether the emphasis in a given session is on structuring, engaging, nurturing, or challenging—the four dimensions of Theraplay that we refer to throughout the book—the sessions are always intended to be playful and fun. Even though the playful activities are designed to appeal to any child, children who are referred for treatment have often developed self-protective defenses that keep them distant from the kind of relationship that the therapist, as parent surrogate, knows they need. Part of treatment is, therefore, to stay in tune with the child through the inevitable period of resistance.

The kinds of problems that Theraplay addresses often have their origins in the earliest stages of a child's development. Although most children who come for treatment are beyond the infant stage, they still need the nurturing touch, the focused eye contact, and the playful give and take that are such important parts of the healthy parent-child relationship. These are the elements that help children learn who they are, what their world is like, who the important people in their world are, and how they feel about them.

There is an explicit emphasis on the child's health and strength. The therapist's optimistic message communicates to the child that there is hope, that at least during her treatment session she can feel "normal," and that no matter how sick, how unattractive, how badly behaved, or how rejected by everyone else, there are many things about her that are lovable. The child must come to see, reflected in the mirror of her therapist's eyes and ultimately in her parents' eyes, the image of herself as special, lovable, and fun to be with.

Logistics

We now look briefly at the logistics and typical sequence of treatment before we describe a Theraplay session. In Chapter Three, we describe the process in more detail so that you will be able to implement it in your work.

SETTING. The Theraplay room is simple, functional, and comfortable. Large floor pillows or a beanbag chair and soft toss pillows suggest that this is a place where you can relax and have fun. Ideally, there is an observation room with a one-way viewing mirror, behind which parents and a second therapist, the interpreting therapist, can observe and discuss what is happening in the child's session. In many settings, however, such as schools, private practices, and homes, a viewing room and an interpreting therapist are not available. Chapter Three explains how Theraplay can be adapted under these circumstances.

NUMBER AND TIMING OF SESSIONS. Theraplay treatment includes an assessment period of three or four sessions; the treatment proper, which ranges from ten to twenty sessions (longer for the most severe cases); and a follow-up period of four to six sessions spaced over a year. Theraplay sessions are thirty to forty-five minutes in length and are typically scheduled once a week.

PARTICIPANTS. Theraplay treatment, in contrast to many other child therapies, includes parents or primary caretakers in the sessions. The ideal pattern is to have at least two therapists: one or more to work with the child and one, the interpreting therapist, to work with the parents. Since two therapists are not always available, a single therapist can adapt the method to work with both child and parents.

The Sequence of Theraplay Treatment

Theraplay treatment, as stated earlier, includes an assessment procedure, the treatment proper, and a check-up period.

ASSESSMENT. The Theraplay assessment procedure includes the following three elements:

- An initial intake interview with the child's caretakers, during which we begin to learn about the history and current functioning of the family. The child is not present for this interview.

- An assessment of the child's relationship with each parent using the Marschak Interaction Method (MIM) (Marschak, 1960b, 1967), a structured observation technique designed to assess the quality and nature of the relationship between a child and each of his caretakers. The MIM is discussed in more detail in Chapter Three. When only one parent is available, there is of course only one observation session.

- A feedback session with the caretakers who were involved in the observation sessions. In this session, we present our initial evaluation of the problem and show segments of the videotaped MIM sessions to illustrate particular points. If we recommend Theraplay treatment and the parents want to proceed, we negotiate an agreement to embark on a limited number of sessions, depending on the severity of the presenting problem.

TREATMENT PROPER. As you will see in the following transcript, Theraplay sessions are designed to be engaging and fun. The therapist approaches each session with a plan based an understanding of the needs of the particular child. As the session proceeds, the plan can be modified to accommodate to the child's responses. Activities within each session vary from active to quiet and sessions typically end with a quiet nurturing activity including feeding and singing to the child.

The initial session begins with a lively greeting and an immediate active effort to get acquainted, during which the therapist "checks out" the child's important characteristics. He may check on the color of her eyes, count the number of her freckles, and test the strength of her arms and legs.

Although each child responds in her own fashion to the experience of playing with her new therapist, most children follow a sequence from hesitant acceptance through resistance to final enthusiastic engagement. We describe this sequence more fully in Chapter Four.

During the first four sessions, the parents observe their child with his therapist and are guided in their observations by the interpreting therapist, whose job it is to help parents understand what is going on and to prepare them for joining their child in the Theraplay room. Parents are given assignments to try out some of the activities at home between sessions. In the remaining six sessions, the parents, along with the interpreting therapist, come into the treatment room to interact with their child under the guidance of the Theraplay therapist. Chapter Five shows how we work with parents.

The final session is an upbeat party at which the child's strengths and achievements are celebrated. A strong emphasis is placed on how much the child and his parents are able to enjoy each other.

CHECK-UP SESSIONS. Check-up sessions are scheduled at monthly intervals for the first three months and then at quarterly intervals for a year. These sessions follow the pattern of sessions in the second half of treatment; the parents join in during the second half of each session. During the first half of the session parents have an opportunity to discuss any problems or issues that have arisen during the intervening weeks, and when they come into the playroom they are able to demonstrate new activities that they have enjoyed with their child. Check-up sessions are discussed in more detail in Chapter Three.

THERAPLAY IN PRACTICE: *What Theraplay Looks Like.* In this example of a Theraplay session, we see how play is used to help an anxious child separate from her parents and begin to develop trust in another caring adult. Following the transcript of the session, we describe how the interpreting therapist works with the parents behind a one-way mirror.

Sara, three years and two months old, is described by her mother as having precocious cognitive and language skills but no social skills; she is afraid of everything and especially new things. Because of her fears, she has great difficulty separating from her parents. The parents feel controlled by Sara's fearful resistance to routines and activities that most children enjoy. Sara had been a fussy baby with persistent feeding and sleeping problems. Recently, she has begun to have difficulty getting to sleep. In her playgroup she clings to her mother's skirts and refuses to play with the toys or the other children. Her parents want help because she seems so unhappy and because life with her is so difficult.

Following the usual Theraplay procedure, Sara's parents came for an initial interview to discuss their concerns and in order for the therapists to learn more about the origin and meaning of the problem. Following that interview, Sara and each of her parents were observed playing together in a structured MIM observation session. The MIM clearly demonstrated Sara's difficulty separating from her parents, her desperate need to take control of every situation, and her inability to accept nurture from her parents. Based on the interview and the observed interaction, the following treatment goals were developed: to help Sara become more comfortable separating from her parents; to help Sara let her parents take over the task of providing structure and safety for her; and to help her accept soothing, comforting nurture from them.

THERAPIST AND CHILD. Sara's parents and their interpreting therapist are observing Sara's second Theraplay session from behind a one-way mirror. Sara and her therapist, Margaret, are entering the therapy room. A beanbag chair is in the corner and large pillows are scattered around. There are no toys in the room because Margaret expects to be the most engaging object there. Knowing that it is hard for Sara to separate from her parents, Margaret attempts to make the separation as easy as possible by taking Sara's hand and encouraging her to jump on the pillows into the room.

SARA: Mommy!

MOTHER: I'll be right here.

MARGARET: Mommy will sit right here. (points to chairs set up for parents and interpreting therapist)

SARA: (begins to cry)

MARGARET: Mommy and Daddy are sitting outside; we're going to jump on some pillows. I'll help you.

Margaret stands Sara on a pillow and crouches down to face her, then picks Sara up to "jump" her to the next pillow. Because Sara is still upset and not really attending to or participating in the jumping activity, Margaret changes her plan and, holding Sara in her arms, sits in the beanbag chair with Sara in her lap. Sara is whimpering. Margaret wipes Sara's face with a tissue.

MARGARET: I know that's hard Sara. Mom and Dad are right outside; after we play for a while, we'll go find them. Hey Sara, did you bring your strong legs today? I remember that you had strong legs. (feels Sara's calf muscle)

SARA: Yeah. (looks more interested; no tears or protest from this point on)

MARGARET: I'm going to take your shoes off so you can give me a push. Hey, those look like new shoes. I'm going to have you sit in the beanbag. (shifts position to place Sara in beanbag, sitting face to face) Now, let's see if you brought your strong legs.

SARA: (looks at Margaret's face, smiles when Margaret places Sara's feet high on Margaret's chest)

MARGARET: Okay, 1–2–3, push!

SARA: (pushes Margaret slightly with feet; Margaret falls backward in exaggerated way)

MARGARET: Wow, now pull me up.

SARA: (reaches out with one hand)

MARGARET: Oh, you brought strong arms too . . . use both hands.

SARA: (pulls Margaret up, really pushes the second time and reaches readily with both hands to pull, smiling)

MARGARET: You know, I bet you could push me with one foot; just watch.

SARA: (pushes, but begins to look around)

MARGARET: I wonder if you know how to play peek-a-boo this way. (holds both of Sara's feet in front of her face)

SARA: (allows and smiles)

MARGARET: (repeats)

SARA: (pulls feet away a bit)

MARGARET: Hey Sara, when we do that I can see your face in the little space between your feet, look.

SARA: (looks at Margaret through space; slides down in beanbag chair)

MARGARET: You know, it looks like you're slipping down, let me help you up a bit. (helps her sit up)

MARGARET: Great! Now Sara, I wonder what you have inside your socks today.

SARA: (smiles, reaches for sock)

MARGARET: Grapes? (emphasizes silliness)

SARA: (shakes head, No)

MARGARET: Popcorn?

SARA: No.

MARGARET: Sara toes?

SARA: No . . . Yes!

MARGARET: (pulls off sock) Oh, there they are, your great toes!

MARGARET: (begins to do "this little piggy . . ." Sara pulls away) You know what? You've got cold feet. I've gotta warm them up. (rubs feet) Now I'll finish. (Margaret finishes rhyme; Sara watches, smiles, finger in mouth, seems surprised, delighted to have this done to her)

MARGARET: You know, last time you left a big foot print right on my leg.

SARA: On a mat.

MARGARET: Yes, we made them on the mat too. Today we have a special way to make them. (gets out a sheet of black construction paper, Sara puts her foot on it) Hey, you've got the idea! (Sara sits up looks at her feet and the paper) We'll do it like that (presses on foot Sara has put on paper) and like that. (takes other foot, places it on paper and presses. Takes lotion; holds foot) This is going to be a little wet and slippery, but I'll help you with it.

SARA: (allows lotion to be spread on bottom of foot, presses down and picks up foot when directed, looks away when footprint is held up for her)

MARGARET: Now I get to rub it in. (Margaret pulls firmly on foot and lets it slip through hands) Oh, you've got a slippery foot. Now we need to do this foot. (Sara allows, leans forward with interest to look) I'm going to put your socks back on so your feet won't get cold. Here, help me with the powder.

SARA: (helps shake the powder. The powder clings to the lotion and makes an interesting foot picture) Why are we putting on feet?

MARGARET: .This is for you to take home, Sara's very special feet.

MARGARET: (shows Sara a handful of cotton balls) Let's see, I'm going to hide them on you, Sara. Close your eyes. (hides a cotton ball in jeans cuff, in her pocket, under her sock. Sara watches, finds each immediately) Oh, you're good! I'm going to hide it on me, close your eyes. (hides in own sleeve. Sara hangs back, then reaches up, searches) Can you hide it on you? I'm going to close my eyes. (elaborately covers eyes)

SARA: (hides at her neck)

MARGARET: Did you hide it?

SARA: Yes.

MARGARET: (starts to look, Sara pulls it out)

MARGARET: I'm gonna hide it on me, again. (hides in pocket)

SARA: (actively sits up, gets it, it pulls apart. Surprised response) Ooohhh!

MARGARET: That's OK, it didn't hurt anything. One more time, you hide it.

SARA: (searches for place, lifts shirt, sticks behind neck, smiles, pulls out cotton ball as Margaret looks for it)

MARGARET: What a good idea! (Sara looks relaxed)

SARA: (looks down [tiring of activities, beginning to think about parents?] Margaret turns to a nurturing activity.)

MARGARET: Sara, I have something here. (shows pretzels)

SARA: (smiles, reaches) You brought me those again.

MARGARET: I did, I brought you those again because I remembered you really liked them. (puts Sara on her lap)

SARA: Is it the same kind?

MARGARET: I think it's the same kind. Let me see if you can take a bite. (Sara bites) Now, let's try some juice. Let's see if it's the kind you like too. You check and see.

SARA: (takes sip from juice box, nods) It's the kind I like, apple juice. (begins to squirm)

MARGARET: I can hear you go glub, glub. I think you need another pretzel.

SARA: (avoids eye contact)

MARGARET: Let's see if this side tastes better. (pretends to crunch with her)

SARA: (begins to refuse pretzel, moves out of lap)

MARGARET: You need to stretch for a minute. (stands in front of her and helps her stretch)

They catch a bean bag off each other's head—a return to engaged interactive play following Sara's beginning discomfort with being held and fed.

MARGARET: (puts Sara's shoes back on, helps her to collect herself)

The final song, a nurturing ritual repeated each session, includes a review of the day's activities.

MARGARET: Twinkle, twinkle little star,/What a special girl you are;/Nice brown hair and soft, soft cheeks/Big blue eyes from which you peek . . . and you like to make footprints, and crunch pretzels, like apple juice, can push me over with one leg, you're a good cotton ball catcher and finder and a fun, fun girl./Twinkle, twinkle little star,/What a special girl you are.
Let's see if I can pick you up and carry you right out to Mom and Dad. (delivers to Father's arms)

INTERPRETING THERAPIST AND PARENTS. Throughout the session, the interpreting therapist is alert to the parents' need for explanation and understanding about what their little girl is experiencing. At the beginning, sensing their uneasiness, the interpreting therapist explains: "Sara still finds it hard to leave you, but she seems more comfortable today than she was in the first session. Margaret wants to make the leave-taking easier by having her jump on the pillows into the room. Let's watch and see how it goes. . . . Well, that didn't quite do the trick, so Margaret changed her plan. Looks like it will take a while before she can settle down.

"When Margaret challenges Sara to push with her feet, Sara forgets her fears and begins to enjoy herself. That's good to know. So when she is having difficulty leaving you, it would help if her teacher got her involved in a physical activity."

And so the interpretation continues. Her parents relax as they see Sara relax and laugh with Margaret and as they watch Sara's pleasure in the silly "find the toes" game. "It feels so good to see her enjoy herself,"

Mother says. "Why do you think she didn't stay long with the feeding?" Father asks. "I'm not sure," the interpreting therapist says. "Perhaps she suddenly thought of you, since you are the ones who usually share such intimate moments, perhaps some uncomfortable feeling was stirred up from all those early times when feeding was so difficult. It often happens that feelings associated with early caretaking experiences are stirred up when children first find themselves accepting care from a new person. After all, this is the first time she has allowed someone else, other than you two, to take care of her. It is a new experience that she likes but is not yet sure of."

Throughout the session, Sara's parents are given as much support and encouragement from the interpreting therapist as they need. In later sessions they will join in the fun so that they can learn to interact with Sara in ways that work for her.

REPLICATING THE HEALTHY PARENT-INFANT RELATIONSHIP

As you can see from the session, Margaret interacted with Sara in ways that are reminiscent of the play of parents with their very young infants. She touched her and held her, she was playful and engaging, and she was attentive to Sara's every response. She used challenging activities to keep Sara interested and nurturing activities to make her feel good. And finally, rather than ask Sara to decide what to do, she took charge of the session to make it safe and fun.

Theraplay treatment involves replicating as much as possible the pleasurable interactions that are an essential part of the healthy parent-infant relationship.[2] If you picture what goes on in the interaction between an infant and her parents, you have the model for Theraplay and how it works:

Daily, parents nuzzle their baby's neck, blow on her tummy, sing in her ear, play "peek-a-boo," and nibble her toes. They pick her up, twirl her, spin her, rock her, and bounce her. They hold her close, feed her, sing to her, and talk baby talk to her. They wash her, pat her dry, powder her, lotion her, and comb her hair. They whisper, coo, giggle, chatter, and make nonsense sounds. They hold her, confine her, restrain her, protect her. They define her life space, her property, her relationships, her use of time. And finally, they remain one step ahead of her, thus encouraging her both to move forward and to enjoy the challenge.

The baby, in turn, coos at her parents, smiles at them, reaches for them, strokes them, worships them, imitates them, and enjoys being mirrored by them; she gurgles with them, and, finally, she names them. Although the child may sometimes protest, she responds to her parents' definitions, limits, and structures, and rises to their challenges. But above all she stares at them and gazes deeply into their eyes.

The baby enjoys the clarity, security, and predictability; the happy excitement, surprise, and stimulation; the easy warmth and tender softness; and the opportunity to strive a little. Most of all, of course, she welcomes the certainty, implied throughout, that there is reliability, empathy, and caring. Though parents are clearly "in charge" of the interaction, it cannot be too strongly stated that the emotional "intuneness," the empathy, with their baby is of the highest priority.

Using this picture as a guide for treatment, the Theraplay therapist models his behavior on that of the attuned, responsive parent. He engages the child in a playful, reciprocal, interactive relationship. He confidently takes charge. And he responds empathically to the child's needs using the Theraplay dimensions as a guide.

To help you understand why Theraplay emphasizes these characteristics in treatment, we discuss in the following section the role that each plays in promoting a healthy relationship and therefore the healthy development of the child.

Using Play

A striking characteristic of the healthy parent-infant relationship, play permeates all of the Theraplay therapist's interactions as well. Play introduces an element of joy and excitement that is essential to the development of a zest for life and an energy for engagement in all children.

Creating Positive Interactions

The ideal parent-infant relationship establishes a positive interaction that is not only playful but interactive and empathic as well. The cycle thus set into motion is a reciprocal one, a "mutual admiration society." Each is eager to please, protect, and cherish the other, and each one responds by showing pleasure and concern. The gratitude at having been given so much pleasure leads to greater and greater efforts to please, protect, and cherish. The goal of the Theraplay therapist is to establish a similar positive interaction between himself and the child in treatment and ultimately to establish it between the child and her parents.

As parents find increasing pleasure in being with their new baby, he in turn becomes more pleasurable to be with. The baby comes to see himself as clearly differentiated, attractive, lovable, and capable of making an impact. In addition, his parents acquaint him with his body parts (as when his mother counts his fingers or plays "this little piggy" with his toes) and help him distinguish himself from the reality of the world at large (as when she plants the soles of his feet against her chest and encourages him to push). They teach him about physical realities such as gravity, time, and motion (as when his father tosses him up high in the air and catches him), or, later, about moral and social realities such as, "It hurts when you pinch me, and I can't let you do that."

As they interact with their baby, parents come to see themselves as loving and giving, and at the same time as resourceful, strong, and competent. They find in their new parenthood the confirmation of many positive personal qualities, including a capacity for intimacy and a firm sense of self enhanced by being able to be a strong role model to their children for confident assertiveness in the world.

These pleasurable interactions not only lead to strong, positive self-images for both baby and parents, they help the baby form a positive image of his parents and the world. The baby forms a picture of his parents as warm, loving, caring, and trustworthy. He knows that they can be counted on when he needs them. He comes to view the world as a place he enjoys exploring and in which he can feel safe and well cared for. Experiencing this happy environment fortifies children with such a sturdy sense of self and resilience to stress that unless something occurs later on to interrupt their healthy development, they seldom need treatment.

Establishing a Confident, Take-Charge Attitude

Just as the good parent takes charge in order to make sure that her infant is safe and well cared for and that his emotional needs are met, the Theraplay therapist takes charge of the interaction during sessions. Because this is a controversial aspect of Theraplay treatment, we go into more detail in Chapter Two to explain its importance.

Parents make choices for their baby all the time—choices based on their sensitive understanding of her needs. One of the major tasks for parents during the first few months of their infant's life is to develop an exquisite sensitivity to their baby's needs, moods, and feelings. They must learn to "read their baby's mind." As we discuss later on, problems can develop at this stage either because the baby is difficult to "read" or the parents, for their own reasons, are unable to read the baby's signals. But when things go well, parents and their baby very quickly develop a dance that is mutually enjoyable and very satisfying. In this dance, the parents confidently take the lead.

Only later does the parents' role shift toward encouraging greater independence and autonomy on the child's part. They then offer simple choices in order to encourage the child's initiative. At no point, however, should children be offered choices that require more knowledge or maturity than they possess. A three-year-old cannot be expected to decide whether to wear boots when going out into the rain. A six-year-old is not mature enough for the responsibility of choosing whether to watch an "adult" television show. Even with an older child, the good parent does not simply go along with what the child "wants" to do but supports what, for the child's best development, he "should" do.

Although the child who comes for treatment may be of a chronological age when it would be appropriate to encourage greater autonomy, his emotional age is usually much younger. His impulses toward autonomy often lead him to distance himself from others and to shrink from new experiences. If given a choice, he would not choose to engage with a new person. The confident therapist knows that he must be wooed, enticed, and drawn into interaction. The more quickly he can be brought to experience a new kind of relationship, the better. Therefore the Theraplay therapist, like the mother of a younger child, initiates the interaction and does not wait for the child to "choose" to relate.

Using the Theraplay Dimensions to Meet the Child's Needs

Having said that the therapist confidently takes charge of treatment, we must emphasize once again the importance of designing treatment to meet each child's individual needs.

Based on their intuitive understanding of their child's needs, parents move from one activity to another with no conscious thought for what particular kind of activity their baby needs next. The Theraplay therapist, however, must plan carefully to meet the needs of the child who comes for treatment. She uses the four dimensions of Theraplay as a guide in making her plan. Each of the four dimensions provides support to different aspects of healthy growth. One child may require soft cuddling, rocking, and singing; another may require vigorous wrestling and pillow fights. The hyperactive child who runs about frantically may need more clear definition of limits, whereas the passive, shy child may need to be encouraged to take the initiative. The following section defines the Theraplay dimensions and suggests the kinds of problems for which each is most useful. In Part Three we provide more detail about how treatment is tailored to deal with different kinds of problems.

The four dimensions of Theraplay are modeled on the interaction between parents and child in a healthy relationship:

- *Structuring.* Parents are trustworthy and predictable, and they help define and clarify the child's experience.
- *Engaging.* Parents provide excitement, surprise, and stimulation in order to maintain a maximal level of alertness and engagement.
- *Nurturing.* Parents are warm, tender, soothing, calming, and comforting.
- *Challenging.* Parents encourage the child to move ahead, to strive a bit, and to become more independent.

STRUCTURING. In the parent-infant relationship, the parent sets boundaries to ensure the child's safety and survival and helps the child to understand the world in which she lives. The adult is attuned to the infant's needs and responds accordingly, initiating playful, stimulating contact when appropriate and offering soothing, comforting contact when needed. As a consequence of the caregiver's structuring of the child's environment, the child enjoys physical and emotional security and is able to understand and learn about her environment. The adult conveys the message, "You are safe with me because I will take good care of you."

In treatment, the therapist is in charge for the same reasons that the parent is in charge with an infant. It is not reassuring to a frightened, unhappy, or chaotic child to experience the adult as uncertain or to feel that he or she must decide what to do next. In Theraplay sessions, the dimension of structure is addressed through clearly stated safety rules (for example, "No hurts!"), through activities such as singing games that have a beginning, a middle, and an end, and through activities that define body boundaries. Although all children benefit from the predictability of structure, this dimension is most important for children who are overactive, unfocused, overstimulated, or who have an anxious need to be in control.

Because of her fearfulness, Sara, whose Theraplay treatment we have described, had a desperate need to take control of every situation she found herself in. Knowing this, Margaret's goal was to relieve her of that burden by taking over the structuring role. Margaret provided structure by confidently taking charge of the session, making sure that Sara was safe, and organizing the session in ways that met Sara's needs.

ENGAGING. The interaction between parents and their babies is a constant pattern of delightful intrusion leading to engagement. The baby signals her eagerness to be engaged by looking, smiling, and babbling. The mother responds and adds her own variety of sensitively timed interactions that maintain her baby's alert engagement with her. Many traditional baby games, such as peek-a-boo, blowing on the tummy, and "I'm going to get you!" serve to draw the baby into interaction with her caretaker and maintain an optimal level of arousal. The activities are unexpected, delightful, stimulating, and engaging. As a result the child learns to communicate, share intimacy, and enjoy interpersonal contact. The message is, "You are fun to be with. You can interact in appropriate ways with others. You can be close to others."

Many children who come for treatment project a surface message that they want to be left alone. Such children need to be enticed out of their withdrawal or avoidance by an empathic intrusion aimed at engaging them in a pleasurable relationship. Unless the adult encourages them to try it out, they may never know what they are missing. Using activities modeled on the playful games of a mother with her infant, the therapist offers adventure, variety, stimulation, and a fresh view of life, allowing the child to learn that surprises can be fun and new experiences enjoyable.

Sara had made it eminently clear that she did not want to let anyone get close to her except her parents—and even that only on her own terms. During Sara's first session, she actively resisted engagement by crying and fussing for most of the session. Margaret planned the second session to provide as many enticing and engaging activities as possible to help Sara overcome her fearful, withholding stance and become able to relax and enjoy the games. The first sign that she was beginning to relax came when Margaret touched her "strong legs" and challenged her to use them to push her over. Both the challenge and the opportunity to use some physical force in pushing Margaret away intrigued her, and she put her full energy into the game. Throughout the session, Margaret used enticing, surprising activities to keep Sara with her. These activities included using surprising variations of peek-a-boo, hiding cotton balls on Sara so that she had to touch Sara to find them, and exaggerating her fall when Sara pushed her over.

NURTURING. In the parent-infant relationship, nurturing activities abound: feeding, rocking, cuddling, and holding, to name a few. Such activities are soothing, calming, quieting, and reassuring. As a result of experiencing the comforting presence of a nurturing adult whenever he needs it, the child gradually develops the capacity to internalize the soothing function of the caregiver and is able to take over these functions for himself. As the child grows older, the caretaker continues to meet the child's dependency needs as they arise while shifting the balance toward encouraging the child's autonomy. The message of nurturing care is: "You are lovable. I will respond to your needs for care, affection, and praise."

To meet the unfulfilled emotional needs of the child in treatment, many nurturing activities are used, such as feeding, making lotion hand prints, or swinging the child in a blanket. Such activities help make the world seem warm and secure and reassure the child that the adult is able to provide the comfort he needs. This dimension is especially useful for children who are overactive, aggressive, or pseudomature.

For many reasons, Sara had been unable to accept and enjoy her parents' efforts to nurture and soothe her. Knowing this, Margaret planned nurturing experiences for Sara that she hoped would intrigue her enough to accept. When Sara showed some discomfort in being touched and cared for, Margaret made the activities into games: making a footprint, or hiding cotton balls on her body. By the end of the session, Sara was beginning to be more comfortable in Margaret's arms as she listened to the song about "what a special girl she is."

CHALLENGING. In the parent-infant relationship there are many opportunities to challenge the child to take a step forward, to master tension-arousing experiences, and to enhance feelings of competence. For example, a mother might "walk" her baby on her lap, or a father might hold his baby high, saying "So big!" When the caregiver handles the challenging aspects of their interaction well, the child develops confidence in his capacity to learn, to accept challenges, and to have realistic expectations of himself. The message is clear: "You are capable of growing and of making a positive impact on the world."

In treatment, challenging activities also serve to encourage the child's sense of mastery. Such challenges are designed for success and are done in playful partnership with the adult. For example, the therapist might challenge a four-year-old to balance on a pile of pillows and jump into her arms on the count of three. Such activities encourage the child to take a small, age-appropriate risk in order to promote feelings of competence and confidence. This dimension is especially useful for withdrawn, shy, timid, or anxious children.

Although Sara's determination to "call the shots" and her unwillingness to allow her parents to nurture and care for her reflect a premature effort to grow up, her difficulty separating from her parents implies an underlying fearfulness and sense of inadequacy. It was this underlying sense of inadequacy that led Margaret to use a number of challenging activities in her session—challenges that helped Sara feel more self-confident and more able to express her needs appropriately.

As we have emphasized, all Theraplay sessions are infused whenever possible with the loving playfulness that characterizes healthy parent-infant interaction. For the child who is too serious, intense, or worried, this playfulness is especially necessary.

Gearing Treatment to the Child's Emotional Age

Because the roots of the development of the self and self-esteem and trust lie in the early years, we return in Theraplay treatment to the stage at which the child's emotional development was derailed and provide the experiences that can restart the healthy cycle of interaction. Therefore activities are geared to the child's current emotional level rather than to his chronological age. Whether she is eighteen months or eighteen years old (or even eighty-eight years old), a human being can always benefit from the experience of being responded to in the engaged, empathic, playful, and nurturing manner that is the birthright of all children. As you will see when we describe the use of Theraplay with adolescents, even with older children and adults we provide many regressive, nurturing activities to give them the experiences they have missed.

Although it may seem that Theraplay, like school or entertainment, should be specifically age graded, this is generally not necessary. There is more overlap than difference in activities from one developmental level to another. Children from two to twelve enjoy the nurturing of being given watermelon chunks to eat or having their feet washed, happily engage in the challenge of wrestling matches and seed-spitting contests, and respond to the structure of measuring and weighing as well as of games such as hopscotch, "Mother, may I?" and "Simon says." Of course, some variations on these themes are more appropriate for some levels than for others. The introduction of the baby bottle, for example, if its use is indicated, will need greater tact and diplomacy with an older child. A two-year-old can be directly held and fed; a five-year-old will need some time to play give-and-take games with the bottle (for example, squirting drops of juice in each other's mouths, closing eyes, and guessing the taste).

UNDERSTANDING THE REASONS THAT THERAPLAY MIGHT BE NEEDED

We have discussed the importance to healthy development of being cared for by responsive, caring parents. Missing such positive early experiences, for whatever reason, can lead to the problem behaviors and attachment or relationship problems that Theraplay is designed to treat. Even though, in contrast to other treatment modalities, Theraplay does not focus on helping the *child* understand her early unhappy experiences, the *therapist* must understand what led to the child's missing out on the healthy experience and therefore why she is behaving as she is. This understanding also points to how the attachment or relationship problem can be repaired.

By the time a child is brought for treatment, the early sources of attachment insecurity may no longer be present. The child may no longer be as difficult to soothe, the mother's illness may be a thing of the past, or the child may have been removed from his chaotic, abusive home. Although an improvement in the environment can make a big difference for many children, those who are referred for treatment often show the long-term residual effects of their early experience. These effects still can be seen in the child's need to maintain control, his efforts to keep others at a distance, or any of a number of other behaviors that prevent parents from meeting their child's needs.

It is important that we know how the baby's temperament, special sensitivities, or particular neurological problems (either in the past or on an ongoing basis) make providing the empathic, soothing, recip-rocal response that the child needs difficult. The infant's inability to respond to the caretaker's efforts can be as disruptive to the parent-child relationship as any failure on the caretaker's part to be available.

We must understand the many things that made it difficult for some parents to provide what their baby needed. We need to be aware of the effect on a child of being raised in an orphanage, or of being removed from a neglectful home and cared for by a series of foster parents. Finally, we need to be aware that in some cases an unfortu-nate combination of caretaker problems and the child's special needs prevent the development of a secure attachment.

If we understand how some children's constitutional sensitivities or problems contribute to the relationship problems as well as all the fac-tors that might have prevented parents from responding to their child, we can avoid the temptation to place blame on parents. Parents are all too willing to shoulder this blame and must be helped to understand that there is no room, nor reason, for blame. If we understand what happened to the child as well as what might have prevented the parents from under-standing their child, we can work together to help the child grow.

The Child's Inability to Respond to the Caretaker

Since the response of each partner has so powerful an effect on the relationship, any condition that results in lowered responsiveness on the baby's part or that makes it difficult to soothe and comfort the child or to engage in playful interaction, can result in relationship dif-ficulties and insecure attachment.

CAUSED BY THE CHILD'S DIFFICULT TEMPERAMENT OR REGULATORY PROBLEMS. Babies are born with a wide range of temperaments (Thomas and Chess, 1977), thresholds to incoming stimuli, capacities for responding, and abilities to self-regulate, any one of which can strongly affect the parents' attitudes and caretaking styles.

Middlemore (1941) found a correlation between infant tempera-ment and mothers' responses to their babies. She observed that nurs-ing mothers handled the "irritably inert" babies in a rough manner. The babies, in turn, reacted to this handling by grimacing and with-drawing, and with "stiff immobility."

A study by van den Boom (1995) provides evidence both that dif-ficult infant temperament can lead to insecure attachment and that mothers can be helped to adapt their responses to their irritable babies so that secure attachment can develop. She found that it was possible to enhance the mothers' sensitivity and effectiveness in relating to their irritable babies and thus to increase the number of babies who developed a secure attachment as compared to a control group who received no help in adapting to their infants' irritable temperament. In reporting on this study, Karen (1994, pp. 309–310) states:

> Because the irritable babies were less responsive to their mothers, smiled and made pleasing sounds less frequently, . . . the mothers tended to become discouraged and give up on them in various ways. . . . Other mothers . . . fearful of disrupting a quiet infant, had stopped interacting with their babies when they were not crying. Van den Boom encouraged such mothers to play with the child.

Recently, regulatory problems and hypersensitivities in various sensory modalities are gaining a great deal of attention (Greenspan, 1992a). Such children are so sensitive and irritable that even the most responsive, attuned parent finds it difficult to soothe and comfort the child. The use of a combination of Theraplay and Sensory Integration Therapy with such children is discussed in Chapter Six.

CAUSED BY THE CHILD HAVING CONSTITUTIONALLY BASED NEUROLOGI-CAL PROBLEMS. Autism and pervasive developmental disorders (PDD) are extreme examples of children whose constitutionally based neurological sensitivities and problems interfere with the attachment process. Shahmoon-Shanok (1997, p. 38) says, "When a child has severe difficulties in relating and communicating, these difficulties affect not only the child's development; they also bear upon the relationship between the child and his or her parents." These children's efforts to cope with what to them must be an overwhelmingly confusing world produce behaviors and responses that disrupt the normal attachment process. It is very difficult to engage with and to soothe children who cannot respond to social cues or who constantly push you away. In Chapter Seven we discuss how Theraplay can be adapted to meet the needs of children diagnosed with autistism or PDD.

The Lack of Responsive, Empathic Care

Attachment or relationship problems can also develop if children perceive their primary caretaker as inconsistently available and unresponsive to their needs. Parents might be unable to respond to their child's needs for many reasons: stressful family circumstances, overwhelming health problems, or the inability to provide adequate parenting because they were inadequately parented themselves.

CAUSED BY STRESSFUL FAMILY LIFE. The pressures of life can seem overwhelming: poverty, a rental lease that forbids children, in-laws who harass, a spouse who resents the baby or who abuses his wife. There may be competing demands from the house, a job, or other children. If there is much external stress and strain, parent and baby may not find the time and freedom to enjoy each other's company.

Meeting the many demands of their lives may be so difficult for the parents that they may find themselves increasingly inclined to prop the bottle, turn on the television set, and attend only to the child's physical needs. Frivolity, fun, surprise, and warm, caring moments become fewer as they tend to the necessary, the routine, and the serious problems of family survival.

CAUSED BY PARENTS' HAVING OVERWHELMING HEALTH PROBLEMS. Various physical circumstances may inhibit parents from establishing a good relationship with their baby. Depression, illness, fatigue, pain, or the use of drugs may interfere with their ability to be attentive parents. Parents also may be unable to attend to a baby if a partner is seriously ill or if a close relative dies.

CAUSED BY PARENTS' INABILITY TO PROVIDE ADEQUATE PARENTING. Many parents who are still children themselves or who never got the attentive care they needed find it very difficult to respond empathically to their baby's needs. Many difficulties in parenting have their origins in the parent's own early experiences of being inadequately mothered (Spitz, 1970; Main and Goldwin, 1984). Some parents have had so little response to their own infantile needs that not only are they unable to respond empathically to their baby's needs, but from early on they expect the baby to meet their needs. Research by Main and Hesse (1990) indicates that a mother's understanding of her relationship and experiences of attachment with her own mother are predictive of the attachment relationship with her own infant. In Chapter Five we discuss how Theraplay can begin to meet the needs of parents whose emotional needs have not been met.

CAUSED BY CHILD BEING SEPARATED FROM PARENTS. Prolonged separations or the death of a parent can, of course, have a profound effect on a child. Children who have been removed from their biological parents and placed in foster care or in later adoptions often show the effects of these disruptions on their ability to relate and to become attached. Many of these children were neglected or abused by their first caretakers, and therefore had formed a very insecure attachment before they experienced the loss of their first caretakers.

But perhaps the most damaging situation for a child is that of being raised in an impersonal institution. In the worst institutions the child has no opportunity to form an emotional attachment to any caretaker. The plight of such children was vividly illustrated fifty years ago by Renee Spitz (1945, 1947) through his writings and films about infants raised in institutions. With the recent influx of children adopted from foreign orphanages, we are once again observing the devastating effect of impersonal care (compounded in many cases by poor diet and inadequate medical care) on the development of young children. Many of these children have significant impairments in ego structure, cognitive functioning, regulation of aggression, and ability to relate to people. The Theraplay approach to working with such children, as well as how we work with foster and adopted children in general, is described in Chapter Ten.

Problems Contributed Both by the Child and the Caretaking Environment

A combination of problems in both the child and the caretaking environment will increase the likelihood that the child will have relationship or attachment problems and will need treatment later on. A hypersensitive child whose parents are under stress will be more vulnerable than a hypersensitive child whose parents are relaxed enough to adapt to his special needs.

An example of this is the child whose irritability or hypersensitivity interacts with some parenting problems (such as the mother's postpartum depression or the unavailability of adequate child-care facilities) to produce anxious attachment. We see an example of multiple causes in the case of Adam in Chapter Three.

Sometimes the problem is a mismatch in temperament between the child and a parent. An active, noisy baby whose mother prefers a quiet, restful life is unlikely to receive the attuned responsiveness that fosters a good relationship. Therefore, it is important when working with a family to consider how well the mother and her baby were matched. Was there perhaps a "mismatch" between them so pronounced from the outset that an early, mutual turnoff was the result? A vigorous, aggressive, demanding, unpredictable, physically robust infant, for example, may have been boisterously catapulted into the soft, artistic, gentle routine of his frail, dreamy mother; or, conversely, a driving, energetic father may find himself with a limp, lethargic child. Even granted the best of all external circumstances, such mismatches can easily lead to conflict if one or the other partner was unable to adapt or was hindered in the adaptation process.

RECOGNIZING BEHAVIORS INDICATIVE OF ATTACHMENT PROBLEMS

Children are referred for Theraplay treatment because of a variety of problem behaviors resulting from their having missed out on (or their having been unable to respond to) the kind of parenting that produces healthy, resilient children. The diagnostic category into which the child's behavior falls is less important than the fact that something has been or is currently amiss in the relationship between the child and his early caretakers and that the child does not feel good about himself or expect good things to happen.

As we stated previously, not all behavior problems reflect a current dysfunction in the parent-child relationship but may reflect early experiences that continue to make it difficult for the child to accept what her parents have to offer. Some of these children do well in the structured environment of school but fare poorly at home, where the potential for intimacy makes them uncomfortable. On the other hand, it is not uncommon for a child to do well at home where she feels secure and well understood and yet have problems in school, where the situation is too stimulating and her special needs cannot always be met.

Because Theraplay is designed to make children feel better about themselves, engage them in new, healthier relationships, and teach parents to provide the health-promoting interactions that the child has lacked, it is ideally suited to the treatment of children with attachment and relationship problems. In Chapter Two we discuss the evidence supporting the broad effectiveness of many of the aspects of Theraplay treatment.

We provide next a brief summary of the behavior problems exhibited by attachment-disordered children. The most extreme behaviors are exhibited by children who have been raised in orphanages or who have had early disruptions in their attachment relationship, followed by multiple foster placements. Children who have developed an insecure attachment to their biological parents have similar but usually less severe behavior problems.

Problems Relating to People

Many insecure or attachment-disordered children have problems relating to people. Either they are unable to get close to any one person or they are indiscriminately responsive to many people. They have poor peer relationships and are unable to maintain long-term friendships.

Problems Accepting Care

Many children have problems accepting care from others. Although some children take adequate care of themselves and insist that they need no help from anyone, others are reckless and accident-prone. Jernberg (1989, p. 400) states, "It is not unusual to find these children covered with little scratches, bumps, and bruises."

Problems with Transitions

Many children have difficulty handling change and transitions. Their experience of being unable to count on others to keep their world safe and predictable leads them to insist on clinging to their own special routines. Even routine transitions may cause them to fall apart.

Lack of Conscience

Many children appear to lack a conscience. Behavioral evidence of this ranges from cruelty to animals and human beings to stealing and lying. Teachers often note a lack of empathy when a peer is hurt.

Emotional Immaturity

Children with attachment problems are emotionally immature, as shown in their impulsive behavior, frequent temper tantrums, and lack of awareness of others' needs. The immature, explosive nature of their anger is also related to their insecure attachment. It is in the process of becoming securely attached that a child develops the capacity to modulate the more violent expression of emotions.

Problems with Trust and Self-Esteem

Some unattached or insecurely attached children, having low self-confidence and little trust in their worlds, are clingy and immature. Others cover their insecurity with a facade of pseudo-maturity and independence.

RECOGNIZING SITUATIONS IN WHICH THERAPLAY SHOULD NOT BE USED

Theraplay is designed to treat a wide range of behavior problems that have their origin in children's early experiences of not having received adequate response to their needs. But not all children's problems are simply relationship problems. Some problems are best treated using more traditional play therapy designed to help the child explore and come to terms, through talking or symbolic expression, with traumatic experiences and internal fantasies and fears.

For example, the first choice of treatment for children who have recently been traumatized or abused would be a traditional treatment modality that focuses on helping them understand what has happened to them. However, as we discuss in Chapter Nine, some traumatized children can benefit from a combination of Theraplay and traditional insight therapy.

Theraplay would be the logical first choice to help a newly adopted child establish a secure and trusting relationship with her adoptive parents (see Chapter Ten). However, most adopted children at some time need to explore issues related to the adoption: "Why was I given up?" "Where is my biological mother?" "Who can I talk to about my sadness at losing her?" When such issues surface for the child, she may need treatment that can help her explore those issues by talking about them or working them out in symbolic play.

In this chapter we have given an overview of Theraplay treatment, how it is modeled on healthy parent-infant interaction, and the kinds of problems it is designed to treat. In the following chapter we examine in more detail all aspects of Theraplay treatment and explain why Theraplay has been so effective.

Notes

1. Winnicott (1965) uses the term "good enough mother" to describe the general style of parenting that he considers essential to healthy development.

He is referring to the responsive, empathic relationship that we emphasize throughout the book and describe most fully in Chapter Two. But he is also emphasizing that parents do not have to be perfect. They just have to be "good enough."

2. There is a tendency when talking of infants to focus on the role of the mother as the primary caretaker. Mothers do have a special role as the primary caretaker, especially at the very beginning and especially if they breast-feed their babies. Fathers, however, if they are available, can have an equally important role in their children's development, adding their own special kind of energetic, playful interaction, helping to expand their child's horizons, and helping them become more independent. Throughout this book we will be talking about parents (mothers and fathers), although we know that there are many children who are being successfully raised by one parent, either father or mother, or by many combinations of parents with partners, and by grandparents. It is important that children have a secure sense of one or two dependable caretakers to whom they can turn for comfort and security.

CHAPTER TWO

Understanding Why Theraplay Is Effective

~~~

Like many approaches to treatment, Theraplay began as an experimental attempt to respond therapeutically to an observed need: in this case, the need of the many Head Start children for effective, time-limited treatment. Recognizing in the work of Des Lauriers and Brody (which we described in the Introduction) an intuitively natural approach that could be understood and implemented by relatively untrained people, and also seeing its potential for making an immediate and lasting impact, we adapted their methods to help the Head Start children. And it worked. In a relatively brief time children who had been withdrawn and unhappy became outgoing and self-confident; children who had been overactive and aggressive became calm and cooperative.

How can we explain why "just playing" with children can have such a profound effect? We have no difficulty accepting that it is good for children to feel special, loved, and cared for, but we want to explore in

Parts of this chapter appeared in "Fostering Attachment Through Family Theraplay" by Koller and Booth, *Play Therapy: Theory and Practice* (O'Connor and Braverman, eds.), New York: Wiley, 1997. Reprinted with permission of the publisher.

more detail what it is about the Theraplay method that is so effective. Rather than accepting a global, "feel-good" view of why Theraplay works, we want to tease out the various strands that are woven into its fabric (and that account for its richness and appeal) and compare them with current theories and research on child development. We hope in this way to gain a better understanding of why Theraplay works. Throughout the following discussion, we look at how the elements of Theraplay treatment compare with other treatment approaches.

Originally, much of the support for our assumptions was anecdotal and theoretical. We have been gratified to discover more and more research in the past thirty years that validates our original emphasis on the importance of healthy parent-infant interactions as a model for successful treatment.

We look first at various aspects of the healthy parent-child relationship, which Theraplay replicates, and cite studies and theories that attest to their importance in the development of the child and therefore why they make significant contributions to the effectiveness of Theraplay. These are as follows:

- Developing relatedness
- Using play
- Engaging the child
- Keeping the caregiver in charge
- Meeting the child's unmet regressive needs
- Developing empathic attunement
- Using touch
- Stimulating the body senses
- Addressing regulatory problems

Next we look more generally at what is known about the kinds of parenting patterns that foster secure attachment and the research that indicates that the healthy parenting patterns we replicate in Theraplay and teach to parents are associated with secure attachment:

- Understanding the importance of the parent-child relationship
- Recognizing patterns of attachment
- Including parents in treatment

Finally, we look at how the interaction promotes a positive view of self and the world, and conclude with our optimistic view of the possibility for change.

REPLICATING THE HEALTHY PARENT-CHILD RELATIONSHIP

We set out to replicate the healthy parent-infant relationship by imitating the active, engaging, playful, and nurturing ways in which parents interact with their young children. We include parents or primary caregivers in our treatment sessions because we want them to learn how to adapt these ways of interacting to meet the special needs of their children. At first parents are observers, then participants, eventually taking their newly learned skills and understanding into the home.

In focusing on the parent-infant relationship as we developed Theraplay, we aligned ourselves with interpersonal theories of human development, especially Self Psychology (the work of Heinz Kohut, 1971, 1977, 1984) and Object Relations Theory (particularly the work of Winnicott, 1958, 1965, 1971). Their arguments for the importance of the parent-infant relationship in the development of the child lend strong support to our work. Winnicott makes the point emphatically: "There is no such thing as a baby . . . [there is only] a nursing couple. . . . Without a good-enough technique of infant care the new human being has no chance whatever" (1958, p. 99).

In the thirty years since we first developed Theraplay, an increasing body of research in the fields of child development and attachment theory has focused on the early mother-child relationship and its effects on the child's development (see Ainsworth, 1969; Belsky and Nezworski, 1988; Karen, 1994; Stern, 1985, 1995). That research has added a more solid theoretical base to our understanding of why Theraplay treatment with its emphasis on the early parent-child relationship and on attachment is effective.

Developing Relatedness

The goal of Theraplay treatment is to develop a healthy relationship between the child and her therapist and as quickly as possible between the child and her parents. This emphasis on the actual relationship leads to a number of differences in treatment practice between Theraplay and other child play therapy modalities. Rather than encouraging the child to *understand* her relationship with her parents and other adults through symbolic play, we encourage her to form a healthy, direct relationship with her parents through playful, engaging activities. Theraplay sessions include many activities borrowed from the spontaneous repertoire of parents that increase the child's awareness of and connection with others, including peek-a-boo, tug-of-war, and push-me-over.[1] Through these kinds of activities the child begins to be more aware of our presence and of the pleasure we can share, and subsequently, can experience the impact of pleasurable play with her parents.

In focusing on developing a relationship, we tap into a basic human need for connection and relatedness. Theraplay assumes (as do the interactional theories of human development) that a primary motivating force in human behavior is a drive toward relatedness. Personality development is essentially interpersonal. The early interaction between parent and child is the essential environment in which the self and personality develop. Being human depends on being raised by human beings.

Bowlby (1969) postulates that the drive toward relatedness is supported in both adults and infants by innate mechanisms that keep the baby safe and ensure that she and her caretakers remain close and interact in a caring way. Parents respond instinctively to their infant's cries, smiles, and babbling. The baby in turn has an instinct to remain close. Once she can move about, she explores her environment as long as she is assured of her parents' availability, and she frequently returns to them as to a secure base (Ainsworth, 1969). The interaction, thus assured, allows the infant to learn what kind of person she is and what it means to be human.

Stern (1985), on the basis of careful observation of mother-infant interaction, describes stages in the development of the self, which he sees as an interactional process between the innately social infant and his engaged, empathic mother. We return to this aspect of the interaction when we describe how our playful interaction replicates the affectively attuned play that he has observed between babies and mothers.

Given the importance of the drive toward relatedness, and of the interaction between parent and child in the development of the self and of self-esteem, the inclusion of parents in the treatment makes good sense and clearly adds to the power of Theraplay. Later in this chapter, we compare our way of working with parents with other treatment models that include parents.

Using Play

Perhaps the most innovative aspect of Theraplay treatment is the nature of the play itself. It is the kind of play that belongs to the earliest stages of development. It is the joyful play of a parent with an infant, play that entices the infant into a relationship. It emphasizes physical, concrete, here-and-now experiencing rather than insight and talking. It neither looks for symbolic meanings nor reenacts old conflicts. There is only the strong message, "I like you. I want to be with you. You are very special. Being together is a pleasure." It is play that both fosters a secure attachment and has a direct impact on the child's view of herself and of the world.

When we first developed Theraplay, the major approaches to child psychotherapy were based either on Freudian or on Rogerian theory. Although Freud had talked about the importance of the dyadic early mother-child relationship, he placed greater emphasis on the later triadic Oedipal relationship as a source both of character development and later neurotic conflicts. Because of its emphasis on internal conflicts, Freudian theory dictates an approach to treatment in which the therapist's role is to help the patient understand his unconscious conflicts and repressed mental contents. Beginning with Anna Freud and Melanie Klein, child treatment had depended on symbolic play with toys as a means of communication and as a substitute for the free-association of adult analysis. Play was seen as a way of understanding the child's view of his experience.

Similarly, Rogerian theory and the client-centered play therapy that developed from it see the therapist's role as that of facilitating the child's expression of his inner experience and view of the world through symbolic play. In both approaches the therapist follows the child's lead and initiates action only to set limits on dangerous or destructive behavior. The child enters a playroom full of toys designed to invite the expression of feelings and the acting out of important themes for the child. The therapist's role varies from quiet observer to active follower of the child's symbolic play.

The differences both in our theoretical base and our goals for treatment dictate a very different way of interacting with the child in treatment. We believe that if we are to change the child's view of himself and the parents' way of relating, we need to initiate the more active play that is very natural in the parent-child relationship but very different from the play of most other kinds of child therapy. We bring the child into a room without toys so that the entire focus will be on the relationship between the child and her therapist. We then initiate activities borrowed from the parent-infant repertoire, which are active, physical, playful, and surprising. We even use play to escort the child into the playroom. (In Chapter One, Sara was reluctant to part from her mother, so her therapist, hoping to change a fearful experience into a fun one, had her jump on pillows as she entered the room.) To many child therapists, our active, hands-on, "intrusive" play is shockingly different.

Both Stern and Winnicott stress the importance of play. Stern writes, "The more games with which a mother can interest and delight an infant, the more practice he will have in experiencing affectively positive arousal . . . in a greater number of human situations" (1974, p. 416).

Winnicott describes the importance of play in creating an intermediate area of experience between subjectivity and objectivity, that is, play that bridges the reality-based play of the mother with her infant and the fantasy-based play that comes later. He writes, "It is play that is the universal, and that belongs to health: playing facilitates growth and therefore health; playing leads into group relationships" (1971, p. 41; italics in original).

Engaging the Child

Since our goal is to improve the relationship between a child and her parents, we initiate games that entice children into interaction with us. We play "blow the cotton ball off each other's nose" with a young child and tug-of-war with an older child. We rub lotion on hurts and make powder handprints. We check how high a child can jump and how fast she can crawl through a tunnel made by her parents' bodies.

Theraplay's playful approach is able to stimulate, entice, and delight children who have turned away out of fear or hopelessness or whose inherent underreactivity (as in the case of some children with regulatory disorders or autistic spectrum disorders) keeps them from responding. Such playfulness helps them risk becoming connected and allowing someone to take care of them and make life enjoyable.

Greenspan, in his treatment of young children with severe difficulties in relating and communicating, also emphasizes the importance of "establishing a relationship with two-way communication" and of establishing "a pleasurable sense of attention and engagement." Although following the child's lead is an important principle in his approach, Greenspan acknowledges that it is necessary with such children to insert one's presence into their play. Working with these resistant, self-isolating children, he sees the need to interrupt their self-absorbed behavior and to make his presence known to the child. In order to do this, he says that "enormous ingenuity and persistence" and even some intrusive intervention is required. "The more quickly these children and their parents are reengaged in emotional interactions that use their emerging . . . capacities for communication, . . . the better they do" (1992b, p. 4). To address the problems that interfere with the child's ability to relate to others in a normal way, Greenspan and Wieder recommend "wooing the low tone, underreactive child; protecting and soothing the overreactive child, creating challenges to facilitate purposeful behavior and circles of interaction in the child who is aimless or fragmented" (1997, p. 8).

Wieder provides guidelines for working with such children that include many of the specific strategies that Theraplay uses. She suggests that it is important to involve children in activities they enjoy. "Especially with children who have low motor tone and difficulties in sequencing and motor planning, you may need to go back to the motor-sensory games of early infancy, like tickling, peek-a-boo, 'This little piggy,' and 'horsie rides.' This is the earliest kind of active pleasure that a child seeks out" (1997, p. 24). All of these engagement strategies are a standard part of the Theraplay repertoire.

Keeping the Caretaker in Charge

To achieve our goal of engaging the child in a relationship, we confidently initiate activities rather than follow the child's lead. Mothers know that this is important and take active steps to engage their babies for periods of intense interactive play. Children who come for treatment often do not anticipate pleasure in interaction with adults and are unable or unwilling to initiate activities that might lead to engagement. They need someone to draw them out and take steps to initiate a new kind of interaction.

An even more important reason for taking charge of sessions is to provide the safety and security of well-defined limits and boundaries. With young infants, parents do not question the necessity of taking charge to make things safe. As their children grow older and become more independent, parents often need to be reminded of the importance of defining and enforcing clear rules as they and their child negotiate the steps toward adult independence.

Questions such as, "Would you like to play with me?" or, "What do you want to do today?," which are appropriate in ordinary social interaction with healthy children, convey uncertainty on the part of the therapist and place a heavy burden of choice on the child's emotionally immature shoulders. Even though the child may protest the therapist's directly involving the child in play, it is what she needs. The adult does her no favor to sit passively by, watching her spin out of control or sink further into her passivity. There will be time enough for the child to grow into more independent, self-initiated activity after she has established a more secure relationship with her caretaker. If this were a healthy child, brimming full of ideas and fully capable of remaining engaged with the world, that is, not needing treatment, such a giving of choices would be appropriate as long as it took place within a structure that provided safety and clear limits.

To provide a clear structure in Theraplay, we take responsibility for the activities carried out within each session and for the progression of activities from one session to another. We plan sessions carefully with an eye to the child's needs, making sure that each session has periods of high energy alternating with periods of quiet and calm. In Chapter Three we describe this aspect of Theraplay planning in more detail.

As a result of living in circumstances where their needs were not met, many children who come for treatment (especially those in foster care or in late adoptions, or those whose hypersensitivities make them difficult to soothe) have learned that they can depend only on themselves. Their need to take charge and call all the shots interferes with their being able to form a secure attachment. It is a heavy burden on a child to maintain this pseudo-adult role. Therefore, an important reason for taking the lead with such children is to relieve them of the need to take charge of their lives. They need to be able to be children again, to play, and to enjoy the nurturing care of an adult who can make the world safe for them.

If the child tries to take charge of the session by suggesting activities to play, we say, "You have great ideas, but today I have some special games I have planned just for you." If he attempts to control or manipulate by talking or arguing (as Adam does in Chapter Three), we ignore the talk and move on to more engaging activities.

It is evident that we differ markedly from other treatment modalities in the degree to which the therapist takes the initiative in planning activities and responsibility for what happens in sessions. The Theraplay therapist sees himself as having not only every "right," but indeed the obligation to intrude into the child's pathology. In this sense Theraplay resembles the problem-solving therapy of Jay Haley: "The responsibility for change belongs to the therapist. He is expected to plan a strategy of change to bring about what the patient is paying money to achieve" (1976, p. 171). The Theraplay therapist's agenda of custom-tailored, relationship-oriented tasks to be done also resembles the agenda of the "structural" therapist Salvador Minuchin (1974). Structural family therapists similarly manipulate the behavior of family members with respect to one another in order to place the parents in an appropriate parental role.

Research suggests that children who grow up in families where clear, appropriate rules are consistently enforced become more self-confident, self-directed adults than children who grow up in laissez-faire or democratic families where children are given more choices.

The opposition between taking charge and following the child's lead is not as clear-cut as it seems. Client-centered therapy, based on the belief in an innate drive toward health, strongly emphasizes respecting the child's ability to work things out for himself. Our approach respects the child's need for developmentally appropriate interaction and engagement. We view this aspect of Theraplay as a precursor to the kind of symbolic play that is the core of most other treatments. The exploration of inner issues is very important for many children, and there are a number of treatment modalities well suited to the task. But as we have stated before, our goal is not to explore inner issues but to change the relationship between the child and her parents.

The intensity of the opposition that sometimes gets expressed about this issue comes from each side having a somewhat distorted view of the other's approach. We oppose a laissez-faire, "leave it up to the child" approach that at its worst allows the child to flounder and fails to address essential relationship aspects of many problems. Our critics are opposed to an authoritarian, take-charge, nonempathic approach that fails to respect the child's potential for self-actualization. The true nature of each approach lies somewhere in between. Each approach has different goals to which it is well suited.

Having emphasized our differences we must note a strong area of agreement. All treatment modalities agree in emphasizing the importance of safety rules and clear limits. Limits and structure are important elements that help the child move from a belief that he magically controls the world and is the only power in his world, to an understanding that he must take others into account and that he is grounded in reality. Landreth and Sweeney, leading proponents of client-centered play therapy, say, "Children do not feel safe, valued, or accepted in a completely permissive relationship" (1997, p. 23). They quote Moustakas (1959, p. 9) in the same vein: "In a therapeutic relationship, limits provide the boundary or structure in which growth can occur."

Meeting the Child's Unmet Regressive Needs

A natural consequence of modeling our approach on the parent-infant relationship is that we use a variety of regressive activities. We adapt baby games for children of all ages. For example, we play peek-a-boo and patty-cake with preschool children. We hold and rock and sing lullabies to school-age children. We feed children of all ages (often using baby bottles with particularly needy youngsters). With adolescents, we provide nurturing care through many playful activities. For example, we might make a trail of painted footprints on a long roll of paper, which we then hang up to look as though the teenager had "walked right up the wall." In order to do this, we first gently put the paint on his feet with our hands, and later wash and powder his feet and help put shoes and socks back on.

Responding to the child's regressive needs is a necessary step in restarting the healthy cycle of interaction. Because the roots of the development of the self, self-esteem, and trust lie in the early years, and because attachment develops when a caretaker responds empathically to a young child's needs, we encourage parents to attend to the child's regressive needs.

Winnicott (1958) emphasizes the importance of regression in the process of cure. It represents a return to the point at which the environment failed the child, and it allows the child to meet early developmental needs. For Winnicott, the curative factor in treatment is not primarily in the verbal interpretations, but in how the treatment setting fills these early needs. "The tendency to regression in a patient is now seen as part of the capacity of the individual to bring about self-cure" (1965, p. 128).

Greenspan (1992a, p. 6) likewise states that because young children with autistic spectrum or pervasive developmental disorder

> often lack the most basic foundation for interpersonal experiences (that is, they are often not interactive in the purposeful way that ordinary eight-month-olds are), much of the experience that they might use to abstract a sense of their own personhood is not available to them.
>
> Therefore, for these children, the earliest therapeutic goals must be geared to the first steps in the developmental progression, that is, to foster focus and concentration, engagement with the human world, and two-way intentional communication. . . .

We are in agreement about the demonstrated need to go back to the very earliest precursors to interpersonal communication.

Developing Empathy

As the Theraplay therapist engages the child in playful give-and-take activities, there are many opportunities for matching her own actions to those of the child and thus creating a finely tuned "dance" of interaction. Some Theraplay activities are designed specifically for this purpose, for example, "peanut butter and jelly"— a game in which the object is for adult and child to match the loudness and pitch of their words. The adult says "peanut butter" and the child tries to say "jelly" in just the same way—loud, soft, with different emphasis, and so on.

To help a parent develop a coordinated physical activity with an impulsive older child, we use what we call a "mirroring" game. The parent and child sit or stand facing each other and the child is asked to mirror his parent's movements. Once the child can follow both fast and slow movements, he can take the lead, giving his parent practice in imitating her child's movements.

In many activities not just the child's actions are matched but also the affective intensity of the activity. In all our interactions we respond empathically to the child's moods, matching our emotional intensity with the child's emotional intensity and generally helping the child learn the new ways of "dancing" with their parents. Even the child's most intense emotional expressions are matched. For example, the shouts of an angry child are matched in intensity and tone by the therapist. In Chapter Three we describe Adam's therapist responding to his angry resistance during his first session: "You're mad!" she shouts, and for a moment Adam stops his protest as though surprised that she has truly understood his feelings.

In Theraplay we help parents understand and match their child's feelings as well as actions. For example, a parent attempting to soothe her easily overstimulated child might rock too fast. We gently put an arm around her and slow the pace of her rocking until it is soothing for both her and her child. If a parent is out of tune with his child's sad or hurt feelings, we ask him how he thinks his child is feeling. Once he is aware, we ask him to do something that would make her feel better, for example, rocking her in a blanket or in his arms and singing her a comforting song. In Chapter Five we describe in more detail how we help parents develop empathy for their child.

Empathy is important to the developmental theories of Kohut, Winnicott, Ainsworth, and Stern. Kohut (1984) argues that the empathic responses of caretakers to the infant's affective states lead to the development of a cohesive nuclear self. Winnicott (1958, p. 219) states that the basis of mental health is "laid down in infancy by the techniques which come naturally to a mother who is preoccupied with the care of her own infant." The baby begins life as an unintegrated receiver of experience. It is the mother's response to the child that allows him to become integrated.

But perhaps most important to our thinking about the development of empathy in Theraplay is Stern's description of affect attunement between babies and their mothers. He argues that the affective attunement between a mother and her baby leads to awareness on the baby's part of its own feelings and the feelings of others and ultimately to the capacity to empathize with others.

He describes a developmental sequence that begins with the mother imitating the baby's actions. By nine months, the mother expands her actions beyond imitation into a new category of behavior, which Stern (1985) calls *affect attunement*. Affect attunement is the "performance of behaviors that express the quality of feeling of a shared affect state without imitating the exact behavioral expression of the inner state." These behaviors are important because they shift the focus from the action (which would be the focus of imitation) to what is behind the behavior, "to the quality of feeling that is being shared. . . . Imitation renders form; attunement renders feeling" (p. 142).

Stern gives the following example: "A nine-month-old boy bangs his hand on a soft toy, at first in some anger but gradually with pleasure, exuberance, and humor. He sets up a steady rhythm. Mother falls into his rhythm and says, 'kaaaa-*bam,* kaaaa-*bam,*' the '*bam*' falling on the stroke and the 'kaaaa' riding with the preparatory upswing and the suspenseful holding of his arm aloft before it falls" (p. 140).

Such interactions occur over and over in the early years and become part of the shared experience of the child and his mother. Rebecca Shahmoon-Shanok (1997, p. 38) describes a beautifully attuned interaction between a two-year-old boy and his mother and comments:

> We can see how, by varying and repeating similar pictures a myriad of times, as happens in a good-enough baby- and toddlerhood, the development of love and play; of attention and shared attention; of cognition and differentiated emotions; of communication and organization; of the use of symbol and narrative; and of an internal sense of safety and hope happens all of a piece, simultaneously, each element woven into all of the others in the context of contingent, reciprocal attachment. How ordinary and how *extraordinary* it is that so much happens within relationship: autonomy grows out of attachment [emphasis in original].

Many children who have missed this early dance of attunement lack two essential ingredients for getting along with peers: they are unable to understand how their peers are feeling and therefore are unable to take their feelings into account; and they are unable to play interactive games in an appropriate give-and-take manner. These are the skills that Theraplay's interactive play can teach.

Using Touch

Just as in the interaction of parents with their children, Theraplay has always emphasized the importance of touch. In all of our interactions, whether playful or nurturing, we make opportunities for touch. We hold and rock and cuddle children. We rub lotion on their hands and feet and make playful games out of how slippery they are and how hard to catch. All of these activities help children become more aware of their bodies and of the value of their bodies. Myrow, describing the importance of touch in Theraplay, says (1997, p. 1), "With the experience of touch from a loving caretaker, the child develops a sense of self; the capacity to relate to other people; essential skills in modulating affect; a sense of being able to master the environment; and a belief in his own worth." When we encourage parents to include more touch in their play with their children, we are helping them foster a secure attachment by becoming the source of comfort and calming for their children. "When a child already has a secure attachment, physical contact is one channel for quickly establishing a therapeutic relationship, from which to help the child and caregivers resolve more contemporary conflicts, e.g., accepting consistent limits from parents. Fun and physical Theraplay activities work quickly to build trust and invite openness to change" (p. 3).

When we first began doing Theraplay, we enthusiastically borrowed physically intimate activities from the parent-child repertoire, including kissing tummies, eating pudding off fingers, and playing with children in their bath. Now that we are all alerted to the prevalence of physical and sexual abuse of children, we are more careful to avoid the appearance of inappropriate touch. For example, we no longer lift children's shirts to expose bare tummies. Although such an activity is in no way harmful to a child when done by a loving adult who has the child's best interest in mind, we do not want to stir up anxiety in those who observe our work.

This accommodation to current fears about touch, however, does not mean that we hesitate to provide the touch children need. Brazelton (1990, p. 561) says, "Touch functions on many levels of adaptation, first to make survival possible and then to make life meaningful." Touch is indeed fundamental to the human experience. Because it is so important, we make sure that we provide it in as many healthy ways as possible. In Chapter Nine we describe how we address the need for healthy touch with children who have been physically or sexually abused. With all children we guard against using touch inappropriately by asking ourselves, "Whose need is being met right now? My own or the child's?" The answer must always be, "The child's."

EFFECT ON SOCIAL DEVELOPMENT. The importance of touch in attachment is well established. Harlow (1958, p. 676), based on his studies of the importance of touch to infant monkeys, states that "contact comfort is a variable of overwhelming importance in the development of affectional responses." Monkeys reared in isolation behave in autistic-like ways. They indulge in stereotyped behaviors and often turn to their own bodies for comfort. We have seen similar patterns of self-comforting behavior in children adopted from extremely depriving environments such as orphanages. The unfortunate outcome of Harlow's early experiments was a group of adult monkeys who were incompetent in peer relationships and were later inadequate parents, if they could mate at all. Montagu (1971, p. 136) states, "The behavior and motivations of all mammalian infants are directed toward maintaining contact with the mother. Contact seeking is the foundation upon which all subsequent behavior develops." As Main (1990, p. 462) points out, the mother's touch has the greatest impact on a child's social development. She starts with Bowlby's premise that physical contact with an attachment figure is the most important signal to an infant that he is safe. She then argues that the accessibility of that primary attachment figure in times of stress (or simply as support for exploration) is an "organizing principle in the infant's behavior" (p. 484). If the attachment figure is not within reach or physically accessible, or especially if she rejects the infant's touch, anger and conflict may develop in the infant.

EFFECT ON PHYSIOLOGICAL DEVELOPMENT. In addition to promoting psychological and emotional well being, touch also regulates physiological development. Clinical data suggest that early tactile experience influences an infant's immunological response, growth rate, weight gain, and ability to withstand stress. For example, Field's (1995, p. 107) research shows that pre-term infants given daily full body massages show a greater weight gain, increased activity, and higher levels of performance on the Brazelton Scale. Furthermore, touch has proved to be a significant factor in guiding perceptual and cognitive development. Research has shown, for example, that touch can increase an infant's sensorimotor performance, learning and activity level, responsivity, and visual recognition capacity (Barnard and Brazelton, 1990).

Although there has not been extensive work on touch in relation to adolescents and adults, preliminary research suggests that contact remains important for the maintenance of both physical and emotional health at all ages (Fanslow, 1990).

EFFECT ON MANAGEMENT OF STRESS. In addition to its effect on social and physiological development, studies indicate that touch is important in regulating infant stress. Babies who were touched by their mothers during an experimentally induced, brief stressful episode showed reduced levels of stress as compared with babies who were not touched. Tronick (1995, pp. 64–65) concluded that "touch is a component of the mutual regulatory process of the caretaker-infant dyad and that it serves as an external regulator of the affective and behavioral organization of the infant." Tronick also theorizes that different forms of touch convey different messages. Gentle holding and stroking, for example, communicate safety, soothing, and comfort. Poking and pinching, on the other hand, convey threat. In this sense, touch may be seen as critical to the communication system between mothers and infants.

EFFECT ON BODY IMAGE. Weiss (1990, p. 428), in a review of the literature on the connection between tactile experience and the development of body perception, reports research suggesting that if a human infant is not touched and handled sufficiently at an early age, he may develop a distorted body image. She also reports research suggesting that bodily contact with autistic children reinforces symbolic representation, thereby correcting distorted body perceptions. "Studies have indicated that an individual who receives body contact from others over most body areas, in contrast to only a few areas, generally feels more attractive, closer to other persons, possesses an accurate perception of the form and shape of his body, and has a more positive liking for himself as a person" (p. 432).

The evidence for the importance of touch in the interaction of parents with their children is overwhelming. Clearly, treatment intended to help a child form an attachment, improve self-image, and regulate or modulate anxiety would do well to include it.

Stimulating the Body Senses

When we jump up and down with a child, lift him high in the air, or firmly rub his arms and legs with lotion, we are stimulating the body senses (tactile, vestibular, proprioceptive)[2] in just the way that parents do. Such stimulation is important, according to Williamson and Anzalone (1997, pp. 31–32), because "the tactile, vestibular, and proprioceptive systems are intimately involved in the infant's developing sense of self and ability to interact motorically and emotionally with people and objects." Intervention with "children who have problems in these systems is designed to enable the child to attain desired sensory thresholds, achieve an optimal level of arousal and attention, and support a more positive affect during social and environmental interactions" (p. 36).

Early in our work, particularly with autistic children, we became aware that some children find it very difficult to "manage their bodies in space," to accept being off-balance or to handle vestibular stimulation. Their difficulty led them to avoid active off-balance movement and to resist letting anyone move them about. We found that by gently introducing children to a variety of postures, we could help them overcome their fears.

Other children's tactile defensiveness made it very difficult to provide the soothing, nurturing touch that is so essential to children's developing sense of body self and to the relationship with their parents. We gradually introduce touch to such children in a variety of ways that help them accept it.

Some children have such a need for proprioceptive stimulation that they are constantly jumping up and down, flapping their hands, and becoming overexcited. Our active physical play in which we organize their frantic, random movements and yet give them plenty of stimulation has proved helpful to them.

Occupational therapists trained to treat children with sensory integration problems have commented that our playful, physical, sensory-based interaction uses many of the techniques that they use in their work. Combining a focus on the relationship with treatment of specific sensory integration problems is helpful to these children. In Chapter Six we discuss how sensory integration techniques can be combined with Theraplay in the treatment of children with sensory integration problems and regulatory disorders.

Addressing Regulatory Problems

In the early days of Theraplay, we approached all children with the enthusiasm and energy that we believed was typical of parents with their infants. With autistic children, in particular, we assumed that it was necessary to provide a high level of stimulation to arouse and engage them. Very quickly we discovered that many children with autism are hyperreactive to stimuli or have shut down in order to protect themselves and therefore appear underreactive. We found that it is essential to reduce our level of stimulation in order for them to risk engaging with us. Children with less serious neurological problems vary greatly in their tolerance for stimulation.

With this awareness we began tailoring our activities more sensitively to the child's comfort with stimulation and capacity for regulating excitement. We looked for ways to calm and soothe the overexcited child, to enliven the lethargic child, and help both children develop a greater capacity for self-soothing. With the easily overstimulated child, we use a preponderance of calming, nurturing activities, such as quietly blowing a cotton ball back and forth rather than having the child push the therapist over and end up in an exciting flip. When a child reaches too high a level of excitement, we slow the activity down to keep him from escalating out of control. With such a child, our goal is to increase his capacity to tolerate excitement without losing control. For the underreactive child, we use exciting, stimulating activities to engage him in interaction with us.

In this way, we help the child modulate his activity level, providing the safe structure and soothing presence that he needs. Only if children have repeated experiences of being helped to modulate excitement by loving caretakers will they develop the capacity to soothe and nurture themselves in later life.

Williamson and Anzalone (1997, p. 36), describing treatment for children with regulatory problems, state, "Intervention is designed to enable the child to attain desired sensory thresholds, achieve an optimal level of arousal and attention, and support a more positive affect during social and environmental interactions." Greenspan (1992b) considers the regulation of sensory experience the first step in communication and affective interaction. Parents of children with sensory modulation problems need help to understand and adjust to their child's regulatory needs.

The role of the parent in providing calming and soothing experiences is very important for both Kohut and Winnicott. Kohut (1984, p. 30) argues that early experiences of being able to merge with the calmness and omnipotence of an idealized parental self-object are later "transmuted into self-soothing structures capable of preventing the spread of anxiety." Winnicott's concept of the maternal holding environment points to the importance of the mother's being able to maintain a calm, safe, nurturing environment where the infant is free from overwhelming stimuli and able to develop a true self.[3]

Current research (Gunnar, 1997) into the effect of stress on brain development underlines the importance of a secure attachment relationship in modulating the infant's stress response. Levels of the stress hormone cortisol were measured before and after infants received their series of immunization shots. Following each shot, cortisol levels spiked. At fifteen months, however, securely attached infants showed no cortisol increase. Infants who were insecurely attached continued to have a spiking of cortisol levels. Secure attachment was thus demonstrated to modulate stress levels.[4]

Having examined in detail the various aspects of Theraplay treatment that replicate the healthy parent-child relationship, we turn now to the more general issue of how Theraplay fosters a secure attachment relationship between the child and his parents.

FOSTERING ATTACHMENT

Beverly James (1994, p. 24) provides us with an excellent definition of a secure attachment relationship. It is "a love relationship that is caring, is reciprocal, and develops over time. Attachment provides the nurturance and guidance that foster gradual and appropriate self-reliance, leading to mastery and autonomy."

Research into the kinds of parenting that lead to secure attachment has provided us with a further strong argument for why Theraplay is effective. Theraplay replicates the style of parenting that has been found to foster secure attachment. We respond warmly and empathically to the child's needs. We are engaging, lively, and nurturing. Since we use healthy parent-infant interaction as our model, this congruence is hardly surprising.

Understanding the Importance of Attachment

The evidence from separations and losses during the Second World War was what first focused attention on the importance of the parent-child attachment relationship. Children who remained with their parents in London during the most intense bombing fared better than children who were separated from their parents and taken into the country to keep them physically safe. This observation raised questions about the then typical patterns of discouraging parent visits to children in the hospital, placing very young children in residential care, and sending children as young as seven or eight to residential schools.

Bowlby (1951, 1969), in his writings, and the Robertsons (1967–1973), in their films, began calling attention to the devastating effect on young children of even short-term separations from their primary caretakers. For example, one film, *A Two-Year-Old Goes to Hospital* (1952), documents the effect on a young child of a two-week hospitalization with very limited visits from her parents. A second film, *John* (1969), shows the decline over nine days of a seventeen-month-old boy placed in residential care while his mother is in the hospital for the birth of a sibling. Many of the children they observed experienced long-term effects of these early separations. Karen (1994, p. 94) summarizes Bowlby's interpretation of these findings: "Separations from the mother were disastrous developmentally because they thwarted an instinctual need. It's not just a nice thing to have someone billing and cooing over you, snuggling you, and adoringly attending to your every need. It is a built-in necessity, and the baby's efforts to obtain it, like the parents' eagerness to give it are biologically programmed."

Experiments by Tronick and others (1978) have confirmed that maternal unresponsiveness for even a brief period produces reactions of increasing despair in their infants, often leading to complete withdrawal. Lorene Stringer (1971, p. 130) reminds us of the consequences of maternal unresponsiveness: "I think we shall find that the adults who are incapable of forming lasting love relationships, in which they both enjoy and feel enjoyed, had been babies whose parents never played with them in loving, and enjoying ways."

In order for the child to move toward autonomy and independence, however, the parent, after the first few months, must stop responding immediately to every need of the child. Through such mild failures, the child learns that he can survive without the parent's constant presence, that he can become angry or disappointed in the parent's failure to respond, and that both he and his parents can survive that anger and return to their former attuned relationship. Greenberg and Mitchell (1983, pp. 198–199) summarize Winnicott's description: "The infant needs the maternal provisions which define good-enough mothering including: an initial perfectly responsive facilitation of his or her needs and gestures; a nonintrusive "holding" and mirroring environment throughout quiescent states; the collusive agreement to respect transitional objects; survival, despite the intensity of the infant's needs; and the failure to retaliate against the destructive features of object-usage. . . . These relational needs are a developmental imperative; if they are not met, no further meaningful growth can take place."

Recognizing Patterns of Secure and Insecure Attachment

Since Bowlby first alerted the world to the importance of attachment in healthy development, there has been a great deal of research into the kinds of parenting that produce secure and insecure attachment, as well as the long-term behavior patterns associated with each category of attachment.

The *securely* attached child has a mother (or primary caretaker) who is warm, sensitively attuned, consistent, and quickly responsive to her baby's cries and who encourages mutually enjoyable interaction. Securely attached infants are affectionate and can be comforted and calmed when distressed. At two years they are enthusiastic and persistent in solving easy tasks and effective in using maternal assistance when tasks become more difficult. By school age they are flexible, curious, socially competent, and self-reliant. They are assertive about what they want and likely to be leaders.

The parenting styles associated with *insecure* attachment are unresponsive, unavailable, or hurtful. There are three basic patterns of insecure attachment: ambivalent, avoidant, and disorganized. At two years, children who are *ambivalently* attached lack self-reliance, show little enthusiasm for problem solving, and are easily frustrated and whiney. By school age they are often seen as problem children with poor peer relations and little resilience. They seem hopeless in response to imagined separations.

At two years of age, *avoidant* children are less able to engage in fantasy play than secure children, but even when fantasy play is present it is full of irresolvable conflict. These children tend to victimize other children. By school age, they are often sullen and oppositional and not inclined to seek help when injured or disappointed (Karen, 1990). Both the *avoidant* and the *disorganized* group of children had parents who showed some aversion to physical contact with their infants.

For the *disorganized* group, however, there was an additional factor. Disorganized children had parents who rejected their approach and at the same time expressed fear themselves or were frightening to the child. When the attack or fear comes from the haven of safety it arouses conflicting tendencies. These children showed tense mannerisms (pulling their ears and rocking) during the reunion phase of the observation. Even when happy they avoided eye contact. Children's angry behavior is highly correlated with mothers' earlier resistance to child-initiated contact (Main, 1990).

In Chapter One we listed the behaviors of children with attachment disorders. Note that many of the behaviors listed there correspond to the descriptions of children who fall into the three categories of insecure attachment.

Including Parents in Treatment

Parents or primary caretakers, if they are available, are always included in Theraplay treatment. They are essential to the process of changing the relationship between them and their child. Because they are the child's primary caretaker, they are the ones to whom the child should turn for security and comfort. Our goals for parents include teaching them how to respond more empathically to their child's needs, helping them interact in new ways that promote their child's healthy development, and providing them with the skills that will enhance their relationship with their child. First they observe sessions, then they participate under the guidance of the Theraplay therapist, and finally they take charge of sessions. We include role-playing and homework assignments as part of our program of preparing parents for their role as Theraplay therapists for their children. Chapter Five explains how we work with parents.

Traditional play therapy, with its focus on the child's inner world, has tended to keep parents out of sessions, but a number of approaches are now including parents in treatment: for example, Filial Therapy (Guerney), Floor Time (Greenspan), and, of course, Family Therapy. Therapists working with abused and traumatized children, for example Beverly James (1989, 1994) and Eliana Gil (1991), also include parents in some of their children's sessions.

Filial Therapy, developed by Bernard and Louise Guerney (Guerney, 1997, p. 131) in the 1960s and 1970s, trains parents for direct involvement in the process, although in a much less physically active way than Theraplay. "The instruction to parents in play therapy skills is based on learning and reinforcement principles, but the instruction is affectively oriented with an emphasis on the client-centered principles of empathy and acceptance." Parents are given practice in observing their child's play in order to gain a better understanding of the child's point of view. The principle is to let the child lead the way, avoiding criticism, judgment, advice, questions, and interpretation. The therapeutic value of limits is stressed, and parents are taught to be comfortable with setting limits. The goal of Filial Therapy is to train parents to assume the internal frame of reference of the child. The result for the child and parents of this new way of relating is an improvement in the parent-child relationship based on the parents' greater understanding of the child's perceptions and feelings. The focus is on current problems and on learning new, positive ways to relate. Treatment is relatively short-term: ten to twelve sessions plus follow-up. The training includes opportunities to practice the skills in role-played episodes. Interactions are videotaped, and parents watch the tapes and are coached in fine-tuning their skills.

There are evident similarities between Theraplay and Filial Therapy in the ways parents are involved as active agents for change. The major differences in our approaches are in the level of activity of the parents and the different goals of the two approaches. In contrast to client-centered play therapy, Theraplay encourages parents to take the initiative in engaging the child in playful interaction. For Theraplay the goal is an immediate change in the way the parent and child interact. For client-centered play therapy the goal is for the parents to gain a greater understanding of the child's perceptions and feelings, which, presumably, would also lead to a change in the way the parent and child interact.

In Floor Time, as in client-centered play therapy, parents are encouraged to follow the child's lead but are given a more active role in attempting to develop an interaction with their difficult-to-reach children. The goal is to entice the child into symbolic play and to complete circles of communication. Greenspan (1992b, p. 5) states, "The primary goal of intervention is to enable children to form a sense of their own personhood—a sense of themselves as intentional, interactive individuals."

Rather than move as quickly as possible to symbolic play, Theraplay focuses on the presymbolic interactive play typical of a very young child. We believe that when the relationship has gone awry or the child's self-image is very distorted, the best way to improve the relationship is to "start over." Theraplay begins as parents do with infants, interacting in ways that truly convince the child that she is lovable, that you are caring, and that the world is a good place to be.

PROMOTING A POSITIVE VIEW OF SELF AND THE WORLD

Beyond the truism that it is good for children to feel special, loved, and cared for, we wanted to understand the many aspects of Theraplay treatment that make it effective. Having looked at each of these aspects, we turn now to consider just what it means to a child's view of herself of having her needs met and being treated as special and loved.

In our playful, positive interaction with children in Theraplay, we give them an experience from which they can develop a new view of themselves. We pay special attention to each child's positive characteristics, the beautiful color of his eyes, the softness of his skin, the strength of his muscles, and the speed of his punch. We accept children as they are and value everything about them. We convey the message, "You are lovable, you are competent, you are special. You deserve to have your needs met and to be taken care of."

We also give them a new view of the world and how people in their world can respond to them. We present them with a world full of fun and surprises as well as full of caring, responsive adults. We change the child's picture of herself and the world and therefore change the way she behaves and the kinds of responses she evokes from others.

To explain the profound and lasting impact of early experience, Bowlby (1973, p. 203) used the concept of *internal working models:* "Each individual builds working models of the world and of himself in it, with the aid of which he perceives events, forecasts the future, and constructs his plans. In the working model of the world that anyone builds, a key feature is his notion of who his attachment figures are, where they may be found, and how they may be expected to respond. Similarly, in the working model of the self that anyone builds a key feature is his notion of how acceptable or unacceptable he himself is in the eyes of his attachment figures." The important issues for the child are, "How acceptable am I in my parents' eyes? How consistently available are my parents?"

Main, Kaplan, and Cassidy (1985, p. 94), expanding on this idea, suggest that early parent-child relationships result in a cognitive "template" that acts as a filter for the "perception of all succeeding experience and direct[s] all succeeding behavior."

When things go well in the relationship, the infant develops an inner representation of himself as lovable, special, competent, and able to make an impact on the world; of others as loving, caring, responsive, and trustworthy, that is, as being reliably available; and of the world as a safe, exciting place to explore. Within a secure attachment, he begins a process of learning about himself and the world that is positive and hopeful and that will have a powerful influence throughout his life.

ACKNOWLEDGING THAT CHANGE IS POSSIBLE

Our conviction that change is possible and that it is never too late to go back and create a healthy new experience for the child leads us to take active, persistent steps to create that change.

Although there is considerable evidence that an early attachment category (secure or insecure) is both persistent and stable, there is also evidence that change, both positive and negative, is possible. Examples of positive change can be found when the child has a good adoption experience, or when family circumstances improve. As Sroufe (1988, p. 23) reports, "When our poverty mothers form stable relationships with a partner, child adaptation improves." And, of course, a child's security can be negatively affected by loss through death or divorce or through long absences due to illness.

Like anyone who embarks on a career as a psychotherapist, we assume that change is possible. The clinical literature is full of anecdotal evidence of change. Indeed, our experience working with the Head Start children convinced us that Theraplay could effect a change and that the essential ingredients of change lie in the creation of a more positive relationship between the child and his or her parents or caretakers.

Notes

1. You will find a list of Theraplay activities with descriptions of how they are played in Appendix C.

2. The tactile system functions both for protection and discrimination. The vestibular system tells you where you are in space and is important in maintaining an appropriate level of arousal. Gentle, rhythmic rocking tends to soothe the infant, whereas fast, arrhythmic movements tend to increase the overall activity level. If this system is not functioning well, it may be difficult to soothe an infant. The proprioceptive system consists of receptors in the muscles, tendons, and joints that provide the perception of movement and position of the body in space (Porges, 1993).

3. For Stern, Kohut, and Winnicott, development involves gradually internalizing the soothing functions of the earlier self objects or, as Stern (1985) calls them, "self regulating others," so that the older child, and then adult, is able to calm and soothe himself.

4. Studies of stress hormone levels of toddlers in the Ainsworth "strange situation" indicate that security of the attachment relationship with the mother is related to the inhibition of cortisol increases among toddlers to brief separations and strange events (Spangler and Grossman, 1993; Hertsgaard and others, 1995; Nachmias and others, 1996).

Strategies for Theraplay Treatment

I n Part One we introduced the Theraplay method and the theory on which it is based. Part Two is a manual for therapists who want to learn how to practice Theraplay. As we stated in the Introduction, however, we do not expect that anyone could become a fully trained Theraplay therapist without going through our regular training process (see Appendix A for an outline of procedures for becoming certified as a Theraplay therapist). The following three chapters are designed to be used as a guide to practice in conjunction with such training.

Chapter Three describes the overall treatment process, including how to set up the treatment, what takes place at each step of the procedure, and how you can plan for each individual session. Chapter Four shows what to expect as treatment evolves, how to tailor treatment to the individual child, how to handle the child's resistance, how to handle transference and countertransference issues on the part of the therapist, ending with specific guidelines for the therapist. Chapter Five describes the complex task of the interpreting therapist, whose job is to guide the parents' involvement in treatment.

CHAPTER THREE

Structuring Theraplay Treatment

I n this chapter we describe the structure of Theraplay treatment from preparing for the intake interview to completing the follow-up visits. We show how you can arrange the physical setup of the treatment room and determine the number and timing of sessions as well as who should be included in the sessions. Next we describe how to do an assessment, including an intake interview, an observation session via the Marschak Interaction Method (MIM) (Marschak, 1960, 1967; Marschak and Call, 1966), and a feedback session with the parents. We discuss how to plan a Theraplay session proper and how to structure treatment. Each step of the process, from intake to follow-up, is illustrated with transcripts of a single case study.

ARRANGING THE SETTING

Theraplay treatment is structured to facilitate the work with both the child and the parents. You need to consider your room setup, arrangements for parents to observe, the number and timing of sessions, and who to include in sessions.

Setting Up the Room

The physical arrangements for Theraplay treatment are very simple. The intense focus on the relationship between child and adult makes it possible to work effectively in less than ideal circumstances. In the early years when we worked in Head Start centers, we did Theraplay with children under the stairs, in the janitor's closet, and between the inner and outer entrance doors to the school. Ideally, however, you should have a simple, uncluttered space approximately ten feet by ten feet with an easily cleaned floor or gym mat. Large floor pillows or a beanbag chair and small throw pillows are useful additions. Access to a sink for water play and cleanup is helpful. Toys or other objects that might distract the child should be out of sight. Any materials that you need for the day's planned activities, such as lotion, baby powder, bubbles, tinfoil, or newspaper, should also be out of sight but easily available to you when you need them during a session.

Arranging for Observation

You will need to make some arrangement for parents to observe the sessions. An observation room with a two-way mirror and sound equipment is ideal. A video camera is also very useful for recording both the parent-child interaction and the Theraplay sessions themselves.

We recommend videotaping the sessions for a number of reasons. You can review your session to get a better sense of what happened in the session and where you need to go next with the child. You can show the session to parents when you have no viewing room for them. You can have supervision based on the tape while you are in training and at any later time when you want to consult with a colleague about the progress of a difficult case. Finally, you have a record of exactly what happened during your session in case anyone challenges you about the nature of your interaction.

If neither a two-way mirror nor video equipment is available, the interpreting therapist and the parents can sit in one corner of the Theraplay room to observe the session.

Determining the Number and Timing of Sessions

Theraplay sessions typically are thirty to forty-five minutes in length and are scheduled once a week. If the family can manage it, a more intensive arrangement of two or three times per week is helpful. This arrangement is particularly helpful for young children with autism or pervasive developmental disorders (PDD). An even more intensive schedule of daily or even twice-daily sessions can have a very powerful impact. We use this intensive arrangement for families who must travel a long distance for treatment.

Deciding Who Should Be Included in Sessions

Unlike many other treatment methods, Theraplay includes more players than simply the child and the therapist. The ideal pattern is to have at least two therapists: one or more to work with the child and another, the interpreting therapist, to work with the parents. In addition to the child, you can include all the people who have caretaking responsibilities for the child. In some cases you may decide to include siblings. In the following section we discuss each of these options and the rationale for including them.

PARENTS OR CARETAKERS. There are important reasons for including parents. The kinds of problems that Theraplay addresses are inextricably connected with the interaction between the parents and their child. Parents need to learn how to carry on the work that you begin with their child. Although we have had success working with children whose parents were unable to participate, the most effective Theraplay treatment includes the primary caretaker at the very least. Therefore you should always include parents or primary caretakers as an integral part of the Theraplay team, if they are available.

There are so many varieties of caretakers these days that specifying who should be included is difficult. If there is only one parent, he should, of course, be included. If there are two parents, you should make it clear that you expect both to be present. If one parent says that she is too busy, you can say, "It is very important that both of you understand and agree on the new approach we are going to be showing you. You are both equally important to your child, and you can help him best by both being here."

In the case of amicably divorced parents with joint custody, you might include both parents along with their current partners, or they may alternate attending sessions. Again, the reasoning is that everyone who has any responsibility for the care of the child should be part of the treatment process in order to learn what works well for their child and to coordinate their approach to the child.

The more people trained to apply the Theraplay method during the hours intervening between formal sessions, the greater the advantage for the troubled child. You can change a child's view of himself and how he expects others to respond to him much more quickly if his experiences with all of his important caretakers are health-promoting. For instance, you might consider inviting the child's teacher, babysitter, or grandparents to participate in sessions.

SIBLINGS. Unlike Family Therapy, which often includes all the siblings from the beginning, Theraplay focuses primarily on the child who is identified as needing help. You want this focus because the intense interaction between a child and her primary caretakers is essential to the formation of a secure attachment, just as it is with an infant and her parents. Therefore, begin Theraplay treatment with the one child the parents have identified as needing help.

When other siblings are present, developing the focused interaction that is a precursor to secure attachment is more difficult. Even in the format used at Blue Hills Child and Family Services in Canada, where more than one sibling is included in sessions, each child has his own therapist with whom he establishes a strong relationship.

Once a good relationship is established between you and the child and between the parents and the child, you can decide whether siblings should be included in sessions. The reasons for including them would be both to help the child you have been working with learn to interact with her siblings in ways that are healthy, and to help the parents learn to be able to respond to all their children at once.

THERAPISTS. Whenever possible, you should plan to have another therapist working with you as interpreting therapist for the parents. If you work alone, you can arrange to play both roles. Parents can sit by themselves in the observation room or in the Theraplay room itself to observe, and you can discuss their observations with them later. A second option is to videotape the session and have the parents watch the videotape with you sometime after the session. These alternatives for working with parents are discussed in more detail in Chapter Five.

Occasionally you may have the luxury of two Theraplay therapists with the child in the playroom. This is most likely to occur when a therapist is in training to become a Theraplay therapist. Two therapists provide more than double the vigor and intensity and more than twice the spirit of fun, surprise, and spontaneity. With adolescents, we strongly recommend that you have two therapists, preferably a man and a woman. This arrangement allows you to engage in some physical activities that would be difficult for one adult with a large adolescent, and it helps diffuse any sexual implications that the physical intimacy of a single adult with an adolescent might raise. Whatever the age of the child, the presence of two therapists has the additional advantage of modeling for two-parent families how two caretakers can cooperate to help their child.

When two therapists are with the child, they must be prepared to operate in synchrony, and thus pre-session planning is essential. Not only must you plan what activities you will be using, you must decide who will take the lead in each activity. You can establish that one of you will always be the leader, or you can take turns leading activities within the session. An ideal arrangement for young children is for one therapist to hold the child and the other to interact. This avoids the confusion of having two sets of eyes to look at and two sets of (perhaps conflicting) directions about what to do. You should practice together to coordinate your movements, and you should both be very clear in advance how you will participate in each activity. For example, if you are having a child balance on pillows, one therapist should take charge, give the signals, and be the person who faces the child. The other therapist can stand behind to help the child balance by gently holding him around his waist or by making sure that the pillows are secure.

When you first begin working with a partner, you should review tapes of your sessions to learn how to integrate your work together. When carefully planned and well coordinated, Theraplay with two therapists can be very effective.

DOING AN ASSESSMENT

The first step in the treatment process is to do an assessment of the problem and make a plan that is appropriate for this particular child and family. The Theraplay assessment includes an intake interview with the child's caretakers, an assessment of the relationship between the child and her parents with the MIM, and a feedback session.

Conducting an Intake Interview

The intake interview covers a range of topics but focuses especially on attachment and relationship issues. It should provide you with useful information regarding the child's biological strengths and weaknesses, the family environment, and the parents' expectations of the child. The following is an outline of the areas that you should explore:

- The reason for the referral
- The developmental history
- Parents' expectations and attitudes
- Parents' experience within their own families
- Parents' relationship with each other

REASON FOR REFERRAL. The first step toward discovering how to help a family is to understand how they define the problem. You should ask each parent to describe the problem as they see it. You can also ask how other adults involved with the child, such as teachers or a pediatrician, see it. You need to learn when the problem first started and why they are coming for help now. Finally, you should ask how they have tried to cope with it.

DEVELOPMENTAL HISTORY. Your inquiry into the child's developmental history should include a strong emphasis on factors that might influence the child's attachment history. You can begin with questions about the pregnancy: How did you feel about being pregnant? What was your pregnancy like? What were your hopes and expectations for your baby? Did it turn out like that? Answers to these questions can give you an initial picture of how well the parents were prepared to respond to their particular baby.

Information about the delivery and the health of the infant (and the mother) at birth is important to an assessment of other factors that might affect the parents' ability to respond to their baby's needs and, equally important, the baby's responsiveness to her parents. "How did the feeding go? How easy was it to calm or soothe your baby? Was she an irritable or colicky baby?" These early experiences set the stage for ease or difficulty in the attachment process.

Answers to questions about developmental milestones, for example, age of walking and talking, give clues to the rate of the child's physical and cognitive development. Questions about time and method of weaning and toilet training, expectations of cleanliness and conformity, and parental attitudes toward autonomy, exploration, and independence tell us the degree to which the child has been allowed to "become his own person."

Information about the child's medical history is important for determining whether health problems have interfered with the child's development or have resulted in hospitalizations or painful medical procedures. You need to assess how such experiences have affected the parent-child relationship.

Information about other disruptions in the relationship such as prolonged separations due to absence or illness of a parent is also important. You should ask about the child's experience with other caretakers. For example, "Who took care of your child when you went to work? When did he first go to day care or preschool? How did he respond to early separations?" All of these questions tell us something about factors that might influence the security of his attachment.

The child's relationship to his siblings also needs to be explored. "Do you have other children? What are their ages? How did this child respond to the birth of later siblings? How do they get along now?"

To assess the child's current functioning, you can ask about his eating and sleeping patterns. Ask parents to describe a typical day.

Finally, you should ask parents to describe their child, her personality, favorite activities, what the parents like best about her, and how the parents enjoy spending time with her.

PARENTS' EXPECTATIONS AND ATTITUDES. Explore the parents' attitudes toward the child's dependency needs as well as toward the child's need for autonomy. How intense is their need for the child to achieve? In their family is it expected that children will stay close and be babied a long time? Do they expect their child to be well behaved and quiet or do they encourage freedom, spontaneity, and nonconformity? You need to assess how their family or cultural expectations relate to the child's current problems.

PARENTS' EXPERIENCE WITH THEIR OWN FAMILIES. Parents' experiences growing up in their own families strongly influence how they raise their children. Explore the parents' view of their own attachment history and their current relationship with their families of origin. "What was it like growing up in your family? Where do you fit in the sequence of your siblings? What was your role? How did your parents handle discipline? What were your parents' expectations for you? How supportive are your parents and siblings now?" You also should explore the family history of problems similar to the child's, as well as assess family patterns that might have affected the parents' growing up or that affect them currently.

PARENTS' RELATIONSHIP WITH EACH OTHER.   You should evaluate the current state of the parents' relationship, how similar their attitudes are about child rearing, and how well they are prepared to work together to help their child.

Since each answer serves as the basis for the formulation and testing of a new hypothesis, exactly what the sequence of questions should be is difficult to prescribe. No one format for interviewing is appropriate for all families. It is up to you to develop the skill to formulate and test hypotheses as you go along, to be free to discard directions of inquiry that lead nowhere, and to pursue those that suggest, "There is more here than meets the eye." Only experience with many parents, an openness to reliving your own childhood, and the freedom to call on your related experiences as parent, teacher, and babysitter, for example, can help you truly supply the backdrop against which a particular family is projected.

To uncover clues regarding marital interaction, direct questions wherever possible to both parents simultaneously. There are exceptions to the rule, of course, and these tend to occur for one of the following three reasons: Questions regarding pregnancy, childbirth, or breast-feeding are generally more appropriately addressed to the mother; a particular hypothesis may need to be tested with respect to a particular parent; or one parent may be monopolizing the interview to the exclusion of his or her partner.

At the end of the intake session, you should tell the parents that the next step in the assessment procedure will be an observation session using the MIM. To help the parents feel as relaxed as possible about this observed interaction, explain that you are interested in seeing how their child responds to a variety of simple activities. "Instructions for the activities will be written out on cards. We will videotape the interaction and then look closely at the videotape to learn more about how to help you and your child get along better. You can tell your child that you are bringing him here so that you and he can learn how to have more fun. The first time you come, you and he will be playing some games together."

THERAPLAY IN PRACTICE: *The B. Family's Intake Interview.* The following is a summary of the intake interview with the B. family, who brought their only child, Adam, for Theraplay treatment because they were concerned about his inability to separate from his mother and because of his impulsive, demanding behavior. Although the family lives at some distance from the Theraplay Institute, the urgency of their need led them to make the trip to Chicago for a week-long, intensive, five-session course of Theraplay treatment. The assessment, feedback, and first Theraplay session took place on Monday, followed by one session on each successive day. The family returned for follow-up sessions once a month for three months.

Adam is an appealing, freckle-faced, curly-haired, blond boy who will be four years old in a month.

Reason for Referral. Adam's parents described him as having a very short attention span—he can't stay with anything longer than two minutes. "He's easily revved up. It's very hard to get him to go to bed. He insists on sleeping in our bed. If we try to stop him from doing something, he becomes very angry and hits and scratches like an angry cat. He has to have everything his own way." But perhaps the most urgent problem for the parents is that he refuses to let his mother out of his sight except to go to his babysitter, who has cared for him since he was a baby. Since Adam is now old enough to go to the very good preschool program near their home, his parents would like to solve the separation problem so that he can enter at the end of the summer.

Developmental History. Adam was the product of a healthy, planned pregnancy and an easy delivery. His mother chose to bottle feed him because "I didn't want to be tied down." Adam was a good baby who "slept a lot and ate a lot." His parents were very proud of how rapidly he developed. He smiled, held his head up, and talked early. "Once he started talking you couldn't stop him." When Adam was six weeks old, his mother went back to work and he was cared for by a friendly neighbor; she still cares for him while his mother is at work. They describe this caretaker as "giving Adam the run of the house." Weaning was late, but potty training early. "He trained himself before he could walk."

The one dark cloud in an otherwise normal development was that Adam developed eczema when he was nine months old and for two years he was miserable. "We did everything the doctors told us to do to keep him from scratching and making it worse, but nothing seemed to work. He was very unhappy during that time. When he was two and a half it got better. What a relief to all of us."

Parents' Families. The parents have good support from their own families, but no one seems to have the solution for Adam's difficult behavior.

Parents' Relationship. The parents are supportive of each other and get along well. They have some disagreement about discipline. "He thinks I should spank him, but I don't agree. Besides he can't bear to do it himself. I talk to Adam like a grownup, 'If you won't listen, go to your room.'" The father admits that he backs down when Adam starts crying. Adam's behavior often makes each of them angry.

When asked what they liked best about Adam, they both agreed that they liked that he is smart and quick at learning, and that he is energetic and lively.

When asked what their goals were for treatment, both parents also agreed that they wanted Adam out of their bed, they wanted him to be able to separate from his mother and especially to be able to go to the preschool program rather than continue being cared for by the babysitter, and they wanted him to be less anxious and hyperactive.

Observing the Parent-Child Interaction Using the MIM

The second step in the assessment is to observe the parent and child in action using the Marschak Interaction Method.[1] The MIM allows you to see patterns in the interaction between a parent and child and to see what works and what does not work in their relationship. Parents often are unaware of the patterns of their interaction and cannot tell us about them. Therefore, there is a great advantage in viewing the interaction first-hand rather than relying solely on parents' subjective reports.

The MIM consists of a large number of tasks from which eight to ten are selected for a particular family.[2] The tasks are categorized according to the child's developmental level: neonate, infant, toddler, preschooler, school-age child, or adolescent. Within each level, tasks vary on several dimensions, which were initially described as the giving of affection, giving of direction, alerting to the environment, and playfulness. To make the MIM more suitable for Theraplay treatment planning, the original dimensions have been revised to correspond to the Theraplay dimensions of structure, engagement, nurture, and challenge, as well as playfulness.

STRUCTURING THE MIM. The MIM observation sessions include the child with first one and then the other of her parents and are usually scheduled one week and two weeks after the initial intake interview. One-parent families, of course, have only one observation session. When families come from a distance, as Adam's family did, the intake interview and both MIMs are performed on the same day. But this schedule is tiring for a young child and it is best to avoid it if possible. Another variation that gives useful information is to observe the child and both parents together for three or four activities in addition to the dyadic MIM. In some cases you might include all the children in the family in order to determine how their presence affects the interaction. You should be aware, however, that the addition of more players in the interaction increases the complexity of the analysis and should not be attempted until you have become experienced in interpreting the simpler, two-person MIM.

MIM sessions are conducted as follows. Unless the child is too young, parent and child sit side by side at a table. With an infant, the parent and child sit on the floor supported by pillows. The session is observed through a two-way mirror and videotaped for later analysis. Lacking either the two-way mirror or video equipment, you can sit unobtrusively in the room and take notes. A stack of cards with instructions for each activity is placed face down on the table in front of the parent. Materials needed for the tasks should be placed in labeled envelopes or boxes near the parent. Activities consist of structuring tasks such as "make a block stucture just like mine," engaging tasks such as "parent plays peek-a-boo with child," nurturing tasks such as "feed each other M&Ms" or "parent powders child's back with baby powder," and challenging tasks such as "adult engages child in three rounds of thumb wrestling."

A parent who refuses to powder a child's back on the grounds that it would "spoil" him or who carries out the powdering but requires the child to spell the word *baby* tells us about his giving and accepting of nurturing. A parent who refuses even to consider the task that asks the child to tell about "when he's a grown-up" or one who, in response to the request to "teach" the child something, puts him on her lap and sits staring off into space, shows us the degree to which she is comfortable with structure and challenge.

A child who refuses to allow her mother to rub lotion on her hands or who becomes restless while her mother tells her about "when she was a little baby," tells us something about her comfort with regressive, nurturing activities. A child who insists on making a design of his own rather than copying his father's block structure ("make a block structure just like mine") shows us how comfortable he is accepting his father's leadership and structure.

Instruction cards not only differentiate these dimensions but also are divided between tasks that are expected to be carried out alone and those that are to be carried out jointly. For example, the activity "parent and child each take one pad of paper and a pencil and each draw something" asks for independent action, and the instructions are significantly violated when a parent grabs her child's hand with the pencil in it and begins to draw. By the same token, a parent who responds to "feed each other M&Ms" by tossing the bag of candies across the table and saying to the child "Eat 'em," is not seen to be behaving in the called-for, mutually sharing way.

With these dimensions in mind, you can determine the degree to which parents are comfortable structuring, engaging, nurturing, or challenging their child, and also the degree to which they operate apart from or in harmony with their child. Furthermore, you can determine the degree to which the child can accept the parents' efforts in the various dimensions.

CHOOSING THE TASKS. The eight to ten activities should be selected to answer specific questions about this parent-and-child unit, based on the hypotheses you formulated during and after the intake interview described above. To compare the child's responses to each parent, some of the tasks should be identical for each parent. Lest the child become bored by the repetition if all the activities are the same, however, some of the tasks should be different. For example, you can have one parent build a block structure and the other make a drawing; both will ask their child to copy what they made.

For Adam's family, we chose activities that would throw light on the parents' ability to nurture and calm him as well as to structure and challenge him. We were interested in their ability to foster a secure attachment that could allow Adam to become more autonomous. At the same time, we wanted to look at Adam's responses to their efforts in all these areas.

Because Adam's family had come from out of town for an intensive week-long course of Theraplay, the MIM was performed at one sitting with only five tasks used for each parent plus three tasks in which both parents participated. The following is a list of the instructions for each of the tasks.

Mother with Adam

1. Adult and child each take one squeaky animal. Make the two animals play together.
2. Adult teaches child something he doesn't know.
3. Tell child about when he was a little baby.
4. Adult leaves the room for one minute without child.
5. Adult and child each take one bottle, apply lotion to each other.

Father with Adam

1. Adult and child each take one squeaky animal. Make the two animals play together.
2. Adult teaches child something he doesn't know.
3. Adult and child comb each other's hair.
4. Adult leaves the room for one minute without child.
5. Adult asks child to tell about when he's grown up.

Both Parents with Adam

1. Make a stack of hands together.
2. Adults and child put hats on each other.
3. Adults and child feed each other.

In setting up MIM tasks, alternate playful and regressive tasks with stressful or demanding tasks. The stressful "parent leaves the room" task should be placed in the middle of the sequence and followed by a task that will help the parent and child reconnect around a playful or nurturing activity.

We chose a playful activity as the first task for each parent ("squeaky animals") because it has the potential of engaging the participants and helping them get past their discomfort at being observed and videotaped. The "teach" task allows us to assess how appropriate the parents' expectations for achievement are and how well the child responds to their expectations. Because Adam has so much difficulty separating from his mother, we wanted to see how he would respond to her leaving the room. We had his father leave the room also in order to compare Adam's response to each parent's departure and return. We were interested in seeing how they related around nurturing activities, and therefore chose the task "rub lotion on each other" (mother), and "comb each other's hair" (father). "Tell child about when he was a baby" was chosen to give some insight into the early relationship between Adam and his mother. "Ask child to tell about when he's grown up" provides an opportunity to see how Adam and his father deal with issues around his growing up and becoming more independent. To see how both parents work together to handle Adam's clinging to his mother and rejecting his father, we chose three tasks that called for playful cooperation: "stack of hands," "hats," and "feed each other." All of the tasks give us an opportunity to observe how well the parents can engage Adam, structure the interaction, set limits, and follow through.

INSTRUCTING THE PARENTS. As the family enters the room (which is usually the treatment room as well), you can point out the camera and show the child how the two-way mirror works. "I will be videotaping the session so that we can look closely at it later. At the end of the session I will ask you to sign a release form indicating that the interpreting therapist and I have your permission to videotape the session and to share it with each other." Adolescents should be asked to sign the permission form as well. Obtaining the signed agreement after the session is completed assures that the participants know what is on the videotape when they sign.

Both therapists do not need to be present for the MIM, but the family should be told that both of you will be looking closely at the videotape and planning their feedback together. Our permission form includes the additional option of using the videotape for training other professionals. Parents are, of course, free to reject this option, though few have done so. Very occasionally a family asks that we not videotape at all.

The instructions you give to the parents should be simple and straightforward: "Here is your chair, Adam. Mom, you sit in the other chair. This is a stack of cards that will tell you what to do. Pick up one card at a time and read it out loud so that we know which activity you are doing. Some of the activities require materials that are in the numbered envelopes here beside the table. You can decide when to go on to the next activity. There are no right or wrong ways of doing these activities. You can decide how you want to do them. I will be behind the two-way mirror (or in the room behind the video equipment) if you have a question. When you are finished, I'll come in to ask you a few questions." Then, to make sure that the parent and child interact with each other and not with you, make yourself as inconspicuous as possible and answer questions very briefly.

EVALUATING THE INTERACTION. At the conclusion of each MIM, ask the parent and child the following questions:

• Is this the way it is at home for you? Did we get a good picture of how things go between the two of you at home?
• Were there any surprises?
• What was your favorite activity? Why?
• What was your least favorite activity? Why?
• Without asking your child, what do you think she liked best? Why?
• What do you think your child liked least? Why?

Responses to these questions can give you insight into the meaning of the activities to both participants.

A close look at the MIM interaction should enable you to answer the following questions:

• What would it be like to live with this child or this parent twenty-four hours a day?
• What works in the relationship and can be encouraged?
• What doesn't work and needs to be changed?
• What does the child need from the parent?
• What does the parent need from the child?
• How strong are they and how much can each be encouraged to change?

THERAPLAY IN PRACTICE: *The B. Family's MIM Sessions.* In this transcript of the MIM conducted with Adam and his family, you can see how quickly the pattern of interaction between Adam and each of his parents emerges. To give you a sense of the interaction, we give full transcripts of three tasks with Adam and his mother, two with his father, and two with both parents.

The comments in bracketed italics throughout the transcript indicate our inferences about what is going on. A question mark indicates the tentative nature of the inference, which must be confirmed or denied by further observation. At the end of the transcript of each task we summarize our interpretation of the interaction to help you learn how to move from observation to inference and analysis.

ADAM WITH HIS MOTHER. Mother sits at a table next to Adam with the stack of instruction cards in front of her. Adam looks expectantly at her and seems interested in what is to come.

1. Squeaky Animals

MOTHER: (picks up a card and reads) Adult and child each take one squeaky animal. Make the two animals play together. (takes the animals out of the envelope) You get one and I get one. *[Hopeful?]* What do you want to play? Do you want to make them meet each other? What's his name? Come on, what's his name? Don't you want to play? *[Disappointed?]*

ADAM: No. (sullen, pouty look)

MOTHER: Well come on . . . what's his name? You don't want to play? Why? You don't like this game? *[Pleading?]*

ADAM: No! (puts the animal down and crosses his arms defiantly)

MOTHER: Well I like it. (picks up both squeaky animals and begins to play by herself) *[Trying a new tactic? "If you won't play, I'll play by myself."]*

ADAM: You put them back in the envelope! (angry, scolding tone)

MOTHER: Are you going to play nice? ("walks" her animal across the table toward Adam; talks with a teasing tone) He's going to take your money . . . (referring to some coins Adam is holding; Adam smiles) *[Playful teasing engages Adam in spite of himself.]*

ADAM: (murmurs inaudibly and hides his face in his mother's arm) *[Can turn to her for comfort after being intrigued by her playfulness?]*

MOTHER: Come on (gently but insistently turns Adam back toward the table)

ADAM: Push me in! Push me in! (Mother pushes Adam closer to the table) Read another card! *[A tyrant?]*

MOTHER: We're doing one at a time. *[Stays firm]*

ADAM: (inaudible)

MOTHER: No, we did that card already. (picks up another card) Let's see what this one says.

[Mother starts the interaction by offering choices to Adam: "What do you want to play?" "What's his name?" Adam immediately becomes resistant and demanding. He scolds his mother as though she were the child and he the adult. After the brief moment when her playful teasing engaged him, he turns to her for comfort. In spite of how difficult he is being, Mother swallows her annoyance, remains calm, and persists in her efforts to engage him. We see already that it must not be easy to be with Adam, but that playfulness can help to win him over.]

2. *Teach*

MOTHER: (reads) Adult teaches child something he doesn't know. What don't you know that you want me to tell you? I've got to teach you something. *[Shifts responsibility to the cards for making this demand?]* What do you want to know? *[Shifts responsibility to Adam for choosing.]*

ADAM: (sullenly) Nothing.

MOTHER: How about if I teach you how to play with two pigs? (picks up squeaky animals) *[A put-down?]*

ADAM: No, you can't do that! You put them back! *[Annoyed by the put-down?]*

MOTHER: Stop!

ADAM: You have to put them back (visibly upset); you put them back.

MOTHER: Stop. *[Agitated, then pulls self together?]* How about if you put them back in the bag (picks up the envelope). I'll teach you to clean up after yourself. That's something you don't know. Let's clean up the pigs. *[Another put-down?]*

ADAM: (throws the animals into the envelope, one by one)

MOTHER: Nicely, please. *[Correcting him]* (Adam puts his elbows on the table, rests his face in his hands, and looks defiantly at mother) That's something you don't know. *[Sarcasm]*

ADAM: (points at one of the envelopes) I want to see what's in there.

MOTHER: No, you have to wait.

ADAM: (points at his mother) No, not for you!

[Like many parents faced with this open-ended request to teach something to their child, Adam's mother turns to him for ideas. When he doesn't respond, she offers suggestions, but her suggestions are couched in hesitant terms: "How about if I —?" Adam responds to all of her questions with a negative. Has Adam's demanding behavior made mother hesitant or has mother's hesitance led to Adam's becoming demanding? Adam's angry resistance stirs up some anger in his mother "I'll teach you how to clean up. That's something you don't know." Yet in spite of this, she remains calm and keeps trying to engage Adam. It is good to see that Mother can be firm in the face of Adam's demands: "No, you have to wait."]

3. Baby

MOTHER: (picks up a card and reads) Adult tells child about when he was a baby. (Adam smiles and looks attentive) You know about when you were a baby, don't you?

ADAM: Yes (smiles). *[Hopeful?]*

MOTHER: What did you used to do? You used to be so quiet and you used to *sleep* all the time. (Adam looks distracted) Are you listening to me? Don't you want to hear about when you were a baby? *[Disappointed?]*

ADAM: No, I don't want to hear about that.

MOTHER: You're not being any fun today.

ADAM: I want to do something else; I want to see what's in that bag. (points to the envelope)

MOTHER: Well, when we get to that card . . . you used to be *patient* when you were a baby. *[Response to his impatience?]*

ADAM: Tell me some more.

MOTHER: Tell you some more? You like that one, don't you.

ADAM: Yeah . . . just tell me what's in that bag. Let's do another one.

MOTHER: You were so quiet when you were a baby. And when Mommy was a baby she used to play all by herself in a corner.

ADAM: Why?

MOTHER: Why? Because I didn't like to go near other people. But it's fun to be with people.

ADAM: (restless) Come on, just read the card. What's in the card?

MOTHER: Well, we'll find out.

[Adam looks pleased at the idea of hearing about himself as a baby, and mother seems relieved at his change of mood. But as soon as she says that he slept all the time, Adam loses interest. Mother's disappointment is reflected in her statement, "You're not being any fun." One could speculate that such a passive picture has no interest for Adam. He might have hoped for a more lively picture of her pleasure in him as a baby. She carries on the passive theme—"You were so patient." "You were so quiet"—emphasizing her dissatisfaction with the present impatient, demanding Adam. And when she reveals that she was a quiet baby who preferred to be alone (followed by her quick reversal, "But it's fun to be with people"), we begin to see why she is so concerned about Adam's difficulty separating from her to go to preschool. Perhaps she fears that Adam is just like her and that like her he will miss out on the fun of being with other children.]

When his mother reads the card about her leaving the room, Adam bursts into tears and begs her not to leave him. After begging and cajoling him to let her go, Mother tries once to leave, then quickly gives up on the task. When Mother attempts to rub lotion on his arms, Adam becomes agitated and pulls away and becomes angry and demanding. It is clear that he cannot tolerate either the messy lotion or her gentle touch.

At the end of the MIM interaction, we asked Adam's mother our standard questions. She said that we had seen a good example of Adam at his fussy worst. Sometimes, when they are alone together and she is not trying to get him to do things her way, they have more fun. It was hard for her to choose a favorite activity; none of them had gone very well. She likes telling Adam about when he was a baby, but not when he won't listen. She doesn't like using lotion on him, because he can't stand the messiness. "Neither can I," she said. It was hard for her to decide what tasks Adam liked best or least. He had been so very resistant to all of them.

The MIM with Adam and his mother begins to point to some of the reasons they are having so much difficulty negotiating the separation phase of his development: it was not easy to soothe him when he was a baby because of his eczema; his mother has her own reasons for remaining aloof and distant; and his way of expressing his distress is so full of anger and resistance that she cannot get past that to understand and comfort him in his distress—even assuming he would let her do so.

ADAM WITH HIS FATHER. Father and Adam sit side by side at the table. Adam is crying from the outset. His father leans toward him in a concerned, caring way. He tries to maintain his composure and remain focused in spite of Adam's angry crying.

1. Squeaky Animals

ADAM: I want to get out of here!

FATHER: (picks up a card and reads) Make animals play together.

ADAM: That's the pig. *[Forgets himself for a moment? Stops crying and takes charge.]*

FATHER: (picks up the envelope) Oh is it? Show me. *[Grateful for his participation?]*

ADAM: (grabs the envelope out of his father's hands and removes the animals; cries) I want to get out of here! (throws the animals down on the table) I don't want to play.

FATHER: Don't you want to play with the pigs?

ADAM: (turns his back on his father) No! I want to get out of here. *[More anger than distress?]*

FATHER: Adam, Adam, let's play with the pigs, O.K.? (soft, pleading tone)

ADAM: No! I don't want to.

FATHER: Why?

ADAM: You have to let me see my Mommy!

FATHER: No, Mommy's going to be all right.

ADAM: I don't want to stay here.

FATHER: (picks up the animals) Come on, let's play with the pigs.

ADAM: (knocks the animals over, then turns his back on his father) No, you leave me alone. I want my Mommy.

FATHER: (speaking to the therapist) Should I move on to the next card?

THERAPIST: (speaks from the background) You can decide.

FATHER: We'll put the pigs away, OK.?

ADAM: (nods) But I have to get out of here. *[Calmer after having won this round?]*

FATHER: No, no, no, not yet. We're going to play a little bit. (puts the pigs away, then picks up another card)

[Adam tries to direct his father's actions, at the same time that he demands to leave. In spite of this, father is calm, patient, and reassuring ("Mommy's going to be all right"). But his tone is pleading ("Let's play with the pigs, OK?") and placating. It must have been very difficult to have Adam reject him so angrily in front of the camera, yet he maintained his focus on trying to reassure and engage Adam.]

2. Teach

FATHER: Adult teaches child something he doesn't know. . . . Let's see . . . what don't you know?

ADAM: (turns his back on his father) Nothing.

FATHER: (smiles with frustration; addresses therapist) Well, right off hand I can't think of anything he doesn't know. He's pretty well advanced, I think. *[Feels hopeless to engage Adam? Appreciates his intelligence.]*

ADAM: (still crying) I don't like this . . . get me out of here!

[As his wife did, Mr. B. turns to Adam for suggestions. But since Adam, in his present mood, is unlikely to help him out, it is not surprising that his father gives up on the task.]

As might be predicted from these two tasks, Adam refused to let his father comb his hair, complained that he wanted to be with his mother while his father left the room, and was unresponsive to the request that he talk about what it would be like when he's grown up. Mr. B. shrugged his shoulders at the end as if he did not feel he and Adam had done well.

In answer to the questions at the end, Mr. B. admitted that Adam's behavior is typical when he has to be separated from his mother. "This is what we were telling you about." He can be even more demanding at home. It was not possible for Mr. B. to decide which were his own or Adam's favorite or most disliked activities.

ADAM WITH BOTH PARENTS. Mother, Father, and Adam sit around the table. Adam is still pouting but no longer crying. Father reads tasks they must perform together.

1. Stack of Hands

MOTHER: Want to make a stack of hands? *[Cheerful effort to engage Adam?]*

FATHER: Me first. (puts his hand in the middle of the table) *[Supporting his wife?]*

MOTHER: Then me. (puts her hand on top) We'll see how tall we can make it. (turns to Adam) Now you put your hand on there.

ADAM: No!

FATHER: Come on, put it on top. Want to see Daddy put his hand on Mommy's? (puts his hand on top of the stack)

MOTHER: Mommy and Daddy are going to play. *[Maybe if we just go ahead, he'll join in?]*

ADAM: (crying) Take your hands off there (tries to remove his mother's hand from the pile) . . . I'm mad at this game. (crosses his arms defiantly) *[Resents their closeness?]*

MOTHER: You're mad at this game? Why? *[Trying to be understanding?]*

ADAM: Because I don't like it.

FATHER: Why? It's just hands . . .

ADAM: No!

MOTHER: (to father) Next.

FATHER: Next. (picks up another card)

MOTHER: (to Adam) If you don't like that game, fine.

[Once again we see how difficult it can be to live with Adam, as he continues his resistance to the activities. With both parents in the room he clearly shows his resentment of Father's involvement with Mother. Both parents support each other in their efforts to find ways to engage Adam in the activities. Both try to be understanding ("Are you mad at this game? Why? It's just hands"). Adam frustrates all their efforts.]

2. Hats

FATHER: (reads) Adults and child put hats on each other. (Adam continues to cry)

MOTHER: (smiling) Hats!

FATHER: (picks up funny hats, laughing)

MOTHER: Oh boy, which one do you want? I want to be the witch!

ADAM: No, *I'm* the witch! *[Mother's assertion engages Adam's opposition? Or are the hats somehow more engaging and less threatening than parents touching each other?]*

MOTHER: O.K., you be the witch. (puts the witch hat on Adam) Which do you want me to be?

ADAM: (points to the sailor hat) *[For a minute, Adam joins in.]*

MOTHER: I'll duck down and you put it on me. (Adam puts the hat on his mother's head). What do I look like?

ADAM: Nothing.

FATHER: Which do you want me to be?

ADAM: I don't like this. (knocks the witch hat off of his head)

MOTHER: Then I'm going to be the witch.

ADAM: No! I'm the witch.

MOTHER: Then why did you knock it off? (puts the witch hat back on Adam's head)

ADAM: I don't like this!

MOTHER: Which one do you want Daddy to wear? (Adam points to one of the hats)

FATHER: You have to put it on me.

ADAM: No.

MOTHER: Do you want me to put it on Daddy? You tell me which one. (Adam points to a hat)

ADAM: Mommy has to do it. *[As long as he directs it, it's OK?]*

MOTHER: (looks at Adam) You look like Winnie from *Hocus Pocus*. (no response) You don't want to look like Winnie? You were a witch for Halloween weren't you?

ADAM: (begins to cry)

[In opposition to his mother's choosing the witch hat, Adam demands it for himself. For a moment Adam forgets himself and allows

his mother to put the witch hat on him. He even points out hats for her and his father. But very soon he pulls back, saying "I don't like this," knocking the witch hat off his own head. Even as he cooperates a bit, he insists on running the show ("Mommy has to do it"). Nonetheless, this playful interactive game has briefly overcome his resistance to being involved.]

THERAPIST'S ASSESSMENT. As we look at the interaction between the family members, we wonder how things got to this state. The parents are caring and loving, they try very hard, they have a lot to offer. How did it happen that such a little boy should come to sound like a scolding mother? He can't bear to be separated from her, yet when he is with her he becomes angry and scolding. How did his father get pushed so far into the background of Adam's interest? What can we do to get them back on track?

To demonstrate the process of looking at an MIM and studying it carefully, we now give answers to the six questions with which we began, based on our observations of Adam and his parents.

1. *What would it be like to live with this child twenty-four hours a day?* Our immediate answer is that it would be very hard. He is so impulsive and easily stirred up, and so desperately needs to "call all the shots." One would always feel as though walking on eggshells. At any moment something might trigger his angry uncooperativeness.

2. *What would it be like to live with these parents?* Although we understand that it would not be easy to remain firm in the face of Adam's demands and temper tantrums, we wonder whether Adam would not welcome their taking greater control. Could their patience feel like weakness to him? Might he be asking himself, "How can they take care of me if they can't stand up to me"?

3. *What works in the relationship?* Both parents are able to remain calm and to persevere in their attempts to engage Adam. Playfulness seems to be a key to engaging Adam and making him feel good. Though there are hints that he might enjoy a more nurturing relationship, at the moment he is very resistant to any overtures.

4. *What doesn't work and needs to be changed?* The most obvious answer is Adam's constant need to be in charge and his parents' inability to take charge. Although his parents make attempts to assume their appropriate parent role, Adam does not make it easy. We need to help them with this problem.

5. *What does the child need from his parents?* Probably the most important thing that Adam needs from his parents is nurturing care, which would help soothe and calm him. His anxiety in holding onto his mother probably stems from his uncertainty that she will be able to meet his needs. His mother's having to leave him with a caretaker when she returned to work so soon after his birth, combined with his hypersensitivity and difficulty being soothed due to the eczema, probably set the stage for the present insecurity in the relationship. Though Adam will surely resist efforts to change these patterns, persistence in those efforts will be very important.

6. *How strong are they and how much can they be encouraged to change?* Both of Adam's parents care a great deal about their child and are highly motivated to change. They seem open and eager to participate in treatment. But they have been missing a clear direction in which to move. Adam is a bright, spunky, engaging child who, though certainly resistant, is sturdy enough to accept the challenge that change will present.

Giving Feedback to the Parents

In preparation for the feedback session, analyze the MIM carefully and make a plan for interpreting it to the parents. Your plan should include choosing segments of the videotape to illustrate your interpretation. The child is not present for this session. If there are two parents, both should be present.

A major focus of the feedback is to point out the positive aspects of the relationship and highlight the interactions that went well. For example, we pointed out to Adam's parents that they were both very patient and calm in the face of his angry, demanding behavior. "It must not be easy. Every time you offer some lovely nurturing activity, he turns you down." We showed Adam's mother that her persistence in finding ways to engage him in the squeaky-pigs activity had paid off and had given him a strong message that she really wanted to play with him. We showed his father the videotaped segment when Adam responded to his caretaking move (reaching out to wipe a tear from his eye—this is not in the transcript) by stopping crying. Clearly, Adam can be comforted by his father. His ability to remain calm and reassuring when Adam was so upset was also very helpful. We pointed out that his supporting his wife in encouraging Adam to participate in the stack-of-hands game led to Adam's becoming more cooperative.

Sometimes children respond more positively to one aspect of their parent's behavior than another. For example, a child who resists her mother's usual educational or intellectual approach may be much more cooperative and responsive when her mother shifts to a more nurturing style. With Adam, his mother's playful, teasing approach engaged him most effectively. Seeing this difference on videotape and discussing it with the therapist had a profound effect. Being able to relate her child's more cooperative response to something she did spontaneously in the interaction made it much easier for her to understand the difference and be able to replicate her behavior in the future.

HELPING PARENTS UNDERSTAND THEIR OWN BEHAVIOR. Discussion during the feedback session often leads parents to fresh insights into their own behavior and to a new understanding of and willingness to deal with their child's behaviors that typically "turn them off." We pointed out to Adam's mother how eager he had been to hear about himself as a baby. We showed her the videotape of that part and asked, "What do you think it was about your response that changed his mood?" She was able to see that talking about his being such a quiet baby had somehow disappointed him. "If I had told him what a cute baby he was and how much I loved holding him and cuddling him, do you think he would have kept on being interested?" she asked.

HELPING PARENTS UNDERSTAND THEIR CHILD'S NEEDS. In the feedback session you also can begin to help parents understand more about their child's feelings and needs. For example, we commented to Adam's mother that even though she was very gentle as she rubbed lotion on him, Adam was very reluctant to have it on his skin. "You have so much to offer, and yet Adam is unable to accept it because he is so very sensitive to touch. We will be experimenting to see what kind of touch works best for him."

With Adam's parents we underlined the need for them to take charge of the interaction more firmly. We pointed out to both parents that Adam's invariable answer to every question was "No!" Since that was the case, we recommended that they reduce their questions to a minimum. We asked them how they would feel about taking more control of their interaction with Adam. They both agreed that they would like to learn how to do this.

We shared our understanding of why Adam had developed into such a tyrant. "His early experience with eczema had left him unsure that anyone could soothe and comfort him. He has come to express his distress by being angry and demanding rather than sad and open to being comforted. His experience with the babysitter, who indulged his every whim, gave him no opportunity to accept rules and limits from a caring adult. As a consequence, he has developed a pattern of demanding that things go his way, but this pattern does not leave him feeling secure and able to grow up. We need to change that pattern. His therapist will not give in to his efforts to control everything. She will look for ways to have fun with him as well as to soothe and calm him. While she works with him, I [the interpreting therapist] will be talking with you about what she is doing and how Adam is responding. When we find things that work with him, we will ask you to try them out at home. From time to time we will give you homework assignments, so that you can practice the new ways we find that work well with Adam."

To help parents anticipate and therefore not become too distressed by their child's resistance to the changes that you will be trying to institute, ask them to predict how he will respond to the playful, insistent presence of the therapist. Adam's parents predicted (rightly, we soon discovered) that he would be very upset, that he would cry and complain and try every way he could to get his own way. Would his parents be able to watch that happen? They thought they could. "We really need to make a change. Things can't go on any longer as they are."

We pointed out that most children who come for Theraplay treatment go through a period of resistance. "For some (and Adam may be one of those), it comes right at the start. For others it comes after a few sessions. We handle it by remaining calm, by staying with the child, and by finding as many ways as possible to engage him and help him have fun."

Thus in the feedback session you begin the process of teaching parents to view their child in a more empathic, understanding manner by pointing the way toward new and more effective ways of relating to their difficult child and outlining the process of treatment. Parents should leave the feedback session with renewed optimism that they will be able to have the relationship with their child that they have longed for.

At the conclusion of treatment, you can repeat the MIM as a way of evaluating progress. When parents see both tapes, they recognize how much they have changed and can observe the impact they have had on their child.

MAKING A PLAN FOR TREATMENT. At the end of the feedback session you should come to an agreement with the parents about whether to embark on treatment. In some cases, you may not recommend Theraplay treatment, either because you judge that the child would benefit more from another treatment modality or because you believe that the family can carry on without treatment. If you do recommend treatment, describe how Theraplay works and agree on the goals of treatment and the number of sessions. Parents can be asked to specify their own treatment goals.

Adam's parents were eager from the start to try Theraplay treatment. They were desperate for a solution to their problem with Adam and thought Theraplay might help. The goals for Adam's treatment were to help him overcome his separation anxiety and to accept structure and nurture from adults. For his parents, the goals were to help them find ways to respond to his needs for nurture, be more firm in setting limits, and be more consistently available emotionally to him.

The goal for any treatment is to provide the kinds of experiences the child needs, as judged from the nature of the parent-child interaction and your understanding of the problem. If it is clear from the observed interaction, for example, that a child has unfilled regressive needs, you should explain to the parents that in treatment you will be doing a lot of nurturing activities to meet those needs. Adam's treatment will strongly emphasize nurturing activities because he needs to have the calming, soothing experiences that he was unable to accept as a baby and that his current hypersensitive and hyperreactive state requires. Finding ways to engage him but not overstimulate him will be important. We also will want to provide a very clear structure, both to help him accept having adults take charge and to help slow down his impulsive behavior. Whereas challenging activities might be useful in catching his interest, this pseudo-mature little boy does not need challenge to encourage him to grow up any faster (we did not see his clinging to his mother as a sign that he was afraid to grow up, but more as a sign that he was not convinced that she would be available to him when he needed her).

PLANNING THE SEQUENCE OF A THERAPLAY SESSION

Once you complete the Theraplay assessment, schedule the first Theraplay session as soon as possible. This session is usually a week later. In preparation for each session, make a plan of the activities you want to use, and the sequence in which you want to use them. Keep in mind the dimensions you want to emphasize for this particular child and consider what will be the best way to capture the child's interest. In the following section we discuss what goes into planning a session. In the final sections of this chapter we describe the sequence of Theraplay treatment.

Although sessions must be planned in advance, taking the goals of treatment and the child's current needs into account, the plan is always subject to change based on the child's response. You must resolve the tension between the need to plan and the need to respond sensitively to the child. Whereas a mother may not plan her playful activities, but simply respond to the child she knows so well, you must plan carefully to have a repertoire of playful, enticing activities for engaging the reluctant child in treatment. The older the child, the more essential is the plan for a variety of playful activities.

Not only should you choose activities according to the dimensions the child needs, but you should also plan the sequence of activities within the session. Begin the session with some checkup activities (for example, "Let's see whether you brought those strong muscles you had here last week"); move into some spunky, lively, surprising (engaging) activities; slow down for some soft, gentle, calming ones (nurturing); build up to a lively, perhaps competitive (challenging) crescendo again; and end, possibly, with feeding and a lullaby (nurturing) in a quiet, integrated mood. Throughout the session, you provide structure by confidently moving from activity to activity, making sure that the child is safe, and clearly defining the rules when needed. Within this general format, specific issues (for example, the child's need to "run the show," his fear of new experiences, his avoidance of body contact, his discomfort with body disequilibrium, or his restlessness and hyperactivity) are dealt with through activities especially designed to help these problems. In Chapter Four we give more details about how to tailor your approach to the specific needs of each child.

Of course, sessions need not follow this suggested format unvaryingly. Sometimes, for example, a child may appear for his session in such an agitated state that it is best to begin, after the greeting, with nurturing activities that "settle" him. Sometimes his life has been such a series of confrontations and conflicts that he requires only order and predictability (structuring activities).

Both greeting and closing, however, are necessary elements of any Theraplay session. Children who require Theraplay often lack spatial and temporal demarcations in their lives. Bedtime and mealtimes, for example, may occur anywhere and virtually at random. The opening and closing of treatment sessions, as well as their physical location, therefore, should be clearly articulated. A child who is permitted to float in at the beginning and drift out at the end of his sessions or who is given sessions that are haphazard or "on the run" may feel even more confused as to his identity and may have an increased sense of diffuseness about the world.

The well-planned Theraplay session includes the following elements. Variations may occur depending on the child's immediate needs.

- The Opening
    Greeting activities
    Checkup activities
- The Session Proper
    Structuring activities
    Engaging activities
    Nurturing activities
    Challenging activities
- The Closing
    Parting
    Transition to the "outside world"

The Opening

The opening includes both greeting activities and checkup activities. In Chapter Four we discuss the importance of greeting activities in introducing the child to the overall nature of treatment. Here we describe how you begin each session throughout treatment.

GREETING ACTIVITIES. The object of greeting activities is to allow the child to experience unrestrained pleasure at being discovered. The initial greeting ordinarily takes place at the location where you first meet the child. In voice, facial expression, and choice of words, you communicate your unambivalent excitement and delight at meeting a new friend or being reunited with an old one. The model for the manifestation of this pleasure is, once again, found in the parent-infant relationship. A mother may greet her baby when she wakes with an eager, "Good morning Merry Sunshine!" "Let me see how big you are today!" or "I'm coming to get you! Here I come! Whee!" (then spinning her around in the air). The Theraplay therapist uses the same happy approach.

The following are samples of appropriate and joyfully stated greetings with which you can usher the child into the Theraplay session: "Oh! If it isn't my friend Paige, with your nice curly hair!" "Well, Ryan, all day I've been waiting to see you!" "You brought that beautiful smile with you again!" "What! Even more of those gorgeous freckles today?"

The greeting should be intense, cheerful, and extremely personal. The child should come to feel that a particular part of himself has been singled out as special and lovable. Most children welcome a gleeful "Oh, I just know there's something inside those socks!" or "Let me taste that ear. Umm . . . yum yum . . . good sugar!" Again, this parallels the mother's cooing to her infant: "You're so sweet I could just eat you up!"

As with a baby, the initial greeting is never formal or perfunctory. It does not include "We're going to play for a little while," "Follow me to my office," "Hello, how are you today?" or even "Did you have a hard trip to the clinic?"

If either the parent or the child looks anxious as they separate for the child's Theraplay session, you can tell the parent, "We'll be back to see you in a little while, Mom. You wait right there until we get back." You can tell the child, "Your mom and dad will be watching right here. We'll come back to get them when we're finished." If treatment takes place in a school setting, the child's anxiety may be assuaged by hearing you say to his teacher, "I'll bring Johnny back right after we've had a chance to play."

In this way, separations are usually accomplished easily. If they are not, you can invite the parent into the Theraplay room for a brief, "Let's show Mom how great you are at balancing before she goes back out to wait for you." Mother looks, is helped to applaud, and then is ushered out. Once again, occasions requiring such concessions are few indeed. If you find yourself frequently resorting to this concession it is probably a reflection of your own discomfort rather than the child's genuine need. In Chapter Four we discuss how you can avoid acting out of your own need or discomfort.

CHECKUP ACTIVITIES. The purpose of checkup activities is three-fold: (1) to reconnect after the week's separation, (2) to give the child a sense of consistency of self as you show that you remember and can still find the same special freckle or the same strong muscles that you found before, and (3) to convey to the child that she is capable of growth as you compare this week's measurements with last.

The checkup typically takes place as soon as you enter the treatment room. As part of the checkup, you examine the child carefully, looking for all your favorite special qualities, or you cheerfully measure and compare the child's height today against a mark on the wall indicating her previous height. You may weigh her and compare a previous weight. You may check out this week's muscle size, number of teeth, breadth of smile, length of hair, and height of kick, jump, or throw.

The Session Proper

In addition to planning for the alternation between active and quiet, you should choose activities from among the four Theraplay dimensions according to the child's particular needs that you discovered during your assessment. Activities from any one or a combination of two or more dimensions may be chosen. (The dimensions are defined in more detail in Chapter One.)

The following is a short list of activities characteristic of each dimension. There is a longer list of activities in Appendix C. An activity may be classified in more than one dimension. For purposes of descriptive clarity, however, it helps to ask, "What is the primary goal to be accomplished?" Peek-a-boo, for example, may serve both to engage and to challenge. The purpose for which it is being undertaken and the manner in which it is carried out determine whether in this particular situation it should be classified as engaging or challenging.

STRUCTURING ACTIVITIES. The purposes of structuring activities are to delineate time and space clearly and to teach mastery through the internalization of rules. Structuring activities include "wait till I count to three, then jump," "Mother, may I?," "walk only on the blue squares," and drawing around hands or bodies.

ENGAGING ACTIVITIES. The purposes of engaging activities are to entice the child into engagement with his caretaker, to maintain an optimal level of arousal, to teach the child where he leaves off and the rest of the world begins, and to enhance his experience of himself as a separate individual. Engaging activities include peek-a-boo, counting freckles, "knock on the door—peek in," hide-and-seek, or any of a number of surprising, unexpected activities suggested by the child's own actions. Parents often create engaging games out of their baby's movements. For example, as her baby lifts his feet toward her, his mother may grab them and unexpectedly peek at him through his open legs. You can be just as spontaneous. Faced with a resistant child who tries to push you away, you can say "Wow! You're strong. Do that again. See if you can push me over. Oh, you did! Now pull me up! Do it again!"

NURTURING ACTIVITIES. The purpose of nurturing activities is to communicate to the child that she can get what she needs without always having to work for it, deny the existence of the need for it, or be rejected for expressing the need. Nurturing activities generally are soothing, calming, quieting, and reassuring. Such activities include feeding, applying lotion or powder, cuddling, singing a lullaby, rocking in a blanket, and, for older children, giving a manicure, face painting, and making powder or paint footprints (which, of course, requires some gentle foot washing when the job is done).

CHALLENGING ACTIVITIES. The purposes of challenging activities are to enhance feelings of competence, provide the frustration that makes it possible for the child to master tension-arousing experiences, and teach that playful combat, competition, and confrontation can release and focus pent-up tension and anger in a safe, direct, controlled way. Challenging activities include balancing pillows on head, feet, or tummy; wrestling (leg, arm, or thumb); tug-of-war, pillow fights, and water pistol duels. They may include, "I'll bet you can't jump over that pillow," or "let's see whether you can throw that beanbag into my arms." You might introduce a challenging activity this way: "Let's see whether this week *I* can beat *you* at leg wrestling," adding mischievously, "You'd better watch out. I've been practicing."

Whereas each dimension serves a distinct purpose, their underlying unity is in their ability to foster an alliance between the child and adult. All the activities can serve to (1) offset the child's chronic experience of mistrust, loneliness, and isolation; (2) enlist the child's cooperation against the time when you and the child must weather the "negative phase" (see Chapter Four); (3) negate the child's "bad," worthless, alienating, or impotent self-image; and (4) allow the child to view himself as a contributing team member.

The Closing

There are two aspects to the ending of a session: the parting from the therapist, and the return to parents or classroom teacher.

PARTING. The object of parting is to provide closure to the session without closing off the relationship and to encourage carry-over into the child's everyday life. While putting the child's shoes back on, you and the child can discuss what was fun about the session and what is planned for the week ahead. For example, "Boy, Kevin, I really liked the way you did that tip-toe trick today. I want you to try that trick out on some of your friends this week."

TRANSITION. As a final step, straighten the child's clothing in preparation for returning to "the outside world." Remind her, "I'll see you on Wednesday," and then, just as you collected her from her caretaker at the outset, you now deliver her directly to the same adult. Do not leave the child alone in a waiting room or allow her to negotiate her own way down a long corridor to her classroom. Instead, take her hand and connect her directly with a responsible adult. Every time, as you do so, give a message to that individual that provides continuity between the two situations. For example, "Mrs. Jones, be sure you let Cindy show you that special little curl in the back of her hair," or, "Mom, don't you think Bobby looks great when he flexes those muscles? And he's got some other neat tricks he's going to show you, too." "Can you hold hands all the way to the car?"

DOING TREATMENT: SESSIONS ONE TO FOUR

In the following sections, we discuss the way treatment is structured. Although it was shorter than the usual ten sessions, Adam's treatment can serve to illustrate what takes place at each step in the process.

In the typical pattern the first four of the ten half-hour Theraplay sessions take place as follows: The parent or parents sit in the observation room with the interpreting therapist watching the child and his therapist. In Chapter Five we give a detailed description of how the interpreting therapist works with parents. We also discuss how, if you work alone, you can work with the child and with the parents at the same time.

For sessions five through ten, parents join the child in the Theraplay room for the second half of each session. In Adam's case, we brought his mother in at the end of the third session and both parents for the final two sessions.

Although it is not invariable, most children go through a predictable sequence of phases in their response to treatment. There is a period of tentative acceptance in which the child seems to be saying, "This is interesting, a bit strange, but it could be fun." Following this comes a period of resistance (the negative reaction phase). Adam skipped the tentative acceptance phase and started right in with a strong negative reaction. At this point the child may pull out all the stops in his efforts to resist becoming involved with the therapist. It is as though he were saying, "I never trusted anyone before, so why should I trust you?" Following this is a phase of increasing trust in which the child seems to be saying, "Well I guess you really are all right. I think I can trust you." When this phase is well established and the parents have become part of the playful interaction of treatment sessions and are able to carry on at home, it is time to plan for termination. Chapter Four describes in more detail how you can guide the child through these phases of treatment. As we describe Adam's treatment, we point out how his responses illustrate the various phases.

THERAPLAY IN PRACTICE: *Adam's Treatment.* In planning for Adam, we anticipated his strong resistance to separating from his mother. Therefore Madelyn, his therapist, planned a piggyback ride as an intriguing beginning. She planned to check him out for freckles, color of eyes, and strength of hands and legs, hoping to get him to kick a pillow with his feet or push her over with his hands. Following the active pushing and kicking games, she planned to do some calming activities such as making lotion hand prints and rocking and feeding him. In the face of his active resistance, she was unable to do any of these activities, but in spite of his protests she continued to attempt more active games, some of which caught his interest and interrupted his resistance. Her planned list of activities included checkup, paper punch, lotion hand prints, pillow push, rocking, and feeding.

SESSION ONE: RESISTING ENGAGEMENT. The session begins, as his parents predicted, with much crying and protest on Adam's part: "I want

my Mommy!" Because Adam's protests show more anger than anxiety and fear, Madelyn calmly persists in her efforts to engage him, first
asking him to kick pillows with his feet, next having him push her
over, cooling and soothing him when he is hot, offering him a drink
of water, all to the accompaniment of encouraging positive statements:
"I'll take good care of you," "You're OK," "How strong you are," "What
a handsome boy you are." When Adam's anger becomes particularly
intense, Madelyn mirrors his intensity as she says, "You're mad! You're
really mad!" Then suddenly in the midst of his protest, Adam stops
short and asks, "What's your name?" In spite of his resistance, he has
realized that here is someone to be reckoned with.

Behind the Mirror. Although his parents are pained by his resistance,
they agree that his cries are not a sign of genuine panic or distress, and
they understand the need for persisting in the face of it. The interpreting therapist points out the moments when Adam's interest is captured
by an activity, the few times that Madelyn's firm touch calms him, and
the fact that in spite of his protest, he is not struggling to escape her
gently enfolding arms. His parents express amazement at the therapist's
resourcefulness in finding interesting activities to engage him and in
her perseverance in staying with him and not getting angry with him.
The interpreting therapist says, "We want him to feel that he's a great
kid just the way he is. If he's worried all the time about being with you,
he doesn't get a good sense of being a competent, solid person."

In the Theraplay Room. The following scene takes place about fifteen
minutes into the session. His therapist cradles Adam in her lap.

MADELYN: (rubbing lotion on Adam's hands) Oh, you have beautiful hands.

ADAM: That's too much cream.

MADELYN: It's lots and lots and lots. Oh, I like this little boy.

ADAM: Didn't my Mommy tell you I have to go home?

MADELYN: (ignores this statement; rocks Adam gently) More lotion
on Adam's hands.

ADAM: (visibly upset; murmurs inaudibly)

MADELYN: You've got lots and lots of questions; lots and lots of questions. . . . Look at this, look what I have. (holds up a strand of curly,

blond hair) I've got a wonderful piece of Adam hair. (Adam continues to resist, but therapist remains undistracted) OK, Adam, here's a piece of paper. Now I need to put a little more lotion on your hands, on your wonderful, soft hands.

ADAM: (turns away from therapist) Mommy? (crying) I want my Mommy.

MADELYN: (presses Adam's hand onto the piece of paper) There's a thumb . . . and this is your pointer . . . and here's your little finger. (holds up the piece of paper, which now has an imprint of Adam's hand) Oh! Look at that! It's Adam's hand! (begins to take off Adam's sock)

ADAM: No! (hesitates for a moment) Look, I have a little boo-boo.

MADELYN: Look at that, you do have a little boo-boo there. Well let's take care of that. Let's put some lotion on it. (rubs some lotion on Adam's foot) Adam, you have five toes! You're just perfect!

ADAM: I am not. (stops crying for a moment and shows interest)

MADELYN: You have one, two, three, four, five perfect toes. Adam, you have just the right number of toes. (rubs more lotion on the bottom of Adam's foot)

ADAM: Mommy! (therapist continues) What kind of lotion is that? It smells.

MADELYN: (doesn't respond; places Adam's foot on a piece of paper, making a footprint with the lotion)

Behind the Mirror. Adam's parents comment on how hard he is working to oppose Madelyn. "It's just like at home." The interpreting therapist points out that with the introduction of the lotion, Adam has stopped crying for a moment and has shifted to using his highly developed verbal skills to control the interaction: "That's too much cream" *[like an adult admonishing a child?]*; "Didn't my Mommy tell you I have to go home?" "But notice," the interpreting therapist says, "that though she acknowledges that he is asking questions, she doesn't let them stop her. When she made the print of his hand, Adam was really interested. And it seems as though Madelyn's focus on his body has made him more aware of it. See how he points out a 'boo-boo' and asks her to look at it. In spite of his protests, he is beginning to see Madelyn as someone who can take care of him."

In the Theraplay Room. Just before the end of the half-hour session, Madelyn cradles Adam in her arms and sings, "Twinkle, twinkle little star,/What a handsome boy you are;/Curly blond hair and soft, soft cheeks,/Bright blue eyes from which you peek./Twinkle, twinkle little star,/What a special boy you are." Adam attempts to distract her with questions, but Madelyn does not get caught up in responding.

In this first session, Adam's protests occur throughout, interrupted only occasionally when his interest is captured and he seems ready to accept Madelyn's attention. His resistance takes the form of angry crying, verbal threats, and sophisticated talk and questions designed to engage his therapist in an argument. He has such an extensive repertoire of ways to resist adults that it is no wonder his parents have had difficulty being firm with him.

As the family left the Theraplay room, Madelyn said, "I'll be looking forward to playing with you tomorrow. I'll be thinking about your bright blue eyes, and your very special freckles. I'll have some fun things planned for us to do." Then placing Adam's hand in his mother's, she said, "Mom, be sure to hold Adam's hand all the way to the elevator. Dad, help him push the button to call the elevator for you."

SESSION TWO: PROTEST AND TENTATIVE ACCEPTANCE. In planning for this second session, Madelyn took into account two things she had learned from her first session with Adam: He is very easily charged up by fast-paced or exciting activities, and he is more easily engaged by challenging activities than by nurturing ones. She therefore planned to modulate her tone of voice and the speed with which she did her activities, find as many activities as possible that are calming and soothing, and add challenge to the quiet nurturing activities to keep him engaged. To help him learn to be less impulsive, she will have him wait for her playful signal before doing an activity. Her plan included a cotton-ball-blow game, which Adam had enjoyed the day before, a cotton-ball-touch (the challenge is for Adam to close his eyes and tell where he is being touched), and a row-boat activity that would lend itself to modulations of tempo.

Madelyn greets Adam at his next session with a challenge: "I'll bet you can't walk on your hands into the playroom." Intrigued, Adam puts his hands on the floor and allows her to pick up his legs and guide him the few steps into the room. Only then does he remember to protest, but this time the protest is less intense.

Five minutes into the session, Madelyn and Adam sit on the floor, face to face, legs outstretched. Madelyn places a cotton ball in the middle of a large pillow that rests between them.

MADELYN: You see if you can blow the cotton ball under my arm, and I'll see if I can blow it under your arm. Ready, set, go. (Adam blows the cotton ball under the therapist's arm and off the pillow) Oh Adam, you're a great blower!

ADAM: (begins to cry) Mommy! Mommy!

MADELYN: (continues with the game, placing the cotton ball in the middle of the pillow) Ready, go! (Adam immediately stops crying and begins to blow; he wins again)

ADAM: (begins to cry) Mommy! Mommy!

MADELYN: You have two big blows and I don't have any yet! (sets up cotton ball) OK, Adam, blow when I say go . . . . Go! (Adam stops crying, blows, and wins again) Great job! You are great!

Behind the Mirror. The parents report that immediately after yesterday's session Adam said he never wanted to come back again, but this morning, he made no protest about coming. They are proud of having been firm about putting him to bed last night. "He settled right down once he realized we really meant it." They notice that here in this session he is making much less protest. When Adam and Madelyn play the cotton-ball-hockey game his father says, "He's really getting into it, isn't he? He seems as though he's enjoying it."

In the Theraplay Room. Madelyn and Adam sit facing each other, playing the cotton-ball-touch game, which proceeds as follows: After the therapist touches Adam somewhere with a cotton ball, Adam must point to where he was touched. Though Adam follows Madelyn's directions (he closes his eyes when asked and identifies where he was touched), he cries for his mother after every response. Madelyn ignores Adam's cries and quickly moves from one round to the next.

Behind the Mirror. The interpreting therapist says, "Notice how he is able to close his eyes while he waits for his therapist to touch him with the cotton ball. That takes a lot of trust. One reason she chose this game is that it is another way to help Adam accept touch without having to protest about it. Although he is still calling for you, there seems less and less urgency about it." When each successful touch was followed by a wail for "Mommy," the interpreting therapist says, "Any time the action stops for a moment, he calls for you. It's almost a habit."

In the Theraplay Room. The therapist cradles Adam in her arms and feeds him frozen yogurt with a spoon.

ADAM: It's melting (referring to the yogurt).

MADELYN: It sure is melting. (continues feeding) Mmmm, yummy.

ADAM: (points to a spoonful) That's too much!

MADELYN: (ignores this comment and goes on feeding)

ADAM: Too much. (eats the spoonful)

MADELYN: (looks at Adam) You are a great-looking boy.

ADAM: What's that white stuff?

MADELYN: (continues feeding) Mmmmm.

Behind the Mirror. The interpreting therapist says, "Even though he is complaining about something at each mouthful, he accepts it. He is beginning to feel much less anxious. Do you think you could do that? Avoid getting caught up in his criticism of what you are doing? That won't be easy, he's so very good at choosing just the right thing to say that might catch you up. Could you two remind each other when you see that Adam has hooked one of you by his clever talk?"

In the Theraplay Room. Adam and Madelyn sit face to face, holding hands. Alternately they pull each other's arms in a "rowing" motion while the Therapist sings "Row, Row, Row Your Boat." Madelyn sets the pace, sometimes slow and sometimes fast. Adam clearly enjoys the game. When the song is over, Madelyn brings Adam to his parents and places one of his hands in each of his parents' hands, asking them to hold on until they get to their car. "Have a good evening. I'll see you tomorrow," she says. Adam smiles and walks out with his parents.

SESSION THREE: GROWING AND TRUSTING. Since Adam has begun to be more comfortable in his sessions, Madelyn can spend less time trying to engage him and more time doing nurturing activities and playful give-and-take games. She plans to repeat the cotton-ball-guess game, this time asking Adam to touch her as well. She wants to have him do some active games such as having him kick the pillow over to see whether she can help him modulate his excitement even when doing something very energetic. Since, in Adam's short treatment, this is the middle session, Madelyn will have Adam's mother come in at the very end to do some nurturing activities with him.

In the Theraplay Room. Madelyn scoops Adam up in her arms and gives him a piggyback ride into the playroom. For the first time, Adam makes no protest when he leaves his parents. They again play the cotton-ball-guess game. This time, however, they alternate roles; first the therapist touches Adam with the cotton ball while Adam guesses, then Adam touches the therapist with the cotton ball while the therapist guesses. Adam smiles and giggles with pleasure.

Behind the Mirror. The interpreting therapist points out to the parents that Adam is now trusting Madelyn and is able to engage in lively give-and-take games. He no longer has to call for his mother after each action. His parents report that Adam said he liked Madelyn: "She has lots of good games to play." The evening had been calmer and more pleasant than usual.

In the Theraplay Room. Adam sits in Madelyn's lap with his feet tucked under a large pillow. On Madelyn's signal, he kicks the pillow and it flips over.

MADELYN: Look at that! Oh boy! How about two pillows?

ADAM: (smiles and nods; he is clearly having fun) Yes!

MADELYN: (picks up another large pillow) Oh, this is a very heavy pillow. Feel this . . . it's too heavy.

ADAM: Yeah.

MADELYN: (places another pillow on top of the first) You have very strong legs. OK, now when I say . . . What would you like me to say?

ADAM: Apples.

MADELYN: Apples. OK, ready . . . peanut butter . . . chocolate . . . strawberry . . . apples!

ADAM: (kicks the pillows and they fall over)

MADELYN: Look at that! My goodness, incredible!

ADAM: (turns around to grab another pillow; Madelyn gets the pillow herself)

MADELYN: With your very strong legs, I think you can do three pillows. (stacks three pillows on Adam's feet)

ADAM: (smiling) It's going to be heavy.

MADELYN: I know. OK, the signal is watermelon. (Adam nods) Peanut butter . . . chocolate . . . watermelon!

ADAM: (kicks the pillows and they all fall over)

MADELYN: Wow! Fantastic! (hugs Adam)

Behind the Mirror. The interpreting therapist says, "I'm sure you've noticed that Madelyn often gives a signal before she asks him to do something. That helps Adam learn to wait before he jumps in. She always makes it funny or surprising, using words like *peanut butter* and *strawberries* as signals, so that it's not boring. Adam is getting better and better at waiting. One of his problems is that he is so fast and so easily excited that she needs to help him slow down. I want you to practice this at home. . . . Did you notice that one time she gave him the responsibility for giving the signal? Since Adam is no longer insisting on taking charge, Madelyn can allow him some say in the proceedings. . . . Adam is so proud of his ability to kick the pillows. Did you see that Madelyn avoided the heavy pillow? That's because she wants Adam to feel successful. While we want Adam to accept being taken care of, we also want him to feel very competent and very good about himself."

To the mother she said, "Madelyn will be calling you to join them toward the end of the session today. She will tell you just what to do. Sometimes children become more resistant when their parents first come into the session. They seem to have to test whether their parents can be as firm as their therapist has been. If that happens, don't worry. Madelyn will help you handle it." To both parents she said, "Tomorrow both of you will be joining in for the last half of the session. So dress comfortably."

In the Theraplay Room. Adam's mother is called into the playroom to help put his shoes on. He asks to sit in his mother's lap, but Madelyn says, "Mom needs to sit there (facing him) so that she can put your shoes on." Adam accepts this and, at the end, leaves the session happily with his mother.

DOING TREATMENT: SESSIONS FIVE TO TEN

The format for the first fifteen minutes of each remaining Theraplay session proceeds as before: parents and interpreting therapist observe the child with his therapist. For the last fifteen minutes, however, the parents join the fun in the Theraplay room.

Because we want parents to enter the Theraplay room in a lively, upbeat manner, the Theraplay therapist often hides with the child under pillows and blankets for the parents to find them. Another variation is to hide notes or special treats on the child for the parents to find. We used both approaches with Adam. In Chapter Five we give more details about how we guide parents in their interactions with their child in the Theraplay room.

THERAPLAY IN PRACTICE: *Adam with His Parents.* It is important to plan well for the ending of treatment. (In Chapter Four we discuss in more detail how this should be handled.) At the third from the last session you should announce that there will be three more sessions and that the final session will be a party. In Adam's case, of course, we were not able to give that much notice. He knew from the beginning that we would have five sessions. His therapist reminded him at the fourth session that the next session would be his last.

SESSION FOUR: PARENTS ENTER THE ROOM, PREPARATION FOR TERMINATION. As noted above, Adam's treatment was very condensed in comparison with the full ten-session pattern. During his fourth session we brought his parents in and at the same session announced that treatment would end the next day. Despite the difference between the usual pattern and Adam's experience, this example still shows how each step is handled.

Our goal for Adam's last two sessions was to give his parents practice taking charge in a playful and engaging manner, regulating his excitement and nurturing him, and, above all, having fun with him. We chose to have his mother come in first, rather than both parents at once, because we wanted to work on her relationship with Adam and did not want to divide attention between the two parents.

In the Theraplay Room. At the beginning of this session, Madelyn reminded Adam that they would be having just one more session this week. "Then I won't be seeing you until just after your birthday."

(Since a month is meaningless to a child Adam's age, his therapist described the time in relation to something Adam could understand, his birthday.) Adam accepted her announcement with no comment. He entered happily into the games she had chosen to play with him.

Fifteen minutes into the session, Madelyn says, "It's time to have your mom come to play with us. Let's hide so she can find us. . . . Mom, close your eyes so you can't see where we're hiding." With lots of giggles and excitement, Adam and Madelyn build a fort with pillows and hide inside it under a blanket. "Call your mom. Call her real loud. Say, 'Come and get me!'" Adam calls with enthusiasm, "Come and get me, Mom!"

The interpreting therapist and his mother come into the room and pretend to look for Adam.

INTERPRETING THERAPIST: I thought Adam was here, Mom. Let's look around . . . do you think he's under this mat? No . . . look at that! I saw those pillows wiggle a little . . . Adam? (Therapist and mother peek into the fort) There he is! Look at his smiling face! Mom, give Adam a big hug. (Adam and Mom embrace, bright smiles on their faces)

A few minutes later Mother, Adam, and the two therapists sit in a circle and make a "stack of hands." At first they go slowly, then faster and faster. Adam becomes excited and pulls his hands out of the stack out of sequence.

MADELYN: Wow! That was exciting. Let's see if we can do it very slowly. (They start again, stacking hands carefully and then, with exaggerated slowness, each hand is moved from bottom to top. Adam goes along very well with the slower pace, looking proud of his accomplishment.) That was great! Now let's see whether we can go from the top down. That's a lot harder, but I'll bet you two can do it. (This time, Adam needs a bit of help with the unexpected order, but he manages without getting too excited.) Mom, look how well he does that. Could you two do that at home? Remember to do it fast and then slow and see if you can manage not to get mixed up. (Adam smiles. He has obviously enjoyed the game and likes the idea that he can do it again at home.)

To give Adam's mother practice in taking charge and making sure that he follows her directions, the therapists next set up a game of

"Mother may I?" With prompting from the interpreting therapist, Mrs. B. directs Adam to take giant steps and baby steps and to do so only after asking, "Mother may I?" Adam is so pleased with the game that he begins to take over—"How about tip toes?"—but Mrs. B. remembers that the object of the activity is to practice having Adam follow her lead, and she gently says, "No Adam, it's my turn to be the leader."

Toward the end of the session the therapists roll Adam in a blanket toward his mother and then place him carefully in her lap. She cradles Adam in her arms as she feeds him a cookie. Then she is given a bottle of juice for Adam and he relaxes into her arms and sucks, seeming to enjoy every minute of it. The interpreting therapist puts her arm around Adam's mother and helps her rock gently to the tune of the "Twinkle Song" ("What a special boy you are"). It is a lovely, relaxed moment, which all enjoy.

At the end of this session, Adam sits in his mother's lap and faces his father while he puts Adam's shoes and socks on.

MADELYN: Adam needs to have his socks put on. Dad, before you put the socks on, you'll need to put a kiss on each foot! (Father kisses each foot, then puts Adam's socks on. Adam giggles with pleasure. Adam is now much more comfortable with his father and is no longer resisting contact with him.)

FINAL SESSION: TERMINATION PARTY. In the usual ten-session pattern, simple preparations for the party would be made during the ninth session. For example, you might ask what the child would like to eat, giving two choices such as cupcakes or cookies. "What color balloons would you like?" The joyous, upbeat nature of the party, rather than elaborate arrangements, should be emphasized. In Adam's case, the party was very simple. Madelyn had arranged a few balloons and streamers to make the room look festive. The treat was Adam's favorite kind of cookie. The emphasis was on all the wonderful things that Madelyn and his parents had discovered about Adam.

In the Theraplay Room. Madelyn greets Adam with a hug and says she has been waiting all day to see him. She takes note of all the special features she has discovered about him: his curly hair, his special freckles, his strong arms. She then revisits some of Adam's favorite activities, such as the pillow kick and the cotton-ball-hockey. She mentions again that this is their last session together until after Adam's birthday. She will remember him during that time and look forward to checking whether he has any new freckles or whether he has grown taller.

In preparation for bringing Adam's parents into the session, she hides four notes on Adam. His parents will find them and lead the activities that are described in each. Adam finds the hiding a bit ticklish, but mainly is excited by the prospect of hiding something for his parents to find. Once the notes are hidden, Adam sits on Madelyn's lap facing his father. He has an expectant look as he waits for his father to find a note. He is so eager that he points to the place where one of the notes is hidden. Remembering not to let Adam run the show, Father continues his search and finds the note in Adam's sleeve.

FATHER: (reads note) Pop cheeks.

MADELYN: Do you know how to pop cheeks?

FATHER: (Nods and moves closer. Adam puffs up his cheeks with air. His father then gently presses them together with his fingers; everyone laughs.)

ADAM: Mommy. Mommy's turn. *[He can't yet give up trying to direct things.]*

MADELYN: OK, this time a tad closer so he can blow right on you. Get a little closer; he's ready for you!

FATHER: ("pops" Adam's cheeks; everyone laughs again)

MADELYN: OK, now Adam's turn. Dad, make your cheeks pop up . . . (Adam leans over and, with a hard, impulsive gesture, pops his father's cheeks) Dad, help him do it very gently. (Father holds Adam's hands and guides him so that he "pops" his cheeks gently.)

Adam's mother found a note telling her to play peek-a-boo with him. Adam sits in Madelyn's lap facing his mother. She peeks at him from behind her hands, then puts her hands over Adam's eyes and has him peek. The interpreting therapist suggests that mother play peek-a-boo with Adam's feet. Adam grins with pleasure at the silly variation.

Father has found a note telling him to have Adam push him over (an activity that Father has seen Adam and Madelyn do together). Adam sits on a pillow in front of his father. The two are holding hands.

MADELYN: Give him a signal, Dad.

FATHER: OK, when I say "peaches." Ready . . . apples . . . grapes . . . peaches! (Adam pushes and his father rolls back, supporting Adam on his knees above his head; Adam laughs with delight as he looks lovingly into his father's eyes)

Behind the Mirror. Adam's parents are delighted with the progress that they and Adam have made during this brief five-day intervention. They report that Adam is much more willing to do what they ask him to do. He allowed his father to put him to bed last night. They aren't sure he is ready for preschool yet, but they are hopeful that he will be ready by the time it starts at the end of the summer. They are especially pleased with what they have learned. Mom said, "I think it had become so hard to be with him, that even when I was with him, I was pushing him away. Now that I can get him to do what I need him to do, I enjoy being with him more. He's more fun to be with. That feels really good." Dad said, "There's a big difference for me. I was worried that he would never let me do anything with him. I thought he would just always be a Mommy's boy. Now I think he can grow up to be a real man."

The family went away knowing that they could call us during the month before their checkup session but feeling that they probably wouldn't need to do so. It was a delightful scene as they skipped away down the hall, holding hands (and the balloons!) all the way to the elevator.

DOING CHECKUP VISITS

Because of the concentrated, intense format of Theraplay, remarkable changes often occur in a short time—as was clearly demonstrated with Adam and his parents. Because it is very important to help families maintain the new ways of relating, checkup visits are an integral part of the treatment plan. Typically we schedule visits quarterly for the first year and annually thereafter (if families wish to maintain contact beyond a year). We have found, however, that many families do better if they come in once a month for the first three months and then once every three months to complete the year. Some families return once a year for a few years for checkup visits. All are encouraged to phone should problems arise in the meantime. Most often these problems are handled in telephone consultation. Occasionally the whole family is signed up for a special session or two. Because Adam's treatment was so brief, we scheduled our checkup visits once a month for three months. We did not go beyond that because of the distance they had to travel.

Checkup visits replicate the format of sessions six through ten, with parents joining in for the second half of the session. At the outset, the therapists express their delight at seeing the child again and look for familiar characteristics as well as those that have changed ("Oh good! You brought those freckles with you . . . except, guess what? Here are some brand new ones. These must have come from those weekends at the beach." "Look at that, you brought your wonderful smile along. And look! Two new teeth! Wow! What beauties!"). With Adam the visits followed this same format. On the first one, he came eagerly into the room flexing the strong muscle he had developed. "Look at my big new muscle!" Madelyn measured his muscle and height, and she found that he had grown a quarter of an inch and that he could now jump and touch a spot on the wall a full inch above the earlier mark they had established. During the session, Adam and Madelyn played many of the games they had enjoyed before and some new ones that she had designed especially for him. In his eagerness, Adam tried to direct the show from time to time, but there was none of the anxious, demanding tone that had so characterized the first sessions of his treatment.

Children seem to love the checkup visits. Parents often report, "We don't know why we bring him. There really hasn't been anything wrong. But he does love to come back here." Adam's parents also said he had been looking forward to coming. They said that they too were eager to return, since they felt the need to bolster their new skills of taking charge and responding to Adam's needs for calming and nurturing.

In the viewing room, during the first half of the checkup visit, parents bring the interpreting therapist up to date on recent developments and may ask for advice on, or approval of, what they have been doing. "We've been having special baby times together [setting firm limits, doing surprise activities, and so on] whenever he gets tense and driven [or wordy and legalistic, or gets too disorganized, or becomes overmethodical], just as we learned to do here. Is it still OK to do?"

Adam's parents recounted their successes (and their failures), emphasizing that they felt very hopeful about the success of the new approach. The final two checkup sessions went much as the first one. Each time Adam seemed more accepting of his parents' attention and more comfortable letting them take charge. Just before the third session, Adam successfully entered the preschool program in which his parents had hoped to enroll him. His mother took time off from work to make the transition go well, staying for the first two days, then shortening her stay until he was able to remain in school for a full day without her (this was the school's standard procedure and not a special concession for Adam). In later phone conversations, his parents reported that his adjustment to school had been very good. "He now goes happily to school. He has made a friend and he seems content. We are very happy with the outcome of our work with you."

Notes

1. For more details about the administration and interpretation of the MIM, see the MIM manuals listed in Publications About Theraplay and the Marschak Interaction Method (MIM).
2. Appendix B gives recommended lists of MIM tasks for young children, school-age children, and adolescents.

CHAPTER FOUR

Working with the Child

Having described the structure of Theraplay treatment in Chapter Three, we now provide more specific guidelines for creating the therapeutic setting and the experience into which you invite the child and her parents.

We first look at the typical phases of children's response to Theraplay treatment. Following this we explain how to tailor treatment to the needs of each individual child. We describe how to handle the child's resistance. Then we discuss how the therapist should recognize and overcome feelings of inadequacy and the hazards of counter-transference. Finally, we provide treatment guidelines for the therapist.

GUIDING THE CHILD THROUGH THE PHASES OF TREATMENT

Although Theraplay emphasizes the importance of responding to each child individually—an emphasis that might lead one to expect that treatment for each child would be very different—in fact the course of Theraplay treatment unfolds in a fairly predictable pattern. A child can make only a finite number of reactions to an insistent, intrusive, interested, and intimacy-seeking adult. When a friendly adult "comes on strong," for example, a child cannot ignore her, continue to "do his own thing," or disassociate himself from the situation. He may accept her, reject her, or try to flee the situation, but any of these behaviors is a response to the adult's insistence and is not simply child-determined.

Theraplay treatment falls roughly into six phases, which may vary somewhat according to age and pathology:

Introduction

Exploration

Tentative acceptance

Negative reaction

Growing and trusting

Termination

We cannot estimate precisely how long a child might remain in a particular phase. Since Theraplay is a short-term treatment, a child is unlikely to remain in any stage very long. Typically, children enter the negative reaction phase after the second or third session. Some children begin their first session by protesting (as we saw with Adam in Chapter Three), then settle into tentative acceptance before entering a full negative reaction. This is especially true of young children who are struggling with separation issues. A few children never show the negative response that we expect.

Although with so much variability, one might question the concept of predictable phases, it is particularly useful to be aware of the likelihood of the negative phase. It is reassuring to therapists and parents to know in advance that the child may have a period of protest and may even become more difficult in her behavior at home before increasing trust and acceptance leads to improved behavior.

Introduction Phase

Although they are never spelled out verbally, the ground rules are clearly set at the very first session:

- Theraplay sessions will be fun.
- They will be clearly directed by the therapist.

- They will be action-oriented, rather than talk- and insight-oriented.
- They will be clearly delineated as to time, space, and therapist and patient roles.

At your first meeting, as at the beginning of every session, move toward the child in a way that tells him, "I know you're basically a strong, fun-loving, and fun-to-be-with person, and right from the start I'm going to present you with the most appealing picture of the world I can conjure up."

After announcing, "I'm Chuck," you might say, "Come on, jump aboard; I have a ride for you," or "I've just been waiting so long for you to hop down this hall with me," or "See, I can make this special 'chair' for you to ride on. Put your arm around my shoulder, and you can sit on it." Thus "hooked" together, you and the child leave the reception area and head for the therapy room. The interpreting therapist and the parents proceed into the observation room. You can tell the child, "Mom and Dad will be watching us from this room. We'll come find them when we're through playing." The action is swift, the level of excitement high. There is little opportunity for the child to dwell on doubts or to verbalize reservations. The period of anxious anticipation is, therefore, cut to a minimum.

Of course, such an abrupt greeting or joyful departure may not always be possible. It may be too noisy and disruptive to begin in such an active manner in a public reception area or in school corridors. If that is the case, you can invite the child and her parents to come with you to the Theraplay door and at that point begin the active, playful introduction of the child into the nature of Theraplay itself.

Occasionally the child herself is too frightened or upset to "allow" such a sudden separation from her parents and introduction to Theraplay. We are not referring here to a child's being resistant or surprised but rather to her being genuinely frightened. Toddlers may need their parents to accompany them when they are first introduced to the Theraplay room and may need to sit in a parent's lap until they feel more comfortable. Some exceptions to this are discussed in Chapters Six and Eight. Also, if the fear is the result of the child's having been traumatized or abused, the approach needs to be very different. We discuss how Theraplay can be adapted to working with such children in Chapter Nine.

Throughout the course of treatment all Theraplay sessions have this same therapist-in-charge, upbeat, playful quality. You do not need to introduce the child to the nature of Theraplay verbally. Every fun-filled action teaches him a little bit more. Some children ask questions or challenge the "rules" by suggesting their own activities, by attempting to engage the therapist in a discussion ("What are we going to do today?"), or by refusing to go along with the activities the therapist introduces. But you should remain steady in your plan to let the child know the nature of the experience you are embarking on together.

Exploration Phase

In the exploration phase, you and the child actively get to know each other. This exploration begins in the very first session as you "check out" the child's many interesting physical characteristics. This is analogous to a mother's checking out her newborn baby by counting his fingers and toes, feeling his soft hair, and seeing how his arms and legs move.[1] In the same way, you and the child get to know who has the largest hands, the curliest hair, the longest toenails, and the strongest muscles. This exploration phase can extend over a number of sessions as you learn about the child's special qualities and the child in turn learns about you and explores the nature of the new relationship you are offering. In the process, the child comes to view himself in a new light. He may not have known before that the hairs on his arms stand up when the therapist blows on them, that he can jump gracefully into the air off a table, reach to touch the ceiling, or that he has twenty-eight knucklebones.

Even negative behaviors can be turned around to show a more lovable side. When she defiantly goes limp, you might use a paradoxical approach, telling her what a skillful "rag doll" she is. Or when she turns her head to avoid eye contact, you might say, "Be sure not to look at me." The chin that stiffens when her mouth closes tight may respond with jolly wobbling to a playful touch; the piercing "no" may change to a musical "no-oh-oh" when you pluck her lips. But, most important, she may not have known before that she is lovable even at her most resistant. She is learning that she does not have to be a "good girl" or master difficult tasks in order to be lovable or acceptable to you.

During the exploratory period, the child must become aware of you as a person, including your facial features, voice, and physical strength. If a session gives him only a vague impression of a shadowy figure that he remembers in some amorphous way, the session is a failure. It is very important that you make every effort to ensure that when the child lies in bed at night after each Theraplay session he will be able to call to mind a clear image of you. Indeed the Theraplay session can be counted a success only if the child has come to perceive you as clearly differentiated from himself, omnipresent, and fun.

The impact of an early exploration session on one little boy was clearly demonstrated when he greeted his therapist the following week with "Look, I found another freckle!" Throughout the week he had carried an image in his mind of his therapist and of the fact that she was intensely interested in his special freckles.

Tentative Acceptance Phase

Following their initial surprise at the special nature of the Theraplay sessions, many children move into a tentative acceptance phase, which may begin in the first session and extend into the following sessions. The child pretends or may actually attempt to "play the game," but tentativeness, even apprehension, is the underlying tone. The child may appear bewildered, excited, reserved, or interested. You must be sensitive to the child's uncertainty and understand that her involvement may be only on the surface. Even when she reacts with enthusiasm and apparent intimacy, however, this reaction is often too premature to be evidence of a genuinely relaxed engagement. Rather, it may be a defensive, apprehensive maneuver intended to keep the intruding therapist at bay.

During this period, you should continue to be engaging and insistent, nurturing or challenging, surprising, appealing, and fun. You should not be seduced by the apparent acceptance into backing away from your efforts to engage the child and move to a more genuine and trusting relationship.

Negative Reaction Phase

In the negative reaction phase, the child becomes clearly resistant to any further efforts at intimacy. The child who had previously appeared so accepting—if not outright cooperative, enthusiastic, and participating—may suddenly become limp and mute or actively resistant and negative. Why does this negative reaction occur? One possible explanation is that the child, like an older adopted child who is beginning to be hopeful about the new relationship, needs to test the reality of the commitment. The child seems to be asking, "If I am going to risk getting close, can I really trust that I won't be hurt again?" "Will you stick by me if you see my ugly, angry side as well as my sweet, compliant side?"

Your response should continue to be insistent and matter-of-fact, conveying to the child that you will stick by him no matter what and that the games you are about to play will be fun. You need to let him know that weeping, tantrums, or refusals to join in do not put you off. (Later in this chapter we discuss how to handle temper tantrums.) The resistance may continue over a few more sessions in the same or varied form. In the face of your firm perseverance and implied hopefulness, however, it will diminish in intensity and eventually disappear. The first clues to its reduction often come in the form of surreptitious eye contact, unintended calm behavior, or even a fleeting smile that appears as though it had broken through in spite of itself.

Because this negative reaction is so important to the outcome of treatment and because parents often find it hard to watch their child go through such a difficult struggle, it is important that you prepare parents in advance to expect such a reaction. Chapter Five describes how Josh's therapist stayed with him during two extended temper tantrums and how parents can be prepared for such an eventuality.

Growing and Trusting Phase

With your warm but firm and omnipresent help, the child has mastered the negative phase and is now ready to move into growing and trusting. During this phase, the child first begins to experience the pleasure of interacting with another human being in a "normal," reciprocally satisfying way. He begins to develop confidence in himself and trust in the world. In this period, which constitutes the bulk of the therapeutic effort, you and the child increasingly become partners in a plan to try out new variations on old themes (including mutual teasing and playful shifts in taking initiative), to enjoy longer and more intense periods of intimacy, and, of course, ultimately to genuinely enjoy each other's company.

At first, the moments of closeness are fleeting, and the laughter will come primarily from you. As progress is made, there is reciprocal laughter, mutual give-and-take, and harmonious times of sitting close and looking into each other's eyes while softly singing rounds or playing patty-cake. Once you and the child have found this high degree of pleasure with each other, it is time to introduce other members of the child's community into the sessions to expand the child's awareness that others can respond to him with as much pleasure and support as you do.

In our usual pattern, the child's parents have been observing from the beginning. At this point, they will join the play for the second half of each session and become increasingly involved in leading the activities. Chapter Five presents the many ways you can help parents prepare to take over the role of Theraplay therapist for their own child.

If the work is being done in a school setting, you can invite a playmate or a teacher to participate. You can accompany the child on tours of the school, stopping to visit librarians, cooks, or other members of the school staff (for example, saying, "Mrs. Jones, Juan and I just came by to see whether you have any of that good chocolate milk today").

Eventually therapy may take place in the classroom itself. To heighten the child's self-esteem through increasing his status in the eyes of his classmates, for example, you might facilitate the child's hosting a party, giving out special treats, or teaching his friends some of the new tricks he has learned while playing with you. This expansion of the child's world to include other loving, interested, and supportive people is an important preparation for termination.

Termination

In one sense, the termination date has been planned from the start, as part of the agreement you and the parents made for a given number of sessions. When children are seen in schools, the contract is based on the school budget that determines the number of sessions children can have. However, the decision to end treatment is always based on how well the child is doing. If the child is not ready for termination when the final session approaches, the original contract should be renegotiated.

For the purpose of outlining the typical sequence, however, we will base our discussion on the standard number of sessions. If the agreement has been for ten sessions, the termination process begins at the seventh session. Although it encompasses a relatively short span of time, the termination of Theraplay treatment consists of three distinct phases: preparation, announcement, and parting.

PREPARATION. Teachers' and parents' reports of decrease or disappearance of symptoms, as well as the child's increasingly harmonious and happy behavior with respect to herself and her world, have led to the introduction into her Theraplay sessions of the other "therapeutic" agents described earlier (parents, teachers, or classmates). Following evidence that these particular expansions of her emotional universe have been appropriate and enjoyable, she is considered ready for termination of Theraplay. Although her relationship with you has become meaningful and intimate and the sessions themselves have become important in her everyday life, the termination period must not be ushered in with gloom, nostalgia, long-term preparation, or tentative misgiving.

ANNOUNCEMENT. In the third week before sessions are to end, announce the termination plans in the context of gains the child has made: "You're getting to be such fun to play with and Michael and Lakeesha enjoy playing with you so much that you won't be needing me to come here and play with you much longer," or "You and your mom and dad are having so much fun together that you don't need to come to see me so often." Then, after a pause to make sure Jimmy has understood, you set the date. "We'll have our sessions this week and next week, and then the week after that on Thursday we'll have our last session."

For the next two sessions, the emphasis is on "tricks" the child has learned in his sessions, such as balancing on five pillows, or doing a backflip with your help. Sometimes you can help the child teach the "tricks" to other children in his classroom. When parents are involved, they take an increasingly central role—planning activities, demonstrating activities that have been practiced at home, and consolidating what they have learned about how to meet their child's needs. The object is to redirect the child's attachment away from you and onto the people who will make up his post-therapy environment.

After each of these termination-phase sessions, remind the child of how many more "times we will have together." You do not need to encourage him to explore his hidden reactions to separation. If he shows clear evidence of anger, sadness, helplessness, or bewilderment, you can label and acknowledge these feelings for him, just as earlier you labeled and acknowledged his body parts (for example, "I know you feel angry that we won't be together any more"). If, as rarely happens, the anger is acted out against you, remind him, "You can tell me how you feel about it, but I can't let you hurt me."

During the course of the penultimate session, remind the child, "Remember, Jennifer, Thursday will be our last time together." As a review of what you have done together, the child may like to replay activities she has enjoyed during her previous sessions. During the quiet time near the session's closing, you can plan for the final party by asking her preferences for food and for special activities. At the end, she is again reminded that the next session will be her last one.

PARTING. By the time of the termination party, an alliance has been established between the child and the friends and family members you have brought into the Theraplay scene. By now you should have disengaged into the position of friendly participant. The theme of the party is a future-oriented reaffirmation of the child's strengths and identity. Guests, child, and you all wear party hats, share party treats, and sing songs about the child's unique attributes. Discussion may include the birthday to come, the school year ahead, and so on. Souvenirs, in the form of footprint or handprint pictures, may be distributed, or a special song taught to everyone. During the session, you might make a T-shirt to send home with the child emblazoned with the brightly colored handprints of all the participants. Or you might make a life-sized drawing of the child with a listing of all the special characteristics that you have discovered about him during his Theraplay sessions.

At the end of this final session, act as anyone would at the close of a meaningful relationship: Give the child a big hug, tell her how much you have enjoyed playing with such a special person, and tell her you know that from now on she will be having fun with her own friends. Then turn her over to her parents or return her to the classroom, making sure that she is immediately incorporated into some favorite group and fun activity. The session ends with a reminder about the date of the upcoming checkup visit.

TAILORING TREATMENT TO THE INDIVIDUAL CHILD

As we noted in Chapter One, even though the general Theraplay approach can be useful for a broad range of attachment and relationship problems, it must be tailored to suit the needs of each individual child. In that chapter we describe the dimensions of Theraplay and how you can use them to help understand and meet children's individual needs. The origins of these different needs lie both in children's inborn temperaments and in the particular ways in which their attachment or relationship difficulties are expressed: for example, in anxious, fearful, withdrawn behavior or in angry, aggressive, pseudomature behavior.

If treatment is not customized, its course may be a hodgepodge of trial-and-error encounters. When there is no purpose and no direction, the benefits of one session or one gambit may be canceled by the blunders of the next. It may be counterproductive to engage a child who requires nurture in an activity that is primarily challenging. It may be unnecessarily rigid to limit a child who needs both challenging and intruding to only one and not the other.

We first address the need for responding within each session to particular behaviors that call for a modified Theraplay approach. Then we address the need to understand the effect of different environmental influences (ethnic, cultural, and family lifestyle differences) that require different kinds and degrees of Theraplay. The assessment of both is necessary if Theraplay treatment is to be responsive to the special needs of each child.

Responding to the Child's Behavior

It is essential that you monitor the child's responses carefully during the Theraplay session for signs of a possible need to revise your treatment plan. The following are examples of behaviors that require such a change.

PHYSICAL DISCOMFORT. Some children are so sensitive to touch that they respond to physical contact with genuine distress. Chapter Six demonstrates how Theraplay can be adapted to the needs of children with special sensitivities or sensory integration problems, as well as the regulation problems we consider next. Although a reaction of distress to physical contact does not rule out the eventual use of touch, you should focus initially on engaging the child through activities that allow some distance while maintaining the interaction. Peek-a-boo, singing to the child, tossing a beanbag, or blowing cotton balls back and forth to each other are examples of such activities.

Since touch is so very important in children's development, we introduce it gradually in whatever form the child can tolerate. A child who is very uncomfortable having lotion on her skin may be able to tolerate powder instead. Firm touch may be more acceptable than light touch for some children, and it has the additional benefit of providing deep pressure to the muscles, pressure that is very soothing and organizing for many children. Such children could tolerate, for example, being rolled tightly in a soft blanket whereas they could not tolerate having their cheeks blown on or being touched with a feather.

If there is any question of whether a child has a sensory integration problem, she should be referred for an evaluation and possible treatment with an occupational therapist trained in techniques specifically designed to help the child overcome her discomfort.

OVEREXCITEMENT. Some children become overexcited by Theraplay activities. These are often the children whose regulatory difficulties (irritability, sensory sensitivities, and hyperresponsiveness to stimuli) contributed to their attachment and relationship problems from the very beginning. In general, you must reduce the stimuli presented to the child as well as carefully monitor his level of excitement so that he can be helped to calm down before he gets out of control. Activities that excite the child within the limits of his tolerance and then help him return to a more calm state are particularly helpful. You can play "Row-row-row your boat" slowly, then faster, then faster still, and finally with exaggerated slowness, ending with a firm hug or firm pressure on the child's shoulders to make sure that he is fully settled after the excitement. After many experiences of being helped to manage excitement successfully, the child will eventually be able to monitor his own excitement level.

UNHAPPINESS. If the child cries or seems genuinely upset, you must evaluate whether the crying is a function of illness, sadness, fear, or anger. (Insincere crying is discussed later in this chapter.)

Illness. If illness is causing the crying, you must determine its severity. Minor discomfort calls for slower activity and an increase in vigilance. Major discomfort calls for discontinuation of the session altogether and for placing the child in the hands of a responsible caretaker. Yet it should be noted that therapists conducting home-based Theraplay can visit an ill child at the bedside. Many Theraplay activities can be conducted with both therapist and child closely confined and relatively quiet. Cool cloths, peek-a-boo, and "messages" or pictures drawn on the back or on the hand in powder, for example, can all serve to make a child feel ongoing, joyful intimacy with his therapist, an intimacy all the more necessary during times of illness and concomitant isolation and worry.

Sadness. If sadness is causing the crying, you must communicate to the child, both verbally and nonverbally, that you understand that he is feeling very sad. You should hold him and rock him and talk comfortingly to him. You should not attempt to cheer him, distract him, or tell him he "will be feeling better soon." You should add playful games only after he is feeling better.

Fear. Sometimes the child appears genuinely frightened. While in theory it might seem difficult to distinguish genuine fear from fearful behavior designed to discourage intimacy, with experience you can distinguish the two quite easily. The cries and physical stance of a truly frightened child clearly convey a message of fear.

If you decide that it is genuine fear, you must determine whether the child's fear is a function of the situation's novelty, the separation from parent or teacher, or the intrusion of the therapist. If the novelty of the situation (for example, the new adult or the strange room) is causing the child to cry, you can acknowledge this briefly ("You never met me before, so you're frightened") but then move on quickly ("But we've got such fun things to do together, like this trick . . ."). If the child shows only mild apprehension, the therapist may ignore the crying altogether.

If separation from mother or teacher is the problem, you can briefly reassure the crying child (for example, "Mommy's waiting for you right outside," or "You'll go back to see your teacher when we're finished playing. First I want to see what you brought to school today inside your nice striped socks . . . ooh, you brought some yummy toes. Here, let me see").

If the child's crying stems from fear of your intrusions and is not simply a way to maintain distance, then you must go more slowly and gently than is generally indicated. Her fear must be acknowledged: "I see that frightened you. Let's make sure you feel safe." If there is someone with whom the child does feel safe, that person should be invited into the session to provide the calming security that the child needs before she can accept the positive experiences that you want to give her. On the other hand, for example, Adam's tears and cries, "I want my Mommy!" were so strongly tinged with angry resistance that it was clear that fear was not an issue.

The possibility that a fearful child has been traumatized in the past or has never felt secure must be considered. Chapter Nine explains how Theraplay can be combined with other approaches to treatment in working with children who have been abused and traumatized. Chapter Eight discusses the special needs of very young children who, because of frequent surgeries and medical traumas, have become unable to separate from their parents.

Anger. When the child cries out of anger, or shows angry behavior that is not just to keep you at bay, you must stop your playful games and acknowledge the child's feelings, matching the intensity of your words with the intensity of the child's anger: "You're really mad at me!" You can encourage a safe physical expression of the anger. For example, in the film, *Here I Am* (Jernberg, Hurst, and Lyman, 1969), therapist Ernestine Thomas tells Pat, "I can see you're angry," and then, extending the palms of her hands for hitting, directs her, "harder than that, harder than that. Bigger than that!" By acknowledging Pat's anger and providing a harmless outlet for its expression, Mrs. Thomas conveys the message that Pat's feelings are legitimate. The palms of the hands allow the therapist to receive the blows without discomfort or ambivalence. Taking the initiative in directing the expression of the anger, rather than being a passive recipient only, she conveys adult control and responsibility and thus ensures that the angry activity will not go out of bounds.

If the child launches into a full-fledged temper tantrum, you must take steps to keep the child safe and stay with him throughout the episode. We describe how to handle temper tantrums later in this chapter.

EROTICIZED PERCEPTION. Rarely, the child responds to the Theraplay activities by becoming sexually stimulated. Often it is because the child has had experiences (sexual abuse or exposure to adult sexual behavior on television or from actual observation) that have made him sexually responsive to physical contact. Occasionally, children who have been raised in a depriving environment, such as in an extremely neglectful home or in an institution, have learned to use masturbation as a self-comforting behavior. When offered an appropriate comforting touch, such children may shift into their earlier pattern of associating comfort with sexual stimulation.

If a child becomes sexually aroused during a treatment session, you must, in a matter of fact manner, help the child distinguish between appropriate nurturing touch and sexually arousing touch. If the child makes suggestive comments or touches you inappropriately, you can simply say; "I won't let you touch me there. You can touch me here and here and here" (hands, cheeks, shoulders, for example). You should avoid the kind of touch that seems to arouse the child but must continually seek ways to provide the child with the experience of appropriate touch.

REQUEST FOR ENLIGHTENMENT. The child may ask for information, not as a means of controlling the session, but because he has a genuine need for information. Theraplay techniques are held in abeyance until the therapist has met the need. Examples of this need would be if the child is uncertain about something important to his security, "Will my mother pick me up today?" or if he is anxious about something that might happen to him, "When I see the nurse, will she give me a shot?"

SHARING AN UNHAPPY EXPERIENCE. The child may tell an unhappy story, not so that the session shall proceed according to his own rather than the therapist's plans, but because he has a genuine need to express his unhappy feelings. For example, many children living in inner cities experience violence every day. They often hear gunfire, they see bullets fly through their windows, and they occasionally witness the shooting deaths of relatives. Such children often have a desperate need to talk about their experiences. Although Theraplay is not a "talking" therapy, you must put aside your plan in order to listen to their stories and help them deal with their fears. To do otherwise would be to fail to meet their needs. Then you must decide whether to refer the child for further counseling with someone who is trained to help children who have experienced trauma. If you are qualified to do so, you may combine that approach with a modified Theraplay approach, as described in Chapter Nine.

Taking Environmental Influences into Account

The model of healthy parent-infant interaction on which the Theraplay approach is based is strongly influenced by American and Western European cultural values and styles of parenting. Whereas we value eye contact as a sign of honesty and straightforwardness and recognize its importance in promoting the development of attachment, in other cultures it is considered rude for a child to look adults in the eye. In comparison with cultures where babies are never out of physical contact with their mothers, we often downplay the importance of touch. American families tolerate a higher level of activity and excitement than is acceptable in many other countries. If an American child is shy, quiet, and withdrawn, we wonder whether she is happy. In some cultures, however, such behavior is entirely acceptable, even valued. In working with families from a variety of cultural backgrounds it is important to understand their values and to adapt Theraplay to their ways of engaging and connecting with their children.

ETHNIC AND CULTURAL BACKGROUND. The consideration of a family's cultural values is crucial to the planning of treatment. A shy little girl from a cultural background that values quietness may require no treatment at all. A withdrawn adolescent from a cultural background that values expressiveness may be quite another story. A mother whose culture defines her role as child caretaker may easily be involved in Theraplay treatment. With a father from the same culture it may be impossible. Body contact or eye contact may be acceptable to a family from one culture, taboo for a family from another.

It is important that the goals of treatment be discussed with parents and that they feel comfortable with the nature of the planned interactions. If the parents want help for their child, and if they agree that part of the solution could be a change in the way they and the child relate to each other, then it should be possible to find ways of engaging the child that are congruent with their cultural values. Fortunately, every culture has ways of helping their children to feel secure and to relate calmly and appropriately to others. By discussing with parents what is acceptable to them, it is possible to modify Theraplay treatment in ways that accommodate to cultural differences and yet achieve the goal of helping the child.

FAMILY LIFESTYLE. When mapping out a Theraplay strategy for a particular child, not only must the child's relationship problems and any cultural differences be taken into account, but lifestyle differences also must be considered. Nothing emphasizes so clearly the danger of following hard and fast rules as the fact that a set of Theraplay principles quite appropriate for a family that uses one style of parenting may be totally inappropriate for a family that uses another. In families that structure arbitrarily and enforce strictly and punitively, the children's needs and wishes are often of only secondary importance. The parents often deal with their children in a practical, short, authoritarian way. In families where children's needs and wishes are paramount, however, structure, rules, and clear authority may be virtually absent. The parents may be overly concerned with "understanding" and with encouraging open expression of feelings. In the process they risk giving in to their child's every mood, need, and inner wish.

The difference between the two groups can be seen in their response to suggestions made by the interpreting therapist. The no-nonsense, authoritarian parent asks, "What do you mean, 'Let him play'? Life is hard. It wouldn't be right to play with him now that he's a big boy. He might think he can play forever." The permissive parent says, "Who are we, his parents, to think we have the right to make decisions for him or tell him what to do?" The results of the two approaches, of course, are quite different and each has its negative side. The strictures enforced by the authoritarian parent may make the child feel impotent. The freedom offered by the permissive parent may make the child anxious. Thus while the child of restrictive parents needs stimulation, movement, and the freedom to explore and to play, the child of permissive parents often needs limits.

Though Theraplay therapists may work to help permissive parents do less listening, discussing, or reasoning with their children, they may advise authoritarian parents to do more listening and discussing. In both cases, the interpreting therapist guides the parents through demonstration, participation, discussion, and the giving of active family homework assignments. While observing behind the one-way mirror as their child is engaged in a Theraplay session, the interpreting therapist may ask a permissive parent, "You see how Aaron keeps trying to engage his therapist in a discussion of why he can't do this and that? Notice what they do each time he does that?" The parent may answer with some surprise, "Why, yes, she seems to be ignoring him. She just goes on about the game she's playing with him. Why does she do that?" And the interpreting therapist explains, "If she responds to the topics he brings up, the session will go exactly as he decrees it should. Then it will be quite predictable from his point of view, and he will have learned nothing. He does too much running of the show that way already. The therapist wants to show him that it's safe to let someone else be in charge once in awhile. She wants him to know that it can even be fun to be surprised."

Authoritarian parents observing their child in Theraplay, however, may be asked, "Notice how Kevin is being encouraged to ask questions and to tell how he feels about what's happening?" The parents may be puzzled, and ask, "Why do they want to know that?" And the interpreting therapist explains, "They want to help him see that what he says and what he wishes and what he feels are important. They want him to understand that because he is so special, he can make an impact on his world." Homework assignments, for both kinds of parents, include the directive to carry out between sessions the kinds of behavior and attitudes toward their children that they have observed from behind the one-way mirror.

HANDLING DIFFICULTIES ARISING FROM THE CHILD

As with any treatment modality, the actual session may be very different from the theoretical understanding that you have about how it should go. Even with the most careful planning and preparation, difficulties can arise that you must handle.

As we discussed at the beginning of the chapter, most children go through a resistant phase in which they test the new relationship. Such testing can pose problems for even the most experienced Theraplay therapist. It can be daunting when you first start practicing the Theraplay approach and still have little experience taking confident control of difficult situations.

The avoidance of intimacy on the child's part may take any number of forms. Any of the dimensions of Theraplay—your efforts to limit, organize, or structure him, to engage him, to nurture him, or to challenge him—may be resisted. Almost all children seen in Theraplay resist acknowledging to some degree that the therapist is in charge.

The child may use all his wiles to escape your efforts. The greater his underlying need for closeness, the greater his determination to avoid it and the more intense his efforts to "escape" will be. With the rationale, "He's too uncomfortable when I come close," you may feel inclined to "cool" the relationship at first. Instead, if you consider that the intensity of resistance reflects an equally intense underlying need— whether it is for structure and limit setting, engagement, comfort, cuddling and nurturing, or challenge—you will persist in your efforts to meet that need.

Given the importance of compensating for the child's earlier deprivations, it becomes your job to be aware of his frustrated needs and to remain therapeutic in spite of determined resistance. At the same time, as we discuss later, you must be certain that in meeting the child's needs you are not motivated to satisfy some unfulfilled needs of your own.

Resisting Structure

Behaviors of children who deny their need for structure tend to be subtle and beguiling. Before the therapist has had a chance to recognize how it happened, for example, the child may have changed the rules. Since the value of Theraplay for a child who has such a need to take charge lies in the child's being the recipient of someone else's rules and structure, the Theraplay therapist must be constantly vigilant and in control of the child's efforts to defeat him. Such children may attempt to take the initiative, defy the therapist, or "engage" him.

TAKING THE INITIATIVE. Initiating may include telling you what to do or deciding what she herself will do. You must be alert to the problem and stay one step ahead of the child. The child who is full of ideas for fun games to play is particularly hard to resist. You need to be prepared to say, "You have great ideas, but today I want to show you all the fun things I've planned for us to do together." In the event that the child initiates what you were about to do anyway, for example, "Let's balance on the pillows like we did last week," you can say, "This week we'll see how many pillows you can balance on your *head.*"

DEFYING THE THERAPIST. In addition to outright refusal, defying the therapist can include countering your suggestion with one of her own, or pleading pain, incompetence, boredom, or obedience ("My mother won't let me"). In the face of the child's resistant tactics, you must persist. There is no need for discussion, apology, or backing off. "This is what we're going to do today," you say, "so let's get started." If the child remains passively resistant, you can use a paradoxical approach, "My, you are quiet, you are as still as a mouse. Let me see whether your nose makes a noise when I touch it." Then, supplying the beeping noise, you explore the sounds that other parts of his body (ears, chin, knee) can make. If the child is actively resisting, hitting or spitting or pushing away, you can use the child's activity to start a new game. "What strong arms you have. Let's see whether you can push me over. Ready, get set, go!" Few children can resist this invitation.

Although flexibility, spontaneity, and alertness to the child's cues are important ingredients of the Theraplay therapist's behavior, do not use them as crutches to avoid unpleasant confrontations with the child.

"ENGAGING" THE THERAPIST. The word "engaging" has been placed in quotes because it represents resistance rather than genuine engagement. Its motives are not to enjoy your company, but to make you a slave. The attempt to "engage" can include "cute" behavior, flattery, scintillating discussion, insightful observations, humorous anecdotes, fantasy or dream revelations, or the bringing of toys, books, or food from home.

Any experienced child therapist will recognize how difficult it is to resist and divert these maneuvers. Indeed, traditional child therapists may welcome them as expressions of the child's real inner life and use them as the key to further exploration of fantasy, wish, dream, and memory. The Theraplay therapist, however, views these maneuvers as tactics employed by the child to maintain his familiar position of vigilant control over himself and his world. Having recognized the maneuver, you must insist on staying in charge. Rather than pause to listen to the child's "engaging" talk, move right ahead with your planned activity. If she charms you with compliments, you can turn the conversation back to her: "You have the softest cheeks I've ever seen. Let's see how soft your nose is too."

Resisting Engagement

Children who clearly try to resist their therapist's efforts to engage them may do this by crying, feigning illness, becoming limp, arching their backs, or protesting verbally. They may refuse to participate, appeal to others, attack you, or try to run away. After acknowledging how the child is feeling, you must insistently try to extricate him from his private world.

Like the autonomy-enhancing parent, you should put a stop to "unhealthy" behavior and redirect the activity toward self-esteem and fun. You must be consistent but not rigid, intent on intruding but not without fun. You must be willing to back off momentarily to allow the child to "save face," but you must not be conned into changing your overall strategy.

In the following example, a mental health worker in the Head Start Program explains how she handled a child's extreme resistance to becoming engaged:

Juan shrank from the world as if expecting the worst. He ducked his head, he twisted his body, and he moved with awkward, jerky motions. When anyone approached him, he shrieked and ran away. An effort to do a neurological examination failed because he was so terrified. As his therapist, I was determined not to let him stay in his fearful, self-imposed prison where he couldn't learn about the world, couldn't get pleasure from being with others, where even the messages he got from his family were negative: his father said, "He just embarrasses me."

Seeing his pain, I could not leave him like that. I pursued him relentlessly. I knew that I must entice him out of his pain rather than leave him as he was. When he hid behind the block cupboard, I found him. When he crawled under the table, I crawled in after him. When I picked him up, he fought frantically to escape and would have thrown himself to the ground had I not held on. He had no sense of the danger, nor could he make use of my encircling arms to keep himself safe.

Gradually my persistence paid off and he began to acknowledge my presence. I put a beanbag on his head, and when he ducked his head to make it fall off, I caught it. I put one on my head and dropped it into his lap, or I held his hands so that the beanbag would fall into them. He began to be interested in this game and would wait for my signal to duck his head to let the beanbag fall into my hands. If he tried to push me away, I pushed back until we had a pushing game going. He was interested when I drew around his hands and matched his hands to the outline we had made. Almost in spite of himself, he began to have fun. He looked at me and laughed when I put a silly hat on my head. He allowed me to put one on him. We looked at ourselves in the mirror and I pointed out how tall he was, how strong he was, and how high he could jump.

After ten weeks of twice weekly sessions it was time to say goodbye. Just at that point, his classroom had a party. As his father and I watched, Juan volunteered to be the first to stand up and break the piñata. He stood proud and erect, his blindfold tipped cockily across his brow. He hit with all his might, breaking the piñata with one blow. What a difference our ten weeks together had made! His father watched him with obvious pride. I watched him with tears of joy in my eyes. I knew that the frightened, cringing little boy was gone forever. In his place was a sturdy, self-confident child who could look forward joyfully to whatever life presented to him.

Resisting Nurture

Behaviors of children denying their need for nurture are clearly recognizable as escape maneuvers. Particularly characteristic of these children is the intensity of their drive. Unhindered, they hit hard, curse loudly, withdraw angrily, run away fast, or ceaselessly reason, argue, and debate. Always in a spirit of fun, you must be as loud, as hard, as fast as they are.

Because "saving face" is so especially important to these children, nurturing activities should be offered both imaginatively and playfully. A child who would not accept having lotion rubbed on her hands, will accept it in order to make a lotion hand print. A child, who usually insists that he be allowed to feed himself, will enjoy a "doughnut challenge" (place the doughnut on your finger and challenge the child, "See how many bites you can take without breaking the circle!"). If a baby bottle is indicated for an older resistant child, you might use it first for squirting the liquid from a distance in the manner of a competitive sport. Even an adolescent, with his surface denial of any need for nurture, will accept having finger paint rubbed on his feet in order to make a path of painted footprints on a large piece of paper. The paper can then be hung up to look as though he had actually walked up the wall. And, of course, it is essential afterward to wash his feet: another opportunity for gentle, nurturing touch.

Resisting Challenge

The child who clings to infantile behavior often responds to your challenges with further regression. Asked to stand, she sits; invited to ask for something, she points. In the following example, the therapist does not allow Tammy to stay in her regressed state. Although she is careful not to make her challenges too demanding, she continues to expect Tammy to rise to the occasion—and Tammy does. Her therapist describes this work with an infantile, clinging child as follows:

> I went to put Tammy down, and she would not straighten her legs. I said, "Hey, let me see those strong legs of yours." She then straightened her legs, and we walked out of the room. I told her what a big girl she was

and tried to guess how old she was. I started at seven and worked down. We did some bouncing, jumping, and flips. I took the flip in stages, first putting her up on my waist, then letting her touch the floor backward. Next I put her on my shoulders and gave her a flip. Yet through her helplessness and nonparticipation she still tried to "control" what we did. When it was time to go, she began to act like a baby. I told her again that it was time to go and that I would be back. She still wouldn't come out of the baby behavior. So I had her act like a soldier. I said, "Let me see how tall you can stand. Look how tall you are. Look at this big girl. Come on, let's go." I had her jump down the steps. And we walked like soldiers back to her classroom.

Some children resist challenges because they are afraid they will fail. For such a child you should present challenges that will produce immediate success. "Newspaper punch" is a good choice. Use a single sheet of newspaper (you can assure success by tearing it slightly at the top). Then, holding it stretched tightly out in front of you, say, "Let's see whether you can punch this paper right through. Make a fist. When I say *punch,* punch your fist right into it. Ready, get set, punch!" If the child is hesitant, help her move her arm back and forth in the gesture she needs to use. If she still hesitates, you can move the paper toward her fist. Most children can easily punch through tightly stretched paper and are very pleased with their success. If the first punch is successful, you can add a second sheet of paper. "This is harder. But you did so well with one sheet that I think you can do two. Ready, get set, go!"

Having Tantrums

When you remain firm in the face of a child's resistance, he is very likely at some point to become angry and even to have a temper tantrum. If this happens, you should stay with the child through the tantrum, holding him firmly so that he cannot hurt himself or you. You may have to hold his hitting fist, constrain his kicking foot, and redirect spitting by changing his position. The most comforting position for an upset child is to cradle him in your lap, holding him so that each of you can see the other's face. If you tuck one of his arms behind your back, you can hold the other with one hand and thus have a free hand to wipe his tears and cool his forehead with a damp cloth. If he is moving his legs about, you can put one of your legs over his. It is important that you find a position that provides security for both of you and that is as comforting as possible. If cradling does not work, either because the child is big or because he is too hard to hold in this position, you may have to place him face up on the floor, straddle him (so that you do not put your weight on him), and hold his hands in order to keep both yourself and the child safe. In either position, you can see the child's face and respond to how he is feeling. The child can also see you and learn that you are not angry with him or out of control yourself. Whatever way you hold him, it is essential that you feel confident in your ability to contain him physically in a safe and secure position.[2]

You need to reassure the child that you will stay with him until he feels better (thereby letting him know that he is safe and that this behavior does not make him "bad" in your eyes). Throughout you can tell him, with confident reassurance, "I know you are upset and angry. I'm going to stay right with you till you feel better. I will keep you safe and I won't let you hurt me. I'll hold you until you're feeling better." You can continue to talk reassuringly, "I know you don't want me to hold you. I know you are angry. It's OK to be angry. When you are ready we can play some more."

You should constantly monitor the tension in the child's body and as soon as he seems to relax a bit, you can gradually release your hold on his hands, saying, "Yes, I think you are ready." If he uses his hands to hit again, you can say, "Oh, I see you weren't ready yet." Some children will bargain, "I'll stop if you let me go." This bargaining is based on the child's assumption that what you are doing is a punishment for his bad behavior. You should avoid this implication by saying, "I'll be able to tell when you are feeling better. When your body relaxes I'll know."

Or you can gently blow on his forehead to cool him. If you have a partner or if the child's parents are available, they can bring a damp cloth or a glass of water. As soon as the child is ready, gradually move him into a more comfortable position, perhaps onto your lap to rock and comfort him. Many children after such an experience do cry and seek comfort.

Holding a child when he is angry has many benefits.[3] He learns that you can keep him safe when he is out of control. He learns that you can accept his anger and not condemn it, and that his anger does not drive you away. He learns that you can survive his anger and still be there to hold and comfort him. Ultimately, he will be able to relax and accept your comfort. When this happens you have created a strong bond with the child. The message is that it is all right to feel what you need to feel and that a safe and caring adult can help you deal with it.

Having described the benefits of staying with a child throughout an angry outburst, we must give a word of caution. It is important to distinguish between the anger of a child determined to resist your efforts to engage him and the panic of an abused child. If the child seems frightened, or if you know that he has been abused, do not restrain him. Instead, you must redouble your efforts to engage him in other ways.

Crying

Before you can respond appropriately to a child's crying, you need to determine the reason for it. Crying during Theraplay may be a genuine, direct response to internally or externally generated pain, as we have discussed earlier, or it may be part of the child's conscious (or unconscious) attempt to keep the therapist away by evoking his pity, shame, guilt, or anxiety. If crying is a form of resistance, the course of action will be as indicated in the above examples of handling resistance; the therapist continues to search for ways to make the child feel comfortable while continuing to try to engage him in a relationship.

HANDLING DIFFICULTIES ARISING FROM THE THERAPIST

In the previous section, we described how you can respond to difficulties caused by the child. We now look at difficulties arising from within you. The most frequent source of difficulty stems from feeling uncertain about how to proceed because of inexperience with this new approach to treatment. A second source of difficulty lies in the possibility of countertransference acting-out. Although we have attempted to be as specific and detailed as possible in describing how to practice Theraplay, a book can never take the place of direct training and hands-on supervised experience. As we noted previously, training is available at the Theraplay Institute in Chicago and from Certified Theraplay Trainers in a few other places in the United States and Canada. Here we describe a few of the most common problems and give suggestions for how to handle them.

Feelings of Inadequacy

Probably the greatest threat to the treatment process lies in the therapist's sense of uncertainty and doubt—her fear that she might run out of ideas or that others might criticize her.

FEAR OF RUNNING OUT OF IDEAS. The very best antidote to running out of ideas is periodic, playful interaction with (or observation of a parent with) a healthy toddler, followed by the same with a healthy preschool child. Not only will this feel refreshing, but it will also generate new approaches and new variations on old themes. Another antidote, of course, is observation of a fellow Theraplay therapist. A further resource is our list of Theraplay Activities in Appendix C.

When all else fails, you can turn to the child's own responses as a ready-made pool of innovative ideas. A leg that pulls away, a face that looks away, or an inadvertent or objecting sound all may provide the foundation on which you can build a new activity. An averted face can lead you to exclaim, "Oh, you turn your head so well! Here, let me see how you did that!" or "Pull it away! Pull your arm away! That's it. You're tricky, you know that? The way you pull that arm away?"

HANDLING CRITICISM FROM OTHERS. If you work in a setting where crying and regressive behavior or boisterous, intimate, physical, and joyful interactions between child and adult are looked on with suspicion, you must expect criticism of your work. If you plan to introduce Theraplay into such a setting, you must prepare well in advance by explaining how Theraplay works and by showing videotapes of Theraplay treatment. Although such advanced preparation is very useful, it will not prevent all later questions and interruptions of your work by people hearing the laughter or the crying coming from your treatment room. If you are questioned while you are in the midst of comforting a crying child or holding an angry one, you can tell the worried bystander, "Josie is going to be all right." Your confidence communicates, "I know what I'm doing." You should add, "I'd like to talk to you about it later on if you have a moment." Given a response like this one, few adults will continue their interruption of the session.

Remember that you are not alone in having these concerns. The more experienced you become, the less these worries will haunt you.

Dealing with Countertransference Acting-Out

In any therapy with children, perhaps even more than in therapy with adults, there is the strong and omnipresent temptation to reenact one's own childhood. In Theraplay especially, the physical contact, the intimate interaction, and the regressive focus all invite many forms of countertransference acting-out. There is, for example, the invitation to do to the child what was done to you as a child, or to do to the child what you feared or wished would be done. The rapidity with which activities are carried out and the amount of physical, mental, and emotional involvement leave little opportunity for on-the-spot self-exploration. Thus, for example, cuddling and bottle feeding a child may stimulate your own oral longings, wrestling or spinning may stimulate your sadism, but there is no time to inquire of yourself about the sources of your anxiety. Yet as a Theraplay therapist, perhaps more than any other therapist, you must make it part of the ongoing therapeutic enterprise to investigate yourself.

As in any therapy, you must be vigilant against the temptation to satisfy your own needs first; that is, to act out in the countertransference. This is not to say that countertransference phenomena do not occur. Racker's (1968, p. 132) requirements for psychoanalysts must apply equally to Theraplay therapists: The therapist must not be so objective that he experiences neither anger nor anxiety, nor must he be so vulnerable that he "drowns" in these experiences. In any case, the therapist should "normally experience these situations with only a part of his being, leaving another part free to take note of them in a way suitable for the treatment" (p. 141).

Becoming aware of the problem and understanding potential dangers are the first steps in avoiding countertransference acting-out.

BECOMING AWARE OF THE PROBLEM. Although this is difficult to learn, during Theraplay you must have a ready set of self-directed questions inside your head, an awareness of the likelihood that counter-therapeutic tendencies are being activated, and a quick resolve to take the matter up in more detail with yourself later on. The questions you must ask yourself include, "In whose interest am I doing this particular activity? Why am I reacting this particular way? Am I or am I not 'using' the child?"

Understanding Whose Interests Are Directing the Activity. The answer to the first question must be "I'm doing it because this child requires it for her improved mental health." If this is not the certain answer, then the implied one very likely is, "I am doing it because of my own neurotic needs," and so the activity should be promptly discontinued. If, for example, the reason for organizing a pillow fight is clearly that the child needs to experience competition in a nonthreatening situation, it is appropriate to continue. If the therapist's own competitive striving is the determining factor in the choice of a pillow fight, there is no justification for continuing the activity.

Looking at Particular Reactions. The important questions to ask are, "What about the child, the activity, or the interaction between us is making me have this reaction? If what I am doing is objectively appropriate for the child's needs, why am I *feeling* guilty, angry, anxious, or abandoned? If the activity I have chosen to do is appropriate, why am I *behaving* in an overprotective, competitive, neglectful or clinging way?"

The answers to these questions will be as varied as there is variety in human personality. For some, the answer may lie in the therapist's identifying the child with some important figure in the therapist's own childhood (for example, a younger sibling), or perhaps with the therapist herself. For others, the answer may lie in the unconscious recollection of an early life experience touched off by the activity as such. Even peek-a-boo may re-arouse an infantile memory of a game with (or the disappearance of) the therapist's mother.

Recognizing Whose Needs Are Being Served. Some questions to ask are, "Am I using the child to reenact, act out, or attempt to resolve my own conflicts? Am I using his or her improved health or success and mastery for my own needs? Is my exhibitionism being fed by hope for public recognition of this child's accomplishments? Is my prolonging the treatment and forestalling termination a function of my chronic anxiety over separation?" These examples are only a few of the many possible ways you might inappropriately "use" the child to satisfy your own needs.

RECOGNIZING POTENTIAL DANGERS. Although other areas may also require alertness, the Theraplay therapist must be particularly aware of anger, dependency, sexuality, and competition.

Anger. Anger may be a natural reaction to someone hurting you physically or challenging your self-esteem (for example, remarking about your areas of vulnerability or causing another to criticize you). It also can be a natural reaction to being rejected. Your raw response to indignity, insult, physical pain, or abandonment will probably include anger. Indeed, your talent for doing good therapy must be in question if you deny having any but benign feelings toward the patient who has just bitten your forearm or spat in your face. Of almost as much concern are therapists whose initial flare-up of reactive anger leaves them so shaken that they cannot deal with it, understand it, or move beyond it. The best therapists experience their anger, understand its origins, then use it to help the patient reintegrate. You should especially examine anger that is not a universal reaction to a particular stimulus (for example, if you become angry in response to a child sucking on a bottle).

Dependency. Dependent longings may be a natural reaction to illness, separation, another's orality, or another's nurturing—so it should be no surprise to find that a therapist's passive, regressive, or dependent longings have been stimulated by a patient's termination of treatment, curling up for cuddling, or offering to guide or feed the therapist. Again, denial is often suspect. More suspect still are dependent longings stirred for no apparent reason.

Sexuality. Sexual arousal may be a natural reaction to prolonged intimacy, seductive behavior, erogenous body contact, or verbalized sexual provocations or preoccupations. Again, both the denial of obvious sexual impulses and their presence in response to apparently non-stimulating behavior are suspect. It behooves therapists to acknowledge the presence of their eroticized responses, then quickly neutralize them and move on, changing the activity if need be.

Competition. Competitive strivings may be a natural reaction to another person's ambition, success, or put-downs, or to another person's not winning. Competitive reactions when there have been no stimuli to arouse them are as needful of self-examination as is repeated failure to rise to the challenge.

Other Issues. Among other nontherapeutic or counter-therapeutic therapist responses—such as projection, exhibitionism, merging, overidentification, sadism, and masochism—two kinds of guilt are of particular interest. First there is guilt over intruding into another's life space or "playing God," which makes it extremely difficult for some therapists to do effective Theraplay. Underlying their difficulty may well be the fear of arousing their own infantile feelings of omnipotence or of the anger that assertiveness may imply to them. Second, there is guilt over "enjoying." Because Theraplay can be such fun instead of dreary hard work, some therapists find themselves very uneasy. They may refuse pay, or they may turn the sessions into onerous burdens.

OVERCOMING COUNTERTRANSFERENCE ACTING-OUT. The following can be helpful in avoiding countertransference acting-out: preplanning sessions, supervisor or peer observation, supervisory discussions, role-playing, and personal psychotherapy.

Planning Sessions Carefully. If you are not yet "onto yourself" or have had minimal Theraplay experience, preplanning is crucial. Preplanning should include not only a list of Theraplay activities for the session ahead but, equally important, also an anticipation of what you will do if your plan goes awry (What if he bursts the balloon before he throws it? What if she spits the orange seeds at me rather than at the target? What if he refuses the bottle?). No amount of preplanning, of course, will account for all eventualities.

Having a Supervisor or Peer Observe. Supervisor or peer observation allows for the objective collecting of evidence of countertransference acting-out. Just as parent observation, this kind of observation ideally is conducted through a one-way window or by means of videotape, but, if necessary, observers can view the session from within the therapy room itself.

Arranging Supervisory Discussions. Discussions with a regular supervisor will allow you to become aware of your tendency to act out in countertransference. A perceptive, nonthreatening senior therapist can help you trace the origins of a particular episode and help you find new solutions.

Using Supervised Role-Playing. Supervised role-playing of particularly troublesome patient-therapist interactions allows for coworker scrutiny of the countertransference. At the moment of inappropriate action, the demonstration is halted while the therapist and his or her coworkers explore the reasons for "doing what he or she did." Reconstruction and attempts at a better solution follow—still within the role-playing framework.

Undergoing Personal Psychotherapy. Although it is not a requirement for Theraplay certification, personal psychotherapy is highly recommended for all who use the Theraplay approach. Your work both with the children and with their parents will be enhanced through your increased awareness and understanding.

TREATMENT GUIDELINES

The following instructions for the Theraplay therapist are, it should be noted, guidelines only.

1. *Be confident and comfortable with taking charge.* Like a good parent you must project a positive self-image and convey the ability to guide and protect. You must not be anxious, uncertain, or meek.

2. *Be appealing and delightful.* You should offer such jolly temptation and such *joie de vivre* that any normal child will find himself inexorably drawn to join with you in your games. You should not be aloof, worried, or even subtly rejecting. Never give messages that say, "Stay away from me" or "What I'm doing you wouldn't want to do."

3. *Be responsive and empathic.* You must be attuned to the child's underlying needs and responsive to them. Avoid being only partially involved with the child or responding in terms of your own unmet needs.

4. *Take charge of the session at all times.* Like the healthy parent who feels no need to make apologies to her one-year-old for organizing the day's activities, you should comfortably take charge of sessions. You need to be aware at all times of the safety and well-being of the child, making statements and carrying out actions with full awareness of the consequences. You must remain fully in control from the moment the child appears in the therapy room until his departure at the end of each session.

You do not need to ask permission, wait for approval or apologize for taking action. Queries such as "Would you like to jump today?" or "OK?" or "May I take off your socks?" communicate to the child that the control of the session is a joint endeavor and thus invite a "No."

As for apologies, if a child has been accidentally hurt as a result of a Theraplay maneuver, of course you apologize, as any respectful human being would apologize for such an occurrence. This is different, however, from an apology to which the child can respond implicitly or explicitly with, "Stop, I don't wish to participate in that." Asking "Do you like this?" is a borderline case. To the extent that it resembles the chattering of a mother (who already reads the answer in her child's delighted response), such a question may be appropriate. To the extent that it invites a vote from the child, however, it is not. The questions, "How do you feel today? Can you tell me what made you do that? What are your thoughts about our terminating?" all may be unanswerable, particularly within the generally noncognitive, noninterpretive, and preverbal focus of Theraplay.

5. *Use every opportunity to make physical contact with the child.* Just as healthy parenting activities involve many kinds of physical contact between child and parent, so should you structure each session to afford multiple opportunities for body contact. It matters little whether these use large or small muscles or whether they result from holding, pushing, pulling, stroking, blowing, or bathing. Do not sit back and discuss, interview, dispute, reflect, or interpret.

Although tickling is often part of a parent's playful repertoire, Theraplay therapists, aware of its potential for sadistic excess, do not tickle children. If a touch inadvertently produces a tickle, you should say, "Did that tickle? Let me see whether I can touch you without tickling."

6. *Use every opportunity to make eye contact with the child.* You should pursue the child's eyes with your own in an enjoyable, playful, and engaging manner. Even if you have to stand on your head, initiate unplanned peek-a-boo's, recruit a second therapist, or focus heavily on games that involve the area around the eyes, let nothing deter you from giving eye contact the highest priority.[4] Children often signal their need for a reduction of stimulation by turning away momentarily. You must respect the child's need to reduce stimulation in this way but be ready to reconnect as soon as possible. Eye contact is important both because it makes the child aware of your presence and because it gives him an opportunity to read your emotional signals in an intense way. We often say to parents, "If he doesn't look at you, he will not know how much you enjoy being with him."

You should not forgo, or permit yourself to be subtly "talked out of," any opportunity for eye contact, no matter how frivolous it may seem. On the other hand, you should not allow eye contact to become a task-oriented, serious matter between you and the child.

7. *Focus intensively and exclusively on the child.* There should be only one focus during your short session together: the child and her potential for health. You must direct all your physical energy and your emotional investment with such intensity that this one half-hour is crammed full of therapeutic experiences. This intensity of focus replicates the focus of a parent with an infant. It forges a connection between the two in a way that less casual interactions could never do.

Do not allow your focus to be fleeting or diluted by other thoughts or messages. If you find yourself daydreaming or even formulating hypotheses, you are not fulfilling the high-intensity part of your commitment.

8. *Anticipate the child's resistant maneuvers and act before, not after, they are set into motion.* In trying to avoid intimacy, the child has a hundred tricks at his disposal. Knowing this, make every effort to initiate action before the resistant action is set into motion. Such a child is very familiar with the experience of having adults chase after him saying, "No, don't do that!" If you are to change this negative pattern, you must be one step ahead of him with an engaging positive experience. If you find yourself frequently saying "No" or constantly redirecting activity the child has already embarked on, you have delayed too long and initiated too little.

9. *Be responsive to cues given by the child.* Be alert to signals that indicate interest in meaningful kinds of activities. Distinguish between situations in which the child is trying to take over and direct activities and those in which your picking up on the cue will be yet another instance of your sensitivity to the child's needs and interests. Select the signals to which you attend; it is you, not the child, who determines the activities that will make use of this awareness. You should not, of course, be wholly guided by the child's cues. Whereas the child's suggestion, "Let's play cowboys today," should not determine the makeup of the session, his coming in with boots or a cowboy shirt might prompt you to give him a piggyback ride.

10. *Use every opportunity to help the child see himself as unique, special, and outstanding.* You should help the child become more aware of her body by identifying and labeling her unique and special characteristics: "You have two long legs," or "What a nice curl you have." To emphasize her uniqueness you can contrast her features with yours: "You have wonderful short curly hair and I have long straight hair," or "Your fingers come right up to my last knuckle!" At no time should such comparisons be "put-downs" (for example, "My hands are big and

strong . . . and yours, why yours are small"). The goal is to help the child develop a strong sense of her own individuality and awareness of others as separate and independent persons. Avoid activities that blur the distinctions or boundaries between the two of you, such as long periods of dreamy rocking in which the child may lose awareness of your presence.

11. *Identify and label the child's moods and feelings.* Just as you help the child become more aware of his body, so you should help the child become more aware of his own moods and feelings. The first step in this, so characteristic of the healthy parent-infant relationship, is an empathically attuned matching of the child's moods and feelings. You should match the child's joyful responses as well as her sad or angry responses.

A final step in increasing the child's awareness of his feelings is to connect the feeling to what immediately precipitated it. Thus you might comment, "You're crying because you're unhappy," or "You want to hit me because you're mad about what I just did." You should not go beyond that to infer unconscious processes or label "deeper" causes. For example, you should not tell a child, "You're hurting me because you're mad at Mommy." Just as such interpretations would be inappropriate in the parent-child relationship, so they are inappropriate in the here-and-now of the Theraplay relationship. There is a place for such sensitively intuited interpretations in traditional insight therapy, but not in Theraplay.

12. *Focus on the child as she is.* Focus on the child just as she is: how she looks, how strong her muscles are, how beautiful her hair is, how well she can jump or bounce or skip. Just as parents' love for their infant does not depend on the baby's performance or compliance, your regard for the child should be unconditional. Your response to the child should not depend on tasks performed, expectations met, or "good" behavior.

13. *Focus on the present and future but not the past.* To consolidate the relationship between you and the child, convey the message that the present matters ("We're together now," or "My, you look pretty today"), that the future is good and imminent ("Tomorrow you're going to be tall up to here," or "Soon you'll be *so* strong"), and that what is really important to both of you is here in this very space you are sharing ("I knew I'd find you right here with me"). Neither concern yourself with, nor ask about, the past or the vagaries of the child's fantasy life. Do not ask about what went on before you met ("When

was your little sister born?" or "How old were you when your grandma died?") or attend to space outside the immediate Theraplay situation ("Does your house have a yard?" or "Does your uncle live with you?"). If a child turns her attention elsewhere (such as to the schoolyard or her home, your response should refocus her attention back to herself, you, and the Theraplay scene: "Your Mommy's at home? I'll bet she is at home. And I'll bet she's thinking about her little girl with these gorgeous dimples, and these curly eyelashes, and these ten cute toes." As we mentioned earlier, however, if the child tells you about a sad or troubling experience, you should listen and not refocus her away from her experience. Do not play "Let's-pretend-you-and-I-are-somebody-else" games. Such games serve only to provide an escape for both therapist and child from what is going on between them in the here-and-now.

14. *Keep sessions spontaneous, flexible, and full of happy surprises.* From the child's perspective, the therapy session itself should be unpredictable, fun, and surprising. Although they are carefully tailored to the child's needs of the moment, the activities within a session flow naturally and spontaneously from one to another. The joyful spontaneity of the activities engages the child and helps him give up his unhealthy need to control things. The session should be neither diffuse nor confusing, nor should it be so rigidly planned as to be mechanical. No one activity should be so repetitiously carried out as to become predictable.

15. *Make yourself the primary playroom object.* You—your actions, movements, words, and noises—must be the major and indispensable "prop" of Theraplay. Move and act vigorously, quickly, alertly, and often humorously. Come across with such clarity and impact that the night after a session—and for the next several days—the child has no difficulty recalling your face or what you did together.[5] Extensive props have no place in Theraplay. Books, dolls, puzzles, and checkerboards distract from the interaction between child and therapist and do not belong in the Theraplay room.

16. *Keep the session cheerful, optimistic, positive, and health oriented.* Barring traumatic happenings or hurts, the healthy parent for the most part remains cheerful, optimistic, and health oriented. You, likewise, should communicate to the child that the world is an appealing, happy, fun-filled place and that the child, being basically strong, has the potential to enjoy it. You should not focus on the gloomy, the discouraging, the sick, or the frustrating. Do not imply that the sadness and obstacles in the world are just too much for anyone to overcome.

17. *Structure the session so that times, places, and persons are clearly defined.* Define the boundaries within which the session will take place and convey clear rules and expectations. Schedule sessions at a certain time each day or week. Each session should last a certain number of minutes. The Theraplay space should be clearly limited to the Theraplay room or to the Theraplay mat in the center of the room. You must be the dependable person who predictably shows up for the child at every session. Do not allow sessions to take place whenever you or the child feels like it. Unless you make a specific plan for them to do so, sessions should not take place at a casual encounter in the grocery store, or spill out into the corridor. Although Theraplay can be very useful in activities with teachers or classmates or a grandmother, these should not be ad hoc casual substitutes for a formally promised Theraplay session.

18. *Make sure that within each session there are many different segments, each one having a beginning, a middle, and an end.* Whenever possible, each segment of each Theraplay session should be a little "playlet" in itself. Each of the many segments within a session should evolve from a beginning to a middle to a conclusion. Thus, for example: (1) You blow on child's ear, and the child squeaks; (2) you say, "Make that squeak again and let's see whether you can blow me over this time," and she does; (3) you fall over. You should not allow the session to be either one diffuse, undifferentiated plateau (for example, long drawn-out rocking) or a collection of sporadic, choppy, undeveloped segments (for example, bursts of irrelevant wrestling).

19. *Make sure that each Theraplay session contains some minimal frustration, challenge, and discomfort.*[6] It is essential for any child's healthy development that she be presented with challenges that encourage her to grow and move forward rather than stay at her present level. In therapy, your job is to challenge the child's no longer functional ways of coping. You must urge her to accept a different view of herself and the world and to perform in a manner healthier than is currently typical for her. The optimism implied by your expectation that the child can reach, stretch, and grow is ego enhancing. To the degree that apparent "comfort" means continuing in pathological ways, you should *not* be concerned with making the child "comfortable." Vacant rocking, avoiding eye contact, or repetitive actions, for example, may seem to make an autistic child comfortable, but because such withdrawal prevents the child from growing, you should not allow it to continue. Rather than protect the child's equilibrium, coax him to try alternatives—even though he may at first resist.

20. *Use paradoxical methods when it is appropriate to do so.* At appropriate moments, you can prescribe the behavior the child is using to resist you in a laughing but mock-serious way. For example, faced with a child who is sitting very still in order to avoid engaging in any activities, you might say, "Don't move. Don't move a muscle!" Or when efforts to calm a wiggling child are to no avail, you might say, "See whether you can wiggle all over. That's right! Wiggle your tongue too." The child then has two choices. He can resist the paradoxical injunction and stop wiggling (which is what you wanted in the first place) or he can wiggle even more and thus comply with your request. This technique is particularly helpful in working with highly resistant children who use "face saving" in an oppositional manner.

Do not overdo paradoxical methods. Used too frequently, this approach loses both its effectiveness and its potential for humor. Also, don't omit the communication that this is nothing more serious than just another playful "wrestling match."

21. *Conduct your sessions without regard to whether the child likes you.* Convey to the child that there is something about him that is likable, regardless of whether or not he views you in the same way. Do not attempt to "seduce" the child by lowering demands, obliterating conflicts, or withdrawing challenge in order to gain his admiration, fondness, or love.

22. *Make your presence felt throughout the duration of a child's temper tantrum.* Help the child gain mastery over a temper outburst by staying in physical contact and by verbalizing your confidence in the child's ability to regain control. Do not lecture the child, encourage him to verbalize his feelings, or banish him to a "time-out" room. The implicit message of "timing a child out" is "It's up to you to control yourself. I don't want to be with you when you are like that."

23. *Prevent excessive anxiety or motoric hyperactivity.* You must maintain a careful watch and firm control so that the child will not experience excessive anxiety or find himself too "wound up." As we have discussed earlier, some children are so easily overstimulated that you must reduce stimulation and excitement to a minimum. You must also intervene before the child's excitement escalates beyond control by changing the activity from stimulating to calming. Provide many opportunities for the child to experience cycles of excitement and calming, so that he can begin the process of learning to calm himself. Your goal should be to attain the optimal level of arousal that will allow the child to engage with you.

Avoid getting caught up in the child's excitement or escalating with the child's anxiety. Neither prod nor "wind up" the child nor pass along your own anxiety. Rather, attempt to convey extra reassurance and calm leadership.

24. *Attend to physical hurts.* However minor the bumps or cuts, nurse them tenderly. Attention to hurts conveys a caring message that teaches the child to value himself and in the long run leads to appropriate self-care and circumspection. Do not focus on the unconscious impulses underlying the hurt. Nor should you withhold attention out of a fear that it will reward self-destructive behavior or that regressive caretaking of this kind might preclude later autonomy.

25. *When at a loss for ideas, incorporate the child's body movements into your repertoire.* Just as parents do with their young infants, you can use the child's slightest movement as a foundation on which to build a Theraplay maneuver. Even mute, immobile, stone-faced children provide programs for Theraplay when they blush, look down, keep their faces expressionless, or plant their feet to the floor. We have given several examples of this strategy in action. All of this should be done lightly, warmly, and with interest: "What have you got there inside your fists? Let me look! Oh, you've got a palm there! Wow! Let me see whether you've got one in your other hand too." In the presence of the child, you should never be at a loss for ideas, never remain preoccupied and silent, and never search to fill your repertoire.

Notes

1. Klaus and others (1970, p. 191) describe typical postdelivery behavior of mothers toward their newborns as follows: There is "an orderly and predictable" progression in inspection and contact "starting with fingertip touch on the infant's extremities . . . to massaging, encompassing, and palm contact on the trunk."

2. If you work with large children or adolescents, do not attempt to hold them by yourself. You should also get training in procedures for providing safe containment.

3. Rosen (1953, pp. 16–17) writes: "The patient's aggression must be brought under control . . . . We explain it this way: The idealized mother must protect her child, and sometimes this protection involves controlling his uncontrollable behavior. . . . If you protect him from his aggression, he will neither be punished . . . nor will he be called upon to suffer the unbearable

guilt feelings that accompany rage and destruction directed against a love object. The patient learns that his aggression is nowhere near the world-shaking catastrophe that he envisioned. Furthermore, he takes another look at you with a new kind of interest, seeing you as a person who can protect him in the real world."

4. Campbell (1978, p. 40) cites a study conducted on a pediatric ward in which the variable that differentiated children who had many visitors from those who had few was the amount of eye contact the child offered. "The least popular children would initially look at the visitor briefly, then immediately look down or away." The children's avoidance of eye contact obviously made visitors feel too rejected (and thus too hurt or annoyed) to want to relate to them. Writing of the subjective experience of interacting with blind children, Fraiberg (1977b, p. 96) says, "The blind eyes that do not engage our eyes, that do not regard our faces, have an effect upon the observer that is never completely overcome. When the eyes do not meet ours in acknowledgment of our presence it feels curiously like a rebuff."

5. In this connection, Pederson, Faucher, and Eaton (1978) have produced a relevant study in the field of education. When Teacher A's pupils were followed into adulthood, they were found to be markedly higher in status than were pupils of Teachers B, C, and so on: "She invariably stayed after hours to help children. Not only did her pupils remember her, but she apparently could remember each former pupil by name even after an interval of twenty years. She adjusted to new math and reading methods, but her secret for success was summarized by a former colleague this way: 'How did she teach? With a lot of love!' One would add, with a lot of confidence in children and hard work" (p. 20).

6. Robertiello (1975, p. 3), writing of young adult failure cases, says the following: "What happened? How did their upbringing fail them? It seems that it failed them in that they were presented with a situation optimal for furthering their emotional growth, but one that was essentially devoid of hardships, deprivations, and challenges that they would have had to fight to overcome. Because of this, they never developed the particular kind of strength necessary for meeting such challenges. That strength is what is essential to the achievement of success in any area."

CHAPTER FIVE

Working with Parents or Other Caregivers

⟨⟨⟨⟩⟩⟩

Ⅰn preceding chapters we emphasize the role that parents or caregivers play in Theraplay treatment. In this chapter we describe in detail how to work with parents to help them first understand and then practice what their child needs to become a healthy individual. Although the initial goal of working with parents in Theraplay is to train them to become Theraplay therapists for their own children, the long-term goal is for the relationship to settle into self-perpetuating, healthy patterns so that there is no longer any need for treatment.

Working with parents is a multifaceted operation orchestrated by the interpreting therapist. In this chapter, we look first at the interpreting therapist's role and then at how we train parents or caregivers to become Theraplay therapists. Training parents includes giving them

An earlier version of this chapter appeared in "Training Parents of Failure-to-Attach Children" by Booth and Koller, *Handbook of Parent Training: Training Parents as Co-Therapists for Children's Behavior Problems* (Briesmeister and Schaefer, eds.), New York: Wiley, 1998. Reprinted with permission of the publisher.

a more positive, empathic view of their child, helping them move through a sequence of steps leading to competence in using the Theraplay approach, teaching them about their child's needs, and, finally, meeting their own unmet needs so that their needs do not interfere with the successful implementation of what they have learned.

UNDERSTANDING THE INTERPRETING THERAPIST'S ROLE

As we have already seen in Chapters One and Three, the role of the interpreting therapist is quite complex. While sitting with parents observing the sessions, she must carry out discussions of Theraplay principles, family dynamics, intrapsychic conflicts, infant temperament, and historical determinants. In addition, she must encourage, redirect, educate, help in selecting appropriate schools or summer camps, provide suggestions for handling in-laws, make referrals to physicians or nutritionists, and more. In other words, in addition to psychological sensitivity, thorough child-development training, personal wisdom and maturity, and sound judgment, the interpreting therapist must also have a good deal of familiarity with the current world of child rearing (for example, carpools, day care, park district programs, and babysitting). The description of this role can easily begin to sound like that of the master of a three-ring circus.

During the child's first four Theraplay sessions, as you may recall from earlier examples, the interpreting therapist sits with the parents behind a two-way mirror (or if that is not available, off to one side of the room). She interprets what the child's therapist is doing and gives possible explanations for the child's responses. She explains the importance of certain activities or interactions the parents observe and advises the parents about how they can translate what they see to what they do with their child at home. She continues to provide support and guidance as they join in the activities for the final six sessions, when she and the parents join the child and his therapist in the Theraplay room.

Once the parents have come into the Theraplay room, the child's therapist usually continues to lead the activities. The interpreting therapist helps coordinate the parents' involvement, is alert to any difficulties they might have, and, because she knows the parents well, suggests changes of plan or special activities to fit the parents' needs. It is very important that the two therapists coordinate their activities and are clear about their goals.

Handling Both Roles When Only One Therapist Is Available

If a second therapist is not available, there are a number of ways that you can act both as therapist for the child and as interpreting therapist for the parents. While a session is taking place, parents can observe the session on their own (either inside or outside the room). Immediately following the session or at a later time (depending on available child-care arrangements and family schedules), you can meet with the parents to discuss what happened and respond to the parents' questions. This arrangement leaves the parents alone as they watch the session but provides an opportunity for later discussion.

If parents must observe on their own, you can give them an assignment to help them focus their observations as they watch. For example, you might ask them to keep track of the activities that their child likes best, or to keep track of the times when the child gives good eye contact. Because they are alone, they should be included in sessions sooner than the usual fifth session. If parents are actually in the room, they can be invited to join in a final nurturing activity at the end of the very first session.

In another pattern, the parents do not observe the session as it takes place, but watch a videotape of it with you either immediately following the session or at a later scheduled meeting. In this arrangement, you are present to comment on an interaction as it is played out on the tape and to respond immediately to parents' reactions. It has the disadvantage for some parents (those who find it difficult to be left out of their child's treatment) of their not actually being present during the child's session.

Once the parents begin to join you and the child for the second half of each session, they must be readily available. By this time, they should be able to watch the sessions by themselves without support. Opportunities for parent-therapist conversations can be made either by telephone or during the fifteen minutes before or after a session.

As you can see, there are many possibilities for a single therapist to manage both aspects of Theraplay treatment. If it seems that these alternate arrangements take a great deal of time, remember that the standard Theraplay treatment takes the time of two therapists. In effect, two treatment sessions are occurring at the same time: one for the child and one for the parents.

Coordinating the Roles of the Interpreting and Theraplay Therapists

When you do have two therapists, an interpreting therapist and a Theraplay therapist, you must work as a well-coordinated team. The teamwork begins with the initial intake interview, where both of you participate in asking questions and following up on issues. Although both of you need not be present for the filming of the MIM, you both should meet the child before the first Theraplay session if at all possible. Together you analyze the MIM (we noted in Chapter Three the value of having more than one person look at the interaction), share insights, and prepare feedback for the parents. Right from the beginning you are equal partners in developing an understanding of the family and a plan for treatment. Being present together for the feedback clearly conveys to parents that you work as a team.

Before each session you should meet to plan the activities for the session based on your shared understanding of the child's current needs. Since you, as the interpreting therapist, must explain what the Theraplay therapist is doing and why, this planning is essential. It is also essential that you share what you learn from the parents about what is currently going on with the child so that the Theraplay therapist can adapt her activities and approach to the child's current needs. Occasionally parents will describe events in the child's life that need to be addressed during the session. Current family crises, special problems or triumphs of the week may warrant a change in plan or at least a response from the Theraplay therapist. In that case, you may enter the playroom and either speak directly to your partner or hand her a note. For example, "Alex won his wrestling match yesterday," or "Marita is not feeling well today." Some issues do not need to be spoken aloud to the child but simply taken into account by the Theraplay therapist.

When you and the parents enter the Theraplay room, all the problems of coordinating the work of two Theraplay therapists that we discussed in Chapter Three apply to this situation as well. You must be clear about who will lead each activity—though in a smoothly working team, if you become aware of an issue that needs to be addressed, either of you can signal to the other for a change of plan. For example, noticing that Dad seems to be sitting back and not participating, you might say, "I think it's Dad's turn to feed Marita." The typical arrangement is that the interpreting therapist is responsible for the parents and the Theraplay therapist continues to focus more on the child. But however you divide up the responsibilities, you must both be aware of the need to give clear instructions to parents about what they should do while you continue to meet the child's needs.

Having five people in the room requires careful planning and choreographing of activities to avoid confusion and mixed cues. Occasionally, for a child who is easily overstimulated and upset, such a big group is too much. In that case, the interpreting therapist does not enter the room, and the responsibility for directing activities for all participants falls to the Theraplay therapist. If you work alone, this will always be the case.

Following each session, take a few minutes to talk about how the session went, share information from the parents, and think about the child's needs for the next session. Make brief notes (the videotapes provide a full account) for your record of what happened in the session, especially about the child's and parents' responses. Note also ideas and plans for the next session. For example, "Alex seemed to be slumping down on the pillows a lot today. Next week let's do more activities with him standing and doing something active," or "I notice that Mom is very hesitant when she gives the signal for Jenny to do something. Next week let's play 'Mother, may I?.'"

This is the time to discuss any problems that might have arisen between the two of you about who should be leading and how to coordinate the activities. It is also an appropriate moment to discuss any disagreements about the approach to take with the child. For example, does the child need a more gentle, quiet approach or a more lively, engaging one? The Theraplay therapist has the best view of how it feels to be with the child, whereas the interpreting therapist has a broader view of the whole picture. The two views need to be coordinated. The longer you work with a partner, the more smoothly your work will go. If you do not find that you are working smoothly together, consult with a supervisor or trusted colleague who can help you work things out.

We turn now to describe in detail the various aspects of our work with parents. Although we describe each aspect separately, many of the steps overlap and the work is spread out over all the contacts we have with parents. Some of the work is done in special sessions without the child—for example, when the interpreting therapist helps a parent plan and role-play a Theraplay session in preparation for the parents' taking charge of an upcoming real session. The rest of the work takes place while the parents are observing the sessions.

HELPING PARENTS GAIN
A MORE POSITIVE, EMPATHIC
UNDERSTANDING OF THEIR CHILD

Throughout the treatment process, beginning with the session in which we give feedback to the parents about our observations of the MIM, the focus is on helping parents understand and appreciate their child. We do this by demonstrating a positive, respectful approach to their child, focusing and guiding their observations of the therapy process, and role-playing the child's part.

Demonstrating a Positive Approach to Their Child

We showed in earlier chapters how Theraplay is modeled on the upbeat, affirmative interactions that take place between a healthy parent and child. From the very first session in which parents observe the Theraplay therapist with their child, they see new possibilities for how they might interact with him. Watching a therapist count the freckles, find and take care of hurts, and rub lotion on the hands and feet of her six-year-old son, one mother said, "Oh, I can see how much he needs this. I wish I had done it a lot more. I think I'll do it tonight before he goes to bed." Another parent, noting the way her depressed daughter brightened up in the presence of her lively, energetic therapist, said, "I see that she really responds when someone is more energetic. It's not my style, but I'm going to try to be more like that." Because many parents who seek Theraplay treatment for their child are stuck in ineffective and sometimes even destructive behavioral patterns with their child, it is enormously useful for them to see a very different approach with a more positive outcome.

As they watch the Theraplay therapist with their child and notice the way the child is valued and respected, parents also begin to see their child as more lovable, more attractive, and more appealing. One mother, as she observed her teenage daughter in her first Theraplay session, poured out her disappointment and frustration. "I hate how she looks. She is so dirty and messy. I think she deliberately dresses like that to annoy me." The mother watched the therapist polish her daughter's fingernails, arrange her hair in interesting new styles, place a soap-bubble crown on her head, and engage her in lively thumb and arm wrestling contests. During the fourth session, the mother said thoughtfully, "What has happened? She is so beautiful. I never noticed that before."

Thus at the same time that we help the child to become more receptive to and accepting of such interactions and to feel better about herself, we demonstrate for parents how they can relate to their child more empathically and help them see their child in a more positive light.

Guiding Parents' Observations

As they watch the Theraplay session, parents have the opportunity, free of the stress and preoccupation of everyday living, to begin to put themselves in their child's place. Such empathic intuiting of their child's feelings is a common experience for new parents with a healthy baby, but it has often been lost by the time a family comes for help.

DISCUSSING BEHAVIOR SEEN DURING THERAPLAY SESSIONS. To increase parents' empathy for their child's experience and feelings, the interpreting therapist might ask, "How do you think she's feeling right now?" or say, "Notice how he smiles and relaxes when his therapist does that."

Some parents recognize how much the child is enjoying an activity, but scorn it or resent it or say that the child is just manipulating. "He'll lap it up all right. He can behave when you're paying attention to him all the time. It's when I can't be with him that he gets into trouble." At first, some parents see the child only as "selfish" or manipulative, as perhaps not even deserving of all this special attention. "But remember," the interpreting therapist says, "does a little baby have to earn the special attention that makes him feel so good? We are trying to fill your child with good feelings that he can hold on to when he doesn't have you right with him."

John's parents understood this after only two sessions. John, a six-year-old adopted boy, had once again "gotten into trouble" at school. Left alone in his classroom while his teacher attended to another child, John had taken the glue bottle from her desk and rubbed it all over himself. From the teacher's point of view, a point of view shared by his parents until just two weeks before, this was just one more of a long series of John's inexplicable, annoying behaviors. Now his mother said, "I understood it. With his teacher out of the room, John needed some help to hold himself together. What better choice than glue! It must have reminded him of the lotion his therapist comforts him with in the sessions." The consequence of this new understanding was that John was not scolded and told he was a bad boy. Instead, his parents told the teacher about John's difficulty controlling himself when he is alone. Together they made a plan so that John could be given something to steady himself whenever his teacher had to leave the classroom.

Another parent, asked how she thought her child was feeling about having lotion rubbed on her hands (perhaps confusing her own feelings with her child's) said, "She hates it. She can't stand to be touched or have lotion put on her." The interpreting therapist responded, "Yes that is what she is saying with her words: 'That's baby stuff.' But look closely. Is she really resisting? Would she cuddle in like that if she were totally rejecting of the closeness?"

DISCUSSING PAST BEHAVIOR. Sometimes it is possible to give parents a more empathic understanding of their child's past behavior. For example, John's parents reported that when he first came to live with them, he would often stand silently next to something he wanted rather than ask for it. In an effort to help John become more "grown up," his parents had refused to respond to his helpless silence and had insisted that he use words to let them know what he wanted. John had never experienced the empathic, attuned responsiveness that is so important in the early life of an infant. No one had been around to "read his mind." What he needed most from his new adoptive parents was that they be able to intuit his needs. This was a hard lesson for his achievement-oriented parents to keep in mind.

Later when John came home exhausted from a soccer game, he was unable to tell his parents that he needed to go right to bed rather than do his homework and chores. His parents, forgetting for the moment their new understanding of his needs, felt that he ought to be able to say he was tired rather than have a temper tantrum.

The conversation with their interpreting therapist went like this: "Think what a toddler would be able to do. He couldn't tell you. It would be up to you to figure it out, and if you weren't able to, he would have a tantrum." "But John is not a toddler, he's six years old!" "Yes, but when he's exhausted, he regresses. He doesn't have the self-control that a six-year-old might have. At those moments he is like a toddler. And besides, this is a wonderful opportunity for you to do the kinds of empathic caretaking that will add one more brick to the structure of his new self-esteem and to his ability to trust that you really care and will take care of him."

Role-Playing the Child's Part

As we describe further on when we talk about the steps leading to competence in using the Theraplay approach, some role-play is designed primarily to give parents confidence in relating to their child in a new way. An equally important reason for role-playing, however, is that it gives each parent an opportunity to experience what it feels like to be the child (as the parent takes the child's role). Often, the enacted scene is of some difficult behavior that parents want help in handling. The father, for example, describes how he handled a situation, while the interpreting therapist takes the father's role and follows the father's script. Next the interpreting therapist enacts a Theraplay approach to the situation. The parent is thus able to experience how each approach feels. He learns, for example, what it feels like to be held when he is upset, to be stopped from doing dangerous things, or to be cuddled and comforted. Such experiences help parents have more empathy for their child's feelings.

One father, playing the role of his hyperactive, aggressive son, sighed with relief when the therapist held him firmly until he relaxed. "I was so glad that you finally stopped me. I felt totally out of control and really afraid that you wouldn't be able to stop me before I did something dangerous. Can that be how Jim feels? Does he wish that I would stop him when he gets wild?"

LEADING PARENTS TOWARD COMPETENCE IN THE THERAPLAY APPROACH

In addition to helping parents understand and empathize with their child, the interpreting therapist's goal in working with parents is to strengthen the relationship and help them become more competent as parents. To accomplish this we follow a series of steps leading to the parents' taking full responsibility in sessions for the interaction with their child.

Using Discussion

During Theraplay sessions, parents observe their child interacting with her therapist. The interpreting therapist explains what is going on and encourages parents to watch how the therapist handles the child's problem behaviors and to ask questions about anything they don't understand.

INTERPRETING THE INTERACTION BETWEEN THE THERAPIST AND THE CHILD. Jamal had been a baby who was difficult to soothe. He was now, at seven, demanding, bossy, and very active. During his first Theraplay session, the interpreting therapist pointed out to his parents how much he seemed to enjoy his therapist's playful attention, but how quick he was to take advantage of any pause in the action to take charge. "In those years when it was so difficult to soothe and comfort him, he formed a very strong 'take charge' pattern. It will take a lot of experience before he can overcome his expectation that it's up to him to make things happen. And since he has such a lot of good ideas it will be hard for you to remember how important it is for you to stay in charge. Watch how his therapist handles it. Sometimes she ignores it, sometimes she says, 'You have great ideas. We'll do that sometime later, but right now I want to do this with you.'"

The first sessions with three-year-old Tracy posed a different problem for her parents to understand. From the very beginning she showed her typical pattern of angry resistance to anyone who didn't let her take the lead. Because it was so typical, her parents were not surprised that it showed up immediately, but they needed help to understand the therapist's approach, which was so different from their own pattern of alternate placating and angry withdrawal. "Watch how her therapist stays with her and continues to try to engage her," the interpreting therapist said. When Tracy suddenly stopped her angry protest and began to enjoy herself, the interpreting therapist pointed out, "She has finally realized that she can have fun and not have to be in charge of it."

PREPARING PARENTS FOR THE DIFFICULT PHASES OF TREATMENT. During the early sessions, the interpreting therapist prepares parents for the inevitable negative reaction. As we have said, most children have a honeymoon period, the tentative acceptance phase, before testing the new relationship. During this phase it is important to prepare parents for the change that is to come. Having the therapist, and later his parents, stay with him, calmly contain his violent behavior, and not retaliate or reject him is a powerful experience (which may need to be repeated many times). Following such outbursts, children often cry and relax into the therapist's (or parent's) arms as though, for the first time, they feel that someone can truly share their feelings and comfort them. You might say, "This is a very important part of treatment because it signals that your child is beginning to hope that an adult will be able to stay with him even when he shows his worst side."

THERAPLAY IN PRACTICE: *Helping Parents Understand Their Child's Angry Resistance.* Such an explanation made sense to nine-year-old Josh's adoptive parents because they knew his history of being rejected again and again by a series of foster parents who had inadvertently confirmed his worst fears by giving him up when he became "impossible to handle."

From the start of his fourth session, Josh began an active, angry resistance that lasted for twenty minutes. He tried to hit, bite, and get away. His therapist, Jane, held him firmly and calmly reassured him, "I won't let you hurt me and I won't hurt you. I know you're mad at me! I know you don't want to be held, but I'm staying with you till you feel better." When Josh found he couldn't hit or bite his therapist, he shouted angry insults: "Let me go, you b—! I'll call the DCFS [Department of Children and Family Services] worker and tell her you abused me. You can't get away with this!" But Jane remained calm and in control. After twenty exhausting minutes of struggle, Josh cried and relaxed into her arms, remaining there till the end of the session. Because his parents had been prepared for something like this to happen and because they felt supported by their interpreting therapist, they were able to watch the scene without too much anxiety. But they were relieved when it was over. "He looks so young, so vulnerable, so relaxed. We never knew it would be possible to reach him like this. On the way here he said he was going to fight her! We didn't know what he meant then, but we see now. He was thinking about Jane and planning this all week. It must have been very important to him." Josh started the next session once again with a "fight." This time he relaxed after ten minutes and again snuggled into Jane's arms for comfort. His parents reported that at home during the week between sessions they had handled a temper tantrum in the same way. "We couldn't believe how much it would change our relationship. He was soft and relaxed and available for hours after it was all over. He was right there with us. It feels as though we now have the key to how to help him!"

REASSURING PARENTS. For Tracy's parents, who had always been there, it was more difficult to understand where her angry resistance came from. The interpreting therapist explained that because of Tracy's hypersensitivity to all kinds of stimulation, no one had been able to soothe and comfort her in the way she needed. She had grown up trusting only herself. No wonder she raged when anyone tried to take over or enter her carefully controlled world. Her parents were reassured that many children like Tracy throw tantrums and must be held until they feel better. "Don't feel embarrassed by Tracy's angry outbursts. See how she is beginning to take her therapist's presence into account. Soon she will no longer need to protest and will be able to enter into the fun." And in fact, Tracy made a remarkable turnaround. By the third session she was laughing and playing with her therapist. By the final session she was sitting comfortably in her mother's arms enjoying being rocked and cuddled like the small child she really was inside.

The discussion with the interpreting therapist helps parents understand their child's behavior and the reasons behind his therapist's responses to it. Such discussion appeals primarily to parents' cognitive understanding, though some parents can put that understanding immediately into practice at home. Throughout Theraplay treatment, the interpreting therapist will continue to discuss and interpret the child's feelings and behavior, but we do not depend on discussion alone to effect change. Parents need practice in order to implement their new insights.

Guiding Practice During Sessions

After observing four or five sessions, parents enter the Theraplay room and join in the fun under the dual guidance of the Theraplay therapist and the interpreting therapist. This step requires careful preparation. Parents must understand that their entrance into the sessions may produce resistance and regression on the part of their child. If parents are not prepared ahead of time, they may think that they have done something wrong or be reinforced in their fears that their child doesn't like them. If they know that this is a very common response, they are able to handle it better.

Explain to the parents that there are probably at least two reasons for such a reaction. First, children find it difficult to accept any intrusion into the relationship that is developing between themselves and their therapist. Rather than see their parents' presence as a gain, they see it as a loss. Second, they need to go back and test their parents, just as they tested their therapist, to see whether they can be as responsive, as firm, and as reliable as the Theraplay therapist is proving to be.

To help the child accept her parents' entry into a session, whether it is the first time or any of the following sessions, the Theraplay therapist plans activities that turn their entry into a game. For example, as we saw with Adam, the therapist and child may hide under pillows or a blanket and call to the parents to find them. In preparation for this step, the interpreting therapist has coached the parents to talk about the wonderful girl they are hoping to find and to respond with joy when they find her. If the child is young and restless, they will be told, "Don't take too long finding her. She really can't wait." With this preparation, the reunion between child and parents is joyful and leads easily to the activities that follow.

Another playful approach is to hide something on the child for the parents to find. Sometimes it is food that they can feed to their child. Sometimes they find notes that describe an activity for the parent to do: "Play a game of thumb wrestling with John," or "Give Susan a butterfly kiss."

In addition to preparing parents for their entry into the session, the interpreting therapist also tells them how to handle particular activities. For example, if the activity is a competitive one, you might say, "Make sure that Alex wins part of the time, but don't be a pushover. He needs to feel how strong you are," or "We will be practicing having you take charge. When we play 'Mother, may I,' be sure that you help Melissa do the actions just as you ask her to."

Once the parents are in the room, the child's therapist takes the lead in giving clear directions to the parents about their role in each of the activities planned for the session: "Mom, you sit here, and Dad, you sit on Juan's other side. We're going to help him get all soft and floppy. Mom, lift his arm and wiggle it a bit to see whether it's relaxed. Good. Dad, how about his other hand? Now that he's all soft and floppy, Dad, you tell him to wiggle one part of his body."

While they are in the Theraplay room, parents are worked with as intensely as was their child heretofore. Depending on their particular conflicts—as these have emerged during the initial intake, MIM, and preceding four sessions of observation—the focus of the Theraplay sessions is carefully designed to confront these conflicts. If, for example, Father cannot tolerate passivity in his son, he is asked to hold or powder him and is enthusiastically praised for the inventive, or strong, or cuddly way he does this. If Mother or her son has difficulty competing, then water pistol fights and mother-son wrestling matches may be the order of the day, with Father acting as cheerleader, umpire, or the cooler-off of perspiring brows. If Father is unable to assert his authority with his child, he is helped to develop assertiveness in a game of "Father, may I?" in which he is required, albeit in fun, to tolerate no violation of the rules he establishes. If parent and child tend to cling together too much, they are encouraged to pillow fight, wrestle, and play tug of war, while physical and other differences between them are cheerfully emphasized by the therapists.

Sometimes a child has been seen by his parents as not very appealing. Your job then is to help parents see how lovable and attractive their child really is. You can have them participate in taking care of every tiny hurt with lotion, warm water, and band-aids. You can help them prevent every chance for an accidental hurt (for example, "Mom, when we hold his head this way he could bump it. See, we have to hold it this way"; "Dad, that time he jumped too hard. He could scrape himself. Let's help him do it again carefully, so he'll be really safe this time").

Giving Homework

As powerful as the interaction in the session is for making a child feel good about herself and for setting the relationship on a better footing, it is essential that the parents reinforce it at home. As soon as we see that the parents are comfortable with the idea, we ask them to practice some of the activities at home that have worked well in Theraplay sessions. The mother described above who said at the very first session that she would try some of the nurturing activities that night with her son, was clearly ready. Other parents may need to wait for awhile. But all parents need to put the ideas into practice at some time.

You might suggest that parents schedule a regular twenty-minute time for Theraplay every day. Some families find it easier to incorporate Theraplay activities and attitudes into all of their daily routines rather than schedule a regular time. The wake-up call can be turned into a wonderful five-minute checkup session (pretending the child is a lump in the bed, needing to be smoothed out; or waking up sleepy fingers and toes with gentle kisses). The bedtime routine can be enhanced by ten minutes of feeding and rocking and singing.

Many parents feel so overwhelmed by how much time it takes to get their child through the daily routines that they wonder how they could possibly spend another twenty minutes each day playing with their child. "It takes Melissa forever to get dressed for school." To such parents you can respond with the question, "How much time are you now spending arguing with her about getting dressed? Use that time to make dressing a pleasant, shared activity and you'll be surprised at how much time you will save."

When making a homework assignment, it is important that you help parents plan carefully so that the experience will go well. You might ask them, "When is the best time to schedule such activities? Can you arrange it while your other children are busy with something else? Where will you do it? What activities would you like to try first?" At the next session, ask how the homework went. If there were problems, you can help the parents modify their approach so that it will work better next time.

Prepare parents for the fact that children are not always as responsive with their parents as they have become with their Theraplay therapist. Since this is the case, before having the parent try an activity out either in sessions or at home, make sure that the child is comfortable with it and that it can be done without undue resistance or out-of-control excitement. Nurturing activities are particularly likely to be difficult for parents and their resistant older child. Even though they have become comfortable with regressive nurturing in sessions with their therapist (that is, having lotion rubbed on their feet, or being fed from a bottle when they are well past the usual age for that), these children often resist when their parents offer it at home. Since you want their first efforts to be successful, suggest that parents start out with playful, challenging activities before they try quieter nurturing activities.

Using Role-Playing

In preparation for a parent's taking a more active role in sessions, the Theraplay therapist and the interpreting therapist meet with the parent (without the child) to plan and role-play the activities that will take place during the next session. During the role-play, you can take the part of the child and play out the anticipated response of the child so that the parents can practice how to handle problems that might arise. The parents must learn, for example, how to move more calmly and slowly for the easily excited child, or move smoothly from one activity to another for the child who has trouble with transitions. Though not all parents need this step, it is a powerful tool that we often use. Parents who have not experienced good parenting themselves find it especially helpful. Toward the end of treatment, such role-play can be geared to the parent's taking full charge of the upcoming session with the child.

Role-playing serves two purposes: the obvious one of preparing parents for taking charge of sessions as well as for carrying on the Theraplay approach at home; and the more subtle one, discussed above, of giving them insight into how the child might feel while engaged in such activities.

THERAPLAY IN PRACTICE: *Role-Playing with a Parent.* The following is an account of a role-playing session with a single parent who was seeking to regain custody of her three-year-old daughter. Carmen had worked very hard to meet the requirements that her Department of Children and Family Services (DCFS) worker and the courts had set up to assure that she could handle the care of her child. She had attended parenting classes, found work, arranged for an apartment, and been consistently available for all supervised visits with her little girl. But the DCFS worker felt that Carmen needed more help to meet her daughter's needs for nurture and empathic responsiveness. She therefore was referred for an MIM and a series of eight Theraplay sessions with her child.

The MIM confirmed the worker's judgment. Although Carmen obviously cared about her daughter, her way of showing it was through teaching. For example, instead of using the feeding task ("Feed each other") as a way of getting close, she asked Selena to name the colors of the candy pieces and to count them. When asked why teaching was so important to her, she said, "Selena needs to know a lot if she is going to get along in the world. She's already had to be in so many foster homes." We felt that she and Selena would benefit from the opportunity to shift the focus of their interactions.

Initially, Carmen was outspoken about her frustration at what seemed to her just another roadblock in the way of getting her daughter back. "I know how to take care of her. I took care of her all the time when she was a baby. I raised all my brothers and sisters. I don't need this." But as she watched the Theraplay therapist taking good care of Selena and having fun with her, she became excited. "I could do that. My mother never played with us kids like that, but I can see that Selena really likes it." Carmen entered into the sessions as a willing and eager participant.

In preparation for Carmen to take charge of the seventh session, we scheduled a planning and role-playing session. Carmen outlined the activities she would like to lead: paper-punch, thumb wrestling, lotion handprints, and other activities. First Carmen played the role of Selena, experiencing what it would be like for Selena to participate in such activities. She was very perceptive in her comments. "That feels good. I really like it when you put the lotion on my hands. And I can't believe how interesting it is to see my own hand prints there on the paper." She also was able to act out some of Selena's resistance and to experience how it might feel to have a calm but firm response from an adult.

Next Carmen shifted to the role of Therapist, with the interpreting therapist playing the role of Selena. Though Carmen had a clear idea of what she wanted to do, she needed help to keep focused on her child and to move quickly enough to stay in charge. As she played out how she would check out her daughter's strong muscles before having her punch the newspaper, her eyes wandered to the other side of the room. The interpreting therapist commented, "Could you look right at her when you do that? You have such lovely warm eyes, and she would feel so much better if she could see them." When she moved slowly to introduce the next activity, the interpreting therapist, playing Selena, slipped away. Carmen said, "Oh, I see that I have to move faster or I'll lose her." And thus the practice session went on, smoothing out the rough edges of her approach, preparing her to be responsive and to take charge when actually faced with her little girl.

As a result of this practice session, Carmen developed a stronger sense of her own powers and benefited, as she played the role of her child, from the experience of being cared for by another adult. This was an experience she had lacked when as a child she had had to grow up quickly in order to take care of her younger siblings.

Following the preparatory role-playing, Carmen was able to take full charge of the session with Selena, having the Theraplay and interpreting therapists there as a cheering section. At the end of eight sessions, she seemed ready to have Selena returned to her care. We recommended that Carmen have ongoing support from her DCFS worker as she began to care for her child and that she continue to come in for monthly checkups for three months and then once every three months for a year.

Helping Parents Take Charge of Sessions

The final step in helping parents feel comfortable in using the Theraplay approach with their children comes when parents take charge of a session, as Carmen did, while the Theraplay therapists support from the sidelines. When this is accomplished the family is ready to end treatment.

The preparation for this final step takes place during all the earlier sessions as parents participate in activities. They are given practice in taking charge or structuring activities in games such as "Mother may I?" or "Simon says," in which their child must wait for a signal before he follows their instruction. They play a variety of surprising and engaging activities, such as peek-a-boo with a young child or hand-clapping games with an older one. They have experience holding and rocking and soothing their child under the guidance of the Theraplay therapist. And they participate in many challenging activities such as helping their child balance on pillows or engage in pushing contests. When it comes time for them to take charge of a session on their own, they are experienced in each Theraplay dimension. They then need to practice taking charge of moving smoothly from one activity to another. That is why a role-playing session is so helpful.

In planning for the session they will lead, parents should choose activities that they enjoy doing with their child. By this time the importance of certain kinds of activities (for example, structuring for an impulsive child, nurturing and soothing for a very active child), should be well understood by the parents. As activities are chosen and planned, you may ask the parents to predict how their child might respond and also to plan for how they will handle it.

During the actual session, the therapists let the parents take charge, but are always prepared to offer a tip or prompt the parent if he needs help. When the session is over, you can show the videotape to the parents so that they can evaluate their own performance. They are often very pleased with what they see.

TEACHING PARENTS ABOUT THEIR CHILD'S NEEDS

This didactic part of our work has much in common with other approaches to working with parents and children. It gains added significance from the parents' having the opportunity in sessions to interact directly with their child and to put the new information into practice under the guidance of the Theraplay therapists.

Keeping Parents' Expectations in Line with Their Child's Needs

It is important for all parents to have realistic expectations that are congruent with their child's needs at each stage of development. Many parents who bring their children for help have either too high or too low expectations. That Hassan's father had very high expectations became clear during the MIM as we watched him teach his five-year-old son about high-energy physics. Being unable to meet these expectations had contributed to Hassan's low self-esteem. Treatment included helping his father match his expectations to his son's very appropriate five-year-old interests and capacity for understanding, which in turn helped bolster his son's self-esteem.

When a child is developing normally and the parents are not caught up in their own agenda, it is not too difficult for parents to understand what their child needs. When a child is insecurely attached, however, she may be clingy and babyish or independent and pseudo-mature. In either case it becomes more difficult for parents to read their child's needs appropriately. Parents of the clingy child may push her to grow up and therefore miss out on meeting her legitimate dependency needs. Parents of the pseudo-mature child may accept their child's maturity as an indication that he doesn't need the regressive nurturing care that he has missed out on. Understanding how to respond to their children's needs is particularly difficult for parents of older adopted children. These children may function physically and cognitively at age level, but they often are emotionally much less mature. It is their emotional immaturity and neediness that causes so many problems. In Chapter Ten we address how Theraplay can help adoptive families.

We begin pointing out to parents what their child's needs are right from the beginning when we view the MIM videotape with them. Together we observe how the family negotiates nurturing activities. Sometimes it is clear that the parents would prefer to be more nurturing but the child resists it heartily. "That's babyish," he may say, or "I'll do it to you instead." Sometimes the parents find it difficult to be nurturing with an older child. "What if she just stays a regressed little baby? Isn't that the way she was when she came to us? Her being more independent now seems like progress." In the feedback to such parents we say, "Look at how much she resists being taken care of. That is precisely what she needs. We will be working to help her feel more comfortable with that," or "In our experience, once a child feels truly comfortable and secure, he is ready to move ahead."

Looking at the Child's Inner Representations as an Indication of the Child's Needs

To help parents understand their child, we introduce them to the idea (discussed in Chapters One and Two) that children develop a picture, or inner representation, of themselves and the world and how they can expect others to respond to them based on all the interactions they have had with important caretakers in their lives. We point out that their child's difficult behavior can be understood as stemming from that inner representation. As they describe some difficult behavior, we ask, "How do you think he was feeling about himself at that moment?" "What does her hoarding of food tell us about the picture of the world that she developed when she was a tiny, neglected child?"

As parents watch their child experiencing a new kind of relationship in the Theraplay session, you might ask, "How do you think it makes him feel about himself?" and comment "We want him to feel special and well cared for," or "We want him to learn that he doesn't have to be in charge in order to get his needs met. The more he believes that, the more he will be able to relax."

With the parents of a foster child who was neglected and abused, you might speculate about how he views himself and the world based on those early years of abandonment and neglect. "He could only believe that he was unworthy and unlovable and expect adults to be unresponsive and neglectful. His insistence that everything be under his control, on calling all the shots, is the only logical outcome (other than despair and giving up) of such a view of himself and of the world."

Parents are introduced to the idea that it is possible to change the child's inner pictures, to go back and recreate the conditions under which the infant in a stable, responsive family learns to feel secure, learns to trust, and develops a strong and positive self-concept. As they watch the Theraplay therapist working with their child, they see how to do this themselves. As soon as they are ready, they are encouraged to do the same things at home.

It is helpful to parents if you point out that every instance of infantile, resistant, or angry behavior by their child offers an opportunity to respond to their child's underlying needs—for nurture, calm structure, or for nonpunitive acceptance of angry feelings. By using these opportunities they can begin to create the kinds of interactions that develop trust and lead to an awareness of the caring, soothing presence of adults.

Showing How Meeting the Child's Needs Leads to Changes in Behavior

The advice we give to parents about how to handle their child's difficult behavior at home is based on the Theraplay principles of having parents meet the child's needs for clear, safe structure, consistent follow through, and empathic understanding of the meaning of the child's difficult behavior. Many problems become easier to handle or disappear altogether when the child feels understood, nurtured, and valued.

To help parents understand the connection between needs and behavior as they sit behind the one-way mirror at each session, the interpreting therapist asks parents how things have gone during the previous week. Frequently a parent will describe some difficult interaction that took place at home. A mother of a "spirited," hypersensitive, adopted six-year-old girl complains that it is always a struggle getting her daughter ready to go to school. "Judy always creates a scene. Her clothes are too tight, her socks have lumps in them, and she can't bear to wear the gym shoes she has to have today. Nothing is right and nothing I do seems to help. It always ends with both of us angry. Then she goes off to school and both of us feel bad."

The interpreting therapist says, "Let's think about what is going on with Judy at times like that. How do you think she is feeling about herself at that moment? How does she feel about leaving you? What do separations mean to her: abandonment, loneliness, pain? Her complaints keep you with her and delay the separation. And finally they create angry feelings that make it easier for her to leave you. Those angry feelings don't help in the long run, though, so we need to find a way to help her get off to school without such a difficult time." Together they make a plan for Judy's mother to dress her daughter in a playful, nurturing way that will help meet Judy's need to feel more secure and enable her to go off to school happily.

MEETING PARENTS' UNMET NEEDS

Just as the Theraplay therapist makes a child feel good about himself by being appreciative and empathically responsive, so the interpreting therapist responds to the parents. Many parents find it difficult to be positive, empathic parents because they have not been parented in a positive, empathic manner themselves. It is essential in working with such parents to meet their needs to be supported, to have early unmet needs acknowledged and responded to, and to feel good about themselves before you can ask them to attend to the needs of their children.

Giving Parents Support

A major component of Theraplay treatment is parent support. All parents need support, understanding, and empathy for the problems they face in raising their children. Parents of children with attachment problems or with constitutionally based problems such as autism and PDD, however, need more consistent and intense support because their children give so little back in response to their parents' efforts. Be on the alert, therefore, to be empathically accepting of parents' feelings and needs.

Some children present a cheerful, friendly face to strangers while behaving like little monsters at home. Parents of such a child are frequently told, "She's such a dear. I don't understand why you find her so difficult." The implication is that it must be the mother's fault. Or the mother may simply observe that the child behaves well with others, and then make her own self-denigrating inference: "It *must* be my fault." Given this dynamic, you must be careful that the child's initial outgoing response to his Theraplay therapist is not interpreted by his mother as yet another confirmation that she is a failure. You can point out that this is typical of many adopted children, and not at all the fault of their mothers. Because they were disappointed by their birth mother, they challenge and test their adoptive mother most of all.

Although empathy and acceptance can go a long way toward relieving an overburdened parent, often parents need more than that. When this is the case, you must help them find the supports in the community that they need. For example, parents of a child with autism or PDD may need information about parent support groups and respite care. Parents of adopted children welcome the opportunity to share their experiences and problems with others through adoptive parent organizations. You need to know what your community resources are and guide parents to them.

Offering Theraplay for Parents

Sometimes parents have received so little good parenting that they find it impossible to give their children the nurturing and positive attention they need. In these cases we offer parents the opportunity to have some Theraplay sessions for themselves. While this can be done partially through the role-playing described above that is designed to help them take charge of sessions, sometimes it is important to have the sessions designed exclusively to meet the parents' needs. Such sessions are very much like the Theraplay sessions with their children. They include engaging activities, such as counting freckles, playing hand-clapping games, and hiding and finding candies on each other; nurturing activities, such as rubbing lotion on hands and feet, making lotion hand- and footprints, feeding, and rocking and singing rounds together; and challenging activities, such as tug-of-war, balancing on a stack of pillows, and punching paper. The therapist takes charge and carefully plans the sessions to meet the needs of the parent. The parent is able to experience being taken care of, nurtured, played with, and valued just as they have seen their child cared for.

Another way of meeting parents' needs for good parenting is through Theraplay Parent Groups. In Chapter Twelve we describe Group Theraplay and give examples of including parents in groups with their children.

THERAPLAY IN PRACTICE: *Using Group Theraplay to Meet Parents' Needs.* Group Theraplay was offered to parents who were public housing residents as one of the components of a program geared toward improving parenting skills, providing knowledge of child development, and increasing the range of choices available to parents for interacting with their children (Leslie and Mignon, 1995). The program was planned to consist of twelve sessions. The first eight to ten were for "Moms only"; with one or more children of each mother joining in for the last few sessions. The goal was for participants to increase their ability "to accept and practice healthy self-nourishing behaviors," and "to have a better idea of how good nurturing feels." Three facilitators led the groups, planning sessions that began with checkups, ended with sharing a treat, and bridged these rituals with active and quiet games.

To reduce any resistance that might occur, the first session was planned to be fast and fun. Activities such as paper-patty-cake, peanut butter and jelly, stack of hands, "Miss Mary Mack," and pudding pictures were not only challenging, but provided the type of silly fun that these mothers had never felt was permissible. Feeding a partner a Popsicle or giving her five licks from a Tootsie Roll allowed group members to be nurtured in a fun, nonthreatening manner. These women were so uncomfortable touching each other that they could not do so unless it was required as part of a game. Passing a lotion squeeze and having your neighbor guess where you touched her with a feather were acceptable. Massaging shoulders all around the circle was more difficult. In addition, the women tended to do the group activities very quickly and did not request a repeat, regardless of their evident enjoyment. The group members were given a voice in how games were played, and they rejected the childish goodbye song for a rap song that one participant created.

Although the plan had been to include children during the last two sessions, the group became "for parents only." When it came time to decide about including their children, the mothers resoundingly voted "No!" The experience filled such an important need that they were not ready to share it even with their children. They needed to have something just for themselves.

Dealing with Parents' Individual Issues and Marital Conflicts

Sometimes parents need help in resolving their own individual issues or marital conflicts, including conflicts over parenting styles that interfere with the successful parenting of their children. In some situations it is possible to respond to the parents' marital or individual issues as part of the discussion behind the one-way mirror. At other times it is not possible. If that is the case, you might want to use an approach developed by Dr. Evangeline Munns in her work at Blue Hills Child and Family Centre in Aurora, Ontario. It provides a more extended opportunity for family work following the Theraplay session. One Theraplay therapist takes the child (or children when more than one child is included in sessions) into another playroom while the interpreting therapist meets with the parents. During this meeting, traditional family and marital therapy techniques are used to help the parents work out their differences and come to a better understanding of their own needs. Another variation is to have the children remain in the room while the family work is being done. In that case, simple play materials are provided for the children, such as crayons and quiet toys, and the child or children are free to interact with the parents and to be involved in the work that is being done. Including children in sessions is a pattern often used in traditional family therapy and can be very revealing of family patterns as well as helpful to both children and parents.

But sometimes parents' issues and conflicts are so serious that they need to be addressed more intensely than is possible in conjunction with the Theraplay sessions. The parents are then referred for individual or marital work separate from the Theraplay sessions. Such work may take place concurrently with the Theraplay sessions or after Theraplay is completed. Very occasionally it has been necessary to stop Theraplay treatment until parents have resolved these other issues.

In this chapter we have explored the many ways you can work with parents in Theraplay treatment. Each family presents its unique problems and challenges, and therefore not all the steps will be followed with every family.

Specific Applications of Theraplay

Part One of this book gives an overview of what Theraplay is and why it works. Part Two describes how it works and what you need to know to practice Theraplay. In Part Three we look at how Theraplay can be adapted for special populations or for children with special needs. Chapters Six, Seven, and Eight are devoted to how we work with children whose relationship problems have a constitutional, neurological, or physical base. Chapter Six deals with children whose difficulty stems from problems in the regulation of their response to stimuli and of their activity level. Chapter Seven discusses children with autism and pervasive developmental disorders (PDD). Chapter Eight treats children with physical disabilities.

The common issue in these three chapters is that a difficulty on the child's part makes it hard for his parents to meet his needs. Anything in the child that interferes with his ability to respond energetically to his parents' efforts to engage him or to comfort and soothe him can interfere with the development of a secure attachment relationship. Although we do not expect to change the basic physical or neurological problem, Theraplay can affect positively the child's ability to tolerate stimuli and cope with experience. By doing so, it can overcome some of the barriers to healthy interaction, thus making it possible for these children and their parents to develop warm, joyful, interactive relationships that can open up the child to further learning and healthy experiences.

In Chapters Nine and Ten we turn to groups of children whose problems stem not from within their own physical nature but from the failure on the part of the caretaking environment to provide what they need. Chapter Nine addresses how Theraplay can be adapted to meet the needs of children who have suffered abuse or trauma. Chapter Ten considers how Theraplay can be helpful with children who have been separated from their birth parents and placed in foster care or adoptive homes. Theraplay must find ways to help these children learn to trust and form a secure attachment to new parents following the loss of their original parents and the varying degrees of trauma that such a loss entails.

Most of our examples of Theraplay treatment up to this point have been of children from eighteen months through school age. In Chapter Eleven we look at how Theraplay can be adapted to working with adolescents. Although we have given a few examples of working with adults, particularly with parents in conjunction with our work with their children, a more detailed discussion of our work with couples and individual adults is beyond the scope of this book.

Finally, Chapter Twelve discusses the application of Theraplay principles to groups. Beyond these applications, Theraplay also has been imaginatively applied in a variety of settings, including hospitals, day treatment centers, and in home-based treatment. The *Theraplay Newsletter, Fall, 1995,* discusses a series of applications of all these forms of Theraplay.

CHAPTER SIX

Theraplay for Children with Problems in Regulation

Early in our practice of Theraplay, we found that children referred for treatment can be roughly divided on the basis of their behavior into two opposite groups: quiet and withdrawn or hyperactive. We found that Theraplay must be adapted to the needs of shy, quiet, withdrawn children as well as distractible, overactive, aggressive children. We recognized also that some children are easily overwhelmed by stimuli of all kinds—visual, tactile, auditory—and that others are uncomfortable being off balance (even in the normal posture for being bottle or breast fed) and managing their bodies in space. Some of the children who are overwhelmed by stimulation shut down, freeze, or withdraw, thus making them appear passive and unresponsive (you will see in the next chapter that this is often true for children with autism or pervasive developmental disorders). Some quiet children are constitutionally underresponsive and require a high level of stimulation to be engaged. At the other extreme are children for whom almost any unaccustomed activity starts an escalating spiral of excitement that is difficult to stop. Many of these very active children also have sensory sensitivities, as we saw with Adam in Chapter Three. In this chapter we discuss how Theraplay treatment can be adapted to meet the needs of children with constitutionally based problems in neurological and physiological regulation:

sensory integration problems (SI), regulatory disorders, attention deficit disorder (ADD), and attention deficit hyperactivity disorder (ADHD).

Very passive, "good" babies, because they don't do their part in asking for it, often get less of the playful give-and-take that is so important to healthy development. Irritable, difficult-to-soothe infants with regulatory disorders often resist being held and cuddled and therefore lack experiences that would be calming and nurturing. As these children grow older, their problems with arousal, attention, and regulation interfere with school work and peer relationships, and continue to disrupt their relationship with their parents. In Chapter One we identified such constitutionally based problems as one source of the relationship difficulties that Theraplay is designed to treat.

In this chapter, we define the problems briefly, consider the underlying causes, show how these special sensitivities affect the attachment relationship, and then look at the basic principles of treatment. We end with examples of Theraplay treatment with a withdrawn child and a hyperactive child.

DEFINING THE PROBLEMS

While the problems we are considering here—sensory integration problems, regulatory disorders, and attention deficit disorder—may contribute to relationship difficulties, they do not prevent the child from relating to others or communicating in an age-appropriate fashion. That is not the case for children with autism who have severe problems in relating and communicating. Since children with autism share many of these same problems in extreme form, the principles of treatment that we discuss here apply to them as well.

The common theme throughout these three classifications is the difficulty in modulating response to stimuli and regulating attention, arousal, and activity level. Children without these difficulties readily achieve an optimal range of arousal for receiving and responding to stimuli. But a child at either extreme is unable to attend or to learn. An important focus in treatment is to arouse the underresponsive, lethargic child and calm the overresponsive, hyperreactive child.

Sensory Integration Problems

Sensory *integration* problems are neurologically based difficulties in regulating and processing sensory experience, including touch, movement, body awareness, sight, sound, and the pull of gravity (Ayers,

1979). Sensory *modulation* refers to the ability of the child's central nervous system to "modulate" the intensity of specific sensory stimuli. The ability to modulate input directly affects arousal, attention, and organization of behavior.

The severity of sensory integration problems varies from mild, such as the child who hates to have her hands dirty or who cannot stand the feel of the labels in her clothes, to extreme, such as the autistic child for whom stimulation in more than one sensory modality can be overwhelming. We adapt techniques designed for treating sensory integration problems to children with special sensory sensitivities and modulation problems whether mild or severe.

Regulatory Disorders

With regulatory disorders, the emphasis is on the child's difficulty with modulation or regulation of response rather than on the child's specific sensory sensitivities. Regulatory disorders are characterized by difficulties in regulating "physiological, sensory, attentional, and motor or affective processes, and organizing a calm, alert, or affectively positive state" (Greenspan, 1992a, p. 601). As with sensory integration problems, children may be either overreactive or underreactive.

The symptoms of regulatory disorder in young children include irritability, aggression, distractibility, poor tolerance for frustration, tantrums, and sleeping and eating difficulties. Infants variously described as irritable, fussy, or difficult to soothe, or as having a difficult temperament, are included in this category.

Young children with regulatory problems are at high risk for later behavior problems of the sort associated with attention deficit hyperactivity disorder (ADHD) or attention deficit disorder (ADD) (DeGangi, 1991a).[1]

Attention Deficit Disorder With and Without Hyperactivity

The American Psychiatric Association: Diagnostic and Statistical Manual of Mental Disorders, Fourth Edition (DSM-IV) criteria for diagnosing ADHD and ADD include inattention, impulsivity, and hyperactivity. Behavior is characterized by high activity level, restlessness, impulsivity, short attention span, and difficulty attending. Undifferentiated attention deficit disorder is characterized by marked inattention without the high activity level.

UNDERSTANDING THE CAUSES
OF THE PROBLEMS

The many possible causes for problems in regulation include genetic inheritance, prenatal maternal drug use, postnatal influences such as trauma and stress, institutional rearing, and family dysfunction. It is difficult to determine the specific cause or causes for any one child. Whatever the underlying cause, problems in regulation affect the parent-child relationship in many ways.

Genetic Inheritance

Research into the neurobiological bases of behavior lends support to the argument that there is a constitutional base for most sensory integration problems, regulatory disorders, and attention deficit disorders. Often other family members have similar sensitivities or attentional and regulatory problems, and therefore it is assumed that there is a genetic component.

Maternal Drug Use

Maternal drug use during pregnancy is associated with the infant's difficulty in regulating arousal (Zuckerman and Bresnahan, 1991). Fortunately, this effect can be mediated by good caretaking. However, many drug-involved caretakers are unable to provide the necessary attuned care and often exacerbate the problems by their insensitive care. The use of alcohol during pregnancy, furthermore, can lead to irreversible effects that include severe regulatory problems.

Trauma and Stress

Recent studies of the effect of trauma and stress indicate that stressful environmental circumstances can affect the neurochemistry of the brain and lead to stress- or trauma-induced hyperreactive behavior. In fact, the behavior of children who have experienced trauma is often difficult to distinguish from that of children with ADHD (Thomas, 1995).

Institutional Care

Children raised in institutions where they have been deprived of consistent caretaking, adequate stimulation, and opportunities for physical activity often have regulatory and sensory integration problems. If their experiences were particularly stressful or traumatizing, they may also exhibit the symptoms of post-traumatic stress disorder. We will return to this issue when we discuss adoption in Chapter Ten.

Current Life Circumstances

A child's current environment can also lead to anxious, hypervigilant, hyperactive behavior or to passive, withdrawn behavior. For example, we often see children whose high activity level seems designed to keep their depressed mothers alert and responsive to them. Or, as another example, a mother's large family and many responsibilities may result in her leaving a child too much on her own, with the result that the child withdraws.

Effect on the Relationship between Parent and Child

In Chapter One we discussed the impact of having a child whose under- or overreactivity makes it hard for a parent to respond in ways that meet the child's needs. The underreactive child is difficult to engage, so parents find themselves hurt and frustrated by their child's lack of response. The parent of an irritable, fussy baby will hesitate to intrude when she is calm and will put her down or prop the bottle when it seems that holding her is making things worse. The child who is hypersensitive to touch, sounds, sights, and movement in space resists engagement in the many activities that stimulate cognitive development, language development, and the attuned responsiveness that is the basis of secure attachment. Such a child is likely to develop the behavior patterns of the insecurely attached child: either avoidant (rushing about taking risks and responding angrily to the world) or ambivalent (being shy, clinging, and withdrawn).

In addition, because they are so easily overwhelmed by a wide range of stimulation, many hypersensitive children develop an intense need to have everything under their own control. As we saw with Sara in Chapter One and Adam in Chapter Three, these children often become tyrants. Theraplay treatment with them involves shifting the source of power to the parents so that the child can be relieved of the burden of perpetual vigilance and the constant need to "run the show."

Constitutional factors set a limit on how much change can be made in the child's basic response pattern and add to the challenge of finding ways to compensate for the sensitivities. As you will see, however, Theraplay can affect the child's ability to tolerate stimuli and to cope with experiences. Careful modulation and well-planned Theraplay treatment can make a real difference. This is an important part of the work in repairing the relationship.

UNDERSTANDING THE BASIC PRINCIPLES OF TREATMENT FOR CHILDREN WITH REGULATORY DISORDERS

As with all children and parents whom Theraplay treats, the goal is to initiate or reinstate a joyful, satisfying, interactive relationship. Treatment must overcome the patterns of disengagement that have developed because of the child's regulatory problems. To do this you must learn what level of stimulation or impact brings the child to an appropriate state of arousal, and what activities help the child organize his sensory functioning. You also must provide the structure that helps regulate his level of activity and excitement. The basic principles are as follows:

- Adjust the stimulus level to the child's needs to achieve an optimal level of response and engagement.
- Use activities that organize the child's sensory system.
- Control the child's excitement and activity level.
- Increase the child's capacity for self-control.
- Increase the child's attention span.
- Gradually increase the child's tolerance for stimuli.

We next look at each of these principles in turn.

Adjusting the Stimulus Level

As part of your initial intake procedure with all children, ask parents specific questions about their child's sensory sensitivities. Even if parents are unable to tell you in advance, it will quickly become obvious during the first few Theraplay sessions whether or not a child is hypersensitive. In the case of more severe sensory integration problems, the specific sensitivities may be masked by the child's extreme reaction to any change in his routine. Thus, as you will see when we describe Tom's treatment, part of your assessment will take place as you work with the child. If you suspect that the child has sensory integration problems, you should refer him to an occupational therapist who is a trained diagnostician. A child with severe sensory integration problems will need sensory integration treatment in addition to Theraplay treatment.[2]

The basic principle in using Theraplay with children who are over- or underresponsive to stimuli is to adjust your level of intensity to allow them to achieve an optimal level of arousal. For the low-tone, underresponsive child, your voice should be louder, the lights brighter, and your pace faster and more emphatic. Activities should be engaging, invigorating, and exciting. The hypersensitive child needs just the opposite: your voice should be softer, the lights lower, and your pace slower. Activities should be calming and soothing, as we now illustrate in the case of Tom.

THERAPLAY IN PRACTICE: Treating a Child with Severe Auditory Sensitivity. Tom was a developmentally delayed two-year-old referred for treatment because he was extremely "shut down," distrustful of new adults, and a poor eater. During his first two sessions, he was so upset at being intruded upon by a stranger that he cried inconsolably. Recognizing that he was extremely sensitive to sounds, and that this was keeping him in a state of hyperarousal, his therapist, Madelyn, changed her approach to accommodate to his need for less stimulation. She did a full session in slow motion and without sound. She silently rubbed lotion on Tom's feet with slow, firm strokes; she gently blew bubbles for him to pop; and she rocked him with a very quiet rhythm. During this session, Tom stopped crying, his body relaxed and his level of comfort increased dramatically.

It took only this one quiet session to calm Tom's panic and to allow him to begin to respond to the playful activities Madelyn presented. During the next session, Madelyn returned to her normal pattern of interaction; she talked, and she resumed her normal speed of movement. Tom showed no signs of distress and was very responsive.

Using Activities that Organize the Child's Sensory System

Theraplay's active physical involvement with children lends itself particularly well to the adaptation of the techniques developed by Jean

Ayers (1979) and Patricia Wilbarger (1984) for overcoming children's sensory integration problems.[3] We adapt Wilbarger's sensory diet activities that organize a child's sensory functioning, such as deep pressure, firm touch, rhythmic rocking, and jumping, in ways that increase the interpersonal, interactive nature of the activities and that add playfulness and fun.

TOUCH. Throughout this book we emphasize the importance of touch in the development of all young children. Since many children with sensory integration problems are hypersensitive to touch, they often lack important touch experiences. It is therefore crucial to find ways of providing touch that the child can tolerate.

Many children find light touch very distressing whereas they accept and are calmed by firm touch. We have adapted the idea of firm touch to a lotion game. With lotion on your hands, hold the child's arm (or hand or foot) firmly and pull toward yourself, saying, "Slippery, slippery, slip." As the child slips out of your hands you can exaggerate your backward fall, thus adding an element of surprise and play to the activity. For most children this surprise is engaging and leads to their asking for more. For the easily startled child, your backward fall must be very slow and gentle.

DEEP PRESSURE. Touch experiences should also include hugging and deep pressure. Temple Grandin reports that as a young child with autism, she both longed for and feared such contact (Sacks, 1994). She invented a squeeze machine that would provide the deep pressure she needed to calm her constant state of arousal. In the following example, you will see how Larry's therapist met Larry's need for deep pressure.

THERAPLAY IN PRACTICE: *Providing Deep Pressure for a Child with Severe Sensory Integration Problems.* Larry's parents brought him for treatment because they were concerned about his speech and language delays and his severe temper tantrums. During the MIM, Larry refused to engage in any of the tasks. Frustrated by their efforts to engage him, he threw himself down on the mat in the treatment room. Finding the mat too soft, he moved to the floor to bang his head harder. His eye contact was very poor but he used it appropriately, along with pointing, to show that he wanted to leave the room. Larry showed severe tactile defensiveness; he was unable to tolerate lotion on his hands or allow his parents to touch or stroke him.

Because he seemed so very fragile, we changed our usual practice of beginning treatment with the parent out of the room. We had his mother hold him on her lap for the first session. But this only seemed to make matters worse. Larry's sensitive nervous system prevented him from tolerating the sensory impact even of sitting on his mother's lap. He became so hyper-aroused that he was in a panic state. But when his therapist, Judy, tucked him firmly in a beanbag chair, thus providing consistent firm pressure all around his body, Larry became calm. The vestibular stimulation of rocking him back and forth to the tune of "Row, Row, Row Your Boat" also was calming. For several sessions, Larry continued to be easily upset, but Judy now knew what would calm him. When calmer, Larry was able to respond to the simple back-and-forth games that Judy played with him, such as popping a bubble with his finger or blowing a cotton ball off her nose.

In his fifth week, Larry stopped crying entirely. He now seemed able to trust Judy and no longer had to avoid her efforts to engage him. Life at home also was going more smoothly as his parents incorporated some of our suggestions for accommodating to his sensory needs and managing his behavior.

Other ways of providing calming deep pressure include pressing down firmly on the child's shoulders (the child must be sitting up straight before you do this) after an exciting activity, placing a heavy pillow on the child's tummy and asking him to knock it off by just using his tummy (if he is successful, you can add more pillows), and rolling the child tightly in a soft (not prickly) blanket. He then can be placed in his mother's arms for rocking or feeding.

RHYTHMIC ROCKING. As we saw with Larry, rhythmic rocking is also very organizing and calming for some children. When rocking a child, adjust your pace to the level that seems the most comforting; some children need faster or slower tempos. If you have access to a swing (though most Theraplay rooms do not), you can swing the child back and forth as you face him, making sure to have some playful contact or impact as he meets you; for example, pushing him by his feet, peeking at him, or touching his hands.

Swinging or rocking a child in a blanket has a surprisingly calming effect on children of all ages and all levels of sensitivity and activity.

You will need at least two adults (four with a larger child). Have the child lie on the blanket and each adult takes hold of the corners of the blanket firmly. It is best to have the child's parents in a position to see their child's face. Singing a lullaby or song about the child adds to the pleasure of this comforting experience.

VIGOROUS JUMPING. Many children with sensory integration problems seek opportunities for jumping up and down, sometimes at the expense of the family furniture and beds. You can incorporate this beneficial activity into your sessions by holding the child's hands and jumping up and down together while the child stands on a stack of pillows or a sofa. If you see many children who need to jump, you may want to get a small, safe trampoline. (You also can suggest to parents that they get a trampoline to use at home.) You should structure a jumping activity by doing it rhythmically, for example, by jumping to a special jumping song.

The familiar baby game of "This Is the Way the Baby Rides" is also useful. Have the child sit on your knees facing you and bounce her up and down to the rhythm of "This is the way the baby [lady, gentleman, farmer] rides, a gallop a trot, a gallop a trot." The lady, the gentleman, and the farmer ride with increasing vigor. Of course you must pace your vigor to the child's tolerance for stimulation and excitement, and you will want to return to the more gentle level in order to finish in a calm state.

SENSORY DIET. Finally, the sensory diet techniques recommended by Patricia Wilbarger can be adapted for Theraplay sessions. The technique, as recommended by Wilbarger, involves using a specialized scrub brush (which can be purchased from an occupational therapy resource)[4] and vigorously brushing the child's arms, legs, and back, followed by "joint compression," which involves applying pressure to each joint: ankles, knees, shoulders, wrists, and elbows. To apply these techniques properly you should be trained specifically in how to do them. Parents are trained to do this at home for several minutes several times a day. If a child cannot tolerate the brushing, joint compression on its own can be very useful. Following this experience, children appear much more focused and can attend and respond better. The following example shows the effective use of brushing and other sensory diet experiences with a three-year-old child with severe sensory integration problems.

THERAPLAY IN PRACTICE: *Adapting Sensory Integration Techniques.* Maria was a child with severe sensory integration and motor planning difficulties. Easily overwhelmed, she often withdrew to her room to jump on her bed. When faced with unfamiliar demands she would space out. Recognizing her need for stimulation that would organize her sensory system, Michael, her Theraplay therapist, incorporated sensory diet techniques in his Theraplay treatment in ways that were very helpful to Maria. Michael used brushing as part of the greeting checkup for each session. The following is a sample session:

MICHAEL: (accompanying his actions with a warm sing-song voice, he identifies each body part as he brushes it) Hi Maria, let's see what you brought with you today. There's your leg, leg, leg, leg, leg. And your foot, foot, foot, foot, foot. (When he finishes brushing her leg and her foot, he grasps her foot in his right hand and, holding her lower leg in his other hand, he firmly presses the foot upward toward the leg several times. He does this for each joint of her legs and arms.)

MARIA: (looks directly at her foot as if interested, then at Michael, and grins)

MICHAEL: You look good today. Oh, you brought your hands too. (brushes palm vigorously) I found your fingers, one, two, three, four, and your thumb!

MARIA: (makes a singing noise almost matching Michael's sing-song tone)

Following this activity, which included joint compression with arms and legs, Maria was much more focused and relaxed than when she first arrived. Michael included a number of sensory experiences in the session. For example, he had Maria make hand prints in play-doh, pressing each of Maria's fingers firmly into the resistant ball of play-doh and then showing the print to Maria. They jumped up and down together, to the accompaniment of the nursery rhyme "Humpty Dumpty." So that she could see his face as they jumped, Michael placed Maria on the couch. When "Humpty Dumpty had a great fall," he helped Maria fall into his arms for a great firm hug as he put her "all back together again."

Although many children with sensory sensitivities could not tolerate the level of stimulation in the next activity, it was the one that Maria loved best. Michael blew up a balloon and let the air rush out against her cheeks, her feet, her hands, and her hair. She even pulled up her shirt to let it blow against her tummy. She waited excitedly to see where the air would swoosh next; looking directly at Michael and giggling with delight each time. Her intense focus and excited anticipation was in marked contrast to her behavior before Theraplay treatment began.

Controlling the Child's Excitement and Activity Level

The goal in controlling the child's excitement and activity level is to help the child learn to regulate patterns of excitement and calm. Being either over- or under-aroused interferes with the child's ability to focus on what is happening, to engage in social interaction, and to learn.

Repeated cycles of arousal and calming are part of the everyday experience of most infants. The experience of becoming excited, agitated, or upset, followed by the helpful intervention of a parent who feeds, soothes, and calms him, enables the child later on to provide calming experiences for himself (though no one gets beyond needing help during times of stress).

Children who have difficulty modulating their response to stimulation or are difficult to soothe, and children in orphanages who have no one to provide the external help, do not experience this comforting pattern. As a result, they experience their world as stressful. They experience others as being of no use in reducing stress. They usually conclude that it is up to themselves to take charge of stress reduction. They may reduce stress by insisting that everything remain the same, by rocking and using other self-stimulating techniques, by withdrawing and shutting out stimulation, or by maintaining a high level of activity in order to manage their excitement. Hyperactive children tend to escalate until they crash—that is, until they have a temper tantrum.

Theraplay provides a second opportunity for the child to experience the help of parents and other adults in managing cycles of arousal, excitement, and calming. Theraplay provides the external regulation, just as a parent does with an infant, until the child is able to internalize the experience of becoming excited and then calming down without having to escalate out of control. Once children are able to accept the external control of other adults, it is possible to teach them specific techniques for managing excitement. We describe these techniques in Chapter Nine.

PLANNING THE SEQUENCE WITHIN THE SESSION. The basic principle of planning sessions to provide cycles of excitement and calm, described in Chapter Three, is especially important for children who are unable to monitor their own levels of excitement. With the easily overstimulated child, you should use fewer exciting activities; you must use some, however, so that the child has the experience of becoming excited and then calmed. As we describe when we discuss the older hyperactive child, you will want to begin with some activities that match his high level of excitement in order to engage him and begin to bring him down into a calmer state. If at any time an activity seems to be getting out of hand, you should stop it and switch to a more calming activity.

USING GAMES THAT REGULATE ACTIVITY LEVEL. Many activities can be adapted so that they provide these cycles of excitement and calm. Some games have this built in, such as motor boat. Standing and holding hands, move around in a circle to the chant, "Motor boat, motor boat, goes so slow . . . so fast . . . step on the gas," and then return to the slow pace. Many baby games, such as "This Is the Way the Baby Rides," use built-in changes in rhythm. The peanut butter and jelly game described earlier provides modulation in sound rather than activity as the child and therapist match each other's level of intensity in whispering or shouting.

You can add cyclic tempo changes to other games such as "Row, Row, Row Your Boat" as you hold hands and rock back and forth. The stack of hands game, which can easily become too exciting as children rush to pull their hands out of the stack, can be used as a modulating activity by changing the pace from fast to slow. "Let's see how very slowly we can do it. Let's do it from the top down."

Slow-motion follow-the-leader can give the hyperactive child an experience of moving more slowly and matching his movements to yours, and it also can include variations in tempo. Facing the child, ask him to imitate everything you do. Then very slowly move your arms, your head, your eyes, and so forth while the child concentrates on matching your speed exactly.

Popping bubbles and throwing cotton balls or marshmallows or crushed newspaper balls likewise can be done in a calm, controlled manner ("See whether you can hit my shoulder with the newspaper ball—ready, get set, go") or in an exciting free-for-all manner ("OK, let's have a snowball fight! See how many cotton balls end up on your side of the room!"). For the underresponsive child or the child who needs to be livened up, the free-for-all approach would be your first choice. For the impulsive, hyperactive child, the more controlled approach would be best. Of course, you can combine the two, making cycles of more controlled and more free activities. You should stop the free-for-all before it gets out of control by saying, for example, "Now let's see whether you can hit this target."

USING CALMING ACTIVITIES. We already have described many nurturing activities that are calming to a child. Rocking, swinging in a blanket, feeding (using a baby bottle while being held in Mother's arms is very calming and provides exactly the experience that many of these children have lacked), rubbing backs, and massaging feet and hands with lotion are soothing activities for most children. Rather than doing full massage within a session (it could easily fill a whole session and is best done with the child's clothes off), we recommend that parents of young children with regulatory problems learn infant massage techniques and use them regularly. This is especially important for children adopted from orphanages where they have had very little physical touch. The massage should be done facing the child and accompanied with soothing personalized talk about the child: "I'm rubbing your soft, warm leg" and "You have such rosy cheeks."

REVIEWING THE QUESTION OF USING MEDICATION. When we first began treating hyperactive children with Theraplay, if the child was on medication we asked that the child's physician discontinue it for the duration of treatment. We did this both because we wanted to be able to deal with the full range of the child's behavior and because we wanted the child to be alert and responsive. In addition, we were concerned then, as we are today, that too many children were being overmedicated. Since that time there has been a tremendous increase in the number of children diagnosed as ADHD and given medication. While medical experts agree that methylphenidate (Ritalin) does help a small percentage of children, there is concern that it is being greatly overprescribed as a panacea for behavior problems (Haslip, 1996). Still, a given child may need medication to control attentional and behavioral problems at school, and in that case we no longer insist that he be off medication entirely.

A greater understanding of the neurobiological bases of the stress response and of post-traumatic stress disorder (PTSD) has led to experiments in the use of medications for calming children who seem to be constantly in a hyperaroused state. These include children with autism[5] as well as children who are suffering from PTSD. In our limited experience with children whose hypersensitivity and hyperactivity stem from early traumatic experiences, carefully monitored medication has helped lower their anxiety level and thus has made them more open to treatment and developing a relationship with their parents.

Until we know more about the long-term effects of these new medications, we continue to be very cautious about their use. Whether the child is on medication or not, we find that a great deal can be done to calm and regulate children's behavior through the Theraplay techniques that we have described.

Increasing the Child's Capacity for Self-Control

Activities that cycle from fast to slow and those that calm the child provide experiences that lead to greater self-control. The following activities and techniques work specifically on the issues of impulse control, following rules, and thinking about what you are doing.

WAITING FOR THE SIGNAL. The technique of waiting for a signal, which we describe throughout the book, is particularly useful for impulsive, hyperactive children. It slows them down, gives them practice at thinking and waiting before plunging in, and thus develops their self-control. As the child gets more comfortable with this idea you can vary the signals by using silly or surprising words—"watermelon," "dinosaur," or any other unlikely word—so that the child enjoys the wait for the special signal. Or you can choose a number—"When I say three!"—and then count, "One, fifteen, four, three!" These variations add playfulness and increase the attention the child must pay as she waits for the signal. To foster more eye contact you can use visual signals: "When I blink my eye" or "wiggle my nose" or "stick out my tongue." The use of signals gives the child a routine and helps him predict what will happen next. With very young or developmentally delayed children, use the simple, "Ready, get set, go!"

"Red light, green light" is another way of helping the child to practice following the rules and starting and stopping on command. Ask the child to walk or hop or move her arms at certain times, with "green light" meaning "go" and "red light" meaning "stop." With very young children, saying "go" and "stop" may be more easily understood. Make sure that with a very active child, you do not use an activity that allows her to be out of physical contact with you until you have confidence that she will not run away.

"Mother, may I?" and "Simon says" also can be used to practice paying attention to directions and following them. For young children we eliminate the tricky part of these games (remembering to say "Mother, may I?" or making sure that the leader has said "Simon says"). For the older child, though, the element of trickiness is an added incentive.

SMOOTHING OUT IMPULSIVITY. Another technique that is useful is having the child repeat an action that was too impulsive or that caused an accident. For example, if a child impulsively throws himself down when it is time to sit, you can say, "Whoops, that was dangerous. Let's try that in a safer way." Then you can hold the child's hands and sit down together when you say "Go." It is best with an impulsive child that you prevent "accidents" by anticipating them and providing a controlled way of doing the activity. But since you cannot always anticipate it, once the impulsive activity has occurred you can respond in the above manner.

Increasing the Child's Attention Span

The impulsive child often has a very short attention span. He is up and ready for a new activity before you have finished the first. With such a child, you need to repeat activities "One more time" and plan variations that extend the activity a little longer: "Pop the bubble with your finger. Now do it with your toe. I'll bet you can do it with your shoulder," or "That was so nice and quiet the way you did that tiptoeing. Now do it one more time." The appropriate length of time to stay with an activity depends on the child's age, as well as on his tolerance for the activity. You will learn with each child what his tolerance level is and how you can extend it just the little bit that keeps him interested without stretching beyond his endurance.

Increasing the Child's Tolerance for Stimuli

Once you have found the level of stimulation that a particular child can tolerate, your goal should be to help him extend his tolerance gradually. This involves techniques that actually change the child's ability to handle stimulation (such as the adaptations of occupational therapy techniques we describe next) as well as help the child see that he can in fact tolerate a higher level of stimulation. Many very sensitive children, having been overwhelmed as infants by sensory stimuli in one modality or another, avoid such stimuli long after their immature nervous systems have developed to a point where they no longer need to be so avoidant. Thus part of your job is to find ways to help the child risk learning from experience that sensory stimuli are no longer so painful. Introducing sensory experience in small doses or in playful ways can help a child come to tolerate a wider range of experience.

We saw that adapting the level of stimulation (remaining silent and slowing down) made it possible for Tom to tolerate both sound and normal activity level in the very next session. One father of a seven-year-old who was oversensitive to sound provided earplugs for his son to wear to his first baseball game. With the plugs in place and with his hands over his ears for good measure, he was able to control the amount of noise that got through to him and to enjoy the game thoroughly. We advise parents to be aware of their child's needs and to avoid taking them into situations that are overwhelming to them until they have achieved some level of tolerance and control.

So far we have dealt with the general issues and specific techniques of how Theraplay can be adapted for children with regulatory and sensory integration problems. Many techniques are applicable to the full range of sensory and regulatory problems, including those associated with the autistic spectrum disorders, which we discuss in the next chapter. We turn now to the special treatment issues that apply to working with the underresponsive child and the hyperactive child.

UNDERSTANDING THE TREATMENT NEEDS OF THE UNDERRESPONSIVE, WITHDRAWN CHILD

For the child who is too quiet, too self-controlled, and too unresponsive, your goal should be to increase spontaneity, liveliness, and the level of activity. Fun, delightful surprises and stimulating activities should be offered to entice her out of her passivity. For example, encourage the use of fingerpaints or chocolate pudding pictures that cover a whole piece of paper, rather than make one thumb print right in the center of the page (as you would with an impulsive child who lacks self-control). If the child easily gets stuck on one repetitive activity, you should move quickly and with surprise to new activities.

The following example illustrates successful Theraplay treatment with a withdrawn child.

THERAPLAY IN PRACTICE: *A Shy, Selectively Mute Child.* Jessica, three and a half, had attended an inner-city day-care center for a week. During that time she did not speak to her teachers at all, though her mother reported that Jessica talked freely at home. She was so shy about speaking that she occasionally wet her pants rather than ask for help. Her teachers were concerned about her silence as well as about her relationship with her mother, Ms. J., who had told them that Jessica was very difficult at home, kicking and screaming when she was upset. Because of their concerns, they referred her for Theraplay treatment. As part of the initial assessment, Jessica was observed in her classroom during her first week in school. A beautiful, fair-haired, meticulously dressed child, Jessica stood on the sidelines observing the other children for a long time. When another child asked her to play, Jessica silently complied.

Jessica seemed to be a child with a slow-to-warm-up temperament (Thomas and Chess, 1977) and a significant need to take charge as a way of managing her anxiety about new things. She maintained control in her new day-care setting by being extremely withholding, as evidenced in her refusal to talk with the teachers. To give her a chance to warm up on her own, a further observation was scheduled for six weeks later.

By that time Jessica still was not talking at school, so the Theraplay therapist, Madelyn, met with Jessica's mother to address her concerns, obtain background history, and discuss the possibility of the two of them participating in Theraplay treatment. From the intake interview it was learned that during her pregnancy with Jessica, Ms. J. had experienced considerable stress due to lack of money and poor housing arrangements but had managed to get the kind of medical care she needed. Toward the end of the pregnancy she had moved in with her mother in order to be sure that she had support in taking care of her baby. While Ms. J. worked, Ms. J.'s mother took care of Jessica until Jessica entered the day-care program. They had continued to live with Jessica's grandmother.

Ms. J. reported that she, like Jessica, is very shy and believes that shyness is a family trait on her father's side. Because she had been depressed as a teenager, she wondered whether Jessica might be depressed as well.

Because her own mother was a forceful and self-assured person, Ms. J. often felt inadequate and uncertain about her parenting skills. In the MIM, however, we observed a very loving, devoted, sensitive mother with excellent parenting skills. Jessica was anxiously watchful but talked freely with her mother; they shared a pleasant, back-and-forth reciprocity. Occasionally Jessica tried to take charge of the interaction, at times taking over the parent role. For example, she insisted on being the first to put lotion on her mother and on taking good care of her.

Based on these observations we developed a strategy designed to help Jessica relax and become less vigilant and to foster spontaneity and active physical and verbal expression. Our goal for her mother was to help her take charge more assertively so that Jessica would feel that her mother provides both safety and calm nurturance. We soon discovered that with a little support, Ms. J could be comfortable taking charge of the care of her daughter rather than deferring to Jessica's grandmother.

Jessica's treatment required only four sessions. With her mother nearby talking to the interpreting therapist, Jessica's anxiety and watchfulness were easily overcome. In fact, she showed no discomfort in relating to her therapist. By the second session she had become fully engaged and had talked freely with Madelyn during the playful activities. They played many active games such as ring-around-the-rosy, push-me-over, and newspaper-punch. She particularly enjoyed peanut butter and jelly. Madelyn deliberately made silly mistakes in order to help Jessica relax her internal demands for perfect behavior. Nurturing activities, such as feeding, rocking, and singing were included in each session, so that she could experience the calming effect of being gently soothed by her mother.

While Ms. J. observed the first part of each session, she and the interpreting therapist talked about how the activities contributed to our goals for her daughter (to overcome her fear of new situations, become more lively and engaged, and allow others to calm and care for her), as well as about how she could continue these activities at home.

In preparation for her taking charge of some of the activities (keeping a balloon in the air using arms, shoulders, and feet, but not hands; making chocolate-pudding handprints; rocking Jessica while singing a lullaby), we conducted a role-playing session with Ms. J. In the process of playing the child role, she received some much-needed nurturing herself. She also practiced how to provide it for her daughter. Throughout, we strongly supported her confidence in her ability to take charge of Jessica's care in order to counter her fear of being a less adequate parent than her mother.

By the end of the four sessions, Jessica was talking freely and was able to carry this sense of trust back with her to school. She talked openly to her teachers and to the other children. We later learned that she became a leader in her day-care classroom. She could have fun and even occasionally get messy.

Jessica is thus an example of a shy, slow-to-warm-up child who, faced with a new and to her overwhelming situation, had "frozen" and become stuck in a pattern of anxious withholding. It would have been easy to assume, as her mother had, that Jessica was depressed and then to treat her with medication or long-term nondirective or psychoanalytic therapy. But in order to move forward, Jessica did not need to deal with complicated family dynamics and underlying neurotic conflicts. What Jessica needed was to be enticed into playful, nonthreatening interaction with a new person (her Theraplay therapist), to be nurtured and soothed, and to be given opportunities to engage in activities with no worry about doing things "right" or about keeping clean and proper.

INCORPORATING THE THERAPLAY DIMENSIONS IN TREATING THE HYPERACTIVE CHILD

As we have noted, children with ADHD are impulsive, easily overstimulated, hyperactive, and aggressive. They have a short attention span and often seem to be running away from engagement. Traditional play therapy, using toys or games or talk, often does not work for such children. Their restlessness and inner tension make them take to their feet and run just as the well-meaning therapist is formulating his impressions. Being interactive and physical, the Theraplay therapist can keep up with the active child, find ways to help the child modulate the high activity level, and, in addition, respond to the child's underlying needs for nurture and calming.

The obvious need of the child diagnosed with ADHD is not for stimulation and excitement but rather for soothing and calming. He has two overriding needs in this regard. First, he needs structure, to know that his world is well defined and that there are bounds beyond which he may not venture. Second, he needs regressive, indulgent nurturing. His tough-guy swagger and his provocative talk are often found to conceal the longings of a needy infant. Rather than challenging these children to grow up, you should nurture and calm the child and respond to his regressive, infantile needs.

Structuring

Structuring should be part of every session with a hyperactive child. From the very beginning, for example, you must keep the child so physically close that an observer might say that the two of you are attached to one another with glue. When you are not holding the child's hand or having an arm around her shoulder, you could be patting her back or encircling her waist. Only after you are sure she will not run, should you release your hold. Rather than as a response to the child's problem behaviors, your contact should be ever-present in order to prevent such problems. Your rule should be to anticipate rather than react to what the child does.

Engaging

In what appears to be an all-out effort to avoid intimacy and to master all unknowns, the hyperactive child is ever on the go, always hitting, throwing, pushing, and running. Before she can be coaxed into a therapeutic relationship with you, she must somehow be "caught," calmed, and attended to. Since such a child will take every opportunity to escape, the obvious first step is "catching" her.

Once you have "caught" her, Theraplay may take any one of a variety of forms. You can label as positive some behavior that heretofore was labeled as bad (for example, "The way you throw those blocks! My gosh, you *are* good at throwing! Here's a Nerf ball. Bet you can't throw this one way over here at my hand!" or "What a good spitter you are! Can you spit real hard right at this Kleenex here?"). Of course, you should never permit or encourage behavior that is genuinely antisocial, like hitting ("No, I can't let you hit me") or otherwise hurting either persons or property. You often present your biggest surprise simply by being the first person in the child's world who does not label her actions as clumsy, inept, bad, messy, or rude and who does not imply that the child herself is a failure.

Although your goal is to calm the overactive child, you may need, in the early stages, to do some lively challenging activities in order to keep up with and get through to her, or sometimes simply to "wear her out" a bit. You may find it useful to wrestle, run, or roughhouse with her, or to spin, swing, or physically challenge her. Even these activities are monitored carefully to determine just how excited she can get before needing help to calm down. Having thereby gotten through to her, earned her interest, and disarmed her suspicions, it is far easier to begin the more difficult job of nurturing, for she will resist this next step with a vengeance.

Nurturing

Knowing that, for all his protest, nurturing is exactly what the hyperactive child—particularly the aggressive child—secretly desires, you must insist on cuddling, holding, comforting, rocking, singing to, and feeding him. This account of Tough Sam, a four-year-old, tells the story.

THERAPLAY IN PRACTICE: *Nurturing a Tough Guy.* Sam was referred for help by his Head Start teacher, the most recent in a string of teachers exhausted by his never-ceasing movement and outlaw actions. When he was not racing around the room on his own, knocking over garbage cans, toppling tables, and scattering toys, he was hitting other children, kicking adults, and cursing wildly. Matters appeared to become even worse with the arrival of the Theraplay therapist. Aware that she had come to attend particularly to him, Sam went into overdrive.

She responded to his attempts to push over the fish tank by inserting herself between it and Sam. "You a motherf—!" he screamed at her. "I am?" she asked. "How does a motherf— walk? Does it walk like this? Or maybe like this?" "Naw!" he answered. "You dumb!" But, momentarily caught off-guard, he had stopped in his tracks and was studying this strange lady who confronted action with action and was not frightened by his apparent power.

A few sessions later, in his chronic wandering he swaggered around the room upending chairs, announcing, "I the only one growed around here. I fifteen years old!" She intervened to make him set the chairs aright, and in the process she held him. He struggled to free himself, shouting obscenities as she half carried, half dragged him off to a chair in a secluded corner of the classroom. There she seated herself, placed the struggling Sammy in her lap, and began to sing a lullaby as she rocked him. After a while, his curses changed to tears, and soon he was quiet, listening to her sing. When she had finished her song and stopped rocking, Sam raised himself from her lap, looked at her threateningly, and thundered, "Goddammit! You sing that again! You hear me? You better sing that song again!" Not yet ready to give up his tough-guy stance, Sam demanded what she was very ready to give—a repetition of the song and an ongoing offer of the nurturing experience he should have had all along. Over the next few sessions, Sam slowly let down his guard and began to accept rather than demand the closeness he so obviously needed.

Challenging

Only after nurturing has been well accepted and the relationship has become truly meaningful can you begin to work on issues related to a child's impulsivity, hypersensitivity to stimuli, and inability to accept structure. Not every child needs to work on this as explicitly as Clem did in the example below, but for many hyperactive children it is an essential stage in treatment.

THERAPLAY IN PRACTICE: Helping the ADHD Child Accept Structure and Manage His Impulsivity. Eight-and-a-half-year-old Clem was referred for Theraplay treatment by his neurologist. In addition to his seizure disorder (which was well controlled by Dilantin), Clem was extremely active both verbally and motorically and was hypersensitive to many kinds of stimulation, particularly to touch and vestibular imbalance. In line with Theraplay policy at the time, it was requested that Clem's Ritalin be discontinued before treatment would begin. The Dilantin, of course, was not altered.

In the early sessions Clem talked nonstop and attempted to direct all activities. When his therapist, Roger, tried to feed him, he resisted at first, then welcomed being held and fed juice from a baby bottle. Once he was able to relax and accept Roger's caretaking, he was ready to be challenged even more explicitly to accept Roger's structure, begin to control his own impulsive behavior, and tolerate more of the kinds of stimulation that he had learned to fear. Because Clem had great difficulty handling his body in space, it was very hard for him to enjoy the fun of being lifted up in the air or swung around. To help him learn to tolerate such experiences, his therapist was holding Clem up in his arms like an airplane, moving him gently and slowly around.

ROGER: I'm going to turn you around just like this.

CLEM: (whimpers)

ROGER: I've got you . . . and you're going to go down . . . I've got you just like this. . . . You did it.

CLEM: I'm scared.

ROGER: Everything's OK. I'll take good care of you.

CLEM: It's all over.

ROGER: It's not all over. But I'm going to take good care of you. I'm going to lay you down just like that. I want you to make that mouth so lazy that it can't say a word.

CLEM: (laughs nervously)

ROGER: Lazy mouths don't laugh, and they don't talk. Nice and soft (stroking mouth and cheeks) and this one (checking hand to make it floppy). Wait! That's a little tight. Make it loose.

CLEM: (talking)

ROGER: Oops! Your mouth is forgetting. You know what? When you laugh, it makes your whole body tight. I'll try not to tickle you. Wait! Your mouth is still wiggling. Your hair is soft, your mouth is soft, your cheeks are soft, your nose is soft. I think you're ready. I really think you are. Let me see. Let me see what you brought today. Your hair's getting longer.

CLEM: (lies still)

[Clem has survived the very difficult challenge of having his therapist hold him up in the air. As he relaxes, his therapist quietly counts his fingers and toes as a way of soothing him. He is now ready for a more active game. In this example his therapist helps him practice "one more time" in order to smooth out an impulsive movement.]

ROGER: Now we're going to see if we can pull each other up. All the way up on our feet. There we go. Sit up. You're going to pull me up.

CLEM: I can't.

ROGER: Yes, you can.

CLEM: (jerks therapist up clumsily)

ROGER: Wait a minute. That was almost dangerous! You pulled too hard. You could have fallen. We'll do it one more time.

CLEM: (repeats action slowly, deliberately)

[Since Clem has done well with this activity, his therapist proceeds with another challenge to Clem's fear of being up in the air]

ROGER: You did it just right that time. Good. Now, stand up real tall. Nice and straight. Put your feet like that. Make your arms real straight and make your elbows stiff. I'm going to pick you up by your elbows just this high.

CLEM: No!

ROGER: Make 'em real straight and stiff.

CLEM: Please don't.

ROGER: Clem, you're all right. Clem, I'm going to take care of you. Make your elbows stiff as you can. You've got to make your elbows stiff. Here we go. Now the other one.

CLEM: (whimpers) I don't like to be picked up.

ROGER: (picks him up) See? You're all right. I'm taking care of you. They're not stiff yet. *You* can do it. There you go. (lifts him higher)

CLEM: (enjoys being up)

ROGER: See? That was just right. Now we're going to sit on the floor. Cross your feet like mine.

CLEM: My stomach hurts.

ROGER: Come on and sit and you'll be all right. I think your stomach hurts because you got scared.

CLEM: Yeah.

ROGER: Well, I'm going to take good care of you. Come on. Lean back against the pillow now. I can't see your eyes. Like this. I'm going to make your tummy feel better. I'm going to fan it with this pillow.

CLEM: That feels so cool.

ROGER: Does it feel good?

CLEM: Yeah.

ROGER: You can tell me it feels good.

CLEM: It feels good.

Theraplay was then expanded to include Clem's father. The father was selected for this session rather than the mother because, although he had already been involved in some sessions, he was still passive and ambiguous in relating to Clem.

ROGER: I'm going to call Dad in to let him help us. Hey, Dad!

DAD: (enters, helps Clem up from lying position by putting his toes to Clem's and holding his hands to pull him up, as he had seen Roger do)

CLEM: (begins to chatter)

ROGER: Whoop, whoop, whoop. (touches Clem's mouth to remind him not to talk) There, we're going to put him right up on his feet, Dad. Look at that. He did it just right. One more time, Daddy.

CLEM: (looks worried)

ROGER: I'm right here. Make your body stiff. Good for you!

CLEM: (distractedly looking away and chattering)

ROGER: Clem is not listening. . . . That's better. Let's play "Father may I?" Dad, I want you to tell us one thing to do, and we'll do it just right. Clem and I will stand over here.

DAD: Clem, are you ready? I want you to skip one time.

ROGER: Try again, Dad. Make it clearer yet.

DAD: I want you to skip toward me one time. Are you ready, son? Are you ready?

CLEM: Yeah. (skips)

DAD: I want you to skip twice.

CLEM: (skips three times)

DAD: Nope, nope, nope.

ROGER: Nope, that wasn't two skips.

DAD: I want you to do it nice.

ROGER: I don't think "nice" means anything, Daddy.

DAD: I want you to skip all the way to Daddy.

CLEM: (skips to Daddy)

ROGER: OK. I want you to sit right next to Daddy. We'll sing our song. Remember our song?

CLEM: Yep.

ROGER: Twinkle, twinkle, little star. (one arm around Clem, the other on father's shoulder; Father has hand on Clem's leg) That wasn't clear enough. OK. Now let's see if we can do it over. (they repeat the song) That was very good. Clem, lie down on these pillows. Now, Dad, can you make him all soft and floppy? And I'll put his shoes on. His toes are still wiggly. Ah, even his cheeks are floppy, now. That's good.

CLEM: (chatters)

ROGER: He might need your hand on his mouth to remind him to stop chattering.

DAD: (does so)

ROGER: You can do it gently. There we go. He's hiding that lip . . . there we go. That's the best I've seen all day. That's perfect. There we go, just like that. That's fine, Daddy. That's fine. (Clem laughs) Nope, nope . . . let's get him real quiet here. Tuck his shirt in. (Clem laughs) We have to be careful about tickles. (Clem is calm and quiet) There we go. Dad, you take Clem's hand in yours and then go quietly down the hall together. Quietly . . . quietly . . . quietly . . . (holding hands, father and son tiptoe from the Theraplay room).

In this chapter we see how Theraplay can be adapted to help children with sensory sensitivities or regulatory problems, including children with ADD and ADHD. In the next chapter we look at how these same principles can be applied to children with more extreme sensitivities and regulatory problems, in particular children with autism and pervasive developmental disorders.

Notes

1. Some of these children also have specific learning disabilities. Formerly the term *minimal brain dysfunction* was used to identify the distractible, hyperactive child with learning problems.

2. Sensory Integration International, 1602 Cabrillo Ave., P.O. Box 9013, Torrance, CA 90501, will provide information about qualified occupational therapists certified in sensory integrative treatment throughout the United States. Nonmembers are charged a small fee for the service.

3. See also Ann Jernberg's (1981) paper on sensory integration and Theraplay.

4. PDP Products, 12015 N. July Avenue, Hugo, Minnesota 55038, has a variety of equipment designed for sensory integrative treatment, including surgical brushes.

5. Temple Grandin (1995, p. 77) discusses the use of antidepressant medication for controlling anxiety associated with sensory sensitivities of people with autism. "My sensory sensitivities became much less bothersome after I started taking the antidepressant Tofranil. My senses are still easily overstimulated, but the medication calms down my reactions to stimuli."

CHAPTER SEVEN

Theraplay for Children with Autism and Pervasive Developmental Disorders

F or thirty years Theraplay has been successful in using playful activities to engage autistic children in healthy social interaction. From the beginning we assumed that a constitutionally based deficit was the source of the problem. We did not accept the then prevailing view that the difficulty originated primarily in parental coldness or unresponsiveness. Nor did we assume that these children are inherently unable to relate to others. Rather we assumed that their neurological problems, which generally include extreme forms of the sensory reactivity and processing difficulties that we discussed in Chapter Six,[1] interfere both with their ability to send out signals to which their parents can respond and with their ability to read social cues and to learn from experience. These children are unable to process experience or to be appropriately aware of others, and therefore they are cut off from the important developmental achievements that follow from awareness of others. They often miss the normal stages of emotional, cognitive, communicative, and even physical development so essential to developing a sense of their own personhood.[2]

Even the most experienced parents find it difficult to achieve engagement with such children. Theraplay helps parents find ways to engage their children in pleasurable social interaction. The earlier we do this the better. This is particularly important since the period from ages twelve- to twenty-four months, when many children with autism or pervasive developmental disorders (PDD) seem to withdraw, normally is a time of rapid learning of social skills such as reciprocal gesturing and understanding the "rules" of complex social interactions.[3]

UNDERSTANDING HOW THERAPLAY WORKS WITH CHILDREN WITH PDD

As we state in Chapter Six, we do not expect to "cure" the neurological problems, though early intervention and well-planned sensory integration therapy can make a significant difference. Theraplay's effectiveness lies in establishing or reinstating a warm, interactive relationship. As long as the child must withdraw in order to avoid feeling overwhelmed, as long as the child remains in her own world, she will continue to lack the important social learning that takes place during interactions with others. Early intervention that sets the child on the path of social give-and-take, of looking to others for models, and of being able to learn about how the world works, goes a long way toward helping the child lead a more normal life.[4]

By developing a warm, interactive relationship with children with PDD, we begin a process that leads to a change in the child's ability to understand and process her experience. Crucial to a good outcome is maintaining the child's focus, keeping the child engaged, and not letting the child drift or space out. Grandin (1995) emphasizes how important it was to her development that her mother found ways to teach her, engage her, and entice her out of her withdrawal.[5]

Although the problems have a constitutional base, the right kinds of playful engagement can make a difference, particularly in the child's ability to relate in a warm and caring way. We help parents understand what makes it so difficult for their child to be open to their advances. We help them accommodate to their child's special needs. We initiate kinds of interaction that will further engage their child and finally establish a joyful, interactive relationship. Theraplay is able to make a great difference in helping children become emotionally alive and spontaneous and capable of enjoying a warm, loving relationship.

Defining Pervasive Developmental Disorders

We use the general term *pervasive developmental disorders* to refer to the spectrum of disturbances in interpersonal relating, communication, and overall adaptation that include autistic disorder, Rett's disorder, Asperger's disorder, and pervasive developmental disorder not otherwise specified. Theraplay treatment issues are the same across this spectrum.[6]

The most common symptoms in young children are lack of speech or abnormal speech, lack of eye contact, a preference for being alone, frequent temper tantrums, oversensitivity to stimuli in a variety of modalities, rocking or other rhythmic stereotypic behavior, and inappropriate play with toys.

Adapting to the Child's Special Sensitivities

The paradoxical problem in treating these children is that healthy development requires the very kinds of physical contact and playful interaction that children with autism or PDD often find overwhelming and difficult to accept. The challenge for treatment, therefore, is to find the right level of impact that will engage the child without overwhelming him and leading him to withdraw further.

Early in our work we recognized the need to adapt the level of stimulation to the child's sensory threshold. Des Lauriers (1969) had emphasized the need to *increase* the level of stimulation in order to activate the unresponsive autistic child. But we soon discovered that many children, although they seem to be underresponsive, are in fact so overresponsive that they have shut down in order to protect themselves from becoming overwhelmed. Thus, more children with autism need a reduction in stimulus level rather than an increase. Nevertheless, all children with PDD need to be enticed into engagement.

We must assess each child's special sensitivities, find the kinds of stimulation that are tolerable to the child,[7] provide experiences that increase their tolerance for the stimulation, and above all persevere in finding ways to engage the child in warm, pleasurable, social interaction. In Chapter Six, we described in detail a number of techniques for addressing the needs of children with sensory and regulatory problems. Although children with PDD generally have more severe problems in these areas, the principles we describe for children with less severe problems apply here as well.

Understanding Why Theraplay Is Especially Useful

Theraplay is particularly helpful in the treatment of children with PDD, because it does not depend on their being able to respond to language and because we use a repertoire of playful, surprising, interactive games that engage even the most resistant child. Because of their difficulty accepting change, stimulation, and surprises, treatment must focus on helping these children become emotionally alive, spontaneous, and able to have fun. We cannot emphasize enough the importance of surprise and silliness in engaging children with PDD.

The inclusion of fun, cheer, empathy, and nurturing, in addition to the insistence on engagement, makes Theraplay a "natural" and a less formalized approach than the more strictly intrusive treatment programs. We have found that treatment methods that break a task down into small units and teach skills as separate steps often work against the goals of spontaneity and warm interaction. What should be a delight becomes a chore. Theraplay's engagement of the child makes it possible to develop empathic attunement with the child, which can lead to greater awareness of others.

The young child with PDD can learn to interpret the dialogic interchange, as a baby does with his mother. Theraplay concentrates on the precursors to cognition and to representational thinking—mutual attention and engagement—making it an ideal treatment for young children with relationship and communication difficulties.

Understanding What Affects Outcome

The outcome of treatment for children with PDD depends a great deal on the severity of the problems, the age at which treatment begins (the earlier the better), and the consistency and intensity of the impact on the child. The treatment of two of the children described in this chapter, Benjamin and Jeff, began relatively late (age five and seven, respectively). The good outcome of their treatment was supported by the fact that both boys were relatively high functioning and both had families and school staff who consistently and intensely interacted with them and engaged them. Some very young children whom we have seen have had less academically successful outcomes, not because their families and school staff have not been energetic and dedicated, but because the children's neurological problems are so overwhelming. Even with our less successful outcomes, however, all children have become more focused, more socially interactive, and much more warm, joyful, and engaging.

In the remainder of this chapter we explain how the dimensions of treatment must be adapted, describe special treatment issues, and note how the phases of treatment differ for children with PDD. We end with a full case study in order to follow the course of treatment.

ADAPTING THE THERAPLAY DIMENSIONS

The following descriptions and case studies describe how the four Theraplay dimensions can be adapted to meet the special needs of children with PDD.

Engaging

The most important dimension of Theraplay in working with children with PDD is engagement. Just as with the hyperactive child, however, you must first capture the child if you are to engage him. (We discuss containment in more detail in the next section.) Once you contain him, you must find a way to intrigue him and make him want to be with you. Because these children are so adept at shutting out unwanted stimuli, the Theraplay principle of making yourself a force to be reckoned with, to be taken into account rather than used for their own purposes, is particularly crucial. When everything goes smoothly according to what the child demands or is comfortable with, no new impact is made. Therefore, you should not let yourself become part of the child's magically controlled world. The goal is to provide maximum impact in combination with fun and spontaneity.

You must tailor your sessions to entice the child to join you as the infant he was when he first "tuned out" the world. You can rock and cuddle and sing to him. You can encourage him to study his mother's face or reach out to touch her cheeks. If he is comfortable on his back, you can lay him down on pillows and hover over him, mirroring his actions and encouraging him to look closely at your eyes. If he is not comfortable on his back (some children are not) you can prop him on pillows or in a bean-bag chair, as with Larry in Chapter Six. In all these ways, you invite him to join you in a relationship that you know ultimately will give him pleasure.

The concepts of "pleasure" and "enjoyment" are critical throughout. Although they certainly are not *always* present for a resistant child with PDD, these principles reinstate in the child-parent dyad the spontaneous warmth and expressive pleasure that has been missed since the child began to withdraw. It is through pleasurable interactions that the child is enticed into a relationship that includes the warmth and joy that should be part of any child's experience with his parents.

In the following example, you see Devon's Theraplay therapist play baby games not only in order to intrigue and engage him but also in order to begin an interactive dialogue.

THERAPLAY IN PRACTICE: *Enticing the Child into Engagement.* Devon, a three-year-old Head Start child, was referred for Theraplay treatment because he had no expressive language and had many "autistic-like" behaviors. He wandered aimlessly about the classroom, stopping occasionally to line up blocks in a row or to twirl the wheels of a toy car. If other children approached, he turned away, flipping his hands in anxious excitement. When his teacher tried to get his attention or to make eye contact, he averted his eyes.

During his first Theraplay session, Devon sits limply on his therapist's lap, his upper body turned away as if to avoid even acknowledging that she is there. His therapist, Margaret, holds his hands up in front of her face and suddenly peeks out from behind them, saying, "Peek-a-boo!" Intrigued, Devon turns suddenly toward her, looking directly at her eyes, and giggles with a deep appreciative laugh as she peeks out at him. Margaret laughs in turn and says, "You have such a great laugh." Devon, excited by the interaction, makes a lovely gurgling noise, which his therapist imitates. Soon this child, who up to this time has made no effort to communicate, begins exchanging playful sounds. He has begun to sample the pleasures of a new interactive experience.

Not all children with PDD respond as readily or as delightfully as Devon does. More often they are so overwhelmed by being close or by anything new that they actively resist even sitting on your lap.

The first Theraplay session with Matt, a young child with PDD, can serve as an example of how his therapist sought and found the right kinds of activities to soothe and comfort him while attempting to engage him and make him aware of her presence. As with most children with PDD, Matt's first response is to cry, struggle to escape, and resist in every way he can. Even though he is very angry, his focus is not on his therapist but on the general problem of getting away from an uncomfortable situation.

THERAPLAY IN PRACTICE: *Finding Ways to Engage the Child.* Matt is a three-year-old diagnosed with PDD and severe language delays. From the MIM, we learned that Matt has a short attention span, shuts people out readily, and is likely to resist new activities, but that he can be engaged by playful, physical surprises and can be soothed by lotion.

SESSION ONE. Lucille, Matt's therapist, greets him in the waiting room and carries him in her arms into the Theraplay room, saying, "Mom and Dad, you sit over there while we play." Surprised by her move, Matt begins to cry and struggle to escape her hold. To keep him safe, Lucille sits down and holds him so that he won't throw himself out of her arms.

While still holding him in her lap, Lucille quickly puts lotion on his hand. His attention captured, Matt stops crying and excitedly squeezes the lotion in his hands, shutting Lucille out. To bring his attention back, Lucille takes his slippery hands and rubs them against her cheeks. For a moment he looks attentively at her. But he quickly turns away, crying and arching his back to get out of her arms.

Lucille then props him on a large pillow, where he seems more comfortable than in her arms. Having taken off one shoe and sock, she lotions his foot with a firm stroke. Matt relaxes into the physical experience but seems unaware of Lucille until she holds his foot up close to her face. He then looks at her and smiles briefly.

LUCILLE: You like that. (leaning down to touch his nose with her nose) You have beautiful toes, and a beautiful nose.

MATT: (indicates that he wants the other shoe off)

LUCILLE: We'll wait till I finish lotioning your nice toes on this foot. *[In order to avoid falling into his obsessive need for symmetry and predictability, she postpones taking the second shoe off.]*

When he becomes restless, Lucille changes the activity, leaning over him and asking him to push her with his feet. Perhaps not understanding, or perhaps feeling that she is too close to him, Matt begins to fuss. But as soon as she falls backward with a great flourish (having helped him push her), he begins to giggle. It is a lovely, relaxed giggle, which invites a repetition of the activity. But after a second push, he turns away.

LUCILLE: One more, one more time. *[Trying to extend his attention span a bit.]*

MATT: (begins to fuss)

LUCILLE: (imitating his fussing tone) You don't like "One more time"!

With the final push, Lucille falls on her back and pulls Matt on his tummy up onto her knees. Although initially intrigued, he quickly becomes uncomfortable and tries to escape (with no regard for danger). In spite of his discomfort, Lucille does the trick quickly one more time in order to help Matt learn that he can tolerate the strange position and even eventually come to enjoy it. But it is too much for him in this first session.

MATT: (screeches)
LUCILLE: (with energy equal to his angry shouts) Oh, that made you so mad!

Following this challenge to his tolerance for unusual body postures and strange new experiences, Lucille turns to an activity she is sure he will enjoy, putting shaving cream on Matt's hands. Again in his excited squishing of it between his fingers, he shuts her out of his awareness. Lucille takes his hands and places them on her cheeks. Seeing the shaving cream on her cheeks, Matt laughs.

At the end of the session Lucille holds Matt in her arms like a baby and feeds him pretzels. His first impulse is to grab the pretzel to feed himself, but when she insists, he accepts it from her while looking briefly at her face.

Throughout the session, Lucille actively attunes her responses to Matt's. She imitates his sounds and his facial expressions, she comments on his moods and responses, and she conveys that she is totally engaged with him. But Matt does not reciprocate; his resistance remains diffuse and unfocused. It will take a few sessions before he begins to see her as a separate person he must take into account.

The following special techniques are helpful in engaging the child with PDD:

MAKING EYE CONTACT. Avoiding eye contact is one of the most common methods that autistic children employ to shut out experience. Finding ways to help them tolerate and even enjoy eye contact is an essential step toward engaging them. But once again, enjoyment is the critical issue. There is no place for making eye contact a task to be rewarded mechanically. Instead, plan delightful, surprising activities that produce spontaneous eye contact (like the peek-a-boo game Margaret played with Devon so successfully).

Do as many of your activities as possible close up to your face, thus ensuring that as the child focuses on the activity, she will be looking at you. For example, as you hold a bottle for the child, place it close to your eyes so that you intercept the child's gaze as she drinks. When playing with bubbles, hold the bubble that you have caught on the wand right in front of your nose so that the child will have to look at you when she pops the bubble with her hand or foot. Or you can, as Lucille did, place the child's hands or feet on your cheeks so that he looks toward your face.

USING REGRESSIVE ACTIVITIES. As we have indicated, most of the activities that successfully engage an autistic child are geared to the level of a very young infant. They are natural and engaging and may be familiar to the child from the time before he began to withdraw. Being simple, these games allow the child to be successful and to feel competent. Games such as peek-a-boo use an element of surprise that captivates the child and focuses his attention. In your first session with the very young child with PDD, you should use a limited repertoire because they need time to become familiar with the activities and to feel comfortable with them. Just as with a baby, repetition of familiar and fun games is appropriate, especially when the child indicates that she wants "more." However, as we discuss in a moment it is important to distinguish this from obsessive insistence on sameness that shuts out awareness of new experiences.

The following is a sampling of the kinds of simple activities that are helpful in engaging the very young child. Whenever possible, they should include taking turns. A number of the activities listed in Appendix C can be adapted to fit the needs of the young child with PDD.

- Pop the bubble (with finger or toe or elbow)
- Slippery-slippery-slip
- Pop cheeks (the child's toes can also be used to pop your cheeks)
- Sticky nose: put a sticker (or use a cotton ball and lotion) on your nose and have child take it off (or blow the cotton ball off)
- "This Little Pig" or any of a variety of playful, rhythmic finger-play games, including patty-cake and "Itsy Bitsy Spider."

FOLLOWING THE THREE TIMES RULE. Whereas simple familiar activities may engage the child, a new or unfamiliar activity may not be accepted at first. It is very important that you keep trying. The child may need time to understand what you expect him to do, he may need time for motor planning, or his conservatism may make him resist anything new. It is therefore important to slow down, repeat the activity, demonstrate with gestures, and present the activity enough times that it begins to make sense to him.

This frequent rejection and slow warm up of children with PDD led us to develop what we call the Three Times Rule. When you first present an activity to a child with PDD she may resist it and scream or turn away; the second time you present it, she may be cautiously interested; the third time, she may be delighted and want to do it over and over again. As long as this has the lovely spontaneous quality of an infant who can't get enough of a playful game, you should stay with it. When you see that the activity has taken on a rigid, perseverative quality and no longer has a joyful, interactive flavor, it is time either to change the nature of the activity or to move on to a new activity.

MIRRORING. We have described the mirroring of a child's affect as a way of engaging an angry, resistant child and of making him aware of your presence. Mirroring the child's emotions is one of the most effective techniques for establishing mutual engagement. This practice can be expanded even further in working with autistic children. The basic principles of mirroring include imitating all of the child's verbal and nonverbal responses and matching or exaggerating the affective intensity of your response so that it truly makes an impact.

The mirroring of a child's sounds is like the playful babbling that parents do with their infants, which is a precursor to communicative language. Mirroring sounds is therefore important for any child with language delays. It calls attention to the child's sounds and indicates that they can be responded to. It begins an active interchange that can lead to true communicative language. Devon, for example, when Margaret imitated his spontaneous gurgle, was immediately engaged, and a lovely "conversation" ensued. Occasionally, parents of children whose speech is well developed (but echolalic or not very communicative) question our willingness to return to the babble of an infant. They fear that their children will lose the speech they have. However, going back to the beginnings of communicative language makes it possible for them to turn their echolalic speech into true communication.

Structure and the need for containing the child with PDD call for a special kind of holding and mirroring that we have found particularly useful with children with PDD and which we will turn to shortly.

USING MUSIC. Songs and music are particularly compelling for many autistic children. The familiarity and predictability of a favorite song gives the child multiple opportunities to remember the words and join in the gestures. Many of the familiar nursery rhymes and rhythmical finger plays are activities that work well to engage the autistic child. As you work with these children, it is helpful to pause so they can insert a word or an action into the nursery rhyme or song. Since many autistic children have delayed auditory processing or poorly developed motor planning skills or both, they need long pauses, lengthy hesitations, and many repetitions in order to have sufficient opportunity to say the word or execute the action.

Structuring

Perhaps more than with any other child, efforts to engage an autistic child require the dimension of structure to provide a sense of security as well as simply to keep the child with you. You must set the stage for the drama to unfold and then sensitively follow the child's lead within the moment of the interaction.

CONTAINING THE CHILD. Because the child with PDD will avoid interaction in every way she can, including wandering away, it is very important that you find ways to keep her with you. Holding her on your lap (or having her sit in her parent's lap), propping her on pillows, or snuggling her into a beanbag chair will organize her and give her a sense of security. Some children enjoy being rolled up in a blanket before being placed in their mother's arms for rocking and feeding. As we saw in Chapter Six, some children find laps too stimulating and do better in a beanbag chair. Simple containment helps to regulate and modulate the child's fragile nervous system. By providing external regulation or boundaries, you help children learn how to regulate their level of arousal. All of the adaptations of sensory integration techniques, such as firm pressure and joint proprioception, are useful with PDD children as well.

DEVELOPING IMPULSE CONTROL. Like all children who have regulatory problems, children with PDD need help controlling their impulsiveness. The techniques discussed in Chapter Six apply here as well.

GUIDING THE CHILD'S ACTIONS PHYSICALLY. Since the young child with PDD often has motor planning difficulties or simply does not understand what is expected of him, it is useful to take his hand and help him execute the action you want him to take. Hold his hands to play patty-cake, or nudge his arms to help him push you over. This guidance helps the child understand what it is that you expect and gives him practice in doing the activity. Soon he will be able to initiate the action without help.

TAKING CHARGE. Because the autistic child often seems so very pained by changes in routine, it is tempting to the inexperienced therapist to back away from activities the child doesn't like, and to shift to a more nondirective approach. Because permissiveness allows the child to withdraw and remain in his autistic state, however, you should not permit him to "turn you off" or "tune you out." Much as he might appear pained by your insistence, you must insist. Remind yourself that you are asking of the child no more and no less than a normal child would enjoy.[8] Not only does permissiveness allow the child to withdraw, it gives him too much power. A child can feel very insecure if he is uncertain about what the limits are.[9]

The general Theraplay rule that you should avoid questions applies doubly to the child with PDD. Questions imply uncertainty on your part (which confuses the child), are difficult for the child to understand, and invite the child to say no.

HOLDING AND MIRRORING TO ACHIEVE FOCUSED AWARENESS. Holding and mirroring is, for children with PDD, perhaps the most structuring and intrusive Theraplay of all and therefore must be used with extreme sensitivity. This is a technique that goes far beyond the mirroring described earlier that briefly engages the child and even delights him. In this technique, you add holding to the mirroring in order to achieve a focused awareness leading ultimately to a delightful engagement. Because the child often resists being held and engaged in this manner, the steps toward delightful engagement can include angry resistance.

With the child held firmly in your arms, place yourself in direct visual range and adopt the child's frame of mind, imitating each movement, gesture, and mood that she displays. If she groans and grimaces, you should do this also. If she squeals with delight, so should you. Maintaining eye contact all the while, mirror the pitch, volume, and rhythm of the child's voice and the frowns, smiles, looks of surprise, despair, sadness, and so on, on her face. As you become more familiar with a particular child, you can pace your responses so that they are almost simultaneous. When you attain this high degree of synchrony, the picture is indeed one of empathic responsiveness.

The intrusiveness is often so great that it startles the child, who, having scarcely uttered the sound or made the grimace, finds his behavior doubling back on him. The child's shock is generally followed by an all-out effort to escape. He may begin to protest, try to look away, or attempt to wriggle free of your restraining arms. You should not let him go, but rather hold him firmly, continuing all the while to "catch" his eyes and mirror his moods. The period of vigorous protest (often including screaming and efforts to bite) eventually diminishes to be replaced in turn by increasing moments of mutual cooing, humming, singing, and giggling.

Because it is so difficult for parents to sustain this intense mirroring in the face of their child's resistance, it is best that you be the one to do the mirroring first. You and not the parents become the first to be subjected to the child's full rage. Only after they have had an opportunity to observe should parents be encouraged to take their turns. They will need your full support, including protection from kicking feet, scratching fingernails, or biting teeth. You can place a comforting arm around a shoulder or a cool washcloth on a forehead, and you should, of course, offer words of praise and encouragement.

After two or three controlled periods of mirroring, parents are usually ready to introduce it into their own Theraplay sessions at home. At first, a few brief moments may be all that are possible in the course of a week. Eventually parents find their impact so powerful and their child's response so gratifying that they begin to enjoy extending these periods. Before long, parent and child are "speaking" softly to one another, giggling noisily, or gazing smilingly into one another's eyes.

Nurturing

Nurturing is essential to Theraplay treatment for children with PDD because of its potential for calming and soothing them. Many such children, however, because of their discomfort with being rocked or held in the usual nursing position, have lacked (or later come to refuse) the most common nurturing experience, being held and nursed or bottle fed. It is therefore especially important to discover how each child can feel comfortable. One child may not be able to tolerate being held in her mother's arms while sucking a bottle but can accept it if supported on a pillow or on her mother's knees face to face.

Since all children need touch, you must find the kind of touch that is acceptable to each child. We saw that Matt responded with intense interest to lotion and shaving cream, but other children might refuse to touch either one. Light touch may send some into a panic, whereas firm, deep pressure is welcome to others. Some children accept touch on their feet but not on their hands or face. Others cannot tolerate having their feet touched. Here, as elsewhere, infant massage techniques can be very useful for parents with their children.

Challenging

Beginning with the simple baby activities we suggested earlier, you must gradually introduce new activities and new challenges so that the child can feel increasingly competent. Some of these new challenges involve being able to tolerate the stimulation she has rejected before. If you introduce these challenges gradually, the child can learn that they are not as overwhelming as she fears.

In presenting challenges, begin just at the point where the child can easily manage and then move him forward a step at a time. Like the parent who provides a finger for her almost-ready-to-walk toddler, you must support the hesitant child to take her first step. A small dab of lotion firmly applied to the palm of the hand of a child who is tactilely defensive, or even, perhaps, a dot of powder first, will move the child forward in her ability to accept new tactile experiences.

In the following example, Laura, a tactilely defensive three-year-old with PDD, begins to enjoy the interactive play with her therapist as her aversion to touch is made into a turn-taking game of "drop the beanbag into my hands."

THERAPLAY IN PRACTICE: The Beanbag Game. Laura sits in her mother's lap and faces Madelyn, her therapist. To help her understand the game, Madelyn first places the beanbag on her own head, asking Laura to catch it as it falls. Laura's mother helps her hold her hands just right for the catch. Next Madelyn puts the beanbag on Laura's head. Laura's natural impulse is to duck her head and let it fall off. Madelyn catches it as it falls, and then puts it on her own head again. As Laura catches it in her hands, Madelyn cheers, "Yaay!" and then says, "Laura's turn." This time Laura places the beanbag on top of her own head. "Good girl! Ready, set, go!" Laura ducks her head and drops the beanbag. "Good for you!" What began as an action on Laura's part to avoid unwanted touch, has developed into an intentional shared game which Laura clearly enjoys.

Other challenging activities in which you can take advantage of the child's impulse to get away are a variety of pushing games. You may have to help him push the first time, but most children are delighted when their slightest push leads to an exaggerated fall backwards on your part. Additional challenging activities for these young children include pop-the-bubble and throwing a beanbag or a ball into or through the therapist's arms.

SPECIAL TREATMENT ISSUES FOR CHILDREN WITH PDD

The following special treatment issues are important in working with children with PDD:

- Fostering language development
- Increasing the amount of time parents spend engaging their child
- Maximizing the impact of school staff and peers
- Making an impact through multiple interventions

Fostering Language

One characteristic common among children with PDD is the lack of communicative speech. Many young children have no language at all or have lost the few words they had earlier. Some children have highly developed speech that has very little communicative meaning. In either case the challenge is to help the child develop communicative language.

Because of its focus on fostering shared attention and engagement and two-way gestural communication, Theraplay is in a good position to foster the beginnings of speech and language in the non-speaking child. Even the child who has well-developed speech but who uses it in a noncommunicative fashion can benefit from what Theraplay has to offer in terms of truly interactive communication.

Your most powerful tool in helping the child develop language is to mirror every sound the child makes and then, if possible, to develop and expand the interaction around the sound. When the child gurgles and you gurgle back, you are encouraging a round of sounds that can be subtly varied and enjoyed. Even the spontaneous sounds of the child with language should be imitated in order to start the process of learning to use language interactively. You can expand this idea by using cardboard towel tubes. Place the tube against the child's ear as you make a sound, and then place the tube to the child's mouth when it is his turn. Noise makers, whistles, and other sound-producing toys also can be used to stimulate interactive play with sounds.

Beyond these spontaneous, natural beginnings the following guidelines can be helpful:[10]

- Reduce your own language to match the child's receptive language needs. With the nonverbal child, encourage the addition of natural gestures and signs. You can use pictures and encourage the child to point to indicate what he wants.

- Use language to refer to what is going on at the moment and to refer to visible objects rather than to talk about the past or distant events.

- Comment on the child's action just as a parent talks for a young baby. As the child moves toward something, you might say, "Oh, you want that," taking a response within the child's repertoire at the moment and making it purposeful. Acknowledge what you think the child is feeling. "You really liked that. That made you feel good."

- Ask questions that allow a "yes" or "no" answer, an indexical or eye-pointing response, a picture or object selection, a physical gesture.

- If the child cannot respond, assist him in an appropriate physical response by using physical guidance or hand-over-hand assistance.

Increasing the Amount of Time Parents Spend Engaging Their Child

We have always emphasized the importance of having parents continue the Theraplay approach at home, but this is absolutely essential for the autistic child, who so quickly shuts down when he is not actively engaged. The child must be intruded upon and engaged as much as possible.[11] Speech therapy, occupational therapy, and well-planned preschool programs can contribute helpful stimulation in addition to that which the parents provide.

Early in our experience we found consistent, active parental engagement to be an important factor in the successful treatment of children with PDD. The following case study demonstrates this point.

THERAPLAY IN PRACTICE: Using Theraplay at Home. Benjamin, an autistic child, was brought by his parents to the Theraplay Institute when he was five. His dramatic progress could hardly have come about without his parents' enthusiastic spirit. During the first half of each weekly session, they observed Benjamin being played with by his therapists, and while they watched they asked questions of the interpreting therapist, discussed the happenings of the past week, and conjured up activities for the week ahead. During the second half of each session, both mother and father joined in, as intent as his therapists on engaging Benjamin in eye contact and on participating in making handprints, lotioning his feet, playing leapfrog, and feeding him with a bottle.

His parents' main contribution to improving his condition, however, came not at the weekly sessions, but during their time with him at home. For Benjamin, home had become one big Theraplay room. When his mother was not romping, rolling, or gently feeding or powdering him, his older sister was. And every evening first Father alone and then Father with the whole family engaged and nurtured Benjamin in ways that were cheerful, imaginative, irresistible, and fun—always with the aim of attaining eye contact and playful engagement. It was not too long, in fact, before they reported Benjamin's wandering in from the sidelines on his own and placing himself in the midst of all the noisy, tumbling, family joy.

After several months of Theraplay treatment, the family moved to another city. Since Benjamin had always reacted to change with temper tantrums, they anticipated the worst with such a big change. To their surprise he adjusted extremely well. On his first day in his new school, his teacher, who had expected a nonspeaking autistic child, couldn't believe her ears when Benjamin greeted her with a cheerful, "Hi, teacher."

Maximizing the Impact of School Staff and Peers

The fact remains that parents can't do it all. These children need to be integrated into a school program where everyone is prepared to continue the playful, engaging approach that Theraplay uses so successfully in keeping these children engaged. This requires that you find ways to explain and demonstrate the Theraplay approach to all the people who work with the child. Although you can invite them to observe sessions, often it is more efficient to go to the child's school and elicit the cooperation of the whole staff.

The following case is an example of the effectiveness of having all the people who work with a child (in this case, school and day-treatment staff) carry on the playful, engaging Theraplay approach.

THERAPLAY IN PRACTICE: *Involving the Whole Staff at School.*[12] Jeff, an autistic seven-year-old, was admitted to a school-based day-treatment program because of problems in social interaction, aggression toward peers and family members, and increasingly oppositional behavior. He made no moves toward contact with peers, and he avoided eye and physical contact in general. His speech was mainly echolalic. His academic skills were well below grade level. After an initial intake and assessment, his therapist, Dave, introduced Jeff to Theraplay. His parents were enthusiastic and committed to the process.

Jeff's more than forty sessions were held once a week over the course of his fourteen-month stay in the program. Dave concentrated on intrusive, engaging, and nurturing activities, such as peek-a-boo, tunneling, lotioning, wrestling, and feeding. Whatever sounds Jeff made were mirrored back to him. Though this mirroring might seem as though it simply replicated and therefore reinforced Jeff's echolalia, it had a very different quality. The sounds that were imitated were not just his rigid speech, but the spontaneous sounds Jeff made as he engaged in activities with Dave. Just as the playful mirroring of sounds between parent and infant lead to later meaningful language, this mirroring began the process that led to Jeff's using more and more spontaneous and appropriate language.

Jeff was at first highly resistant to the sessions. His resistance was not violent. Instead it involved attempting to wiggle out from Dave's grasp and burying his head in Dave's chest to avoid eye contact. Dave maintained a gently insistent pursuit of Jeff, attempting to keep physical and eye contact at all times. Given Jeff's size and physical strength, it was occasionally necessary to bring in a second therapist. This had the salutary effects of preventing sessions from becoming predictable and making it more difficult for Jeff to escape physical contact.

Gradually, Jeff became more comfortable with this interaction and began to allow the therapist to touch him without resistance. His eye contact improved, not only in sessions, but with peers, family, teachers, and other staff members. Indeed, it was the use of intrusive engagement by Jeff's peers, staff, and family that made his progress so dramatic.

The principle of intrusive engagement was carried over into the broader milieu of Jeff's day treatment program. It became a deliberate, systematic principle that all staff should engage and interact with him as often as possible. They would engage him in conversation or playful activities, make physical contact with him, and insist on eye contact. They wanted him to be continuously aware of them and to relate to them. He was seldom allowed to withdraw or retreat.

Additionally, the other children in the milieu, many of whom were hyperactive, were powerful therapists for Jeff. Their high levels of activity and natural intrusiveness were tailor-made to draw him further out of his shell. Group Theraplay was used extensively with Jeff and his peers. Activities such as having the youngsters rub lotion on one another's hands or cheeks, pass a hand squeeze around the circle, or name someone and throw a soft ball to him across the circle, kept Jeff on the alert and constantly engaged. This boy who had mastered the art of evasiveness now found that all the important people in his life were no longer willing to let him slip away.

By the end of his stay in the program, Jeff had improved dramatically in social skills. He was one of the more popular members of his peer group. He made and sustained several friendships. His eye contact had improved, and his echolalia was only manifested in times of stress or uncertainty, such as when meeting new people. His academic skills also had improved greatly. Jeff was "mainstreamed" into the second grade in his local school, where, because his teachers were willing to intrude on him, he continued to do well. He is currently in a private residential school for children with learning problems where the smaller teacher-to-student ratio supports his excellent progress.

Increasing the Impact Through Multiple Interventions

Because of their many special needs, children with autistic spectrum disorders often require multiple treatments designed to address their specific disabilities. Although Theraplay can make a great difference in the child's ability to relate to others and in her ability to understand and respond to social signals, there is still room for special help in the particular areas of the child's vulnerabilities: occupational therapy to deal with the sensory integration issues, speech and language therapy to address the communication problems, physical therapy to develop muscle tone, and so forth. We see Theraplay as providing the basic "humanizing" foundation for the child. But we know he will need other treatments, which he will be able to accept more readily once he has had some Theraplay experience. We often recommend starting with Theraplay and then moving on to other treatment modalities as the child becomes more open to interventions. In Timmy's case (at the end of this chapter) you can see how this was implemented.

GUIDING THE CHILD THROUGH THE PHASES OF TREATMENT

The process of treatment for children with PDD takes longer than with any other children. Though the change from isolated aloneness to tentative interaction may begin within a few sessions, the underlying constitutional problems continue to make it difficult for the child to interpret cues and to be comfortable relating to people. Treatment may take anywhere from six months to three years.

In the beginning, and especially with very young children, more frequent sessions (two or three per week) are helpful. And as for Benjamin, Jeff, and all children, the more intensely the Theraplay activities can be carried on at home and at school, the better the outcome. The phases of treatment also differ both in timing and in style. There are three basic phases: a phase of unfocused, impersonal resistance; a phase of focused, personalized resistance that may include focused rage; and finally a phase of acceptance and growth.

Phase of Unfocused, Impersonal Resistance

Because they are so easily overwhelmed by sensory stimuli and so very resistant to changes in routine, children with PDD resist right from the beginning. Their resistance, though it may be either violent and angry or passive and avoidant, lacks focused, personal intent. The child simply wants to get rid of whatever is making him uncomfortable, but he makes little distinction between you and all the other things in his life that he tries to avoid. He will try all his usual ways of shutting out unwanted experiences: avoiding eye contact, twiddling his hands, arching his back, banging his head, spacing out, or running away. When you persist in intruding on him, he will scream and cry. But no matter how intense his response, you will feel that it is not you, personally, that he is fighting.

If you allow the child to continue in this phase of unfocused, impersonal resistance, very little progress will be made. Although you should look for ways to accommodate to his sensory needs and to make your activities as enticing as possible, you must continue your attempts to make him aware of your presence even if your persistence leads to increased resistance. Only when he can resist in a personalized way, thus "becoming" more of a person himself, will he be able to move into the final phase of acceptance and growth.

The Phase of Focused, Personalized Resistance

As you continue to intrude on the child, you will be amazed at the amount of energy he puts into avoiding any specific awareness of you. Your goal should be to find ways to stop his extravagant dispersion of energy. This may require holding him close, stopping his wiggles, and insisting on eye contact. A more tender-hearted approach that seems to say, "I know this bothers you; I will wait till you're ready," simply postpones the child's getting better. As the child moves into the phase of more focused, personalized resistance, he will redouble his efforts to shut you out of his awareness.

The following is an example of a child who, after a period of impersonal resistance like Matt's, suddenly makes a highly focused gesture to shut out his therapist. It is an earlier phase in the successful treatment of Benjamin that we described above.

THERAPLAY IN PRACTICE: *Benjamin's Focused Resistance.* From the beginning, Benjamin's impersonal efforts to shut out his therapist included multiple body movements and hand twiddles, avoidance of eye contact, screaming, and turning away. In his fourth session (before his parents joined in), faced with his therapist's persistent attempts to engage him in playful activities, Benjamin suddenly shut her out with such a focused, intense gesture that there was no doubt that he had become aware of her. Using both hands, he put his thumbs in his ears, his little fingers up his nostrils and his other fingers over his eyes— shutting out every chance for sensory intrusion except touch. At the same time he stuck out his tongue and made a high-pitched repetitive noise, "La, la, la, la." He was using all his energy to make one last attempt to shut out this intriguing, insistent person who was trying to enter his world. Excited by the evidence that Benjamin was beginning truly to be aware of her, his therapist hugged him and repeated his wonderful "La, la, la, la" song. Soon after this episode, Benjamin became much less resistant and began to engage in the interactive play that his therapist and his parents and sister at home were eager to offer him.

Not all focused, personalized resistance, however, will be as ingenious or as nonviolent as Benjamin's. Over the weeks of treatment, as activities are introduced, embellished, and insisted upon, resistance may give way to focused rage. The enraged child begins directly and visually to confront his "enemy," the intrusive therapist. For moments at a time, he looks fiercely—yet intently—at you. He may, along with the angry looks, lash out at you in a purposeful, integrated gesture that is distinctly directed to a human being who must, to him, feel bothersome at best. When this occurs it is cause for jubilation. The child is now truly "alive."

During this period of angry lashing out, you must firmly take charge and contain him physically. He should feel you holding him, protecting him, securing him in a position that allows maximum eye contact with a minimum of threat (as we described about holding and mirroring). This period of rage evokes for the first time the picture of a human child feeling appropriately angry toward a frustrating human adult.

Just as for other children, holding a child with PDD when he is angry has many benefits. Ultimately, as his therapist acknowledges his angry feelings and holds and comforts him, he is able to relax and accept the safety and comfort. Another step has been taken toward his becoming more connected, more human. Often at the end of the angry struggle, the child begins to cry and truly turns to his therapist for comfort.

It is often difficult for parents to watch the intensity of these sessions. As the interpreting therapist you support the parents, expressing your understanding of how difficult it is for them to see their child so upset. You will need to put a supportive arm around a parent's shoulder or hold a hand. Above all you need to help them see that their child is safe, that it is a vital part of treatment that the child be able to express his anger directly at someone who does not back down or run away.

The Phase of Acceptance and Growth

Once this phase of angry confrontation is over, the final phase of acceptance and growth begins. The child is now able to relate to you and to her parents in a comfortable, relaxed manner and begins to enjoy the playful activities that you present. Because even this period will not be all smooth sailing, you must be alert to the need to keep the child engaged and interacting. Further, because treatment with these children takes a long time, you will need to keep refurbishing your repertoire with new activities to keep both yourself and the child looking forward to sessions with anticipation and excitement. Also, as you saw with Jeff, there remains a continuing need to keep all the people who interact with the child prepared to intrude and engage him when he withdraws into isolation.

We turn now to a case study that demonstrates the full sequence of treatment with a very young child with PDD.

THERAPLAY IN PRACTICE: *Following the Course of Treatment.*[13] Timmy was a difficult baby from the start. Throughout his first year of life, he had colic and was inconsolable most of the time, except when his mother held him tightly in her arms to nurse. By eighteen months his mother noticed that Timmy was not progressing like other children. He showed little interest in people and made poor eye contact. Although he had spoken a few words before this time, he suddenly stopped talking. At twenty-one months, Timmy's behavior took a dramatic change for the worse and he screamed most of the time. His parents were emotionally and physically drained by their son's inflexibility and raging temper tantrums, which could be triggered by almost any change in routine. Going to the grocery store or the doctor's office had become a nightmare. They also were concerned about his extremely delayed language development.

At this point his parents began to seek help. After an exhausting search for a conclusive diagnosis, a pediatric neurologist gave their twenty-five-month-old son a preliminary diagnosis of "pervasive developmental disorder—autistic type," with a developmental language disorder. When Timmy was twenty-six months old, the family came to the Theraplay Institute for treatment.

MIM WITH BOTH PARENTS. For the MIM session both parents remained in the room, sitting on the floor with Timmy and taking turns with the tasks. Throughout the session, Timmy showed little interest in his parents (he sat on his mother's lap and occasionally looked up at her face but mostly maintained his insistent gaze aversion). Timmy's emotional reactions ranged from hysterical laughter in tickling games, to rage-filled temper tantrums when his juice was taken away or when his parents left the room. He showed sensory integration difficulties: dislike of light touch and lotion, discomfort with changes in position, and poor modulation of sensory stimulation. His play with toys consisted mainly of matching objects by color and lining them up. Based on our observation of the parent-child interaction, we decided that engagement, structure, and nurture were the dimensions of interaction most likely to lead to our goals of increased interpersonal relatedness, acceptance of changes in routine, and reduction of temper tantrums and perseveration.

His therapist, Madelyn, saw Timmy weekly for twenty-six half-hour sessions with one or both parents either observing or directly participating in each session. His parents were encouraged to carry on the Theraplay activities at home. Because Madelyn was working alone, she phoned Timmy's parents after each session to discuss what had transpired, to talk about behavior management issues, and to learn about changes in Timmy over the week.

As he became more open to a wider range of experiences, she recommended that he be enrolled in other programs: speech and language therapy, occupational therapy, early intervention educational services, a special recreation summer program, and Kindermusik. The parents also participated in a parent support group for children with autism. In spite of his young age and extreme difficulty accepting changes in routine, Madelyn decided to meet with Timmy alone for the first few sessions in order to develop an intense, personal relationship with him.

SESSION ONE. Timmy responded to Madelyn's carrying him into the treatment room with angry crying. She acknowledged his feelings saying, "You are mad!" She held him tightly and rocked him back and forth to assure him he was safe. When she mirrored his anger, he momentarily looked at her face and his crying diminished. She tried several playful activities such as peek-a-boo and rubbing lotion on his feet, but he resisted her efforts by throwing himself down on his back. Only her mirroring of his sounds and feelings caught his attention.

Instead of being disturbed by Timmy's distress, which she observed from behind a one-way mirror, Timmy's mother later told Madelyn that she was relieved. "His kicking, screaming, and pushing away is so typical of his temper tantrums at home. I was glad to see someone hold him and stay with him during one of his angry outbursts. I knew you weren't hurting him."

SESSION TWO. Timmy did not fight as hard against Madelyn's efforts to engage him as he had during the first session. This time as he cried he snuggled into her lap seeking comfort. As before, she mirrored Timmy's affect. When she laid him down to lotion his feet, he protested more loudly and deliberately looked away. To help with his extreme sensitivity to touch and his other sensory integration problems, Madelyn adapted some of the sensory diet techniques (described in Chapter Six) to her work with Timmy. Timmy's mother was already familiar with these techniques, and Madelyn encouraged her to make use of them on a regular basis. In spite of his angry crying, Madelyn persisted in her attempts to engage him, playing patty-cake, peek-a-boo, and pop-the-bubble. The bubbles caught his attention, and he stopped crying and looked directly at her. Since Timmy was not yet ready to take turns, Madelyn took turns for both of them, raising his hand to pop the bubbles.

SESSION THREE. Today Timmy's crying lasted only the first five minutes. When Madelyn brought out the bubbles, Timmy looked at them intently and with real interest. He had liked them from the beginning, but today there was a new shared quality to his pleasure. Recognizing that even this shared experience quickly took on a rote quality, Madelyn moved on to another activity in order to keep him alert and engaged. She next tried feeding Timmy a bottle in order to recreate the early mother-infant nurturing experience that is so soothing to most infants. But Timmy was not ready to accept this and he adamantly refused. However, he was able to tolerate having baby powder rubbed on his feet accompanied by the song "Rub-a-Dub-Dub."

Timmy's mother came in for the first time toward the end of this session. While his mother held him on her lap facing Madelyn, he spontaneously patted his knees and Madelyn imitated his gesture. Soon they were engaged in a delightful turn-taking game. Timmy would pat his knees and wait for Madelyn to repeat the gesture. He giggled when she did so. Next, she held his feet in front of her face and peeked out at him, saying "Boo!" He smiled widely, said "Boo!" several times and briefly stole glances at her during this game. His mother was surprised and delighted with how engaged Timmy had become after only three sessions. She spoke with relief about the changes that were occurring at home. He had become more manageable and his tantrums were dissipating more quickly. She was happy to report that for the first time Timmy was able to have lunch at McDonald's and to be pushed around K-Mart in a grocery cart. She recognized that Timmy's emotional needs were those of a much younger child, so she put away his two-year-old toys and began playing interactive Theraplay games with him at home.

SESSION FOUR. Timmy was very upset when his mother brought him to the session today. Once Madelyn had imitated him, however, Timmy stopped crying and was in a much better mood. He became alert and made sustained eye contact. For the first time he initiated the game (which they had played before) of holding out his arms to receive Madelyn's exaggerated kisses, giggling all the while. Timmy became really excited when Madelyn imitated the nonsense sound he was making, and he soon began to experiment with more sounds. Signs of language seemed to be reemerging along with reciprocal turn-taking. Timmy developed a word approximation for ready, "eya yah," and said "pop" to bubbles. Next Madelyn placed a beanbag on her head and held Timmy's hands to catch it as it dropped off, taking turns catching and dropping the bag. Madelyn had to move quickly to keep Timmy from lapsing into perseverative, self-stimulating play (squishing and twiddling the bag) and thus losing their emotional connectedness.

Aware of his hypersensitivity, Madelyn had all along modulated the intensity of their interaction in order to reduce his excitability. As Timmy began to feel more comfortable and his need for globally shutting out all new experiences decreased, his sensory integration problems became more specifically identifiable. Light touch was intolerable for him. Firm, deep pressure helped calm him down. He did not like to have lotion on his feet or hands; postural changes (horizontal rocking and being placed on his back) were difficult for him; and he pulled his hands away when his mother and Madelyn tried to help him clap his hands. Recognizing these problems, Madelyn experimented with moving at a much slower pace to see whether that would reduce his excitability and help him modulate his excitement level. But she continued to look for activities that would gently challenge him to be more comfortable with a wider variety of activities. While Timmy still occasionally arched his back and tried to push away, it was not the same battle as in earlier sessions. Timmy remained emotionally quite volatile. He moved rapidly from being overreactive (crying) to underreactive ("tuning out" and looking away).

To help Timmy deal with his hypersensitivities, Madelyn recommended to Timmy's mother that she increase the amount of time spent using the Wilbarger Sensory Diet techniques and suggested that she include some infant massage techniques along with Theraplay activities at home. Madelyn also suggested that she get a small trampoline and a swing to encourage gross motor activities and provide proprioceptive stimulation at home.

SESSION SEVEN. This session seemed to be a turning point. Timmy left his mother without crying, and he was emotionally connected for most of the session. He withdrew only momentarily by averting his gaze.

His mother described an incident at the park where he tried to grab a girl's popsicle. Instead of having a tantrum when his mother told him he couldn't have the popsicle, Timmy just stamped his feet. She also reported that he seemed much better adjusted to his summer day camp. Last week, he only fussed for a couple of minutes after she dropped him off there, and he even began to play next to other children with toys.

SESSION NINE. Separations seemed to be getting easier. Timmy left Mom without any crying or protest, and when Mom was in the room, he even got off her lap at one point during the session to pop the bubbles. Timmy took the sticker off Madelyn's nose when she told him to "get my nose." He gazed into her face and touched her eye as she rocked and sang "Rock-a-Bye Baby." He talked more, saying "bubble," "boo," "juice," "weady," "bye," and "go."

Timmy's autistic behaviors had also decreased. He only flapped his hands or flicked his fingers when overstimulated or really excited. Transitions were easier for him. His unfocused temper tantrums were being replaced by more focused, personalized aggressive behavior directed toward the offending person, either Madelyn or his mother.

Over the next few weeks, he began pinching and hitting his mother when she wasn't paying attention to him or when she was not as readily available as she had been before. She reported that Timmy would now look at her when he was angry, and that the quality of the anger had changed to being much more like that of a normal child. She could now hold him and help him calm down. Madelyn suggested that she acknowledge his feelings at the same time that she stop him from hurting her: "I know you're angry! But I won't let you hurt me!"

SESSION TEN. Timmy's communication skills continued to improve. During the session, he either grabbed his mother's clothes to get her attention or pointed to what he wanted to do. He also had gained five new words in the last two weeks. His hitting and pinching decreased.

Timmy and Mom began a Kindermusik class at the Park District. As with most new beginnings, Timmy threw a huge tantrum his first time there, banging his head and screaming. Mom calmed him down by holding him firmly, reassuring him, and slowly bringing him closer to the group. By the end of the half hour, Timmy sat on Mom's lap just a foot away from the group.

She reported that Timmy waited his turn with the other children recently at a picnic and acted almost like a normal two-year-old. Most of the autistic features and the tantrums were now gone. "He has come farther then I ever could have imagined."

SESSION FIFTEEN. Timmy did not protest at all when he left his mother to come into the Theraplay room. As Madelyn took his socks off, he smiled but kept his eyes averted. He momentarily shifted his gaze to look at his foot as she said, "Whoa, come on sock." As she pulled harder, he grinned, laughed, and actually turned to look directly at her. When Madelyn imitated his movements and sounds, he imitated in return, "I gotcha," and a nice turn-taking game developed. When they played pop-cheeks, which resulted in having his face blown on, Timmy said "bo" [more], looked directly at Madelyn's face and laughed. After the sixth time, he spontaneously signed "more."

SESSIONS SIXTEEN THROUGH TWENTY-FOUR. Timmy, Mom, and Madelyn continued to meet weekly. His eleven-year-old sister joined in for some of the sessions, as did his father when work permitted. The sessions included playing the beanbag game, the slippery-slippery-slip game with hands and feet, singing a song together, playing sticky nose, patty-cake with hands or feet, popping bubbles, and hiding under a blanket or behind a pillow so Mom could find him. Perhaps the most striking change was Timmy's increased comfort with being held and nurtured like a baby. He now enjoyed being swung in a blanket, being rocked and fed by his mother, and having his special "Twinkle Song" sung to him. Timmy became more responsive during each session, although there were ups and downs. At home his behavior continued to improve.

SESSION TWENTY-FIVE. This was Timmy's last session because he would be attending an early childhood special education program five mornings a week. This seemed an appropriate time to stop direct treatment because he was now ready for a wider experience. He was comfortable interacting with people, able to enter into new activities easily, and able to express his needs. His babysitter, a special education teacher, said, "While Timmy still has a lot of difficulties to overcome, he now has a wonderful personality and a great sense of humor not usually found in children with PDD, and he responds to approval and affection."

CHECKUP SIX MONTHS LATER. Timmy made good eye contact and interacted well. He laughed heartily and appropriately to the game of push-me-over and said "weay" (ready) and "go" when we played "Ready-Set-Go." As he tired, instead of screaming, he called out for "Mommy."

INTERVIEW WITH MOTHER. We asked Timmy's mother to describe her reactions to the Theraplay experience.

> Before Theraplay, I felt as though I was losing Timmy; he was regressing so, and I didn't know how to grab him and hold on. After a month of sessions the regression seemed to stop. And then we started to work on getting him to move forward with eye contact and to interact, to tolerate different positions, to tolerate transitions (that was a big one!), and also to play on other peoples' terms, not just on his own.
>
> What made the difference was that you were not put off. You persevered. If you had simply followed his lead, you wouldn't have gotten anywhere. You made him interact; it opened up his world. I think one of the major things too was it gave him an identity. It started to make him realize that he was a person.
>
> I think the nurturing was very important: going back to where he was emotionally and doing the things you would do with a child that

age; holding him and looking at him. Thinking of him as a six-month-old helped me when I would get frustrated with where he was. The structure helped a lot too; he still needs that today.

I personally feel that without Theraplay we wouldn't be where we are today. It was the first step. That was what brought him back and stopped him from regressing. After that he was more able to make use of occupational therapy and speech therapy.

Theraplay thus had established the foundation of social interaction that allowed Timmy to change from being isolated, fearful, and perseverative to being sociable, engaging, calm, and interactive. Theraplay, with its emphasis on empathically meeting the child's needs, with its ability to challenge and structure the child, and above all, with its ability to entice the isolated autistic child into engagement, can provide the experiences the child has so sorely missed. Once he has moved through the phase of focused resistance, he can accept his parents' offer of a warm and loving relationship. When this relationship is established, many more good things follow, not the least important of which is the wish to communicate. While systematic teaching of skills may still be necessary (as it is for most children), he is now spontaneously interested and eager to learn. Theraplay helps these children take the crucial step of learning to become human in a world of human beings. Once this is achieved, the children begin to have their own internal motivation to learn, to imitate, to fulfill their own potential.

Notes

1. Greenspan, describing children with autistic spectrum disorders, says, "Each child has his or her own unique profile for processing sensations (i.e., 'regulatory' profile). This includes differences in sensory reactivity (e.g., tactile, auditory, visual), sensory processing (e.g., auditory/verbal, visual/spatial), and motor tone and motor planning" (1992b, p. 2).

2. Greenspan states, "the primary goal of intervention is to enable children to form a sense of their own personhood—a sense of themselves as intentional, interactive individuals. . . . This sense of 'personhood' seems initially to organize itself around physical sensations, a sense of connection to others and a sense of intentionality (two-way communication, involving the use of simple and complex gestures). Next it would define itself in terms of emerging representations or symbols as they become organized and differentiated.

As the sense of personhood evolves, earlier and more fundamental levels serve as a foundation for newer levels" (1992b, p. 5). For a more recent account of Greenspan's approach to working with these children see Greenspan and Wieder, 1998.

3. Greenspan suggests "that there are biologically based regulatory difficulties which contribute to, but are not decisive in determining, the relationship and communication difficulties. When problems are perceived early, caregivers and children, with appropriate professional help, can learn to work around the regulatory dysfunctions and their associated relationship and communication problems, and form varying degrees of warm, empathetic and satisfying relationships" (1992b, p. 4).

4. For a sampling of books describing the successful treatment of children with autism using a variety of intrusive and engaging approaches, see Maurice (1993), Kaufman (1975), and Copeland (1973).

5. For very enlightening accounts of personal experiences as autistic children, see Grandin and Scariano (1986), Grandin (1995), and Williams (1988, 1993).

6. In developing a classification system for children under four years of age, Greenspan introduced the term *Multisystem Developmental Delay* to avoid the "negative connotations of autism or PDD" and the "questionable assumption that these types of children are not capable of love, warmth, and comfort with dependency" (1992b, p. 4). Although many children we work with might fit his definition, we do not use Multisystem Developmental Delay here because it adds to the confusion of labels.

7. Greenspan and his colleagues also emphasize the importance of modulating sensory impact for children who are hyper-or hyporesponsive. "As one fosters focus and engagement, one must pay attention to the child's regulatory difficulties. For example, if he is overreactive to sound, talking to him in a normal loud voice may lead him to become more aimless and more withdrawn. If he is overreactive to sights, bright lights and even very animated facial expressions may be overwhelming for him. On the other hand, if he is underreactive to sensations of sound and visual/spatial input, talking in a strong voice and using animated facial expressions in a well-lit room may help him attend. Similarly, in terms of his receptive language skills, if he is already at the point where he can decode a complex rhythm, making interesting sounds in complex patterns may be helpful. On the other hand, if he can only decode very simple, two-sequence rhythms, and perhaps understands a single word here and there, using single words (not as symbolic communication, but as gestural communication) and using simple patterns of sound may help him engage" (Greenspan 1992b, p. 6).

8. As Clancy and McBride (1969, p. 242) have so aptly put it, "Permissiveness is actually harmful to the autistic child. In the autistic process, as we see it, the child actively shapes the family's behavior so that he achieves isolation. This is most clearly seen in his use of cut-off and the family's acceptance of it. The temper tantrum is clearly used to demand relationships on the child's terms. This is the reverse of normal socialization, which requires leadership and control by the parents, not the child. Accordingly, we reject permissiveness and would argue for forceful demands by parents, to intrude and to reinforce negatively both cut-off behavior and temper tantrums."

9. Jay Haley (1973, pp. 212–213), writing of the tyranny of the autistic child, says: "Even when dealing with severely disturbed children, such as an autistic child, [Milton] Erickson does not approach them as children who need love as much as children who have more power than they can tolerate. He feels that a child's insecurity can come from an uncertainty about what limits are set upon him, and the therapeutic approach is to enforce limits."

10. These communication strategies are a compilation of ideas from several authors, including Prizant and Wetherby (1989), Weitzman (1994), and Bruner (1984) in his concept of scaffolding.

11. Parents using the Lovaas method (Lovaas 1977; Maurice 1996) hire therapists to spend up to forty hours a week with their child. Greenspan and Wieder (1997) also emphasize the importance of spending as much time as possible interacting with the child in a variety of ways, including interactive play, speech therapy, occupational therapy, and enrolling the child in an integrated preschool program (where one fourth of the class has special needs and three fourths are normal children).

12. This case study originally appeared in somewhat different form in "Theraplay as a Treatment for Autism in a School-Based Day Treatment Setting" by Fuller, *Developments in Ambulatory Mental Health Care: Continuum: The Journal of the American Association for Partial Hospitilization,*1995, *2,* 89–93. Reprinted with permission from *Continuum.*

13. This case study originally appeared as "Theraplay for Children with PPD/Autism" by Rieff and Booth, *The Theraplay Institute Newsletter,* Fall 1996. Reprinted with permission of the Theraplay Institute.

CHAPTER EIGHT

Theraplay for Children with Physical Disabilities

W e turn now to look at how Theraplay can meet the needs of children with physical disabilities. As we emphasize throughout, healthy parent-infant give-and-take is crucial to the development of the child and to the ongoing attachment relationship. As we have seen in the previous two chapters, any problem in the child that reduces her responsiveness or makes her less appealing and engaging can have a negative impact on that relationship.

Although many of the same issues we discussed before apply here, physical disabilities present some special problems to therapists and parents. For example, you must understand and support parents as they mourn the loss of the "perfect" child they had dreamed of having. This is an issue with any child who does not fit a parent's notion of an ideal child but is especially true with a physical handicap that cannot be expected to change. You need to understand how this mourning can make it difficult for them to respond positively and energetically to their child.

Parents of a child with a disability often end up focusing on remedial lessons and therapies that fill the child's time and take precedence over play time with their child. Both the parents' mourning and their focus on work, combined with the child's inability to respond in the normal full-bodied manner of a healthy infant, can reduce the playfulness and joy of the interaction between parent and child. Thus the child can miss out on the kinds of interaction that normally lead to a secure attachment, a positive self-image, and feelings of competence in her physical body. In addition, parents often become cautious and protective, which, compounded by the child's lack of confidence, often delays the child's growth toward independence and autonomy.

As you treat children with physical disabilities you will also experience many of the same problems. If the child is unresponsive, whether because she cannot hear, cannot see, or cannot respond in an active, physical manner, you can easily become discouraged and back off. Just as parents fear the physical fragility of their disabled child, so you may find yourself holding back as you work with such a child. Or you may even be repulsed by the child's physical difference. And just as parents find it hard to challenge a disabled child to try harder and to reach farther, you may find it difficult to challenge the child to have fun.

In this chapter we look at how to deal with these problems. We do not, of course, expect to change the physical disability, nor do we attempt to train the child specifically to work around it. Many special services are available to physically disabled children: physical therapy, speech therapy, sensory integration therapy, signing for the hearing impaired, Braille for the blind. In fact, there are so many special kinds of remedial work for disabled children that it is often a full-time job for parents to get their children to their many therapy sessions. What Theraplay can offer to the disabled child and her parents is the opportunity to build or restore the normal parent-child interaction with all its benefits to the child's self-esteem, self-confidence, trust, and secure attachment.

Following a brief consideration of how to deal with the special problems you face in working with a physically disabled child, we address the various problems that disabilities present to parents and their children. We give examples of Theraplay treatment for children with two specific physical disabilities—hearing impairment and cerebral palsy. Our work with these two groups of children can serve as guides in using Theraplay with children with other disabilities.

BEING AWARE OF POTENTIAL REACTIONS TO A CHILD'S DISABILITY

In working with the physically disabled child, you face special countertransference issues that go beyond those you face with other children.

Once again, the best way to deal with these issues is to be aware of them and to get supervision from someone experienced in working with such children. Here we identify the issues and suggest how you can deal with them.

Frustration Due to Lack of Response

Probably the most important problem you face in working with a physically disabled child is the lack of response. Just as a mother can be "turned off" if her baby fails to respond, so you can be "turned off" if a child fails to respond to or, even worse, fails to perceive your efforts. If the child cannot hear your words, how do you communicate with him? If he cannot see you, how can you establish eye contact? If he cannot move his arms or legs, how can you play with him? And missing the usual responsiveness of a healthy child, how can you maintain your confidence that you are making an impact? Thus you may be as much challenged with respect to your competence and resourcefulness as is the mother who has given birth to a baby who cannot see her, or hear her, or reach up to touch her. As Selma Fraiberg (1977b) describes her experience in relating to blind children, talking to a blind child can leave the therapist with a "sense of something missing, something that should be coming back to [you]" (p. 94).

To protect yourself from feelings of incompetence resulting from the child's lack of response, be sure that at least some of your caseload is made up of more responsive children. You need, also, to remind yourself that with very unresponsive children, even the slightest response is a triumph, as you will see in the case of Rose Marie.

Fear of the Infirmity

A more subtle response, one that is almost automatic for most people, is the unconscious fear that this particular infirmity or one like it could happen to you—a revived childhood fear of mutilation. Being aware of the source of this fear can help you overcome it. A related conscious response is that you may be physically repulsed; a tracheotomy that needs to be cleared out seems more disgusting on first encounter than a nose that needs to be blown. The older child who drools or is still in diapers can turn off any fastidious therapist. As you become better acquainted with the child, you will find that you no longer have these feelings.

Fear of the Child's Fragility

You also may fear the child's fragility. Like some parents, you may find yourself immobilized by your fear of hurting or harming the child and then hesitate to challenge him to move toward greater autonomy. The best cure for this fear is to learn as much as you can about the nature of the disability and about what the child is physically capable of. You can consult with his doctor or physical therapist and learn what to avoid and how to protect the child, as well as how far you can challenge him.

Feelings of Impotence

Because the physical disability is here to stay, you may well feel impotent about being able to make a difference. If so, you may respond with impatience and annoyance at being confronted both by your own unacceptable fears and apparent incompetence and by the imagined rejection in the child. Finally, you may feel guilt and shame over your own annoyance. "After all," you say to yourself, "how can I feel annoyed when this person has it so much worse?"

Thus, when working with a physically disabled child, perhaps more than with any other group of children, it is necessary to be in touch with your own underlying conflicts and anxieties and with your consequent reactions. For this reason, you will need to have a perceptive supervisor available. All of the foregoing, of course, applies to any professional working with persons with disabilities. It applies as much to physicians, school teachers, and traditional physical, occupational, and speech therapists as it does to Theraplay therapists.

UNDERSTANDING THE NEEDS COMMON TO PARENTS OF CHILDREN WITH DISABILITIES

In this section we look at issues and problems common to working with all parents of children with disabilities.

Coping with Their Sense of Loss

Having a disabled child is most parents' nightmare. When the nightmare becomes reality, parents must deal with it in their own way and in their own time. Often parents first deny the disability or attempt to diminish its importance. Professionals working with parents during this phase in their response to the disability are often frustrated by the parents' apparent unwillingness to accept the fact and move on to treatment. When parents come to you during this phase, you must remember that they need time to accept what the disability means to themselves and their child.

Beyond the denial phase, parents have a great deal of work to do to come to terms with the fact that they have produced a less than perfect child. They must mourn the loss of the healthy child they had so hoped for, and they must deal with the psychological implications to themselves of having a child with a disability. You must be supportive during this phase and not attempt to move them too quickly beyond it. Accept their feelings, including their anger. You might help them find a support group for parents facing similar problems. You may even want to suggest that they have some therapy sessions of their own.

Relating Harmoniously as Co-Parents

Another common problem is that parents often have different ways of dealing with the fact of having a disabled child, and they may be experiencing real tension between themselves. Often it is the mother who dedicates her full time and energy to providing remedial services for her child, while the father works long hours to pay for the many required treatments. Putting all his energy into work may be his way of dealing with the pain. The roles may be reversed, but either way, the pattern leaves one parent feeling unsupported in the work with the child and the other parent isolated and out of touch. You must be aware of this and find ways to support each parent. Including both parents in Theraplay sessions can bring them closer together and help them find pleasure in sharing their relationship with their child. If the tensions are very great, you should encourage them to work on the issues in marital therapy.

Shifting from a Remedial to a Playful, Nurturing Approach

The effect of intense focus on "lessons" or remedial treatment is that the relationship becomes overly serious and work oriented: There is little fun, and the child may become angry and resistant. In the following example we see how Theraplay changed a serious, "stuck" relationship between a mother and her five-year-old son into a positive, fun-filled one that is now fertile ground for further healthy development.

THERAPLAY IN PRACTICE: *Making It More Fun.* Jeremy, a five-year-old with spina bifida, has been referred to the Theraplay Institute because of his negative, resistant behavior, high distractibility, tactile defensiveness, immature speech, and nonresponsiveness to his surroundings. He receives a variety of special services, including speech, music, physical, and occupational therapy. His oppositional behavior makes him frustrating to those who work with him. Paralyzed from the waist down since birth, Jeremy has difficulty performing simple arm and hand maneuvers; all movements require much effort. Life has become totally serious; the fun has been lost and only the struggle remains.

Jeremy's mother is deeply committed to helping her son attain his maximum potential. The interpreting therapist's goal is to help her become more aware of Jeremy's emotional needs and to develop more ways to have fun together. Our Theraplay goal with Jeremy is to help him see himself as a fun, lovable, competent person, and to inspire him with the courage to face his challenging situation. In an atmosphere that is fun and relationship-oriented, Jeremy's emotional needs must be met with engagement, nurturance, and challenge.

MIM WITH JEREMY AND HIS MOTHER. Jeremy and his mother sit on a mat and play with two small, squeaky animals.

MOTHER: Can I see one? (squeezes the animal) Did you hear that? Can yours do that? Let me hear yours. (holds the toy up in front of Jeremy) What are these called?

JEREMY: (inaudible response)

MOTHER: No, I think they're called pigs. Can you say that? Let's take the pigs and pretend they're going for a walk, OK? I'm going to walk down this leg (points to one of Jeremy's legs) . . . and you walk down that leg. (walks her animal down one of Jeremy's legs, but he doesn't follow suit)

MOTHER: What kind of pigs are these?

JEREMY: (inaudible response)

MOTHER: Are they tired? Did they have a tiring day at school? Do you think they can kiss each other? (touches the animals together and makes a kissing sound) (squeezes one animal while holding it over Jeremy's arm) Feel this? See, there's air that comes out of the little hole. (squeezes the toy in front of Jeremy's face) Feel that on your face. (takes Jeremy's finger and runs it over the pig's back) Does this feel smooth or rough?

JEREMY: (no response)

MOTHER: How does that feel? Is it rough or smooth?

JEREMY: (murmurs inaudibly)

MOTHER: I couldn't hear the answer. What was that? Can you say that again?

JEREMY: (no answer)

MOTHER: I think it's smooth. Can you feel that? (runs Jeremy's finger over the pig's tail) It's the pig's tail. And he has two ears. How many eyes does he have?

JEREMY: (points to one eye)

MOTHER: One. (Jeremy points to the other eye) Two . . . and there's his nose and there's his mouth. And he has feet: one, two, three, four. Would you like to put them back in the envelope? (opens the envelope and Jeremy deposits both pigs inside) . . . Good.

This mother is clearly caring and she makes some lovely playful attempts to engage Jeremy. But because he is so unresponsive, she becomes more and more insistent on teaching: asking questions and seeking answers. Given his unresponsiveness, there is no fun, spontaneity, or joyfulness. The plan for treatment was to find a variety of activities that Jeremy could easily respond to and that would entice him into playful interaction.

SESSION ONE. One therapist, Jane, sits on the couch supporting Jeremy in her lap, while the other therapist, Clara, kneels in front, engaging with him face to face. Although it is not essential, it is very helpful to have a team of two therapists with a child as disabled as Jeremy: one to support him physically, and the other to lead the activities. If you do not have a co-therapist, you can prop the child against pillows if necessary.

In this first get-acquainted session Clara takes charge, using persistent, positive, and engaging activities and remaining undeterred by negative responses. Clara keeps Jeremy focused and responsive by holding his hands, touching his cheeks, and talking to him in a playful way. "Hello, there, Jeremy. Oh, you brought your soft cheeks and your beautiful brown eyes. . . . Peek-a-boo, I see you. There you are. What a great boy you are!" Clara makes no demands on him to respond but proceeds whether he responds or not. Jeremy is alternately intrigued (he grins when she peeks at him from behind her hands) and resistant (he turns away with irritation when she touches his cheek) to the close contact.

Sessions are scheduled for once a week and include a variety of engaging (patty-cake, peek-a-boo, and "where did I touch you?"), nurturing (feeding, rubbing lotion on his hands and feet, rocking and singing to him), and challenging (pop-the-bubble, newspaper-punch, and push-me-over) activities. Because he is already too shut down and rigid in his approach to life, structuring activities are not emphasized for Jeremy.

Behind the one-way mirror, the interpreting therapist helps Jeremy's mother deal with her sadness and disappointment about his disability, gives her practical suggestions about how to organize Jeremy's various remedial therapies (including having his father take charge of the physical therapy), and helps her plan for refreshing breaks and brief vacations with her husband. As she watches Jeremy begin to have fun with Clara, she quickly picks up ideas for activities with Jeremy at home. She especially likes some of the active games—newspaper-punch and push-me-over—which she brings home for Jeremy's father to try as well.

After the fourth session, Jeremy's mother enters the Theraplay room. As her son has become more playful and cooperative, she has become more lively and engaging. She comes to sessions ready with new ideas for activities that would be just plain fun. At one point she says, "I think I'll leave the teaching to all of his teachers. He doesn't need another teacher, he needs a playmate."

SESSION TWELVE. Jeremy is now accepting nurturance and closeness. As you see in the following scene, his oppositional behavior has become more focused and is dealt with directly, as well as with paradoxical humor. Jane holds Jeremy in her lap, while Clara faces him.

CLARA: I saw those fancy toenails you brought with you . . . (points to each toe) one, two, three, four, five painted ones on this foot and one, two, three, four, five on this foot! What a fancy boy you are today! (Jeremy laughs) And oh, boy, I see that new tooth coming in (Jeremy opens his mouth wide). There it is! Now I want to see something. I want to see how high you can make your hands go up today. All the way up (Jeremy stretches his arms over his head). You're touching my fingers (touches her fingers to Jeremy's). A little bit higher . . . wow, what a stretch! (puts out her palms, face up, and holds Jeremy's hands on top of her own) When I say go, lift your hands up and clap them right down on mine. Ready, set, go! Clap them down! (Jeremy claps his hands down; therapist catches them) I caught you! Now pull your hands out (Jeremy pulls his hands out from her grasp). OK, now hold your hands out and I'll clap mine down on yours. Here I go (claps hands down). See if you can catch them. You caught them! Good.

JEREMY: (pushes Clara's leg)

CLARA: I felt that push; it's not time for pushing, it's time for catching (catches Jeremy's hands).

JEREMY: No!

CLARA: Oh, that was a good "No"! Do you have another one in there? Let me see . . .

JEREMY: No!

CLARA: Oh, you do! Now I have you caught in my hands. Pull your hands out. That's it. Now the other. Now let's see if you can wiggle your hands in here . . . (forms an opening with her fingers)

JEREMY: No!

CLARA: . . . and say "no" at the same time. Let's see if you can wiggle and say "no" at the same time.

JEREMY: No! (they all laugh)

CLARA: Oh, I love that "no" of yours. (catches Jeremy's hands) I've got your hands.

JEREMY: No!

CLARA: Great. Louder!

JEREMY: No!

CLARA: Louder!

JEREMY: Nooo!

CLARA: Now say "no" and pull your hands out.

JEREMY: (pulls one hand out and says "no," then pulls other hand out without saying anything)

CLARA: Where's that "no"? Is it under here (peeks under Jeremy's arm)? Is it here? (looks under her sleeve, etc.)

JEREMY: No!

CLARA: There it is! (they both laugh)

The session ends with Jane cradling Jeremy in her arms and singing "Rock-a-Bye-Jeremy."

THREE MONTHS LATER. Jeremy now shows his ability to be focused, to respond to challenges, and to be successful. Most important is his pleasure in himself and his enjoyment in interacting with others. Jeremy and Clara sit next to each other on a mat.

CLARA: (points to Jane, across the room) Now when she says "go!" we're going to start scooting over there.

JANE: Go!

CLARA: That's us. Okay, scoot! (they both start "scooting" on their bottoms across the mat) I'm going to follow you because it looks like you know where you're going. (Clara and Jeremy continue to play the game, both smiling and laughing)

SECOND MIM WITH MOTHER. In this post-treatment diagnostic session, Jeremy and his mother are sitting on the mat playing with two squeaky animals as they did in the first MIM. They are both laughing and having fun. The pigs are playfully engaged in dancing up and down Jeremy's legs, in blowing airy kisses back and forth between Jeremy and his mother, and in a variety of imaginative, playful interactions. Because Jeremy is so responsive and talkative and the atmosphere so full of joy, there is no need for his mother to struggle to elicit verbal responses from him or to teach him anything.

In an interview after the session, Jeremy's mother says, "I've seen such changes in Jeremy. He is enthusiastic and much more aware of his surroundings. Jeremy is also more fun; we always found him lovable, but now he jokes, he loves to tease, and he laughs more."

Theraplay had restored the loving happy interaction that had been lost because of the overemphasis on teaching and on working to overcome Jeremy's disability.

Overcoming Their Fear of Injuring Their Child

Both parents and therapists often hold back from energetic interaction with disabled babies. For example, a mother, knowing that her baby has a weak heart, fears imposing on him, startling him, or making demands on him. This fear prevents her from engaging in the usual energetic interaction so essential to the baby's learning about himself as a competent person able to have an impact on the world. It also interferes with the child's being able to negotiate the steps leading to greater autonomy.

As you saw with Jeremy, even though he was unable to move his legs, when playfully challenged there was no limit to what he could do using his arms to scoot about. Once you know what a particular child's physical limitations are, you can encourage active involvement up to those limits.

Coping with Their Anxiety over Separation

Knowing their child's limitations and fearing that they will be unable to communicate their needs to others, parents often find it difficult to separate from their child. They are thus unable to convey a sense of confidence to the child that it is all right to venture forth. When this is compounded by the child's fears, the family can truly become stuck. The best cure for the parents' fear is to see their child successfully handling separations. Therefore, focus on helping the child feel secure with you and able to separate from her mother. When we present Rosa's treatment, you will see how it is possible to help even a very young child overcome her fear of strangers.

UNDERSTANDING THE NEEDS COMMON TO CHILDREN WITH PHYSICAL DISABILITIES

In this section we look at issues and problems common to all children with physical disabilities.

Overcoming Fear of Strangers and Separation Anxiety

Children who have experienced surgeries and painful medical procedures develop an exaggerated fear of strangers and a tyrannical unwillingness to separate from their mothers. Based on their experience they expect all intimate contact with strangers to be painful. When the child's fears combine with the mother's sense of her child's fragility, an impasse develops in which the child is unable to separate from her parents. The following case illustrates how Theraplay is able to help in such situations.

THERAPLAY IN PRACTICE: *Dealing with Separation Issues.*[1] Rosa G. was a developmentally delayed, physically disabled two-year-old who would not separate from her mother. Because of her very low muscle tone (she was unable to sit without support, crawl, or walk) and her language delays, Rosa received homebound services once a week from one to two years of age. Her occupational, physical, and speech and language therapists routinely reported that Rosa was impossible to work with because of her crying and desperate clinging to her mother. At two years of age, she entered an early intervention program, which she attended with her mother. She refused to participate in any classroom activities and she was very upset when anyone tried to play with her. The staff at the early intervention program referred Rosa for Theraplay treatment.

The goal of Rosa's treatment was to gain her trust and overcome her resistance to adults and to new situations. In the MIM observation session, Rosa and her mother showed a lot of mutual affection. Her mother, however, seemed depressed and uncomfortable playing with her daughter; she did not take charge of the interaction. Whenever Rosa wanted her mother's attention, she would point, grab at her mother's blouse, or make a noise. In the classroom, she tyrannically controlled her mother through frequent hitting, scratching, and pulling at her. Mrs. G. reported that Rosa's behavior was better at home. Her greatest concern was Rosa's unwillingness to leave her side. This was particularly important to her since she needed to return to work.

It seemed clear from these observations that the focus of Rosa's treatment should be on engaging her and nurturing her. Another major goal of treatment would be to help Rosa separate from her mother. Although it might seem less stressful to a young child like Rosa to begin Theraplay sessions with her mother in the room, we have found that it usually works best right from the start to work with the child separate from her mother. Specifically, in Rosa's case we knew from the experience of the early intervention specialists, who had spent a fruitless year attempting to work with Rosa in the presence of her mother, that keeping them together would be of little help.

Because Rosa's intense crying would be painful for her mother to watch, we did not have her mother observe the first two sessions. Her mother was so eager to get help that she agreed, without hesitation, to our arrangement. She was well prepared for the fact that Rosa would strongly resist. Because there was no interpreting therapist available, the Theraplay therapist, Madelyn, arranged to talk, after each session, with Rosa's mother about her progress and about other management issues. Rosa participated in a total of seventeen sessions. During the course of the sessions, as Rosa got better, her mother returned to work. Theraplay sessions were ended when Rosa turned three and enrolled in public school.

SESSION ONE. Rosa cried hysterically and yelled for her mother for most of the session. She stiffened her body and screamed even louder when lotion was rubbed on her feet. Madelyn's efforts to interest her in popping bubbles or in playing peek-a-boo were to no avail. Madelyn simply held her and rocked her like a baby, and talked soothingly to her, "I've got you, you're safe." Because Rosa was so upset, Madelyn ended the session after fifteen minutes.

SESSION TWO. Rosa's crying was still uncontrollable. She stopped momentarily when Madelyn pretended to fall over as Rosa popped a bubble: "You popped the bubble and knocked me over!" The element of surprise had captured Rosa's attention for a moment. Because Rosa was so passive, Madelyn had to move her hand to the bubble in order to help her pop it. Very quickly Rosa was crying again. As she persisted, Madelyn mirrored her affect, sometimes imitating her crying, sometimes matching her anger, "No, No, I'm mad!" she shouted in Rosa's tone of voice. The mirroring usually produced a momentary pause in the crying and an intense look at Madelyn. (As you saw with Adam in Chapter Three, mirroring has the profound effect of making the distressed child aware of your presence and it conveys the message that you understand how angry or upset she is.) But soon Rosa would be crying again. By the fourth session, when the crying was still ongoing, and when Rosa burst into hysterical screams upon seeing her, Madelyn began to have doubts about her approach. After consulting with her supervisor, however, she persisted, continuing to mirror Rosa's affect and to attempt playful, nurturing activities. Later, when we looked at the videotape with the sound turned off, we could see Rosa's body gradually begin to relax and to cuddle into Madelyn's arms for comfort even as she continued crying.

SESSION FIVE. In the middle of this session there was a sudden upturn. Against mild protest, Madelyn had taken Rosa's shoes off (a first) to massage her feet with lotion. Then, as part of a playful way to put her shoes and socks back on, Madelyn put a sock on Rosa's head. Rosa laughed at this unexpected and surprising silliness. Gradually her crying stopped and she was able to pop bubbles without any help. Madelyn always chose activities that were well within Rosa's ability to respond and gave her some "control" over the games to give her a sense of success and competence.

Soon after this session, Rosa's mother returned to work and Rosa was picked up at her home and transported to the center on the center's special bus. It was now possible for Rosa to manage this separation from her mother.

SESSION ELEVEN. Giggling with delight and talking up a storm, Rosa enjoyed the give-and-take of Theraplay games. She was much more relaxed and enjoyed being swung in a blanket. She even teased a bit, hiding the beanbag behind her and cocking her head while saying, "Nooo." She showed a clear understanding of the simple baby games such as peek-a-boo, "Row Your Boat," and "throw the beanbag into my hands."

SESSION TWELVE. Mrs. G. joined in the session for the first time. (Because she was working, it had not been possible to bring her in sooner.) As we had expected, Rosa reverted to crying for part of the session. Madelyn took turns with Mrs. G. in rocking and singing to her. She encouraged Mrs. G. to take more control of her interaction with Rosa. By the end of seventeen sessions, Rosa was comfortable with the familiar adults at the center. She was happy and talkative. She was now more willing to participate in physical and occupational therapy and was making progress toward greater muscle control. She showed less stiffness in her arms and legs. She tolerated different kinds of physical activities and was now able to walk when someone held her hand. Mrs. G. was delighted with Rosa's progress. Rosa's trust in Madelyn had generalized to other adults. Now, as they saw their efforts well rewarded, the staff of the early intervention center fully enjoyed working with Rosa. Some staff members, who had been resistant to the Theraplay approach initially, began to incorporate the fun, interactive, and nurturing games of Theraplay with other "difficult" children.

Overcoming Passivity and Developing Responsiveness

The early sections of this book describe the reciprocal nature of the early parent-infant relationship and how important the baby's babbling, cooing, and gurgling responses are in stimulating the parents' continued playful verbal interaction. They describe the importance of recognizing the baby's eye, facial, and overall body responses in helping the parent maintain her own high state of engagement. A blind baby, a hearing-impaired baby, or a baby unable to respond physically will inhibit parents' responsiveness. As we saw in Jeremy's treatment, Theraplay can increase a passive, resistant child's responsiveness.

Developing a Positive Self-Image

Recently a mental health worker in the Head Start program was asked to see what he could do to help a four-year-old girl feel better about herself. Lateesha had been born with only the stubs of fingers on one hand. Although she was expert at using both her hands and was otherwise an attractive, active, and competent child, her teachers and the other children were finding it difficult to relate to her because of their uneasiness about the malformation. Sensing that it would help the child as well as her teachers and the other children if he could make the malformed hand less frightening, the mental health worker decided to make painted handprints of several children's hands including Lateesha's. Roberto gathered a group of five or six children around a table in the Head Start classroom, and had them rub paint on each other's hands in order to make prints on a large piece of paper. Each child's special hand print was identified and commented on: different sizes, different patterns of lines at the knuckles, different length of fingers. Lateesha entered in with interest and excitement, noting how the fingers on her two hands were different. Then Roberto began checking the many ways the children could use their hands: Lateesha could pick up a pencil with her thumb and her short fingers, Samantha could hold scissors in her left hand, and Kester could touch his thumbs to his little fingers. Following this brief intervention, the atmosphere in the classroom was much more relaxed about Lateesha's "difference."

Body image problems can arise not only because children perceive their bodies to be different, but also because the disability has necessarily prevented them from engaging in the physical interaction that leads to a healthy body image. Because it is playful, physical, and interactive, Theraplay can teach parents how to find comfortable ways to touch, hold, and physically interact with their child and thus help their child develop a more positive body image.

The approaches that we have been discussing can be applied in working with any disabled child. We now discuss two specific disabling conditions, hearing impairment and cerebral palsy, in order to demonstrate how you can adapt Theraplay to meet the challenges of a particular disability. These representative disabilities can point the way to understanding how to apply the principles to any child.

It requires a radically different set of techniques and expectations to conduct a Theraplay session with a person who is deaf or a person who is blind. (A game of "wink," for example, obviously would be without meaning for a child who is blind.) And techniques useful for both of these in turn may be quite impractical in working with a child who is nonambulatory or multiply disabled. To assume otherwise would prove seriously disadvantageous to patients and frustrating to the therapist.

ADAPTING THERAPLAY FOR CHILDREN WITH HEARING IMPAIRMENT

The main problem in working with a hearing-impaired child is finding a way to communicate without spoken language. Fortunately, since Theraplay is primarily a nonverbal (or preverbal) treatment, it is an ideal modality for the child with hearing impairment. Naturally, signing should be part of the interaction as soon as possible. Even without signs, however, communication through facial expression and body language is possible.

Talking When the Child Cannot Hear

Ingenuity and self-confidence are required to behave playfully, intrusively, and "in charge" with a child who cannot hear what you are saying. In addition to all the compensatory games and ways of stimulating and relating to him, you must learn, just as a mother must learn with her baby, that a hearing-impaired child's inability to understand speech need not keep you from speaking to him. It takes a skillful therapist indeed to be free enough to keep up a happy chatter while challenging his young deaf charge to a seed-spitting match or a pillow fight. It takes more skill yet to carry out some of the Theraplay activities that are nurturing, such as singing a lullaby. But if you do not make the sounds that an adult normally would make with a child, you will appear to the child as wooden, restrained, and half-human, and the child will miss the comforting vibrations of your voice as she cuddles up to your chest while you talk or sing.

Avoiding Surprises That the Child Cannot Hear

Since the hearing-impaired child's casual suspicion that "others are talking about me" could evolve too readily into a paranoid conviction, you must avoid activities that might reinforce such fears. You should avoid surprises, such as creeping up from behind or any back-to-back activities (such as walking backward into position for a water pistol duel).

Increasing the Impact

The absence of sound should not preclude stimulation as a way of making significant impact. The hearing-impaired child needs compensatory input, and the therapist must give it by exaggerating what the child *can* perceive. To quote James Thomas, who has worked with many children through the Chicago Hearing Society, "If you're working with a hearing child, you can communicate with your tone of voice what a fabulous impact he is making on you. With a deaf child, you have to *act* it out instead. When I arm wrestle, for example, and lose at it, I put on an exaggerated form of defeat. I don't just allow him to plant my arm down on the tabletop; I literally let him bowl me over. That way I let him know I just marvel at the strength of such a little fellow knocking over a great big guy like me. If he were a hearing child, my tone of voice would tell him that. Facial expression tells it all" (personal communication).

Establishing Trust

When you work with children with hearing impairment, even more than with children who can hear, you must be aware of how the child perceives you. You must be ever alert to potential mistrust. For this reason, your initial greeting should not be carried out in the bold, quick, intrusive way usually characteristic of Theraplay. Instead, you must go more slowly and give as many indications as possible that you are a friendly, trustworthy person. For example, a clear, nonverbal, friendly—but not surprising—greeting such as a cheerful "high-five" is appropriate.

Although, as you will see when we discuss Nicholas's treatment, it is not necessary to know sign language, it can be a great help. If the child understands signs, the following might be your first communication: "My name is Jim. I want to get to know you. What is your name?" If you are working with hearing-impaired children, the learning and teaching of signing—in as joyful, gratifying, relaxed, and playful a manner as possible—should be your first priority.

The following dialogue from a sample signed Theraplay session shows the use of exaggerated physical response plus a respectful, nonthreatening way of communicating with a child who knows some signs:

THERAPIST: Stand up. Now jump. Fine (applauding). Climb on my knee. Wonderful (applause). Now let's arm wrestle. I'll show you. Try again. (putting arm down for arm wrestling)

CHILD: ("wins" round)

THERAPIST: I'm trying hard. (in mock determination) Maybe OK this time. [But] I'll show you.

CHILD: ("wins" round)

THERAPIST: Try again. (grimacing in "agony")

CHILD: ("wins" round)

THERAPIST: Again.

CHILD: ("wins" round)

THERAPIST: Again (as though to convey "I don't believe this happened"). Try again.

CHILD: ("wins")

THERAPIST: Wonderful. Stop. We have to do something else now.

At the end of the session, the therapist applauds, signs "We've finished," adds, "I have to go now. I'll be back tomorrow," and gives the child a big hug and leaves.

THERAPLAY IN PRACTICE: *Communicating with a Hyperactive Hearing-Impaired Child.* Frankie, a six-year-old hearing-impaired child, was referred for help because of hyperactivity. He was seen in his home by Steven, a Theraplay therapist. Grandmother, mother, and aunt presented Frankie at the first session, as if to say, "There he is. Now let's see what *you* can do." Throughout all the sessions, all three were present and seemed bewildered by the fact that Steven never echoed their typical refrain of "No," "Stop that," "Don't do that." Instead, Steven caught Frankie's testing behavior and gave it back to him with fun and joyfulness. As hard as he tried, Frankie never could get into trouble with Steven because he made everything into an OK, fun activity.

Communicating with signs was very difficult, and Frankie didn't know what to anticipate. Steven had to show rather than tell him what they were going to do. At first Frankie was very anxious and tried to run from one side of the room to the other. Steven caught him firmly as he ran and swung him in the air for a merry-go-round. Frankie laughed and tried to run again. When he did so, Steven caught him and flipped him and finally jumped up and down with him. A few sessions later, after he had calmed down, Steven showed him how to walk up his body, starting at his knee and finally making it to shoulder height. He was scared at first but then got more confidence and jumped to the floor with Steven holding him safely.

One day, holding him upside down by the legs, Steven walked around the room as Frankie lifted Steven's feet up and down. Frankie clearly loved the feeling that it was he who was controlling *Steven's* walking. After that, he was much more willing to work as a team—to be stiff when Steven needed him to be, to wait before jumping, and so on. He began looking forward to the sessions and began having more fun every time. Although initially he was seldom calm and anyone watching thought he would never stop, at the end (fifteen sessions later) he often sat quietly for long periods. His mother and his grandmother described him as a different person.

It is clear from the foregoing that a child's failure to hear the happy chatter of a Theraplay therapist need not preclude growth and self-confidence any more than a small baby's inability to hear his mother's voice necessarily leads to stunted personality development.

THERAPLAY IN PRACTICE: *Forming an Attachment with a Deaf Adopted Child.* Next consider the case of Nicholas, a profoundly deaf four-year-old adopted from an Eastern European orphanage at the age of three. The work was very challenging because it combined all the difficulties you encounter in treating unattached children who have been raised in orphanages (which we discuss in Chapter Ten) with all the problems you face in working with children who cannot hear and respond to your voice.

Nicholas was a charming boy with dark brown hair and bright brown eyes. Removed from his biological home as an infant because of neglect, Nicholas was placed in an orphanage where he spent the first three years of his life. His American adoptive parents, who originally intended to adopt only one child, brought Nicholas home to the United States when he was three, along with his two sisters, ages six and eight. It is unknown exactly when and why Nicholas lost his hearing.

Upon meeting Nicholas, his new parents were confronted with continuous screaming, hitting, biting, and throwing; if they were not quick to catch him as one of his tantrums hit, he would destroy everything in sight. Whenever they held him, Nicholas would struggle with all his might to free himself, while yelling at an unbelievable pitch. Feeding was impossible and bedtime was a horror. Changing his diaper was a major event, particularly when his adoptive parents tried to clean him. As Nicholas never made eye contact, his parents could not rely on facial expressions to communicate their love and support. They tried everything, but nothing seemed to work. Prior to Theraplay, patience was their only resource.

Theraplay was started as soon as possible after the initial MIM, which simply confirmed how frantic and out of control Nicholas was. Since his therapist, Helen, works alone, she asked his mother to observe the first sessions and to be available to help if she was needed. Nicholas's father was unavailable for the sessions, but his wife kept him informed about what went on in Theraplay, and he did Theraplay activities with Nicholas at home.

SESSION ONE. When Helen first met Nicholas, he screamed "Hello" and lunged for her animal crackers. When she captured him, he thrashed and kicked to be released. Upon seeing this behavior, she reorganized this first Theraplay session around one objective, namely, to hold and comfort Nicholas no matter how much he resisted. Needless to say, after forty-five minutes she was a very tired therapist, she had several new bruises, and her ears were ringing from Nicholas' incessant screaming. She now knew what to expect, however, and was fully prepared for the next session.

SESSION TWO. Two days later, Helen greeted Nicholas with a full embrace, swinging him into the air as they entered the office. While struggling to take off his coat and shoes, she looked him straight in the eyes. Although he continued to scream, she knew her first priority must be to hold him in her arms. He often tried to hurt her, as he struggled to get away, but Helen kept herself safe, especially in this case to model self-protection for his mother. It was very difficult to maintain physical control over Nicholas. By holding him across her lap with his legs secured under one of hers and one of his arms behind her back, she was able to look at his face and hold his other arm in front of her. While she touched and lotioned his free hand, she kept her face within inches of his, letting him know without question that she was in charge and that he would be safe. This message had to be conveyed entirely by her facial expression and manner.

At this point Helen had not learned to sign, but it was just as well, as she needed both hands to hold Nicholas securely in her lap. Finally, after using up half a bottle of lotion, Nicholas's free arm began to relax, and she placed it gently on his tummy. Pulling his other arm out from behind her, she started the nurturing process over again: more lotion and more attention. After repeating this routine many times, Nicholas got the message that the calm hand was to stay on his tummy while the other one received Helen's tender loving care. She also established eye contact, which was critical for communication. So unaccustomed was Nicholas to giving up control, he seemed to stare at her in disbelief.

After forty-five minutes, the session was over and Nicholas had to leave. When Helen released him to his mother's arms, he immediately broke free, escaping out the door and down the hall. Helen quickly ran after him, caught him up in her arms, and repeated their holding routine before passing him back to his mother.

The next day Nicholas's mother called Helen to say he was calm and playful; he didn't even scream until bedtime. Two days later, she called to report that Nicholas had diarrhea. Strangely enough, she was excited over this news, as she had been able to change his diaper without incident. Though it had been hard to hold him down, she had successfully maintained control using firm eye contact and a loving expression.

SESSION THREE. Five days later, Nicholas approached Helen while holding his mother's hand and pulling her toward the Theraplay room. Helen quickly took over, preparing Nicholas for the session with a safe, nurturing hold. He immediately placed one arm on his tummy and offered the other to Helen. Seeing her smile of delight, he matched it with a scream. Unlike his usual yells, however, this one wasn't ear piercing. Helen smiled warmly and continued to explore his tongue, teeth, eyes, and ears, mirroring his emotions.

Helen then invited his mother to lotion Nicholas' legs while she took care of his upper body. This worked very well, until Nicholas was ready for something to eat. Knowing that he could become wild while being fed, Helen slowly put one cracker in his mouth. As expected, Nicholas bit into it aggressively and then began to thrash and scream. Since affect matching had proved successful before, Helen tried it again, now gazing at Nicholas with a firm expression that equaled his own. He appeared to be shocked, as though he had never seen such a look. Establishing eye contact, Helen pointed to the crook of her arm, and gently moved his head back into it, looking at him with a nurturing expression.

That worked for a moment, but he soon struggled to sit up. Nicholas responded to a repeat of Helen's "point and put" gesture and accepted another cracker. This routine was repeated at least ten times. The technique worked: Nicholas now sat up, indicated that he wanted another cracker, and put his head back down on her waiting arm. They smiled and laughed, enjoying every second.

Nicholas's mother, watching this happy scene, longed to be part of it. Since children just beginning to trust a new relationship are often not ready to relax with their own mothers, Helen reminded her that Nicholas might still need some time before he could be calm with her at home. After completing their getting-ready-to-leave ritual, Helen gave Nicholas some gummy bears for the long ride home. Later, Nicholas' mother said he insisted on sharing his gummy bears with her in the car, something he had never done before. Mom, of course, was thrilled.

SESSION FOUR. Two days later, they returned and the routine from the previous session was repeated, this time with Nicholas's total compliance. Now the play was less constrained. Nicholas seemed to enjoy being fed and allowing someone else to be in charge. It was time now for his mother to participate more fully. She and Helen sat on the mat with their feet touching, making a space within which Nicholas could move. Helen made sure his mother was comfortable and ready to take care of him without getting hurt. They rolled him between them, allowed him to crawl from lap to lap, and every so often gathered him up in one or the other's arms. He happily accepted the crackers they fed him, and they all simply enjoyed one another.

Since holding Nicholas had such a calming effect, his mother decided to try holding and nurturing him several times a day at home. Helen asked whether she was really up to this; she said she was. Indeed, her commitment showed, as Nicholas was even better behaved the following session.

SESSION SIX. Earlier in the week, one of Nicholas' teachers had called to say that his screaming in class was driving everyone mad (except for the hearing-impaired students). Since holding and nurturing him had stopped his throwing everything he could get his hands on, Helen wondered if the same technique would stop his screaming? After many experiences of being held, Nicholas did stop screaming. However, he also added a new twist: Out of the blue, he would let out a yelp, look into Helen's eyes and lie down, waiting to be held. This was such a transparent appeal for love and attention that his mother and Helen couldn't help but laugh; after all, Nicholas is a charmer.

Over the next few sessions, although it was not always smooth sailing, Nicholas became more and more open to the playful, nurturing games his mother and Helen offered him.

SESSION SEVEN. During this session, Helen sensed something different about Nicholas; he wasn't as aggressive as usual and his underlying affect was flat. He did laugh and play, but something was troubling him, and he didn't have the words to express himself.

SESSION EIGHT. After making sure his mother was following, Nicholas came into the office without hesitation. Expecting the usual routine, he went directly to the play mat. He seemed calm and able to enjoy the intimacy of being fed and rubbed with lotion. Then suddenly he had the urge to play. He was impulsive and his movements were jerky. He was signing to Helen, but neither his mother nor she could understand him. Fortunately, Kate, the therapist for hearing-impaired children, had agreed to join the session. She approached the mat, made eye contact with Nicholas, and began signing (Nicholas was familiar with Kate as she did the initial assessment and referral). Happy to communicate, he immediately engaged in conversation. When they discussed obeying his mother, he hid his face with his hands (a developmentally appropriate behavior). Soon it became obvious that Nicholas was starving for communication at a higher level.

As a result of this discovery, the need for some changes at home was discussed. First, all family members needed to use sign language when speaking to each other so Nicholas could understand what was being discussed. Second, at the dinner table, he should sit facing the person with the most signing skills. Third, the family needed to catch up to his signing level; he had obviously surpassed them. Perhaps the void or emptiness Helen had perceived over the past several sessions could be explained by the simple fact that he was lonely, lacking the communication that he needed. During the rest of the session, Helen and his mother continued to provide nurturing and play, but Nicholas was sad when Kate had to leave. Helen matched his sadness, and communicated through affect for the remainder of the session.

In a following consultation with Kate, it was decided that Nicholas' treatment should be structured to include more challenges. Kate was to meet privately with Mother for the first twenty minutes of his session, while Helen provided nurturing and structured play. Kate and Mother then were to join the session; Kate would provide communication while Helen provided intimate and challenging play. The new plan was implemented at the next session.

Nicholas thus moved a long way from the angry, impulsive, isolated child he was when treatment first started. He became a calmer, more interactive child eager to communicate and enjoy others. When he was overstimulated, however, he reverted to his earlier wild behavior. Following one such episode, his mother commented, "I forget how much progress he has made until I see him again as he was in the beginning. Most of the time now he is truly a changed child."

ADAPTING THERAPLAY FOR CHILDREN WITH CEREBRAL PALSY

The Theraplay goals of increased self-confidence, affirmed body boundaries, and improved coordination make it an appropriate method of treatment for children with cerebral palsy. Since it is so decisive, direct, and cautiously challenging, it cannot help but encourage the child to "do his best." But certain modifications must be made in the usual strategy.

Understanding Cerebral Palsy

Cerebral palsy is defined by S. Nichtern (1974, p. 120) as a "disorder of the nervous system characterized by disturbances of motor function [which] may be accompanied by sensory disturbances, seizures, mental retardation, learning difficulties, or behavioral disorders." Children with cerebral palsy are limited not only by their own stereotyped movements, but also by their reactions and responses to being moved. The child cannot respond as a normal child does to being dressed, fed, or carried. Rather than moving in synchrony with the adult who does the caretaking, he can only cry and become stiff and frightened.

In engaging in active physical play with a child with cerebral palsy, you must bear in mind that the condition makes it difficult for these children to contain their excitement, control their movements, and make contact in appropriate ways. Because of this you must monitor time and tempo carefully to reduce excitement. Activities must be smoothly flowing, contain only few and small surprises, avoid quick shifts and movements, and proceed without upsets.

RECOGNIZING ATHETOID CEREBRAL PALSY. It is important to distinguish between two types of children with cerebral palsy: athetoid and spastic. Known by workers in the field as "floppy," the athetoid child is unable to maintain body tonus. Her involuntary movements and the constantly changing tone of her muscles make her easily lose her balance and fall over. Unless she is propped up against a firm surface, she will "flop" down; unless she wears braces, she will "crumble"; unless she is supported and held, she will collapse. Passivity, not activity, characterizes her day. Unable to carry out most activities, her tendency is to lie down rather than sit. Generally, she gives the picture of being poorly defined with respect to her body. Occasionally she screams or yells, but the sounds she makes are for the most part guttural.

RECOGNIZING SPASTIC CEREBRAL PALSY. The characteristics of the child with spastic cerebral palsy are quite the opposite. Rather than being floppy, he is rigid. Rather than being passive, he is often agitated and eager to move. Jerky and uneven in movement, his very overactivity is sometimes his downfall. In the excitement that is both responsive to and generative of his high activity level, he may "lock" in position and remain thus frozen until someone comes along to "unlock" him. If not handled well he becomes more rigid.

These two kinds of palsy obviously require different kinds of treatment, different lengths of attention, different tempos, and different Theraplay activities. You must first observe the child to determine whether and to what degree he is "floppy" or spastic. In either case, you must handle him slowly so that he can make his own adjustment, supporting him when necessary but always trying to keep him active.

Treating Children with Cerebral Palsy

Before looking at specific activities for each of the two groups, we need to understand some general guidelines for working with children with cerebral palsy.

FOLLOWING GENERAL GUIDELINES. The following recommendations, based on Nancie Finnie's (1975, pp. 17–18) primer for parents of cerebral-palsied infants, contain clear elements of structure, engagement, nurture, and challenge and thus are made-to-order directives for Theraplay therapists working with children with cerebral palsy:

1. Impose your "talking face" in front of the baby in order to teach him "the vital skill of concentrating on one set of meaningful and associated stimuli, rather than vaguely scanning the world in general. [In this way] he learns to filter out confusing and irrelevant sensations and to pay attention to one problem at a time."

2. Play with the child in a way that is mutually pleasurable for both of you. "If the child is smiling and excited, he is playing and learning. Physical contact games (cuddling, . . . stroking, rubbing noses, kissing); visual games (approach and retreat of adult's face, movements of mouth, tongue, and head, hiding and reappearing); and vocal games (singing, gentle talking, lip and tongue noises, blowing and puffing air)" lead on to more active games such as clapping hands, wrestling, and rough-housing.

3. Always talk to the child. He should hear "the singsong rhythm of normal speech, and the flow of normal language." Avoid focusing on single words that he has to imitate.

4. Imitate every noise he makes—"even a burp or a chuckle." If you wait a little while and repeat the noise again, the child later on will listen for that response and smile when he hears it. "He is now playing with sounds! Still later he will make his noise in order to get you to copy, and then you are 'throwing' sounds back and forwards like a ball, with enjoyment. You can then vary the sound and he will try to follow you . . . (you are teaching him to enjoy learning to control his speech organs to make the

sounds he wants). If he tries to imitate your play or your voice, repeat the procedure and wait again, so that he knows it is his turn."

5. If the child is to be helped to complete tasks on his own, you must gauge carefully how long to let him struggle and when it is appropriate to step in. "He must be shown the task, and then helped to go through the movements with his own hands or body. . . . After he begins to move with you . . . gradually withdraw your effort, particularly at the end of a sequence so that he completes the task by himself."

6. Rather than back down for fear of a battle, maintain your position. The child with cerebral palsy both resents pressure for conformity and enjoys upsetting grown-ups. *"Don't let him enjoy upsetting you* (and don't relent). In the long run, it is kinder to be firm."

7. You must be patient with the slow-to-respond child. Even though he may be unable to respond quickly, he still may be quite able to understand.

8. You must persevere even if improvement is very slow. Often signs of progress will be very small.

9. You must learn to concentrate on helping the child now rather than worrying about the future. "What is needed is a determination to help him develop to the maximum of his capabilities," not a preoccupation with whether he will ever approximate the normal.

10. You must be firm and consistent in requiring reasonable conformity. "Disabled children must develop socially appropriate behavior like everybody else."

11. As with any child, you must insistently make your presence felt. If the child with cerebral palsy receives "little attention, stimulation, or social contact [he] will tend to occupy himself with body manipulation, especially if he has partial or complete loss of vision or hearing or in some cases is severely mentally disabled."

12. You should encourage interest in the environment through peek-a-boo games and the hiding and finding of objects.

PLANNING APPROPRIATE ACTIVITIES FOR CHILDREN WITH ATHETOID CEREBRAL PALSY. Having determined what kind of palsy you are dealing with, you must plan your activities accordingly. If the child is "floppy," you are not so likely to encounter disorganized behavior but you will have to motivate, mobilize, energize, and activate. To keep the child attending, you should use a wall as back support and position yourself squarely in front of the child. Furthermore, your activities must be particularly well defined. You must realize that work with children who are "floppy," unlike work with those who are spastic, will take a long time and will bring few rewards.

Anthony Vitiello (personal communication) makes the following suggestions for Theraplay therapists:

- Plan longer-lasting activities.

- Imitate the child's sounds, even her screaming.

- Encourage lower- and higher-pitched screaming, to practice control.

- Encourage the child to imitate you.

- Engage in simple, repetitive activities. Even though as rudimentary a motion as patty-cake may take months to teach, it provides an important experience.

THERAPLAY IN PRACTICE: *Working with a Child with Severe Athetoid Cerebral Palsy.* Working with children with severe athetoid cerebral palsy can be very difficult. They are extremely unresponsive and difficult to reach. The following example shows how persistence and patience can pay off in working with such a child.

Rose Marie is a twelve-year-old child with athetoid cerebral palsy. Her reflexes are that of a very young baby, and it is generally thought she will never get beyond that. Like a small baby, when she turns her head, her hand goes with it (asymmetric tonic neck reflex). During the first ten years of her life, Rose Marie lay on a carpet on the living room floor, her loving family having no awareness that there could be any alternative for her. She was so floppy and hypotonic that it seemed nothing could be done with her.

Faced with this passive child in her day-treatment center, her therapist, Amy, tried to figure out what could be done. She came up with the idea of warmed massage oil. With Rose Marie seated on her lap (which is tricky in itself because Amy must flex Rose Marie's knees up and cross her arms in front of her on her stomach), Amy began massaging her arms. This brought a mild positive response.

Next Amy tried to get Rose Marie to imitate her. First she blew on her cheeks over and over, trying to get the child to copy the activity. After half an hour, Rose Marie was able to get all her muscles working at last, and she blew back at Amy's face. Amy threw back her head and acted as though struck by a great west wind. It was the first time Rose Marie had given any response more than an undifferentiated holler.

Amy then began including other people on the ward. Long-time workers with severely unresponsive children tend to forget that "there's someone in there." Amy spent time with each child worker teaching her to fall over backward. It wasn't long before Rose Marie was blowing every one of them down. Rose Marie gained a sense of personal power that she had never had before. She now could make an impact on her environment.

One week Rose Marie missed her Theraplay session because she had the flu. As Amy came to see her the following week, Rose Marie screamed at her angrily. When Amy came close and put her face next to hers, Rose Marie blew with such force and "knocked Amy down" so hard that it seemed clear that she wanted to "punch" her in the face.

Two months later Rose Marie was observed by Terry Koller, Amy's supervisor from the Theraplay Institute, who noted: "What I saw was impressive. The quality of the interaction indicated that not only was this child able to 'blow' on command but that this blowing was done in a manner which indicated that Rose Marie (who had apparently related to no one) now recognized her worker and enjoyed engaging in this game. She laughed, lost her limp posture, and made intense eye contact with her new friend. I was then told that this child could now communicate her preferences for food at mealtime. By placing a small flag by items on a plate, she could blow the flag indicating her preference. The staff is so enthusiastic that they are exploring the possibility of buying an electric board which can be used to communicate with others by blowing."

PLANNING APPROPRIATE ACTIVITIES FOR CHILDREN WITH SPASTIC CERE-BRAL PALSY. If the child is spastic, you should avoid activities that might increase the spasticity and cause the child to "freeze." Freezing, however, is not catastrophic; it only takes time and soothing activity to release the tension and get the child "unlocked."

Theraplay for Children with Spastic Cerebral Palsy (Vitiello):

- If "locking" occurs, shift activity to fluid, down-and-out movement for relaxation.

- If a spastic stance occurs, encourage child to "stay put" while you help him out. Discourage the "running around" he may wish to do instead.

- Avoid surprising, jerky, or too-quick activities. A spastic child, attempting to follow, may become "locked."

- Be careful in holding the child. Carry him on the side, straddling your hip. A spastic child may lock his legs if carried from the front.

- Plan short, not long, activities—a spastic child may become "flooded" if worked with too much.

- Keep activities flowing evenly and smoothly.

- Emphasize soothing activities (such as lotion, powder, and bubbles), but remember the child may be hypersensitive to tactile stimulation.

- If the condition is not too severe, some surprising (silly) activities such as pulling a pretend "something" out of the child's ear may be possible.

- Predictions or announcements of activities to come are not necessary.

- Poking or playful jostling is unwise.

The following Theraplay activities can be used in working with a child with spastic cerebral palsy. A typical session would include first making hand- or footprints, then measuring her size and having her crawl under the therapist for "tunnels" (difficult but not impossible; the "wheelbarrow" usually is impossible). Then you could shift to something soothing like hiding and finding candy or blowing bubbles. Timing is always important; these children act up if an activity continues too long. After a soothing activity, you could switch to something active like arm wrestling (difficult with a really spastic cerebral-palsied child), then back to quieting down, putting on shoes, and leaving.

INVOLVING FAMILY MEMBERS. Helpful as one-on-one treatment can be in engaging the child with cerebral palsy, the power is doubled if his family can be involved as well. There is no place for condescending pity or recriminatory guilt. Indeed, within the Theraplay session itself a new and healthier balance of forces may develop within the family. Brothers and sisters may be freed of their burdens as they are told, "Holding Jim steady is Mom's job, Jane, not yours," or "So you moved a mite too fast, Jack; you haven't really hurt her, see? All you have to do is wait a bit and she'll be quite OK." But mostly, with the take-charge confidence of the Theraplay therapist you encourage, "Come on, Dad, he's not going to break if you play a little," or "Come on, Mom, you can help him to help himself . . . like this, see? He doesn't *have* to be helpless, you know. . . . Come on, surer than that, surer than that . . . don't let him talk you out of it now, come on. . . ." As it gains in momentum, a healthier family climate follows.

Only through the Theraplay experiences of "letting go"—within a playful setting—can many parents begin the difficult process of encouraging independence. Challenge is very often the name of the game.

The message has been the same throughout this chapter on Theraplay for children with disabilities. Whatever the disabling condition, the analogy between the relationship of the "good enough" mother with her disabled infant and the Theraplay therapist with his patient applies: Growth-promoting harmony, regardless of the obstacles, should be the goal.

Notes

1. An earlier version of this case study appeared in "Theraplay with Developmentally-Disabled Infants and Toddlers" by Rieff, *The Theraplay Institute Newsletter,* Fall 1991. Reprinted with permission of *The Theraplay Institute.*

CHAPTER NINE

Theraplay for Children Who Have Been Abused and Traumatized

T he first edition of this book made it clear that Theraplay was not the treatment of choice for children who have been traumatized, whether by the loss of a parent through death or abandonment, a painful medical procedure, a natural disaster, or by physical or sexual abuse. We recommended instead that the child receive treatment designed to help her come to terms with the experience—to understand what happened, to express the feelings that the trauma aroused, and to be reassured both that she did not cause the trauma and that she will not be punished for it. We acknowledged, however, that a modified form of Theraplay, primarily involving nurturing and self-esteem-enhancing activities, could be a useful adjunct to the more traditional treatments, particularly if some time had passed since the traumatic event.

In the two decades since the book was first published, we have become much more convinced of Theraplay's positive contribution

---

Part of this chapter first appeared as "Touch with Abused Children" by Fuller and Booth, *The Theraplay Institute Newsletter,* Fall 1997. Reprinted with permission of the Theraplay Institute.

to the treatment of traumatized children. We see more clearly how trauma can disrupt the parent-child relationship as well as how the disruption of a parent-child relationship (as when the child is placed in foster care) can cause trauma. We see that traumatized children and their families often are unable to play. We have become more aware of the physiological effect of trauma on the child and therefore of the need to engage the child in physically calming activities that include nurturing touch. We also have had more experience with the effectiveness of combining Theraplay with trauma work. Although Theraplay does not replace insight and coming-to-terms with the experience, we now see that Theraplay has much more to offer than was originally evident.

Theraplay's emphasis on building relationships makes it an ideal treatment for children who have been traumatized. Treatment that includes caregivers in order to repair disrupted relationships or develop new relationships is essential to the child's healing. By including caretakers in the treatment process, we help them understand their child's anxieties and negative behaviors and learn to interact with their child in a healthier manner. When children experience their parents as empathic, caring, comforting, and trustworthy adults who can provide safety and structure in their lives, the process of cure is well on its way.

Theraplay's ability to teach parents and children how to play also makes an important contribution to the healing process. Play makes it possible for children to integrate and transcend everyday experiences, whether good or bad. Play helps them go from feeling weak and bad to feeling strong and good through physical activities such as jumping, running, pushing, and pulling, through quieter give and take interactions with playful adults, as well as through symbolic play that acts out the vanquishing of the "bad guy."

For a number of reasons, many traumatized children don't play: They fear the loss of control that play and fantasy imply; they don't know how to play because they never learned or were not allowed to play, or because it is thought to be unseemly to play (especially following a trauma such as the death of siblings or parents). For many of the same reasons parents do not play with their children. Additionally, parents are often fearful that if they play they will compromise their parental authority.

Theraplay helps the traumatized child learn that it is good to be a child and that it is safe to play. It also teaches parents how to play and still be parents. It teaches parents how to take charge in a nonpunitive way in order to provide safe limits. We thus reassure parents and children that play can be both safe and enjoyable.

The traumatized child's need to be physically calmed and soothed can also be addressed through Theraplay. Through a variety of calming, soothing activities as well as appropriate, nurturing touch, we help the child modulate her hyperaroused state and become more calm. We describe this in more detail later in this chapter.

A great deal has been written about the important part of the healing process that involves the child's emotional and cognitive understanding of her experience. The works of Beverly James (1989, 1994) and Eliana Gil (1991, 1994) are excellent examples of discussions of treatment of traumatized children. For most children who have been traumatized, this aspect of the healing process must be addressed at some time through focused trauma work. A child therapist experienced in working with the child's specific traumatizing issues—abandonment, death of a loved one, sexual or physical abuse, and so forth—should provide such treatment.

Sometimes the child is not ready to do the work or needs to form a more secure and trusting relationship with her therapist and her caretakers before she will be ready. All treatment of traumatized children must be customized to meet the child's needs and planned on a case-by-case basis. One child's strong need to talk about a traumatic event (such as being kidnapped, or seeing her mother killed by an intruder) would best be met by primary trauma treatment. Another child, fearful and withdrawn following placement in a temporary foster home, would benefit from Theraplay, with the trauma treatment coming later when life is more secure. As we discuss in Chapter Ten, Theraplay may often be the primary treatment for an adopted child because establishing a strong attachment to the new parents takes priority over dealing with past trauma, even though the trauma was significant. Sometimes focused trauma work can take place concurrently with Theraplay. In other cases, Theraplay treatment comes first and builds enough trust for the child that he is later ready to embark on trauma work.

In this chapter we look at the special adaptations of Theraplay that you must make when treating traumatized children. In Chapter Ten we consider the role of Theraplay in repairing or building new relationships for children who have been adopted or are in foster care.

To understand fully why Theraplay is useful in meeting the special needs of abused and traumatized children, we must first understand in some detail how trauma affects the relationship between the child and her parents. Especially helpful in this understanding is the work of Beverly James (1994).

UNDERSTANDING THE IMPACT OF TRAUMA

James (1994, p. 9) defines trauma thus: "Psychological trauma occurs when an actual or perceived threat of danger overwhelms a person's usual coping ability." Whether an event is experienced as trauma depends on its meaning to the child. This fact was brought home forcefully during World War II when, contrary to expectations, children who remained in London with their parents during the blitz fared better psychologically than those separated from their parents and taken to a safer place in the country. Adults, thinking of the welfare of the children, had assumed that they needed to remove them from the daily threat of bombing in order to protect them from physical and emotional trauma. They had not anticipated how the children would interpret the experience. For most children the separation from parents was much more traumatic than spending nights with their parents in a bomb shelter. Clearly, having a familiar comforting adult available during or immediately following a traumatic event is of great help and can prevent problems from developing.

How Trauma Affects the Attachment Relationship

Beyond understanding the importance of a familiar, supportive caretaker in minimizing the effect on a child of a traumatic experience, we need to understand how trauma can disrupt or undermine the parent-child relationship and thus interfere with the parent's ability to help the child.

A single traumatic event can lead to child or parent behavior that seriously interferes with the attachment relationship. A mother's own response to the death of her husband, for example, may make her less responsive or attuned to her child's needs in dealing with the loss. The child, in turn, may not be able to express his needs. Because the traumatized child's presence stirs up painful thoughts and feelings, family members sometimes avoid contact with him, thus unnecessarily isolating him. On the other hand, some parents smother their child with attention in the mistaken attempt to help mitigate the effects of trauma. If these inappropriate responses continue past the initial crisis stage, attachment problems will develop.

Chronic and repeated traumatizing events, such as ongoing physical or sexual abuse or violence in the family or in the surrounding neighborhood, also affect attachment relationships. Abuse by a parent has a profound impact on the relationship with that parent. James writes: "There is the pain, confusion and fear of the abuse itself; there is the mind-boggling experience of having the source of danger and the source of protection residing in one person. Most terrifying of all is the fear of loss of the attachment relationship, a loss children often believe is likely to happen if they try to protect themselves from being abused by a parent" (1994, p. 8).

Trust in the nonabusing parent is affected as well, both because he or she has been unable to protect the child and, in the case of sexual abuse, because the abusing parent often deliberately has isolated the child from the other parent by insisting that she keep their relationship a secret. If the nonabusing parent does not believe the child when she dares to reveal the secret, or, believing, insists that she forgive the abusive parent, the child's trust in the nonabusing parent is again undermined.

If the child is living not only in a violent home but in a violent community, his trust in his parents' ability to protect him will be further eroded. Often children turn to peer groups or gangs for power and strength when they feel that their parents are failing them. In turn parents may become "restrictive and punitive, and the children perceive that behavior as unloving" (James 1994, p. 9).

How Trauma Affects the Child's Behavior

Chronic traumatizing experiences can have neurodevelopmental, physiological, emotional, social, and behavioral effects. The symptoms arising from the impact of trauma fall into three major categories: persistent fear state, disorder of memory, and dysregulation of affect (James 1994, p. 11). All of these symptoms can interfere with the child's functioning. In addition, many of the child's coping strategies (for example, the avoidance of intimacy, the need to be in control, provocative behaviors, and the alarm/numbing response), though serving an immediate survival function, may, in the long run, cause problems in the parent-child relationship, thus preventing the parent from being able to help the child. Since the primary caretaker is the child's best source of safety and ability to cope, this poses a serious problem that must be dealt with.

To understand how these symptoms and coping mechanisms affect the parent-child relationship, we now describe them in some detail. Parents often misinterpret them as "bad" behavior and focus on correcting the behavior rather than on providing the attuned response to the child's needs that would calm the underlying fears and reestablish the child's trust. The focus of Theraplay treatment is to repair the relationship and restore trust between the child and her caretaker.

TRAUMA ENGENDERS A PERSISTENT FEAR STATE. Our recent increased understanding of the effect of abuse and trauma on the central nervous system of the victim (Perry, 1993, 1994a, 1994b) underlines the importance of helping to calm hyperarousal and of dealing with the dire consequences of a child's remaining in such a state. Perry (1994a, p. 3) points out that trauma precipitates the "fight or flight" reaction, the initial stages of which he refers to as the "alarm state." In this state, there is an increase in activity of the sympathetic nervous system, which results in "increased heart rate, blood pressure, respiration, a release of stored sugar, an increase in muscle tone, a sense of hyper-vigilance, and a tuning out of all noncritical information."

The acute fear state arises rapidly and is reversible, but if children are not quickly calmed or comforted, or if the trauma is ongoing, they may remain in a persistent low-level state of fear. In that state, they may be "behaviorally impulsive, hypervigilant, motorically hyperactive, withdrawn or depressed, have sleep difficulties (including insomnia, restless sleep and nightmares) and [be] anxious" (Perry 1994a, pp. 7–9). Perry (1993, p. 14) points out the long-term consequences of remaining in a hyperaroused state. "When the stressful event is of sufficient duration, intensity, or frequency, . . . the brain is altered. . . . The traumatized child's template for brain organization is the stress response." Often the child's responses to trauma, such as tantrums, aggressive behavior, dissociation, and hyperreactivity, are not recognized for what they are. They can be mislabeled as conduct disorder, oppositional-defiant behavior, lying, and disrespect for or not loving the parent.

TRAUMA CREATES A DISORDER OF MEMORY. The brain does not process and store traumatic experiences in memory in the same manner as other events. They are not integrated with past memory but remain separate and partly or fully out of conscious awareness. Intense recollections of the traumatic event can intrude into awareness as though occurring at the present time. Protective dissociation is another disturbance of memory that allows trauma survivors to function in their environment without being overwhelmed by emotions, thoughts, and sensations. Trauma-related memory disorganization is often misinterpreted as "lying, unexplained aggression, withdrawal, or weird or spacey behavior" (James, 1994, pp. 13–14).

TRAUMA CAUSES A DYSREGULATION OF AFFECT. Trauma survivors cannot regulate affect well. This difficulty is reflected in an all-or-nothing emotional style. A good example of this is the play of traumatized children, which is often severely restricted in affect but interspersed with out-of-control affective storms unrelated to the play. Parents of such children complain that they may be apparently calm and happy one moment and in a rage or totally out of control the next moment. It is often impossible for parents to discover what triggered the outburst. Dysregulation of affect can lead to oppositional, defiant, uncooperative, anxious, depressed, impulse-ridden, and unpredictable behavior.

TRAUMA LEADS TO AVOIDANCE OF INTIMACY. Because closeness leads to feelings of vulnerability and loss of control (and therefore represents a threat, rather than safety), many children begin to avoid intimacy. James says, "clingy behavior, hyperactivity, avoidance of eye contact, withdrawal, oppositional behavior, and disgusting personal habits can all be in the service of avoiding intimacy." Other behaviors related to the effort to avoid intimacy include an "inability to trust adults and an aversion to physical or emotional closeness. These children can be guarded, hyperactive, or controlling and often exhibit pseudo-maturity" (1994, pp. 15–16).

James comments, "It is extremely difficult to parent children who engage in behaviors related to a persistent fear response, disordered memory, and affect dysregulation; it feels impossible to parent children who actively avoid intimacy and who mightily resist dependency, both of which are inherent parts of primary attachment relationships" (1994, p. 15).

TRAUMA PROVOKES A CYCLE OF ALARM AND NUMBING. James suggests that many of the puzzling behaviors seen in traumatized children serve the function of "helping them to cope with intolerable anxiety. An alarmed child consciously or unconsciously engages in provocative or otherwise dangerous behaviors in order to increase his state of anxiety to the level where a numbing response is automatically invoked. The numbing response provides relief that cannot otherwise be attained" (1994, pp. 22–23).[1]

For traumatized children, feelings of terror and helplessness are constantly being restimulated by sensory and symbolic cues associated with traumatizing events. The child who cannot modulate affect may attempt to go into the numbing response—a kind of spaced-out, dissociated state that provides temporary relief—in order to interrupt the escalation of alarm. But if the child can't achieve the numbed state he may "up the ante" by seeking out negative and dangerous situations and responding to positive and neutral events with provocative, destructive behavior. The intent of both the negative and provocative behaviors is to obtain relief from unbearable anxiety. It is clear that an important part of treatment, therefore, must be to help the child learn to modulate anxiety.

TRAUMA LEADS THE CHILD TO REJECT POSITIVE EXPERIENCES. A similarly puzzling pattern is often seen in which traumatized children respond negatively to apparently positive experiences. For example, a child may respond to getting new clothes by immediately destroying them, or she may have an outburst of bad behavior immediately following a happy family outing. These behaviors occur because the child doesn't believe she deserves anything good and needs to ruin things and sabotage positive experiences. Parents, however, often experience such behaviors as rejections of themselves and all the good things they are trying to do for the child. It is very hard to keep offering positive experiences in the face of such angry rejection.

Trauma can thus have a profound effect on the relationship between a child and the very people (parents and caretakers) who are most important to the healing process. It undermines the child's trust in his parents, creates a state of hyperarousal, and leads to behaviors that prevent parents from understanding and responding empathically to their child's needs. Therefore, a major focus in treating such children should be to help caretakers understand their child's negative behaviors and begin to have more positive feelings toward them.

In addition trauma can have an impact on the child's self-esteem, it may make her passive and unable to stand up for herself, and it may cause her to fear touch as though it were painful or unsafe. These are all aspects of the impact of trauma that Theraplay can be helpful in treating. As we have said, whether Theraplay should be used before, after, or at the same time as focused trauma work, depends on how recent the trauma is, the child's readiness to make use of the opportunity, and the level of trust the child is able to establish with her therapist.

UNDERSTANDING HOW THERAPLAY HELPS THE TRAUMATIZED CHILD

In light of the above discussion of the effects of trauma on children and their relationship with their primary caretakers, we see that the traumatized child has the following treatment needs (beyond the need to understand and resolve issues related to the trauma experience) that Theraplay can address:

- The need to feel safe and be comforted by a trusted caretaker
- The need to reestablish trust
- The need to modulate affect
- The need to develop a positive self-image
- The need to feel empowered to stand up for herself
- The need to experience nurturing touch that is not exploitive or abusive
- The need to have the disrupted attachment relationship repaired, or to form a new attachment relationship

This final need is the overriding one and, just as in Theraplay with any child, many of the other needs can be addressed in the process of building a better attachment relationship. In discussing adoption and foster care in Chapter Ten, we give a number of examples of how we do the work of repairing the attachment relationship or building a new one. Here we discuss the other specific needs in order to describe the role Theraplay can take in responding to each.

Helping the Child Feel Safe

It is clear that the immediate need of a child who experiences a traumatic event is to be returned to safety and to be calmed and comforted by a familiar caretaker. As we note above, there is considerable evidence that the presence of a secure attachment figure can lead to a rapid reduction in physiological hyperarousal and can prevent the long-term negative effects of the child's continuing in the alarm state.

Once the child has been restored to the safety of familiar caretakers, his primary need is to understand and come to terms with what happened. As we have said, other forms of therapy, designed to help the child deal with his feelings about the experience (by talking about it if he can, by acting it out with toys, or by expressing it through art) have important roles to play in meeting this need. However, because trauma and abuse can be so undermining of trust, and because children are so easily precipitated into a hyperaroused state by talking about their experiences, often they are unable to make use of the opportunity offered to them in traditional insight therapy. Perry (1994a, p. 3) says, "A frightened child doesn't 'hear' words—they 'hear' (process) emotions."

For such children, a modified form of Theraplay treatment can be used, both to help them move out of the alarm state and to help them develop a trusting relationship. The focus should be on making the child feel safe, calm, and comforted. Nurturing activities, such as rocking, feeding, and singing, can be very helpful. Structuring activities that provide predictability and safety are also important. Even more than for other children, you must pay special attention to any "hurts" the physically abused child brings to the session. You need to make a caring ritual out of checking on him and putting lotion on bruises and Band-Aids on scratches, so that the child gets the message that his body is worthy of loving care. Accidental bumps or hurts that occur during a session should be attended to and the activity should be repeated more safely: "Let's do that again more slowly, so that it's really safe." The current caretaker should be actively involved in the Theraplay treatment and participate in the nurturing activities.

WHEN THE ABUSE IS RECENT OR ONGOING. Helping the child *feel* safe means, of course, that she should *be* safe. If recent or ongoing physical or sexual abuse is the source of the trauma, the abuse must be stopped and the child must be safe before treatment can begin. In the past this often has meant removing the child from the home. Because removal from the home carries many unfortunate negative consequences, experiments are increasingly being made to provide in-home support so that the child does not have to be separated from the only caretakers she has ever known. However, if there is any possibility that the perpetrator might continue the abuse, the child should be placed in the care of a familiar and trusted adult where the perpetrator is unable to reach her. James suggests, "It might be appropriate, for instance, to remove the child from the direct care of the parent and provide supervised parental contact that is emotionally and physically safe in order to temper the wrenching separation experience for the child" (1994, pp. 26–27).

WHEN THE ABUSE IS IN THE PAST. Children now in foster homes and in adoptive placement who were abused in earlier family settings make up a large proportion of traumatized children in Theraplay treatment. Because the abuse is long past, the first priority is not making the child feel safe, or even offering the child an opportunity to explore and understand the trauma; the first priority is to help the child form a secure attachment with his current caretakers. We describe this work in Chapter Ten. Safety is only one of many issues that need to be addressed. The overall goal is to form a secure attachment to the new parents by recreating the normal, healthy infancy that the child should have had. The focus is on helping the child feel more lovable and on helping the new parents find ways to impart that lovable image as they interact with their child. For the child, the goal is to help him abandon abuse-evoking behaviors, such as teasing, testing, and provocative mannerisms.

Those children, however, who have formed a "trauma bond" to an abusive parent may not respond to efforts to form an attachment until the bond with the abusing parent is resolved. In that case, other modes of treatment should be used to identify the nature of the bond to their abusive parent, to process the abuse, and thus allow the child to detach from it while allowing them to keep whatever positive feelings toward the parent they might have. Until they can allow themselves to detach from the trauma bond, they cannot allow themselves to feel more lovable and cannot allow themselves to attach to new parents.

Helping the Child Reestablish Trust

As we have said, many traumatized children cope with their experience by resisting intimacy and trying to stay in charge. They struggle mightily to avoid getting close to anyone or being dependent on anyone for fear of being hurt once again. As long as this remains the case, it will be impossible to repair the attachment relationship between the child and his parents. The Theraplay therapist, with her many ways of engaging a child and with her ability to provide a safe, trustworthy environment in which the child's needs are fully respected, can begin the process of helping the child learn to trust. Surrounded with an atmosphere of nurture, structure, and predictability, children can begin to build new attitudes of trust and self-confidence. Theraplay can play an important part in creating this healthier environment for the child.

You must be particularly attuned to the feelings and needs of a child who has recently experienced a trauma. Theraplay's usual emphasis on playfulness and fun needs to be modulated to meet the needs of a child who is mourning a loss, in a state of panic over a recent trauma, or emotionally constricted and wary as a result of traumatizing experiences. Theraplay's energetic, intrusive approach must also be modified to avoid reactivating the trauma for a child who has been inappropriately intruded on in the past. You must adjust your approach sensitively to the child's current mood, use a variety of soothing and comforting activities, and remain positive and accepting.

It is, of course, essential that you respect the abused child's feelings and experience. Since it is impossible to know what might remind the child of the abusive interaction, be especially alert to the child's reactions. "Oh, that startled you," and "You didn't like that. Let's see whether I can do it in a way that feels better," would be appropriate responses. As you engage the child, you thus demonstrate respect for her feelings and begin the process of developing trust. To hold back until the child signals her readiness for engagement would be to delay the moment when she learns that being close to someone can be safe and reassuring.

Because it is so very important to be respectful of the traumatized child's needs, we are often asked how we can protect a child in Theraplay treatment when we do not know that he has been abused. As we now know, children may show no outward signs of having been traumatized and yet at the same time there can be physiological evidence that they are in a state of hyperarousal.[2] Occasionally we have begun Theraplay treatment with a child who we later learned had been or was still being abused, as is the case in the following example. Fortunately, we have found that Theraplay, sensitively done, does not harm the child. In fact, in a number of cases, the trust that developed in Theraplay led to the child's being able to reveal the abuse to an adult or to the abuse being discovered. Once the abuse is known, the child is then ready to shift to treatment that focuses on the trauma experience. In some cases, modified Theraplay continues at the same time, either in separate sessions or with the session divided clearly into two parts: a "working" part and a "playing" part.

The following is an example of integrating Theraplay with trauma work. Unaware of ongoing abuse, the therapist began using Theraplay. Once it became clear that the child was being abused, she shifted her approach to focus on the issue of the abuse.

THERAPLAY IN PRACTICE: *Using Theraplay to Develop Trust.* Vanessa's mother, a single parent, brought her six-year-old daughter for Theraplay treatment because she was concerned about Vanessa's aggressive behavior with other children and her increasingly non-compliant behavior at home.

At the time treatment began, Vanessa was moving back and forth between mother and grandparents every week. Vanessa's response to this unstable arrangement was to try desperately to control whatever of her environment she could. Faced with the prospect of going into the Theraplay room without her mother, Vanessa clung to her mother and screamed. Because of this extreme lack of trust, her therapist made her first modification of the usual Theraplay pattern: She asked Vanessa's mother to join them in the Theraplay room. Even with her mother there, Vanessa often refused to participate and clung to her mother.

A second modification, which was quite effective, was to play out each new activity first with her mother in order to entice Vanessa to join. By watching from a distance, Vanessa could see what the activity was like and not take any unwanted risks. This opportunity to observe and to see the fun in an activity made it possible for Vanessa to overcome her fear and join in.

As part of the overall strategy for providing a safe, trustworthy, and caring experience, her therapist used a variety of structuring and nurturing activities, such as newspaper-punch, powder-prints, "Row Your Boat," cotton-ball-blow, measuring muscles and height, feeding, and rocking and singing. This safety and predictability made it possible for Vanessa to establish a bond of trust with her therapist (as well as with her mother, who actively participated in all the games) and offered a sense of security that Vanessa needed very much.

As she became more open to the Theraplay experience, Vanessa began to reveal the frightened little girl who had been hiding behind her controlling, angry behavior. During several sessions Vanessa seemed to regress to a younger age. She would crawl away from her mother, curl up and suck her thumb, whimpering like an infant. Seeing her fearfulness, Vanessa's therapist became even more aware of the need to make Vanessa feel safe and to lessen her fear of new activities.

After only five sessions of Theraplay, Vanessa had become much less fearful. Her behavior had improved so much that her mother decided they no longer needed to continue. The sessions had helped Vanessa and her mother develop a closer relationship and have more fun together. She was no longer as oppositional at home and her play with other children had improved. The treatment had made the mother aware that she needed to spend more time with her child and she felt that she could carry on the Theraplay approach at home. Treatment was ended with the understanding that it could be resumed should any more difficulties arise.

Sometime later, Vanessa's mother called to ask for more assistance. Vanessa's sexualized behavior with other children at school had alerted her teachers to the possibility that someone might be abusing her. The situation was referred to Child Protective Services and on the basis of their findings the mother took immediate steps to make sure that Vanessa was safe. She now wanted Vanessa to have further treatment.

Nearly eight months had passed since Vanessa and her therapist had seen each other, yet the trusting connection they had made in Theraplay remained strong. In contrast to her first sessions, she now was quite comfortable and eagerly participated in the sessions. Her mother was present for many of the sessions, but there was no longer the desperate clinging and fearfulness that had occurred in the earliest sessions. Knowing that Vanessa had been sexually abused, her therapist shifted her approach to focus on the traumatizing experience. Nevertheless, at Vanessa's suggestion ("Let's play some of those games we played before"), they often added Theraplay activities to their trauma work. Part of the work involved Vanessa orchestrating actions in which she played the helpless child and had her mother and the Therapist rescue her. Toward the end she was able to take a more active role in attacking "monsters" and "bad guys." All of this was made possible by their having established a trusting, playful relationship in the earlier Theraplay sessions.

The earlier sessions had also helped Vanessa's mother learn new ways of being with her as well as understand that she needed to spend more time with her daughter. The fact that the sessions were playful, friendly, and nonthreatening allowed Vanessa to trust her therapist as a safe and caring adult. In the light of what was later learned about Vanessa's experience, this trust was extremely important.

Although the therapist had not known about the sexual abuse when Theraplay treatment began, her sensitivity to Vanessa's fearfulness led her to adapt Theraplay in ways that are appropriate for any child for whom sexual abuse is known; that is, to make it more nurturing and less directive. Had she known from the beginning that Vanessa was being abused, she would first have made certain that the abuse was stopped and she would then have begun treatment using an approach that would invite Vanessa to work on the trauma. In addition, because of Vanessa's extreme fearfulness, she might have used some nurturing and engaging Theraplay activities as well.

Helping the Child Modulate Affect

Our recent increased understanding of the effect of abuse and trauma on the central nervous system of the victim (as outlined above) suggests that an important focus of treatment should be on helping the child modulate affect.

As we have said before, children learn to modulate arousal as a result of being held, rocked, and physically nurtured by their parents. Theraplay uses these same physically soothing activities and is therefore an ideal way to produce the physiological de-escalation that is so important for traumatized children. This is especially important for traumatized children who are emotionally numbed and afraid to feel. As you work with anxious children you will recognize Theraplay's power in soothing and calming them. The effect of being rocked in a blanket, being held firmly, or being sung to and fed can be observed in decreased heart rate, slower breathing, and decreased muscle tension. Activities that encourage a child to modulate his behavior from fast to slow and from loud to soft, such as motor-boat, "Row, Row, Row Your Boat," and peanut butter and jelly, can also be part of your plan. Providing these experiences in Theraplay sessions for traumatized children can elicit a calming response in both the short and the long run.

Once you have established a trusting relationship and the child is in a calmer state, you can add more cognitive approaches to these standard Theraplay practices. These can include

- *Helping the child identify the cues that raise anxiety.* For example, you might say, "Have you noticed that whenever your foster mom tells you that you did something you shouldn't do and gives you a consequence for it [or whatever the trigger is for this particular child], you feel extremely upset, as though you were being harshly punished or abused. Let's help your feelings learn the difference between being disciplined and being abused. And let's practice some things you can do instead of letting your anger take over."

- *Teaching her specific techniques for managing the anxiety, such as learning how to become "soft and floppy," or how to take slow, deep breaths.* To help a child become "soft and floppy," have her lie quietly on pillows or on the floor; gently shake each arm and leg, saying, "Make your arm soft and floppy. Let it be very heavy in my hand. When I let go, just let it fall right down." If the child has difficulty relaxing, ask her first to get "stiff as a board." Then, when she is very stiff, ask her to "let go. Let yourself go all soft and floppy." The contrast between deliberate stiffening and letting go can sometimes help a very tense child recognize the difference and gain more control over the relaxation process. Once the child is soft and floppy, it is possible to extend the sense of calm and self-control by asking her to wiggle just one part—her tongue, her tummy, or her right big toe. Parents can be involved in this activity and the family can practice it at home.

- *Helping her understand her feelings.* This can include understanding the internal cues that signal her tension and anxiety, such as "butterflies" in her stomach or pounding in her head, as well as the thoughts and fears that trigger the physical response. Once she knows the cues, she can practice the relaxation techniques you have taught her.

Helping the Child Develop a Positive Self-Image

As we have noted above, the experience of trauma and abuse is devastating to the child's view of himself and of the world. Treatment must help the child develop a new view of himself and the world and help him see himself as lovable and worthy of good care. When you use challenging activities, such as pillow-push or newspaper-punch, you help the child experience his own strength and power and therefore develop a more positive view of himself. As you care for him in a loving, nurturing manner, you convey the message, "You are worth caring for." As you appreciate and comment on his good qualities, you help him change his inner working model from "I'm bad. I was to blame. I deserved it," to "I'm OK. I'm strong. I'm lovable. I'm worthy of being cared for."

Empowering the Child to Stand Up for Herself

Children who have experienced ongoing abuse need to feel empowered to stand up for themselves. For such children Theraplay treatment should incorporate activities that help them feel strong, powerful, and effective. The case of Anna serves as an example of such treatment.

THERAPLAY IN PRACTICE: Teaching the Child to Be Assertive. Two Theraplay therapists were working with an adolescent girl, Anna, who had experienced ongoing sexual abuse from age seven until it was discovered and stopped shortly before treatment began. The first effort at treatment with client-centered play therapy had been thwarted by Anna's passive refusal to engage in the process. When all efforts to engage her had failed, her therapist decided to try Theraplay and asked a second female therapist to join her in the work. Still Anna resisted all of her therapists' gentle attempts to engage her and nurture her. She curled into a ball, withdrew eye contact, and refused to engage with her therapists in any way other than by repeatedly saying "No" and "Leave me alone" in a voice so soft it could hardly be heard.

Realizing that Anna needed to feel that she could take a strong stand against anyone who mistreated her, they began affirming her negative resistance, encouraging her to say "No" more loudly and with more feeling. Her "No's" were turned into yelling contests: "I bet you can say, 'No' louder than that." Soon Anna was intrigued and she began to enjoy the game of shouting as loud as she could. Her therapists remained in charge throughout, providing Anna with a safe, nurturing, predictable environment. Once she felt the power that her shouted "No's" gave her she was able to participate in games that exercised her physical power: push-me-over, newspaper-punch, and tug-of-war. Anna became more open to the relationship that was being offered. She could now accept healthy, nurturing touch and had became more animated, lively, and hopeful.

Helping the Child Experience Healthy, Nurturing Touch

Children for whom touch has been associated with pain and the misuse of power need to experience touch that is not exploitive or abusive.

Theraplay can change the child's experience of touch from bad to good. The child who has been abused before is now gently cared for. Bruises are lotioned, and scratches are kissed, blown on, and bandaged. The child is cradled, rocked, and sung to. During the course of treatment, the child learns that touch and nurture from an adult can be a safe, enjoyable experience.

As already noted, in the case of sexually abused children you should take special care to provide a climate of nonsexual, safe touch. Your touch must be matter of fact and nonthreatening. Touch should be confined to nonintimate parts of the body. Thus you should not lift up a shirt to blow on a child's tummy as you might with children who have not been traumatized, and until the child is very comfortable with you, you should not remove shoes and socks. Powder may be more acceptable than lotion.

The child's response to any touch should be carefully monitored. For example, you might point out to him that your fingers are "walking" toward his sock. "Those fingers are moving toward your sock. Would your foot like that? What does your foot want to do?" In this way you give the child some say in what happens and become his ally. For example, if the "foot" doesn't want to be touched, you and the child can tell the fingers, "We don't want any surprises today, go away and come back later."

To avoid touch with children who have been touched inappropriately in the past is to deprive them of the opportunity of learning the pleasure of touch that is loving and caring with all of its implications for self-definition, self-care, self-soothing, and self-love. It is your continually calm, nurturing, soothing presence that can transform the touch experience into one that ultimately leaves the child free to accept appropriate nurturing, as well as to give appropriate, not hurtful or sexualized, touch.

Repairing the Disturbed Attachment Relationship

The above discussion has outlined the many ways that trauma and abuse can disturb the child's relationship with her parents. As we have seen, even an intact, secure family may need help dealing with the effect of traumatic events that disrupt their usual healthy ways of interacting. Caretakers who have neither experienced the trauma themselves, nor perpetrated the abuse, still feel a great deal of stress as they try to respond to the needs of the traumatized child. Therefore, parents need a great deal of help and support as you work together to repair the disrupted attachment relationship or build a new one. All of the Theraplay techniques that we describe earlier in the book apply as well to working with families where the attachment and relationship problems stem from the child's experience of trauma or abuse.

Families in which the parents themselves are the source of the physical or sexual abuse need even more help. Many agencies specialize in helping such families in a variety of ways that are beyond the scope of the usual Theraplay approach. Next, we discuss the special contribution that Theraplay can make to this work.

UNDERSTANDING HOW THERAPLAY CAN HELP PARENTS WHO ABUSE

The majority of parents who have physically abused their child did not intend to hurt him. They simply wanted to make him behave. Theraplay can often help such parents. Parents who abuse while under the influence of drugs or alcohol, however, must have their own rehabilitation first. Parents who abuse because of life stresses need help finding ways to relieve those stresses. Theraplay should not be used to treat the small percentage of parents who hurt their child intentionally. It is important that all parents who have abused their children receive help to understand what drives their abusive behavior. They may need parenting classes to teach them about children's developmental needs, about child discipline, and about their own anger management.

Many parents who physically abuse their children while trying to get them to mind do not experience pleasure in parenting. Theraplay can help by teaching parents how to have empathy for their child, how to respect the child, and how to play. They can learn that it is safe for them and the child to have fun and to regress temporarily. By including parents in Theraplay sessions, you can help them see their child as lovable and themselves as loving parents. An important part of our work includes treating parents in a positive, nonshaming manner that they can transfer to their children. Theraplay can also teach parents to set limits with their child without resorting to force or anger.

Helping Abusive Parents See Their Child as Lovable

Including parents in Theraplay sessions with their children is a powerful factor for change. Theraplay is often effective in helping parents see their child as lovable and themselves as loving parents. As they observe the therapist working with their child, they see him no longer as a demanding, annoying nuisance but as a child with feelings and needs that can be responded to. In sessions parents can learn how to soothe and nurture their own children. Love-evoking behavior supplants rejection-evoking behavior. The vicious pattern in which abuse provokes yet more abuse is broken.

Helping Parents Set Limits Without Anger or Abuse

In addition to learning how to relate in a loving, nurturing manner, an abusive parent needs to learn how to set limits without becoming angry or resorting to harsh punishment. Often the child, like the parent, has poor control of impulses. Often his own outbursts follow a period of frustration and uneasy "testing," just as the parent's outbursts follow the same period of dreary "nagging." Neither parent nor child hears the other, and neither knows how to stop. The important but simply stated rule of "no hurts" can create a new frame of reference for both parent and child. Theraplay for abuser and abused (in addition to providing the ever-present fun) adds the element of structure.

As described in Chapter Five, parents first watch the Theraplay therapist as he sets limits and structures the sessions, then participate in role-playing sessions in order to practice setting limits, and finally take charge of the interaction with their child under the guidance of the therapist. The following example demonstrates this sequence in practice.

THERAPLAY IN PRACTICE: Theraplay with a Physically Abused Child. Grant was five years old when he was referred for Theraplay treatment because of his disruptive and violent behavior in his kindergarten classroom. With a smile on his face and a twinkle in his eye, he kicked, elbowed, punched, or scratched his classmates at every opportunity. Peers avoided him and, as a result, he generally played alone. Unfortunately, this did not prevent him from coming into contact with peers in his busy and very active class. Since each experience of proximity to them triggered an abusive demonstration of his seething anger and sense of entitlement, he got into trouble continuously. Both his teacher and the principal of his school referred him for individual Theraplay treatment.

Two years earlier during a particularly difficult period in family life, Grant had expressed his anger and anxiety through tantrums that included kicking, hitting, and biting. Frustrated, stressed, and not knowing better ways to respond, his mother used harsh physical punishment and, more than once, hurt him enough to leave marks. She was now remorseful and wanted to learn other ways to set and enforce limits, but she found it almost impossible to do so. Bright and charming, Grant had learned he could talk himself around anybody. During the MIM his mother was totally permissive. Grant had become a tyrant, arguing for and winning whatever he wanted and yelling if his mother made any attempt to set limits. He yelled so long and loud that she would eventually relent.

Grant was in need of structure and nurture in his Theraplay treatment. Watching his sessions, his mother learned positive ways of stating and enforcing limits but learned also about the critical importance of providing nurturing, especially following an aggressive outburst. Rather than leading to more angry outbursts, the reestablishment of a loving, accepting relationship following an episode in which the child feels he has done wrong or behaved badly provides the basis for the child to feel better about himself, to learn more self-control and ultimately to have fewer angry outbursts. Increasing structure, discipline, and efforts to control the child's behavior without increasing the level of nurture and empathic responsiveness leads to more problems in the relationship.

Because his therapist was aware of the earlier harsh physical punishment, she was particularly careful to monitor Grant's responses to her interventions. However, since Grant constantly challenged authority and tested the capacity of adults to set limits, she was aware that she would need to demonstrate to him that she could stop his out-of-control behavior.

SESSION ONE. The following excerpt demonstrates the dance of testing that occurred as his therapist focused on the dimension of structure. The session took place in an empty school classroom with his mother watching. The videocamera was in full view and had been explained to Grant. His mother had given permission for all sessions to be videotaped.

PATRICIA: (holding Grant's hand) We're going right over here. (on the mat) Have a seat.

GRANT: (looking at the pillow on the mat) Lay down?

PATRICIA: No. Have a seat. (bending Grant's knees so he could sit on the pillow) Hi there. Hello, Mr. Grant! (holding Grant's leg around the ankle so he cannot get away from her) Hello!

GRANT: I want some water.

PATRICIA: I remember you said that downstairs and I said I would decide when we got up here. Now come right up here and I'm going to take a look at you. (pulls Grant onto her lap and puts her arms around his back to contain and support him)

GRANT: (smiling and turning to point to the video camera) How come you're doing that?

PATRICIA: (ignoring his attempt to distract and take charge) I get to check some wonderful things. Grant! You have a wonderful nose! (gently wiggling Grant's nose with a finger) And look at these wonderful shiny teeth!

GRANT: (suddenly twists his body and leans away, trying to get out of Patricia's grasp)

PATRICIA: Oop-oop-oop! (holding and pulling him up again) I got you.

GRANT: (smiling) That was close.

PATRICIA: I got you.

GRANT: Wasn't that close? I almost got away from you! *[He is proud of himself for almost getting away. He is also trying to elicit Patricia's disapproval, anger, and rejection.]*

PATRICIA: You almost did, but do you know what?

GRANT: What?

PATRICIA: You didn't! And you gotta come back up here (into Patricia's lap; he is lying back as far as he can) Come here! *[Instead of rejecting him, she tries to bring him close]*

GRANT: (asking questions and stiffening against being pulled up to face her)

PATRICIA: (deciding not to enter a physical power struggle) I'm going to let you stay down, but I'm going to get a pillow for your head. *[She adds nurturing rather than disapproval.]*

GRANT: My feet are cold.

PATRICIA: Oh no! That's because you don't have your socks on. Remember, they were wet because you were standing up in the water-play table. Here, feel them.

GRANT: (punches at the sock)

PATRICIA: (holding Grant's hands) Oop. That could hurt somebody. I'm going to help you remember that we want no hurts here. Now, do you want to feel your sock? (brings the sock back for him to feel while still holding both hands) Yuck! I can't put them on you because they're still soaking wet.

GRANT: (starts to make a fist and punching motions)

PATRICIA: I'm not letting your hands go, Grant. But I can check your fingers while I'm holding them. One, two, three, four, five. And your hands are warm!

GRANT: OK. Count my fingers! *[Interrupting to get control.]*

PATRICIA: You know what!

GRANT: Count my fingers! Oooo! *[Since Patricia does not let him go or respond to his demand, he turns and twists away.]*

PATRICIA: (not letting him go) I've got to check your feet. Not too cold! Oh, Grant! You have a bump on your head!

GRANT: I don't care.

PATRICIA: I do! I don't think it's a "hurt" bump. (reaches for the lotion)

GRANT: (sees the lotion and begins to shake his head from side to side) No, no! *[Grant invites and anticipates punishment but rejects nurturing.]*

PATRICIA: Oh, do you have a wonderful shaky head! And I can hear your teeth chomp when you do that! Do it again! (he does it, then stops; Patricia quickly puts some lotion on his head) Shake it again and see if you can get the lotion to come off!

After the session, Patricia talked to Grant's mother about safe ways to hold him in order to set limits on his resistant, defiant behavior. His mother returned the next week to report that she had been following through with limits and had been able to hold him when necessary.

SESSION TWO. The second session moved quickly from activity to activity to give Grant as little time as possible to try to control things.

The activities chosen (newspaper-punch, beanbag-toss, motor-boat) were challenging and structuring but age-appropriate in order to keep him focused. At the end of the second session, Grant once again made a concentrated effort to take control. When Patricia returned with him to his classroom, he pulled, resisted, and attempted to run into the room wildly. Patricia held on and took him into a small room nearby to calm him down. She had to straddle him and hold his arms to prevent him from kicking, hitting, or biting her. Since he never seemed panicked and always had a challenging look that suggested he was in a contest to win, she felt that it was appropriate to continue to hold him.

Grant's mother eventually came downstairs as planned to discuss the session with Patricia. But since Grant was still struggling, she immediately sat down next to him, held his hands and told him he needed to stop fighting. Mother and therapist stayed with Grant through a very long protest after which they fanned him and stroked his head, giving him the nurturing that is so essential after an aggressive episode. After he quieted, they stood him up and held his hands to return to his room, but once again, he began to pull back and try to escape. Immediately, mother and therapist brought him back to the room and held him again. His tantrum was shorter this time, and when he calmed, he began to fall asleep. Patricia put his shoes and coat on, and his mother picked him up in her arms to take him home.

SUBSEQUENT SESSIONS. Grant's mother reported at the next session that two significant things had happened. First, Grant, who through childhood had been uninterested in soft, stuffed animals, had begun to bring all of his animals with him into his bed when he went to sleep. During a school sing-along, his mother had physically contained him instead of allowing him to run around the room. In the presence of his classmates, teacher, and other parents, Grant then asked her to pick him up and hold him on her shoulder like a baby. By the next week at bedtime, Grant had begun asking his mother to tell him about when he was a baby, and she had responded with Part I of the story, Part II the subsequent night, and more during each night of the week! Grant was allowing himself to feel and be vulnerable with his mother.

Much later in Grant's sessions, explicit trauma-repair work was initiated. The therapist suggested that his mother tell Grant of her memory of having hit him. She did, and then she lotioned the old hurt, speaking soothing words of apology and concern. Although Grant was somewhat suspicious of her offering of atonement to him in that session, she continued healing his hurts at home. Grant eventually asked if her mother had also hit her when she was a little girl. She acknowledged that she had. This experience of atoning for and healing past traumas represented a turning point in their relationship. During the next session, one month later, Grant played in synchrony with his mother, and he gazed at her with genuine love and happy anticipation in his eyes.

The new school year began soon after this watershed session. Although there had been a question (because of his behavior problems) whether Grant would be able to manage in a regular first-grade classroom, his mother and the school staff agreed that with intensive special education support, he could be advanced with his peers to first grade. To everyone's surprise and delight, Grant began the school year "like a different child." The behavior resource teacher assigned to monitor him and provide intervention, after observing him in class for a week, stated that this was the easiest job she had ever had. According to her and his teacher, Grant demonstrated no significant problems in class. Occasionally, he still grabbed or went his own way without asking permission, and he showed a good deal of resentment toward peers who took the same liberties he had previously relished. By the third week of school, there had been only one instance of mild aggression toward a peer. Grant handled this by giving himself a "time-out" period during which he sat in a corner and composed himself. He very quickly was able to return to his class.

That night he told his mother about the experience and had a positive discussion with her about it. His mother recognized this as a major accomplishment that signified the progress he had made. Theraplay sessions were reduced to approximately one per month to monitor Grant's needs and consult with his mother on parenting issues.

Theraplay can make a significant contribution to the treatment of children and families who have suffered trauma. It can help children develop trust and feel safe. It can help by modulating anxiety, improving self-image, and developing self-assertion. It can provide experiences of healthy, nurturing touch to replace memories of unhealthy touch. Above all it can teach them all to play. Theraplay serves these children and their parents alike to develop healthy interactions and repair their disturbed attachment relationship.

Notes

1. James's alarm/numbing response model is based on and elaborates the work of van der Kolk (1989).

2. Shapiro (1996), describing three little girls who had witnessed their older sister shot in the head the night before, says, "However calm the girls appearances, their physiology tells a different story. Their hearts are still racing at more than a hundred beats per minute, their blood pressure remains high, and, inside their heads, the biological chemicals of fear are changing their brains."

CHAPTER TEN

Theraplay for Children Who Are Adopted or in Foster Care

Sandra Lindaman

T heraplay's strength in promoting relationships and attachment has led to its successful application with foster and adopted children and their families. These children, more than many others, require sound parenting and large doses of empathy, fun, and guidance. Theraplay, with its emphasis on building relationships through playful interaction, can act as a healthy antidote to a painful past. In the past decade, Theraplay has been of increasing interest to parents and professionals working with two special groups of children within this population: the significant number of internationally adopted children who spent part or all of their pre-adoptive life in institutional care; and the increasing number of neglected and abused children removed from their birth families and placed in foster care, awaiting a permanent home.

The children we describe in this chapter have experienced caretaking inconsistencies, failures, or losses early in their lives that have disrupted or prevented the development of a secure attachment.[1] We first consider what these losses have meant to the children and to those who care for them. We then turn to how Theraplay can help. The discussion is organized around the particular kinds of behaviors and problems that adopted and foster children present. Following that we describe a case illustrating the general principles we have described. Next we discuss how we work with foster and adoptive parents. Finally, we present case studies illustrating Theraplay treatment with post-institutionalized children and children in foster care.

UNDERSTANDING THE CHILD'S EXPERIENCE

A child of any age who is in foster care or has been adopted has sustained a number of losses, beginning with the loss of a continuous relationship with the birth parent. The child's awareness of and understanding of those losses at each stage in her development will have an impact on her attachments.

All adopted children share the following experiences (even those adopted as infants) (Jernberg, 1990, p. 271):

- They have "experienced a discontinuity between the physiological and emotional style of their original mother and the physiological and emotional style of their later one."
- They "have to make an adaptation that very few children are called on to make. Adopted children must adapt not only to two women's physiologies and psychologies but often are expected to do so with the least possible show of stress."
- They "know loss, rage, and the feeling of grief."
- They "have experienced a serious threat to their self-esteem."

Depending on the age of the child at the time of the separation, the experience of loss will have different psychological meanings. We do not know what the experience means to a young infant beyond having to adapt to changes in physiological rhythms, sounds, sights, smells, and perhaps temperatures and textures. It is only later that he will need to come to terms with the meaning of having been given up by his birth parents.

Children adopted as older infants or toddlers feel keenly the loss of a caregiver and familiar caregiving routines. These young children also have to cope with the inability to express themselves, and the inability to understand completely what is told to them. Toddlers are at the stage in their development when they would ordinarily be taking their first tentative steps toward independence. Many children who have been removed from inadequate homes or raised in orphanages have not experienced the period of healthy dependence that provides the secure base from which to negotiate this step.

Older children are able to participate more fully in the transition to a new home, but their understanding of events and explanations is limited by their level of cognitive development, which may include magical and concrete thinking. Magical thinking (eighteen months to six or seven years) includes a tendency to personalize events; children believe that their thoughts, wishes, and actions are the cause of whatever happens; they assume cause and effect between unrelated events; and they have difficulty discriminating reality from fantasy. Concrete thinking (ages six to eleven or twelve or older) includes literal interpretations and thinking in absolutes.[2] At different ages, therefore, children will understand their experience in different ways.

Many of these children have later shared their childhood beliefs about why they were given up. "What's wrong with me that she gave me away?" "Maybe I cried too much, or didn't eat right, or something. . . . I keep thinking that I did something wrong . . . like it was my fault" (Brodzinsky, Schecter, and Henig, 1992, pp. 43, 79). This kind of thinking, combined with early negative experiences, leads to a view of themselves as trouble-makers, unworthy and bad.

Many children when first in foster or adopted homes are mourning the loss of parents or earlier caretakers. New parents may have difficulty understanding this, since they know that the child did not receive good care. What they often don't realize is that the need to become attached leads children to bond with even the most untrustworthy caretakers. No matter what the quality of care, children will have strong feelings about the only caretakers that they ever knew and will experience a love that must be acknowledged and resolved. It is important that new parents respect their child's need to mourn that loss. It is also important that the child be given permission from his biological parents and earlier caretakers to become attached to his new parents.

At some time in an adopted child's life, he needs to be able to talk about his experience, his theories about why he was given up, and all the subtle meanings to him of being adopted. Many very young children are not ready to do this, yet their adoptive and foster parents must respond to behavior fueled by these concerns. Theraplay helps parents understand how their children's inner experiences affect their behavior as we work to build a secure attachment relationship between these children and their new parents.

CONSIDERING HOW THERAPLAY CAN HELP

Theraplay builds relationships between parents and their adopted or foster children in the same way that it does with any child. But we face special challenges when we try to form an attachment with a child whose hopes have been shattered. Given this disappointment, forming an attachment takes time, patience, energy, and commitment on the part of adoptive and foster parents. The normal attachment process has an eager and trusting child participant. The adoptive or foster care attachment process has a wary child participant who readily reverts to the tactics she developed to survive on her own. Because it is so much more difficult, adoptive and foster parents need a great deal of support throughout the process.

Understanding the General Principles

Whatever the age of the child, Theraplay dramatizes that the child is special and lovable, that the world of the child is now a place of responsiveness, lively experiences, and growth, and that the child can count on others. Rather than talking about these assurances, the parent and child enact the assurances in the session. With its emphasis on the child's emotionally younger needs, Theraplay recreates the early attachment process for the parent-child pair. Just as a biological child comes to rely on and trust her responsive parents, so adopted children begin to experience their new parents as reliable and trustworthy.

Theraplay is beneficial in foster and adoption work because of its directness and because it involves all members of the family. The importance of working with the family system rather than the child alone is supported by experienced adoption clinicians (Reitz and Watson, 1992; Grabe, 1990).[3]

Deciding When to Use Theraplay

All of the children we discuss in this chapter have suffered the trauma of the absence or loss of a caregiver. In addition, most children in foster care and many children available for adoption have suffered neglect as well as physical, sexual, or emotional abuse (or all of these), and consequently their attachment-trauma problems are severe. Although such children can benefit from Theraplay treatment adapted for traumatized children in the ways we discuss in Chapter Nine, and they all need to build playful, trusting relationships with their new parents, some may need more comprehensive programs that include an opportunity to address their attachment-trauma problems more directly.

Two comprehensive and effective treatment models for trauma and severe attachment disorders are Beverly James's (1994) attachment-trauma therapy and Daniel Hughes's (1997) method for facilitating developmental attachment. These models share aspects of Theraplay's directness, engagement, and appropriate use of touch.

As we discuss in Chapter Nine, Theraplay should be custom-tailored for each child's needs; for instance, changing the nature of the physical contact for children who have been sexually abused, or focusing on comforting and acknowledging sad feelings for children who have experienced a recent loss. We indicated that decisions about when to use Theraplay must be made on a case-by-case basis and depend very much on the child's most pressing need at the moment. For children who have been adopted or are in foster care, often the most pressing need is to build a better, more trusting relationship with the new caretakers.

Carrying Out the Assessment Process

Because many of these children have led complicated lives, it is important to obtain a detailed social history, including the child's and family's involvement with the birth parents. When interviewing parents about their experience as a family, ask how the decision was made to become a foster or adoptive caregiver and how the decision has changed the marriage and family.[4] Topics for exploration that are especially pertinent to the Theraplay process include parents' expectations about parenting prior to caregiving; their experience with children and knowledge of normal development; their knowledge of the attachment process; their own experience of being parented; their parenting styles and conflicts; their comfort with being in charge; their comfort with regression; their plans for the future for the child; their family schedules; family sleeping patterns; whether other caregivers are involved; types of separation from the parents; and the time, desire, and potential to carry out the Theraplay approach at home.

We use the Marschak Interaction Method as described in Chapter Three to assess the interaction between the foster or adoptive parent and child.

Considering the Length and Nature of Treatment

Theraplay sessions with adopted and foster children are much like those with biological children. Since the resistance is greater, the treatment process is generally longer and changes are slower. Structure, engagement, and nurture are emphasized more than challenge in order to create an attachment experience in the session. A great deal of the focus with parents is on helping them understand the child's emotionally younger developmental needs and helping them find ways to become the caretakers the child will turn to for comfort and security.

UNDERSTANDING CHARACTERISTIC BEHAVIOR PROBLEMS

Five clusters of behavior problems, noted in the literature about foster and adopted children,[5] have been observed in children referred for Theraplay: accepting adult control, engaging and relating, accepting care, feeling competent and worthy, and regulating and expressing emotions. As we discuss each problem we consider how it reflects the child's inner experiences related to these behaviors, as well as the adult's corresponding experience of caregiving. In each case we present examples of how we use the Theraplay dimensions to respond to the child's needs as expressed through these behavior problems.

Problems Accepting Adult Control

Most children who have experienced caregiving failures adapt by trying to stay in control at all costs. They do not accept other's authority, particularly that of their new foster or adoptive parents. Control issues are so prevalent that they usually are first on parent and professional lists of difficult behaviors. Parents say, "She's defiant, she does her own thing, she doesn't follow the rules, she refuses to cooperate," or "He wants to do what he wants to do—he'll do exactly what he's told not to do." While some children seek control through passivity, acting out behavior is more typical.[6]

It is as though the child says, "I must take charge of things or no one will. . . . I must make others do what I want so that they won't do the abusive, neglectful things that I fear."

UNDERSTANDING PARENTING ISSUES. Obviously it isn't easy to parent a child who insists on doing everything his way and on his own terms, and who won't let you take charge, enforce rules, or provide limits and structure. A controlling child threatens adoptive parents' sometimes-shaky belief that they have the right to parent the child (Reitz and Watson, 1992). Often feeling devalued by infertility or other losses in their own lives, they now feel devalued as adoptive parents. And since they have gone through a rigorous evaluation process to adopt the child, parents may also feel that they have to be perfect. It is therefore hard for them to admit that they need help.

ADDRESSING CONTROL ISSUES. Issues of control and behavior management can be addressed through the Theraplay dimension of structure: putting the adult in charge, setting limits, keeping the child safe, and completing sequences of activities. It is especially difficult for the child who perceives herself responsible for her own survival to let the adult be in charge, but this is exactly what she needs to do if she is to develop a secure attachment.

In Theraplay sessions, parents can practice being in charge, helping the child to accept that leadership for relatively brief periods while engaged in a pleasant game or activity, as in the following example.

Eight-year-old Jana's foster mother has watched Jana and her therapist play an "up fast–down slow" game and now the mother is called in to share the fun. Jana sits on a beanbag chair on the floor and her mother crouches in front of her, holding her hands. Mother decides that her signal will be a nose wiggle. When she gives the signal, Jana is to pop up to a standing position while holding her mom's hands; when Mom gives the signal again, she is to lower herself slowly to the beanbag chair with Mom's help. When Jana starts moving before her mom signals, or begins to suggest her own signals, the therapist reminds Mom that it's her job to be the leader. If Jana moves quickly or roughly, the therapist suggests that Mom have Jana "do that one again slowly or gently." To maintain Jana's interest, more complicated signals are added for moving at different speeds. The therapist marvels at how coordinated this pair can be. Jana and her mom look closely at each other, laughing at the silliness of the signals and the slow motion movement, but working together all the while.

You can help parents complete activities, defuse sabotage, and ignore distractions so that they feel successful. Parents must understand the importance of structure and predictability in the home setting. You should encourage them to choose a few important "battles" to fight rather than picking on many small issues, to give consistent, united messages on key disciplinary issues, and to practice pleasant adult-in-charge activities at home.

Engagement and Relationship Problems

Older foster and adopted children often resist true engagement; they may avoid eye contact, shrug off or avoid physical contact, display a superficial friendliness, appear distracted, and seem not really "there" with you. They may be impulsive, unpredictable, hard to get along with, and have difficulty making and keeping friends. Hughes (1997, p. 3) points out that they often "avoid reciprocal fun, engagement, and laughter" and that they have limited skills for engaging with others.[7] James (1994) describes trauma-related patterns of dissociation. Lacking an "authentic" self, the child displays a "survival" self, characterized by hiding her feelings and mimicking the behavior of others. She creates a phony unreal, manipulative facade (pp. 67–68).

It is as though the child says to herself, "I'm not comfortable with people—I don't know how to enjoy myself with others, I can only do so on my terms."

UNDERSTANDING PARENTING ISSUES. Parents find it very difficult to claim the child as their own, or to develop a mutual feeling of belonging, as long as the child rejects their every overture, doesn't look at them, avoids enjoyment, or seems unreal. Parents may also experience a distance because of their own grief over the loss of the child's infancy and young childhood, their guilty feelings that they might have saved the child from pain if they had adopted him sooner, and the knowledge that their child has been parented by others (Hopkins-Best, 1997).

ADDRESSING ENGAGEMENT AND RELATIONSHIP ISSUES. Theraplay uses very basic and sometimes novel ways to engage the child. The checkup at the beginning of sessions has the special power of providing foster and adoptive parents an opportunity to do what birth parents do naturally with their infants, check out their child's special qualities in minute detail. You can focus on the exact blue of a child's eyes, the length of his eyelashes, how much a scratch has healed since the last session, or how much fingernail polish has worn off. This usually captures the child's attention and he responds with great pleasure at being noticed in this way.

Parents frequently are surprised at the power of these simple observations. They take pleasure in the special qualities the therapist "discovers." Sometimes the child's reaction, while initially interested and engaged, cannot be comfortably maintained and becomes more superficial, distant, or rejecting. You can then acknowledge, "You might think it's silly to spend so much time checking out how your elbow pokes out just so, but I just think you're so neat."

You can use the tug-of-war game to enact the process of claiming the child and drawing him into the family. With parents on one side and the child and you on the other, parents pull as hard as they can to bring the child to their side. Once the child is on their side, all three can work together to pull the therapists to them. Whether you succeed in pulling the family to you or the family pulls you to them, the end result is the same: a lively, engaged team.

You must have self-confidence and a repertoire of age-appropriate engaging activities that can entice the resistant adopted or foster child. Repeated experiences of engagement with you and with her new parents provide moments of authentic connection. Your goal is to prolong the sense of connection over time through a variety of activities.

THERAPLAY IN PRACTICE: *Engaging a SeverelyTraumatized Child.* Jimmy was an extremely withdrawn sixteen-month-old child in foster care. He had been grossly neglected and had suffered burns from lower back through mid-thigh when his biological mother dipped him in hot bath water. In his foster home Jimmy did not walk or vocalize, except to cry; he did not make eye contact or reach for a toy. He sat in a protective position with his arms and legs crossed most of the time. He was understandably very resistant to risking engagement with anyone. Because he had been so severely traumatized, his therapist used a modified Theraplay approach, which was engaging but very gentle.

In the first three Theraplay sessions, the therapist, Jean, held Jimmy facing her in her lap. She gently "beeped" his nose, and played peek-a-boo and "This Little Pig." Jimmy gave her one brief smile during the first session. During the second session, Jean played more lively activities but still in a slow, calm manner: horsey-back ride or push-me-over, pull-me-up. Jimmy smiled several times but still cried on and off during the session. Jean held Jimmy and comforted him when he cried, but this did not seem to calm him. During the third session, Jimmy cried for most of the thirty minutes; Jean rocked him gently, held him close, and spoke to him in a reassuring tone. At the fourth session, Jimmy began to look at Jean, smiled many times and even began to laugh at her antics. By the end of his twenty Theraplay sessions, Jimmy had became fully engaged with Jean; his affect went from flat to happy, and he sought out and initiated social play. His foster parents participated in the sessions and carried out similar activities at home.

Problems Accepting Care

Like all children with insecure attachment, children who have been adopted or are in foster care often reject their parents' offers of care. If they fall and scrape themselves they say, "It doesn't hurt. I can take care of it." They may be quite good at taking care of themselves and may even try to take over the role of caretaker to their parents. Some children, in contrast, may be reckless and accident-prone. When gum got tangled in the hair of one older adopted child, he cut it out with scissors, leaving a bald spot, rather than asking for help. Hughes (1997) describes these children as trying to avoid being loved, feeling special to someone, or needing anyone. James (1994, p. 15) also reminds us that for trauma survivors, "intimacy represents a threat, not safety."

The child seems to be saying to himself, "I can't count on anyone to take care of me so I will do it myself."

UNDERSTANDING PARENTING ISSUES. It isn't easy to soothe, comfort, and nurture a child who has learned that no one would comfort or nurture her. These children may allow comforting if it is their idea, but frequently reject the parents' initiation of care, or they may turn to the parent on one occasion and ignore them the next time they need help. Nevertheless, parents must move to meet the child's needs as quickly as possible and do this repeatedly, in spite of receiving very little positive feedback.[8]

ADDRESSING CARETAKING ISSUES. Finding ways to nurture foster or adopted children either directly or indirectly is a major emphasis in Theraplay treatment. Direct methods include caring for hurts (and preventing additional hurts), lotioning, powdering, singing to the child, rocking in a cradled position, swinging in a blanket, and feeding favorite foods and drinks (from a baby bottle or squeeze bottle that acts as a baby bottle).

Indirect methods can be used initially with a child who will not allow direct caregiving, and then throughout treatment because they are pleasant and intimacy-building. These include such activities as "painting" lotion or powder on hands or feet to make a print, using fingerpaint to make such prints (which requires that you wash and dry hands or feet); trying on and admiring the child in a variety of hats; putting on paper decorations or costume jewelry; and hiding a powder touch for the parent to find and rub in. Additionally, because it is *responsive* caregiving that forms the basis of the attachment process, we emphasize noticing the child's facial and bodily cues, acknowledging feelings, and making attuned responses that mirror the child's reactions. The following is an example of moving from indirect nurturing (fanning the child after a vigorous game) to direct nurturing (holding and feeding an older adopted child).

Following a lively tug of war with eleven-year-old Michael and his adoptive parents on one side and his two Theraplay therapists on the other, Mom and Dad are directed to sit on either side of Michael on the couch. The therapists grab large pillows and fan the threesome, asking each to check how the other's hair moves in the breeze. They discover that Mom's hair moves the most, Dad has used some mousse and his hair doesn't budge, and Michael's hair wiggles right at his forehead. The therapists spread out a blanket on the floor and tell Michael to sit in the middle. The therapists hold the blanket corners near Michael's head and Mom and Dad take the corners by his feet so they can see his face. Michael can't quite believe that he's going to be swung in the blanket, but as the four adults pick up their corners, he readily stretches out. While Michael is swung back and forth, the therapists lead the parents in singing "My Michael lies over the ocean/Bring back my Michael to me." Michael smiles and laughs and asks for a second swing. After a soft landing, Mom and Dad sit on the couch again. Michael is wrapped in the blanket and his therapists place him on Mom's lap; Dad supports his feet. Mom feeds Michael his favorite juice from a squeeze bottle. Michael laughs and says, "like a baby," but accepts the bottle and looks up at his parents as they notice the way he drinks it, the sounds and bubbles he makes, and the neat way he burps when he's finished.

The younger the child, the easier it is for you or the parent intellectually, emotionally, and physically to provide direct nurturing, but at any age it has a profound effect. Because it is so important, it also can make children feel very vulnerable, and it may be fought off. Parents may not be comfortable themselves providing this experience, or they may be concerned about the child's rejection of the nurture and of them. You should not ask parents to hold or feed a child without doing it first or assisting parents so that they can be successful.

Parents who have the impulse to nurture their older adopted child as they would a newborn are often ridiculed by friends and family members who say the child is "too old for that baby stuff." A mother, hearing about the Theraplay method at a conference on adoptions, said, "I feel so validated! When I brought my six-year-old home, it just seemed like the right thing to do to hold her and rock her and feed her, and she loved it, but everyone else said I was crazy."

Problems with Competence and Self-Worth

Many foster and adopted children feel incompetent, bad, and unworthy. These feelings stem partly from a conviction that they deserved the bad things that happened to them and partly from not having experienced themselves as the object of loving, attentive caretaking. Many also have cognitive and developmental problems, which can further fuel their feelings of worthlessness. Hughes (1997, p. 31) suggests that these children define themselves as unworthy and exhibit "pervasive shame" due to a distortion of healthy developmental attachment patterns.[9] When an adopted older boy won a prize at camp, his scout leader reported that he acted as though he did not deserve it, as though he didn't want even to be noticed.[10]

It is as though the child says, "I'm no good. I can't have been worth much if they hurt me, or if they didn't want me."

UNDERSTANDING PARENTING ISSUES. In order to counteract the child's low self-esteem, it is essential that parents' expectations of the child be geared to the level at which the child can be successful. Adoptive parents may form an impression of a preschool or school-age child's abilities based on his age, size, and school placement. Cognitive and motor development in adopted children ranges widely from above average levels to those having severe developmental delays (often due to lack of stimulation), but because of the disruption in their attachment relationship all of them have much younger emotional needs. They often are unable to maintain self-control in situations that other children their age could handle, and they are not capable of as much reciprocity in relationships as parents might expect. Koller (1981) noted that parents may expect the child to experience the feelings of closeness and mutual satisfaction appropriate to a reciprocal level of attachment, when the child actually is functioning more like an infant or toddler who is only able to receive the parent's care and not able to respond in kind.

ADDRESSING COMPETENCE AND SELF-WORTH ISSUES. Theraplay accepts the child as he is in the warm, caring, attentive manner that we have described throughout this book.[11] Often this means providing more nurturing and caretaking than challenge. When you use challenging activities you must gear your expectations so that the child can succeed and experience his competence. You must ignore the message of the child's physical size and attune yourself to the needs of the emotionally immature child underneath. You can, of course, use mildly challenging activities to engage children who might otherwise be resistant to accepting your structuring, engaging, or nurturing approaches.

Counsel parents to expect inconsistent performance, differences between intellectual and emotional competence, and differences between "performance" at school and behavior at home. Some parents are pleased with precocious talents and may reinforce inappropriate and premature independence without realizing that a child may be using these talents to maintain distance and discourage adult caregiving.

THERAPLAY IN PRACTICE: Meeting the Child's Younger Needs. Paul, described in our introduction, was adopted at age four after two foster placements. At age eight, his behavior was age-appropriate as long as he was in good spirits and feeling well connected to his parents. But when he was tired, in the midst of a transition, or feeling unconnected, he appeared babyish. He forgot what he had learned, he could not handle criticism, he had tantrums, and he became cold and distant. At those times his parents felt that he was not attached to them at all, and they wished he would "try harder" to maintain more self control.

Sessions with Paul and his parents focused on playful, nurturing, and mildly challenging cooperative activities. His parents were brought into a more active, helping role through caring for Paul's bruises with lotion, helping him balance on a stack of pillows and jump off into his dad's arms, making a family handprint, blowing bubbles back and forth in the air until they popped, or feeding Paul a doughnut by having him take bites around it while his mother held it on her finger.

The interpreting therapist encouraged Paul's parents to shift their style of talking and teaching and waiting for Paul to behave appropriately to one of "being with and doing." She focused on helping them understand, anticipate, and actively meet Paul's younger needs; for instance, bringing a snack for him when picking him up from school because he always complained of being hungry at that time. Once they became more responsive to his emotional needs, his parents found that Paul's episodes of babyish, out-of-control behavior diminished and he became much more likeable and more connected to them.

Problems with the Regulation and Expression of Emotions

Like all children with attachment problems, adopted children have great difficulty regulating and expressing emotions. Parents report that often for no apparent reason their child will "totally lose it." They may have temper tantrums like a two-year-old, impulsively hit or hurt others, or run away. In contrast, some children appear unfeeling and unable to experience their emotions at all. Sometimes alternating violent outbursts and unfeeling lack of response can be seen in the same child. Many of these children have difficulty naming their feelings.[12]

The child seems to experience his emotions as frightening. He may say to himself, "I can only handle feelings in certain limited ways or they will spill out; even feeling good can be scary."

UNDERSTANDING PARENTING ISSUES. It isn't easy to calm a child who has missed out on early experiences that lead to self-regulation, to the ability to concentrate, and the ability to respond to stress. Faced with an out-of-control child, parents often panic, fearing that their child will grow up to be violent. Or they may become angry and feel out-of-control themselves. Anger stirs up corresponding feelings in everyone.

Even less violent emotions such as the child's sadness and grief can stir up parents' own feelings of grief and make it hard to respond to the child's needs.

ADDRESSING PROBLEMS IN REGULATION AND EXPRESSION OF EMO-
TION. The child's difficulty regulating and being in touch with his own emotions can be addressed through the dimension of nurture and through multiple experiences of affect attunement and acknowledgment of the child's feelings by the therapist and parent throughout Theraplay sessions. In Chapters Six and Nine, we describe a number of techniques that you can use to help children modulate affect. You can teach parents how to use these with their children.

Two ways of helping children to be more accepting of their feelings are (1) to acknowledge the child's feeling states, including how they have displayed that feeling and what people call the feeling ("You're having a hard time today . . . seems like you're feeling a little sad," or "I can see a sparkle in your eye and you've got a big smile . . . you look happy today") and (2) to validate their feelings ("That must have made you really mad!" "I'd be upset if something like that happened to me"). When children or their parents have difficulty expressing feelings or are hard to "read," you can play a game with the child and her parents of identifying feelings from facial expressions. You and the child choose a feeling to express on your faces and ask the parents to guess what the feeling is. Parents can take turns showing a feeling on their faces and having the child identify it. This can be followed by a discussion of what makes each person feel that way.

The following case study illustrates most of the principles discussed above. In Rebecca's treatment the focus was on helping her accept her adoptive parents' care, helping her feel worthy to have a permanent family, helping her regulate her emotional outbursts, and helping her adoptive parents ignore the message of physical size and respond to her younger emotional needs.

THERAPLAY IN PRACTICE: *Preparing an Unattached Child for Adoption.* Five-year-old Rebecca was removed from her biological home because of neglect, inconsistent parenting, and suspected but unconfirmed physical abuse in the family. In her first foster placement, Rebecca reacted with stubborn opposition to instructions and displayed escalating behavior problems before and after visits to her biological mother. She received some brief counseling. In the next three years, Rebecca had four failed foster placements.

At the age of eight, Rebecca was in her fifth foster placement with pre-adoptive parents; a four-year-old foster child also resided in the home. Rebecca's behavior was described as not significantly problematic in the foster home or at school. A psychological evaluation as a part of the pre-adoptive process revealed functioning in the average range of mental ability and significant unresolved issues including anger, avoidance of negative emotions, fear of being rejected, anxiety, and attachment issues. It was felt that the attachment issues, while mild at the time of the evaluation, could become moderate to severe if Rebecca had to deal with the possibility of permanency in her life. Indeed, when Rebecca was told that the family would adopt her, her behavior deteriorated to the point of having temper tantrums, during which her parents could barely restrain her. She threatened to run away, threatened to jump out of a window, and kicked a hole in a wall at home. Rebecca attended a few individual, child-centered therapy sessions and she and her new parents participated in family sessions. Although Rebecca made some progress as a result of these sessions, it was felt that the direct structuring and nurturing experience of Theraplay sessions could best meet her needs. Therefore, Theraplay was recommended and authorized by the social service agency.

ASSESSMENT. An observation of the interaction between Rebecca and her foster parents using the MIM revealed fairly positive interaction. There were a number of behaviors, however, that are typical of insecure attachment: Rebecca initiated no eye contact, she seemed unconcerned when her parents left the room, and she was quick to take the lead and control or initiate an activity if the parents hesitated or were uncertain. In nurturing tasks, Rebecca often reduced the intimacy of the interaction by talking about other events. It was decided that the focus of Theraplay treatment would be on putting the parents in charge of playful, affirming activities and helping Rebecca experience and accept their structure and nurture.

TREATMENT. Rebecca and her foster parents participated in fourteen Theraplay sessions over a period of seven months, during which time the adoption was finalized. Because of the pressing need to build an attachment to the parents, they were included for a portion of each session right from the start. The first session included a checkup, caring for hurts, powdering her toes, "This Little Pig," "Ring-Around-the-Rosie," hiding with Rebecca under a pile of pillows for her parents to find, and having her parents feed her. The parents were surprised and pleased at Rebecca's responsiveness. They were sent home with the assignment to powder Rebecca's toes at least once during the week. At the next session her parents reported that Rebecca had had fewer tantrums. She did, however, have one extremely intense tantrum immediately following their powdering her toes. This was interpreted as Rebecca's anxiety concerning the attachment process.

Each session emphasized nurture and engagement, while maintaining the structure of therapist and parent-led activities. Activities included a lengthy checkup and caring for hurts at the beginning of each session, a number of engaging activities focusing on body contact and caretaking, such as family handprints/hand wash, toe painting, feeding and singing to Rebecca, hair combing, passing a touch of powder around the circle, swinging in a blanket, and face painting. Each session ended with Rebecca cradled in her parents' laps as they sat close together; in this position the parents fed Rebecca her favorite foods, sang to her, and cuddled and calmed her. The parents were asked to do these nurturing activities three times a week.

By the fourth session Rebecca's engagement had shifted from a compliant, eager-to-please demeanor to a sense of real connection and pleasure; her parents reported fewer and less intense confrontations. At this time, Rebecca was thrilled by a celebration of her one-year anniversary of placement with the family. Her outbursts at home continued to decrease in intensity and length and were no longer violent, but the foster parents were concerned about a possible relapse with the impending finalization of adoption of the younger foster child in the home and the movement toward Rebecca's own adoption.

Sessions seven and eight were modified to talk about these issues during the checkup time. Special activities were carried out, both in and out of session, to emphasize Rebecca's connection to her parents. For instance, on the day of the younger child's adoption the parents drew hearts on the hands of all family members. The parents reported that Rebecca was upset several times on that day but that the family carried out the activities as planned and Rebecca did not have a significant outburst.

During the period of the final five sessions, the parents reported that when Rebecca became upset, she was able to leave the conflict, calm down, and come back to discuss it or apologize if necessary. At the eleventh session, Rebecca brought invitations to her therapists to attend her own adoption and began calling the other child in the home her "sister." Sessions were continued beyond the adoption to solidify the gains that had been made. In the second to last session, when her hands, feet, and height were remeasured and compared to initial measurements, Rebecca was delighted with her growth. The final sessions focused on fun activities such as doing the Hokey-Pokey, trying hats on each other, passing a series of touches around a circle, and making painted handprints and decorated headbands. The parents reported that they felt the treatment had been extremely successful; the change in Rebecca was nothing short of a "miracle." The therapists felt that the time and importance they gave to nurturing activities in this treatment allowed the parents to meet Rebecca's self-esteem and dependency needs head on and to demonstrate and assure her that they were capable of taking care of her.

WORKING WITH PARENTS

We have described how hard it is for foster and adoptive parents to understand and handle the difficult behavior of their children. Work with such parents includes all the steps we outlined in Chapter Five. However, because of the special challenge that these children present, these parents need much more support, understanding, reassurance and guidance than almost any other group of parents. The following case illustrates our work with these parents.

THERAPLAY IN PRACTICE: *Reassuring and Empowering Parents.* We begin with the parents' description of their experience with their adoptive children prior to treatment. The description of treatment and the work with the parents is then given by the interpreting therapist who worked with the family. We end with a final statement by the parents describing the outcome of treatment from their point of view.

PARENTS' DESCRIPTION OF THE CHILDREN AND THEIR PROBLEMS

When we decided to adopt five-year-old Daniel and his three-year-old sister Lisa from the foster care system, we found that neither six years of experience in mental health nor eleven years of parenting our two biological children prepared us adequately for parenting children with severe attachment problems.

Daniel, Lisa, and their eight-year-old half-sibling, Geoffrey, were placed in foster care when Daniel was two and Lisa was six months old. Geoffrey, who had been the primary caregiver of the younger children, went to live with his biological father and the two younger children were thus separated from him. The children were removed from their home because of extreme neglect and physical abuse (as evidenced by multiple bruises and cigarette burns in varying stages of healing at the time of the investigation). The biological mother reported that she had used drugs and alcohol while pregnant with Daniel. In the next three and a half years, the children lived with one foster family for two and a half years and with six other foster families for periods of one to three months; several of the removals were due to abuse by a foster parent or other children in the homes.

Reports of the children's behavior while in foster care (which we heard only after the problems began to surface in our home) were a litany of the behaviors we later learned were typical of neglected, unattached children. Both children would hide food in their rooms and overeat to the point of becoming ill. Daniel had to be supervised constantly so that he did not injure himself. He sometimes banged his head on surfaces and purposely ran into trees or walls on his bicycle at full speed. Both children were aggressive with pets, lied "about everything," and were described as "overactive." Both had tantrums, but especially Lisa; she bit and pinched when she did not get her way.

To our surprise, when Daniel and Lisa first entered our home, they immediately began calling us "Mommy" and "Daddy." Lisa constantly crawled in our laps to shower us with kisses and hugs. However, it wasn't long before problems began to emerge. We soon realized that the titles of Mommy and Daddy were not used for us alone; Lisa was just as affectionate with people on the street or in the grocery store. Displays of affection could be accepted when Lisa initiated them; if we tried to hug or kiss her, Lisa would pull away or would have a tantrum that could last for more than an hour.

Daniel also avoided affectionate approaches by turning them into a wrestling match or a game of catch. He refused to complete any class work in kindergarten. At home, Daniel repeatedly wrote his name and the alphabet on his bedroom walls. He destroyed his clothing and toys, especially those we had purchased, as well as those of the other children. Daniel's customary greeting for adults was to run at them full force and then head butt them in the stomach or back. There were constant reports of aggression and injuries at school and church. All of our attempts at setting limits failed.

After four months the stress of these behaviors had affected our entire family. Because Daniel and Lisa were always charming and loving when extended family members or friends were present, people began blaming us for their bad behavior. Daniel would beg for food and complain of being hungry in front of our family and friends. If we didn't give in to his pleading, family members would leave, angrily accusing us of being cruel and harsh disciplinarians. We began to limit contact with others and did not socialize if it meant leaving the children with a babysitter. We could not sleep because we feared Daniel would wander and hurt himself. We finally installed a motion detector and baby monitor outside of the children's bedroom doors so that we could rest easier.

The stress affected our older children as well. Much later, our oldest child told us of the resentment he had felt because of the stress on me and our inability to go certain places because of the children's behavior. Daniel appeared to target our oldest boy, who was the same age as Daniel's half-sibling Geoffrey. Daniel would purposefully aggravate him, take his belongings, and destroy things that he knew were important to him.

Throughout this terribly stressful period when our self-confidence hit rock bottom, the only thing that kept us going was our biological children, who were both well behaved and honor roll students. In order to reassure ourselves, we kept returning to the fact that we had successfully parented our first two children. That fact assured us that there had to be something more than parenting techniques at issue and we began to look for help with our problem. Having investigated various treatments and becoming more aware of the role that attachment issues played in our attempts to parent the children, we chose Theraplay as an approach that seemed "family friendly." The playful activities could be adapted to our family life. We began treatment first with Daniel, because his behavior problems were more severe.

THERAPIST'S DESCRIPTION OF TREATMENT. The work with Daniel and his parents followed the typical pattern for children with severe attachment problems. Because of the many possibilities for neglect and abuse with such children, a more extensive intake interview than usual is needed; the parents particularly need to be supported and assured that the problems are not their fault; and the child needs longer and more intensive treatment.

ASSESSMENT. Because there was such a long history of problems with Daniel, extra time was given to the details of Daniel's life before coming to live with his adoptive parents. We even called the therapist he had seen prior to adoption. The information we obtained was useful both to help the adoptive parents understand why Daniel behaved as he did and to prepare for any unusual or odd responses to the therapy (for example, if a child had a bottle given to him each time he was sexually abused, we would not use one in Theraplay without careful consideration).

By the time many parents of children like Daniel come for help they are frustrated and often angry. Because these children behave so differently in public than at home, or because they solicit sympathy and pity, saying their parents "don't understand" them or are "mean" to them, their parents (as Daniel's parents were) have many times been blamed for the child's disruptive behaviors. Therefore the advice they have received from friends, family, and even other professionals has rarely been healing. Your first job is to dispel the belief that the parents are to blame for the child's unusual and manipulative behaviors.

With Daniel's parents, much of the intake interview was spent listening to and appreciating their experience. They were reassured that they were doing the best they could under the circumstances and that in therapy we would work on Daniel's perception of the world and of what parents can be to children. Since the methods the parents had used to set limits—taking away toys, witholding privileges, timing out, and even, in their desperation, spanking—were not working, alternate ways for the parents to manage Daniel's behaviors would be considered.

The feedback session following the MIM is an opportunity to point out some of the subtle (and not so subtle) ways the child manipulates the parents into inviting intimacy, which he then rejects. You can also point out to parents how patiently and persistently they attempt to build a relationship with this difficult child. An important goal for this session is to begin building a supportive relationship with the adoptive parents and to establish a therapist/parent team.

Based on his history and his current behavior, Daniel was accepted for Theraplay treatment with a diagnosis of reactive attachment disorder.

TREATMENT. An interpreting therapist was behind the mirror with Daniel's parents throughout the sessions, a total of fourteen over a three-month period. Two therapists, a male-and-female team, worked with Daniel. Because Daniel was so resistant to establishing a relationship, his parents were not brought into sessions until the eighth session. The first session was a typically engaging, getting-to-know-you session. Daniel was comfortable with the challenging activities but less comfortable with the nurturing, engaging activities such as feeding.

Beginning with the second session, Daniel showed increasing discomfort with not being in charge, especially when being fed. The feeding activity was becoming frantic, with Daniel attempting to consume an enormous amount of food and drink at a record rate.

By the fifth session, Daniel was clearly in the resistant phase. His attempts to control sessions both verbally and physically were increasing. He was striking out at and head butting the assisting male therapist. During feeding he attempted to bite whatever hand was feeding him. In spite of this upsurge of angry behavior in sessions, Daniel's behavior in school had improved.

The eighth session was remarkably calm and Daniel's mother was brought in briefly for the feeding. Daniel responded well to his mother's nurture. This eighth session showed the beginning signs of the growing and trusting phase.

To prepare the parents for full participation in sessions, we had a special session for them. Without explanation, we took them directly to the Theraplay room and engaged them in their own session, including a "checkup," playful games, and feeding. During feeding, the parents took turns acting as therapist and as child, and thus were able to feed and nurture each other. Daniel's parents were playful and receptive to this all-adult Theraplay session.

Some parents have difficulty with this method of teaching. When this happens you can briefly back off to discuss the principles of Theraplay and get some feedback from the parents on their feelings about the therapy and the progress toward the goals. The parents' discomfort with particular activities, for example, nurturing, provides an opportunity to help them understand their own resistance in that dimension. As they experience your confidence in handling their discomfort and resistance to the activities, they learn how they, too, can handle their child's resistance to their own efforts to nurture and to set limits for their children.

During Daniel's ninth session, the parents and the interpreting therapist entered the Theraplay room for the feeding. The interpreting therapist cued the parents as to what to do and when, including what to say or not to say to Daniel. When Daniel would attempt to wrest control of the session from his parents, the therapist cued them to take charge, "Mom, you decide when Daniel gets the bottle. You'll know when he's ready." Or when Daniel tried to distance himself by asking about school, the therapist said, "You do not have to respond to his question, just look in his eyes and tell him just what color of cinnamon brown they are." In the following sessions, the parents were introduced earlier and earlier into sessions, allowing them to set up and direct more of the activities.

Following their introduction into the sessions, Daniel's progress began to move much faster. In the eleventh session, we began to prepare for termination. Often at this point a child's resistance will resurface but usually fades before the final session. In Daniel's case, his termination anxiety, which included some of his original behaviors of striking out and head butting, was not seen until the fourteenth and final session. This was attributed to the excitement of having Daniel's three siblings present for the termination party.

During the termination party, responsibility for managing Daniel's behavior was turned over to the parents. His excitement required some extra structure but his parents managed with no cues from the therapists. Daniel's increased self-esteem was clearly demonstrated in his response to the listing of all the wonderful things everyone could think of about him. Daniel contributed to this list that he was a good ball player, a good "tagger-outer," and a good hitter. But perhaps the most telling contribution came from his nine-year-old brother, who stated that Daniel was a good brother, both helpful and loving.

Over the next year Daniel returned for a checkup therapy session every three months. These visits are especially critical with a child with severe attachment problems because of their fear of abandonment. At first Daniel's mother would telephone frequently for support and advice, but these calls decreased over the year as his parents became more confident in their skills. The mother reported that the entire family often participated in Theraplay type activities at home, which helped the relationship between the parents' biological children and their adopted children.

PARENTS' DESCRIPTION OF THEIR EXPERIENCE FOLLOWING TREATMENT

Although it took a few sessions before Daniel's behavior began to improve, we immediately felt reassured about our parenting skills. We were encouraged to engage Daniel and Lisa in games and activities that our two older, biological children had delighted in when they were infants and toddlers. We were naturally inclined to do these activities but had not done so because of Daniel's and Lisa's avoidance and rejection, and also because of misleading advice we had received from well-meaning friends, family, and mental health professionals. Daniel began to make changes at home and in school. His teacher commented that better behavior followed each session. Formal treatment sessions were held weekly, but Theraplay became a "way of life" at home.

We began to seek out eye contact and nurturing physical contact even when the children resisted it. Whenever it was necessary to discipline either child, we tried to help the children see that we were trying to take care of them and keep them safe. On the advice of the Theraplay therapists, we identified the children's destructive behavior as a "bad choice." We said that we were afraid the children might make a bad choice and get hurt, so we had them stay within sight to ensure that they were safe. Although it wasn't always easy, we looked for positives to comment on. When Daniel would not look at us, we would look for his "chocolate brown eyes."

When we began to rock Lisa while giving her a bottle, she would kick, scream, spit, and attempt to bite and pinch. We told her how much we cared for her and reassured her that we would stay with her. At times, she would scream, "Don't say that. You don't love me! You'll leave me, you will!"

When we attended a potluck dinner at church or an extended family gathering, we would fix the children's plates and make sure that we all sat together as a family. If one of the children were injured, I would be sure to be the one to comfort him. Theraplay became a way of thinking, not just a therapy.

Two-and-a half years after the end of treatment, Daniel continues to thrive. Although he is somewhat accident prone, he no longer purposefully destroys things. His second grade teacher describes him as one of the best readers in class and he is repeatedly on the honor roll. While both Daniel and Lisa continue to need a great deal of structure, they are now eager to please us and are as well behaved as most other children their age.

WORKING WITH POST-INSTITUTIONALIZED CHILDREN

In the past ten years, many children have been adopted from Eastern Bloc countries, South America, and Asia. These children usually have spent part or all of their pre-adoption life in foster care, group care, or large institutions where multiple caregivers, gross neglect, and a lack of stimulation were the rule. Fraiberg said, "We must look upon a baby deprived of human partners as a baby in deadly peril. This is a baby who is being robbed of his humanity" (1977a, p. 62). To one degree or another the emotional development of these children was put at risk by the absence of a responsive caregiver. As these children come to live with their adoptive families, they present developmental and behavioral profiles ranging from essentially normal functioning, to specific deficits in cognitive-sensory-social functioning, to attachment disorders, and to pervasive developmental disorders.

The first post-institutionalized child for whom we provided treatment was referred to the Theraplay Institute in 1992 by her therapist, who had been using nondirective play techniques with little success. This child made such significant progress during a brief, intensive period of Theraplay treatment that we were encouraged to use the method with other post-institutionalized children as well. Intuitively, it makes sense that Theraplay would be useful to these children and families, promoting attachment through the very activities that they had missed. We then learned a great deal more from the parents who had been searching for answers and advocating for their children through such groups as the Parent Network for the Post-Institutionalized Child.[13] Children in various parts of the United States and Canada were treated with individual and Group Theraplay, as we describe in Chapter Twelve, with good results.

The development of children adopted from institutions is influenced by many pre- and postnatal adverse factors in addition to social-emotional deprivation. These factors include genetic predisposition for psychological problems and learning disabilities; harmful prenatal environments; prenatal exposure to toxins; prenatal

alcohol exposure; postnatal exposure to chemical pollutants; low ges-
tational birth weight and premature birth; infantile malnutrition;
chronic otitis media; and physical and sexual abuse, with resultant
post-traumatic stress disorder (Tepper, 1997, pp.1–2). A study of the
functional neuroanatomical and neurocognitive correlates of early
severe deprivation (Eastern European orphanages) via positron emis-
sion tomography (PET) has revealed abnormal PET scan findings in
the initial nineteen children studied (Behen and Chugani, 1997). Federici, a neuropsychologist with extensive experience with post-institutionalized children, advises against thinking of these children as
having only attachment or behavior disorders, noting that the impact
of deprivation on brain development itself can account for some of
the children's attachment characteristics (1995).

In addition to the relationship difficulties that have been discussed
earlier in this chapter, children adopted from institutions also frequently have significant problems in the following areas: motor development, cognitive development, sensory processing disorders, central
auditory processing disorders, language delays, and second language
acquisition disorders. The longer that children remain in institutions,
the more cognitive and behavioral difficulties they display (Ames,
1997). Federici has proposed that some children display a subgroup
of pervasive developmental disorders and reactive attachment disorders that he defines as "institutionally induced autism" after spending
years in these depriving and emotionally damaging settings (1997, p.
3). All of these developmental problems require thorough evaluation,
and coordinated and early intervention services. Clinicians working
on attachment issues must be aware of the impact of these various
problems and their appropriate treatment.

Another issue faced by these adoptive families is that many parents
did not fully realize the potential negative impact of social deprivation on their child's development. A study of Romanian children
adopted by Canadian families revealed that before adopting, most of
the parents were concerned about health problems, some were concerned about developmental delay, but only 18 percent said they were
concerned about behavioral, emotional, or social problems. When
interviewed several years later about the "most troublesome problems," the concern about developmental delay and medical problems
was low, but 72 percent of the responses concerned behavioral, emotional, or social problems (for example, "passivity, rocking, not making needs known, not eating solids, being indiscriminately friendly,

being slow to attach . . . peer problems, fear/crying, hyperactivity/distractibility, and disobedience/defiance" (Ames, 1997, p. 62).

The study recommended that all parents should have specialized pre-adoption preparation and post-adoption programs concerning the short- and long-term characteristics of orphanage children and their special problems. The researchers advised: "All adoptions of orphanage children should be considered by both prospective parents and adoption officials to be special-needs adoptions . . . [involving] extra commitments of parents' time, energy, acquisition of expertise, and willingness to work with helping agencies" (Ames, 1997, p. 115). Parental awareness is improving due to the continuing efforts of parent groups and the relatively recent publication of research studies on post-institutionalized children (Groze, 1996; Ames, 1997); however, the initial lack of information continues to have an impact on current parental expectations for those who already have adopted. We also continue to see prospective adoptive parents who do not realize the impact of institutionalization on the children they hope to adopt.

The following case studies of post-institutionalized children focus on how Theraplay can be used to create and strengthen attachments between very young and older children and their parents. As we have described, many children who have been separated from their birth parents develop the need to maintain control at all times and assume that no one will be available to comfort and care for them. When a child is raised in an impersonal institution, this pattern is even stronger. Treatment must find ways to help the child see their parents as a source of comfort and security.

The following case of a toddler adopted from an Asian orphanage demonstrates both the problem—the child had learned to depend only on himself for comfort—and the solution—finding ways to place the parent as a source of comfort.

THERAPLAY IN PRACTICE: *Helping Parents Become the Source of Comfort.* Li was abandoned at the age of three days and spent six months in a Vietnamese orphanage before being adopted by his American parents. Pictures they received as part of a pre-adoption description of him showed "a very sad face." While in the orphanage, Li shared a crib with another child in a large room full of babies. He had scabies, which made him very uncomfortable, but he was otherwise healthy and well developed. Sleep was a problem when Li first came home; he experienced frequent night terrors. It took four months to clear the scabies, and during that time he contracted chicken pox as well. While he had mild motor delays, his cognitive development was within normal limits. When Li was sixteen months old, his parents contacted a Theraplay therapist because of their concern about Li's very frequent masturbation.

ASSESSMENT. The Marschak Interaction Method evaluation showed a lively, independent toddler who clearly had formed an attachment to his parents. Both parents were very comfortable with physical contact and very attentive and loving. They readily initiated engaging activities, but if Li was not interested they allowed him to follow his own lead. One episode of masturbation occurred while his parents' attention was turned to answering the interviewer's questions.

TREATMENT. Li and his parents were seen for three Theraplay sessions, during which the therapist demonstrated activities, made suggestions to the parents, and coached them in how to carry them out. Session activities focused on engaging, interactive games such as playing peek-a-boo with Li's feet, catching a beanbag dropped from the therapist's head, making Play-Doh impressions of Li's fingers and toes, having Li push the therapist over with his feet and then pull her up, popping bubbles blown by the therapist, and using songs and finger plays such as "Row, Row, Row Your Boat" and the "Itsy Bitsy Spider." These livelier games were interspersed with calming, soothing activities such as putting lotion on Li's feet or arms, massaging him with firm pressure, and feeding and singing to him while cradling him. Massaging his feet seemed to be the most comforting of all activities. Li became calm and relaxed and very focused and content.

The therapist recommended to the parents that they use baby massage techniques particularly with him facing them so that Li could clearly identify his parent as the source of the comfort. Li's mother began getting into the tub with Li for his bath. Li appeared to enjoy the skin to skin contact, having water squeezed on him from the sponge and being swished in the water. He became very calm and sometimes almost fell asleep on his mother's tummy as she held and sang to him. Each bath experience was followed by a period of calm play with no masturbation.

To help his parents understand and respond to Li's needs, the therapist explained that the masturbation was one way that Li had developed to calm and soothe himself as an infant. Because he wasn't able to have a truly responsive caretaker during his first six months, he developed a way to soothe himself. She suggested that the masturbation, like any baby's thumb sucking, was a sign that Li was tired, bored, or in need of physical contact and sensory stimulation. They could then respond in a calm and helpful manner to his need, comforting him, and helping him find something else to do. As a "preventive" program, they should try as much as possible to be the source of comforting sensory stimulation. The other advice had to do with their taking the initiative to engage him in interactive games and to find ways of making themselves a very interesting and indispensable part of his daily life.

Following these three sessions, the parents reported that there was much less masturbation. Li eyed likely objects to masturbate against, but followed through less frequently. Additional sessions were not immediately scheduled due to other family commitments. In a follow-up phone call one month later, Li's mother reported that the masturbation had almost completely disappeared. Li was now turning to her for comfort, rather than masturbating. "In the midst of playing, he will jump up and come to me saying, 'Mama, Mama.' Then he cuddles in my lap, puts his finger in his mouth, and strokes my hair. He doesn't need to stay very long before he's ready to go back and play."

She said that prior to the Theraplay sessions she had been giving Li a lot of love and physical contact, but that the engaging activities of Theraplay had helped Li become more focused. "I hadn't realized how abnormal my life had become. I was so distracted by having to be on the alert to distract Li from masturbating. Now I feel there is a real human connection . . . it feels so good."

Li was adopted when he was six months old. The longer a child remains in an orphanage, the more difficult it becomes to overcome the adverse effects of being raised in an institution and to form an attachment. In the following case, we describe Theraplay with a child who spent his first six *years* in an institution before being adopted by his American parents.

THERAPLAY IN PRACTICE: *Forming an Attachment with an Older Post-Institutionalized Child.* Sasha, a tall, wiry, fair-haired twelve-year-old boy, was brought by his adoptive parents for Theraplay treatment because, even though six years had passed since they adopted him from a foreign orphanage, he had been unable to form an attachment to them. When he first came to live with them he had nightmares and experienced so much distress that they sought treatment to help him deal with his early traumatic experiences. This work, plus medications to reduce his anxiety, had been helpful, but he still had many of the problems typical of older adopted children, which we described earlier, including violent temper tantrums, insisting on having things his own way, and refusing to accept any caregiving, especially from his mother. A bright, quick-witted boy, Sasha was doing poorly in school and seemed to have few friends except one or two with whom his parents wished he would not associate. As Sasha approached adolescence, his parents became more concerned about his future.

In Theraplay treatment, Sasha worked constantly to wrestle control from Don, his therapist, or from his parents if they had been assigned a supervisory role. If an adult said the sky is blue, Sasha said it's green; if Don offered him strawberry ice cream, Sasha wanted vanilla; if Don commented on how well he had done something, Sasha said, "No big deal." Since Sasha was very clever at engaging adults in verbal arguments, Don kept talk to a minimum and did not get involved in countering his oppositional words. When he refused food or asked for another flavor, Don said, "Oh, I guessed wrong about which flavor you like. Next time we have ice cream, I'll make sure it is vanilla." When he discounted Don's comments on his success, Don simply repeated them: "Well, I think it was great the way you were able to balance on ten pillows!"

Sasha seemed to go out of his way to show adults that he didn't like himself and that he expected adults not to like him either. To counter this Don found ways of making Sasha feel good about himself—commenting on his strength, his cleverness at figuring things out, and his attractive appearance—but above all having him experience himself as successful and very much appreciated. A clear sign of change in Sasha's feelings about himself and his willingness to share them with others came toward the end of treatment, when Sasha came to a session proudly wearing a special costume he had designed and made himself (as part of a school project). His ability to take pride in his work and in his appearance had changed dramatically.

Initially, Sasha resisted any intimacy and avoided even casual touch. Although he frequently came to sessions pointing out a hurt finger or a painful back muscle, he would not let Don do more than put a small band-aid on a finger, and he asked to have that removed almost at once because it hurt. In order to get past this resistance, Don tried every enticing and engaging Theraplay trick he could muster. Lotioning was difficult due to Sasha's sensitivity to touch, but Don was able to have Sasha teach him which spots to avoid (his feet especially), and then they explored which touch felt best. He made handprints by rubbing lotion all over Sasha's hands (in the firm way that Sasha preferred) and pressing them firmly onto black construction paper. Don put powder on Sasha's feet (being careful not to tickle), and he and Sasha's father supported Sasha as he "walked" up the door leaving a trail of powder foot-prints. Together they made moustaches for each other using shaving foam. Although Sasha seemed to enjoy this initially, when it came time to make a moustache for Don he lost control and spread the foam all over Don's face and into his hair. Don calmly put the foam away and had Sasha help with the job of cleaning both of them up.

Because Sasha was so tense and so easily overstimulated, Don worked directly at helping him relax. He had him lie quietly on the floor and practice getting "soft and floppy," first getting "stiff as a board" and then letting go. At first this was very difficult, but Sasha began to get the feel of it and was able to let his arms and legs go limp. He liked the challenge of wiggling only one part of his body—his big toe, his tongue, and his nose—while keeping the rest of his body quiet. His parents learned how to help him with this and began using the technique with him at home.

Sasha liked best to be challenged—especially by competition with others. Don and he wrestled using thumbs, arms, and legs. In these matches, Sasha's need to control was channeled into using all his energy to win. Because Don was large and strong, he could maintain the physical control necessary to keep things safe, but he had to work hard at it. And Sasha achieved a satisfying number of wins. Later he demonstrated wrestling holds to his therapist and practiced trying to push his therapist off balance as they held their right arms tightly together. His dad coached him in strategies he could use to achieve better balance and more leverage against Don's larger size and greater strength.

Challenge was also used to help Sasha accept nurture, for example, when he was asked to see whether he could crawl out of his mom or dad's encircling arms. His parents were instructed to hold on tight, and although he struggled mightily, he was careful not to hurt them as he escaped. The game of tug-of-war also allowed him to accept his mother's putting her arms around him, as together they pulled Dad and Don to their side of the room.

As trust developed, Sasha became more playful, more easily calmed when he became upset, and much more willing to let others have some measure of control. Even when it clearly bothered him not to be in control, he no longer appeared to panic when things did not go his way. As treatment progressed Sasha learned to verbalize his dislike rather than to act out his struggle to escape the limits set by others. At times he even seemed to take some comfort from having clear boundaries set.

In order to help Sasha's parents practice taking charge in the face of his determined efforts at control, we had them play "Mother or Father, May I?" and coached them to make sure that Sasha did just as he was told. Mom and Sasha played the eye-signal game keeping a pillow between them as Mom indicated with eye blinks which direction he should go.

With practice, Sasha's parents became increasingly resilient, not wilting in the heat of his sometimes scathing attacks and not giving in for the sake of peace—which was almost always more a promise than reality. At home, Sasha's mother began to hold him close to her when he got most out of control. Even though these incidents were difficult, they were usually followed by a more relaxed, pleasurable period of calm after the upset passed. Sasha's father became more relaxed and more comfortable with being direct; he was less likely to bargain to gain cooperation. For example, when Sasha refused to do a chore at home, Dad said simply, "Now is the time to do it. I'll stay right here while you take the garbage out." Sasha and his father developed a very nice attunement and are now able to predict each other's reactions and preferences. When asked to describe what Sasha likes best to do or to eat, Dad knew precisely what makes him happy, what his favorite records are, and what his favorite foods are. And Sasha was equally good at describing his dad's preferences. They were now more at ease, teasing and enjoying each other and showing real affection.

Finally, Sasha's tolerance for—even open enjoyment of—playfulness and intimacy appeared to awaken. Sasha's manner with his younger siblings became increasingly gentle and caring. He started to seek out his mother for holding when he needed reassurance, saying, "Mom, would you hold me during the scary part [of a movie]—and hold me real tight when it gets really scary."

THERAPLAY FOR CHILDREN IN FOSTER CARE

Theraplay has been used for children in relative and non-relative foster care and family reunification programs. Clinicians attending Theraplay training often ask whether this method should be used to promote attachments between the child and an adult who will not be the permanent caregiver. We believe that developing attachment between children and temporary caregivers is appropriate and necessary. As Fahlberg notes, "Given the potential long-term effects that lack of attachment can have on a child, it is crucial that the foster care system respond in ways that help the child develop attachments with their primary caregivers whomever [sic] they may be. . . . [T]he development of an attachment to foster parents should be encouraged" (1991, pp. 23–24).

The experience of forming an attachment, even to a temporary foster parent, gives the child an opportunity to break out of the emotional isolation imposed by trauma and loss and begin to reach out again in order to complete their grieving and healing. Attachment is a skill that needs to be developed and used in all relationships.

We know that attachment to the primary caregiver makes it possible for children to make a good connection with other caregivers, family members, and teachers. Similarly, attachment to a foster parent helps the child form an attachment to adoptive parents. Hughes (1997) notes that some poorly attached children need to have the experience of forming an attachment to a therapeutic foster parent before they can be ready to form an attachment to adoptive parents.

For Theraplay treatment to be truly effective, foster parents must come to understand their importance in the child's life and must make a commitment to attend and participate in sessions. In fact, in addition to using Theraplay with individual foster families, child welfare workers have found the Theraplay model useful for foster parent training programs. Use of the Theraplay dimensions of structure, engagement, nurture, and challenge can form the basis of an explanation of children's needs and helpful caregiver responses. In addition to working with foster parents and children, Theraplay treatment also has been effective with caseworkers and their clients and group home staff members and their residents. Although the ideal setting includes a parent figure, children can still benefit from the unconditional regard, the structure, the nurture, and the self-esteem building of the Theraplay experience.

Children who have had multiple placements in foster care have developed very strong defenses against forming an attachment. Many are referred for Theraplay after having years of treatment in other modes of therapy with little effect. This long experience with ineffective therapy can result in the child's not trusting the therapist and being able to manipulate adults and the system. When working with these children, be prepared for extreme displays of passivity or aggression, which may include outbursts of rage. You must prepare caregivers as well for these displays of rage so that they continue to support treatment and do not withdraw the child. If treatment ceases when the child expresses his anger and despair, the child will feel rejected yet again, and will feel that adults are unable to protect him.

Working with these children is both emotionally and physically draining. Treatment is usually extended to perhaps twenty or thirty sessions over a period of six months to a year, and it should follow the child if and when he moves to a more permanent placement. You must be willing to accept slow improvement in small steps. On a positive note, therapists working in child welfare, who have for long periods of time used other approaches, frequently tell us of significant improvements in child behavior, child-caregiver closeness, and caregiver satisfaction when Theraplay treatment is initiated.

This final case study of three siblings in foster care illustrates how Theraplay was able to encourage the children's growing use of and dependence on the foster mother's emotional stability and availability. It happens that these children were placed in permanent foster care with this mother; however, if their plan had been to move on to an adoptive placement with another parent, the treatment goal would have been the same: first to promote a secure attachment to the foster mother and then to help the children transfer that attachment to the adoptive parents. The foster mother would have been part of the transition to the adoptive home through giving support and permission to the children to attach to the adoptive parent; she might also have continued contact with the children as an extended family member.

THERAPLAY IN PRACTICE: *Developing an Attachment to a Foster Parent.* Katie, a lively four-year-old, the youngest of three siblings, was brought to therapy by her foster mother. Two years earlier Katie and her two brothers had been removed from their home and placed in permanent foster care with this foster mother because of sexual abuse, neglect, and abandonment by their biological mother and father.

Although Katie had been in treatment previously, she still showed signs of indiscriminate and shallow attachments. She showed no preference for being with her foster mother over being with a stranger. Katie initiated contact with strangers and would sit in their laps or hold their hands. When she sat in her mother's lap, she would not cuddle or make eye contact but would be restricted in her emotions and rigid and agitated in her behavior. She often ignored what her mother said to her.

Katie and her foster mother were initially seen in joint, nondirective play therapy sessions, and she had begun to enact through play the fear she had of being close to anyone. After a year of this therapy, she had made some progress but was still maintaining distance; for instance, she would pretend to be a baby but adamantly insist on taking a baby bottle to a corner to feed herself.

Also, the foster mother had become aware that there was sexualized activity occurring among the three siblings. Treatment was hampered by the fact that all three siblings had formed an alliance against the outside world, including the foster mother. The children were staunchly independent and looked to the older brother to provide leadership, as he had done when they lived with the biological parents. (This child, an eleven-year-old boy, was currently in therapy elsewhere.) The children would not disclose or talk about the sexual behavior. Because the behavior had been reported to the child welfare authority, there was a concern that the children might be separated.

At this point, the therapist received training in Theraplay, and a new plan was developed with the foster care agency and foster parent to initiate a Theraplay treatment program. The foster mother enrolled all three children in the treatment program in order to coordinate treatment. This highly invested, loving foster parent agreed to attend five sessions per week in order to help the children progress. Each child had a weekly individual Theraplay session with the foster mother and a weekly family Theraplay session; the foster mother also attended parenting consultations once a week.

TREATMENT. In the Theraplay sessions Katie's ambivalence to attaching to the foster mother rapidly surfaced. Although Katie was intrigued by challenging activities such as balancing and then jumping off a tower of pillows, she struggled for control in nurturing activities, grabbing the lotion and saying, "I'll put the lotion on myself." Undaunted by Katie's attempts to withdraw, Beverly persisted. She playfully but insistently retrieved the bottle of lotion and gave it to the foster mother, saying that Mom would be so disappointed if she couldn't put the lotion on Katie's wonderful hands.

Using a combination of warmth, humor, and fun—for example, putting lotion on Katie's toes while singing a song about "going up and down the mountain"—her foster mother was able to reengage and delight Katie. After such a moment of shared intimacy, Katie would try to run to the other side of the room and play by herself. Beverly would follow Katie, "corralling" her in a playful manner. Lifting Katie gently, she would say, "Whoops! Oh, that Katie is a slippery character when she has lotion on her feet! We're going to have to slide her back to her mom!" Katie would protest and her feelings would be acknowledged: "I can see you want to hide away in that corner but Mom and I really want you back here so we can have more fun together. Mom, wouldn't we miss Katie if she hid away from us?" The foster mother, following the cue, made a playful and dramatically sad face and agreed that she would be so unhappy if she couldn't play with Katie.

Crises seemed to erupt as Katie flew around the room, occasionally bumping herself and then crying inconsolably. Again both therapist and foster mother would reinforce the message that no hurts should happen and soothe Katie's hurts, both physical and emotional, holding and comforting her until she felt better. By the seventh session, Katie was calmer and more engaged, staying with her mother and enjoying having her arms lotioned and, in turn, lotioning her mother's hands. In the eighth session, she curled up in her mother's lap for the first time, made eye contact and said, in baby talk, "You feed me."

The middle child, Louis, age nine, had also been in traditional play therapy for a year with no progress. He had developed a smooth, pseudo-congeniality that effectively kept people at a distance. In treatment he maintained a glib defensiveness, while at home he was extremely disrespectful to caregivers and also cried easily. When Theraplay began, his emotions rapidly surfaced.

While Louis engaged quickly in games of challenge such as newspaper-punch or tug-of-war, he just as quickly tried to take the lead by creating a new game and attempting to engage Beverly in "his" game. Beverly expressed interest but insisted on maintaining the leadership: "What a great idea; we'll have to try that sometime, but I have something really special for us to do today. We're going to . . . " As Louis realized that he would not be able to take control, he put up a playful but very earnest struggle, darting around the room, hiding under pillows. Beverly reflected his feelings but stayed in charge. Louis eventually sat on the floor pounding a pillow and directly expressing his anger: "I don't like this!" This was the first time he had allowed himself to express anger directly and authentically in a session. His feelings were validated: "Oh Louis, you really are angry. I'm so glad you can share your angry feelings with us. Mom, is it okay for Louis to have these angry feelings?" His foster mother agreed that it is fine for Louis to feel angry. Beverly then encouraged Louis to express his angry feelings. "Let's both pound the pillows and say how angry this makes you feel!"

At times Louis actively fought for control, hiding under the pillows and taking the cookie that his mom had fed him out of his mouth so that he could then feed himself. His mom responded by pretending to pout because she didn't get to feed him and eventually won him over. At other times he eagerly joined in such activities as bean bag toss or foil prints.

In the fifth session his control issues peaked and began to lessen as sessions continued. By the seventh session, he stated that he liked to be fed and was earnestly talking with his mother. He stated that he preferred the (Theraplay) sessions in the new room (which had no toys other than those materials chosen by the therapist for that session) to his sessions in the old play therapy room (which had many choices of art and play objects). Following session twelve, the foster mother stated that his disrespectful attitude had decreased significantly. Louis was now able to control his anger and to apologize; she felt that she was able to tolerate the anger he did express.

William, age eleven, began Theraplay without having had earlier treatment. The MIM evaluation of William's relationship with his foster mother highlighted issues of trust. In treatment he responded with skeptical wariness but did not actively resist the activities. He made a point to hide his feet behind him and stated a strong distaste for taking off his shoes. By the third session, he showed signs of warming up as he allowed his foster mother and Beverly to give him a "flying ride" down the hall. In session eleven, he initially responded with disdain to his foster mother's pretending to "paint" his face with a soft brush, but then entered into the spirit, asking her to "put silver on my eyebrows!" By this time he was shedding his shoes easily. During this session, he agreed to lean against his foster mother for support as he shared a scary nightmare. In parenting consultation, the foster mother stated that she saw a marked improvement in the quality of his attachment to her at home.

The nurturing and accepting atmosphere of the individual sessions created a sense of intimacy in which the children could begin to explore their difficult feelings around issues of trust and sexuality. As the children drew closer to the foster mother, there was a decreased need for secrecy and independence, and each child formed a more appropriate attachment to her. The individual sessions laid the foundation for the family sessions; the sense of playfulness, acceptance, and nurturing in both types of sessions helped the children feel more secure and less defended.

Family sessions began after each child had at least three individual Theraplay sessions with the foster mother. In the family sessions the children were asked to take turns feeding each other; this was difficult as they were uncomfortable allowing themselves to be fed by anyone. When the children were reminded of the "No hurts" rule, one of the boys said humorously, "It hurts me to have to be fed, so that means I can feed myself!" Beverly matched his humorous tone: "Good try, Louis; you've got it right about no hurts, but I don't believe you will die from eating a chocolate chip cookie, even if your sister feeds it to you!" She then acknowledged how difficult it is to be fed, and asked the children to trust her and their foster mother that accepting food from someone who cares for them is an important experience for them to have.

Beverly and the foster mother carefully monitored the children's feeding of each other so that the "feeder" fed the other child appropriately and received praise when he was able to do this. When a child failed to feed appropriately, he was helped to try again and it was acknowledged that it is a difficult thing to do. Mom also explained to the children that she hoped they would learn to treat each other well by learning to feed each other in a respectful manner. Eventually, one of the children remarked that this was like the Golden Rule: "Feed others, as you would want to be fed." This bit of wisdom became part of the family tradition and was quoted and remembered in other sessions.

The feeding also helped the children verbalize their own needs, for example, "Don't give me too big a piece of cookie." This set the state for expressing other boundaries and needs.

In the secure, nonjudgmental, and nurturing environment created by the family Theraplay sessions, the children began to share their painful family history, as well as to discuss the inappropriate sexual behavior. To tackle these issues, family sessions were grounded in Theraplay but incorporated other therapeutic methods to address specific issues. For instance, in the individual sessions, the children created their own charts of touches they personally would allow or not allow. In the following family session, the children each shared their own preferences and then chose whether to receive an "OK touch" from the others. Theraplay activities such as "pass the lotion" or "pass the touch" gave opportunities for appropriate touch and ways to have fun, thus providing a corrective experience and alternatives to sexualized behavior.

Through activities such as these, sexualized behavior became a topic that could be discussed. For example, one session began with Katie taking center stage as everyone settled in, putting her hands on her chest and wiggling suggestively. The boys laughed at Katie's behavior, egging her on, but also making a show of complaining to their mom about her behavior. Beverly asked all the children to look at what had occurred: "Let's look at the interesting way that things work in your family. Katie learned from you that breasts are exciting and she is acting this out for both of you. But I wonder if you really want Katie to act like this?" Both boys said they didn't think it was a good idea for a four-year-old to behave in this way. Then she asked, "Katie, if you could get attention another way, could you stop doing it this way?" Calmer now, Katie agreed that she doesn't want to act like this if she can have fun other ways. Beverly set up a plan for each brother, with help from his foster mom, to teach Katie something nonsexual that she could have fun showing off in future sessions. The foster mother supported all of this.

In the safe atmosphere of these sessions, the children shared more about the sexual behavior that they were exposed to in their family of origin, responded to discussions of how they would like that to change in their new family environment, and were helped to identify problem areas without needing to place blame on each other for the sexualized behavior. The foster mother as well as the children report that incidents of this behavior at home decreased.

As we predicted, with the decrease in inappropriate intimacy, there was an upsurge of angry, often vicious, sibling rivalry, which seemed to be in the service of helping the children break the emotional enmeshment that was so strong among them. Unfortunately, since these children had seen only angry and chaotic detachment behavior in their early life, this is the model they turned to in order to separate from each other. In order to help the children find healthier ways to individuate, Beverly began incorporating assertiveness techniques in her work.

Their conflicts peaked in the ninth family session with an outbreak of quarreling and difficulty engaging in games together. Beverly commented on how frustrated they all seemed and accepted their feelings. The foster mother had established excellent boundaries with the children over the years by using consistent rules and consequences firmly yet lovingly enforced. She was therefore able to command their attention in a quiet and nonthreatening manner: "Thank you Louis, for sitting nicely on your pillow." Establishing meaningful eye contact with William, she said, "Please come back to your place now." She ignored attempts to distract her, reminded them that they had only thirty minutes left for the session and that they were wasting their own time.

Katie, however, was unable to calm down and continually interrupted activities. This had the predictable outcome of annoying her brothers, who began to complain that she was ruining the session. As Katie was not able to respond to efforts to engage her, Beverly and the foster mother decided that it would be best if Mom took Katie out of the session while Beverly continued to work with the boys. The foster mother made sure to let the children know that she was taking her out, not as a punishment but because Katie needed time to calm herself. Beverly said, "Wow, you children are really having a hard time today. Maybe just this time Mom needs to take Katie back to the waiting room. We can stay here and figure out how to help everybody feel OK."

Beverly then helped the boys to express their frustrations, and together they worked out strategies they could use to stop themselves from reacting so strongly to Katie's provocative behavior. They made a chart of behaviors that "helped" and behaviors that "didn't help" to keep conflicts at a minimum. In the next session, the children were eager to show that they could cooperate and asked the foster mother to use a hand signal to quiet the family. The children are working on moving beyond this conflict into more appropriate sibling bondedness.

The foster mother was elated with the changes that occurred as a result of the Theraplay sessions. She felt that all of the children became more securely attached to her. The foster care worker noted that Theraplay treatment made a big difference in the way the children related to their foster mother. The foster mother attributes some of the change to the way in which Theraplay (and Beverly) supported her efforts to nurture these wonderful but challenging children.

Now that the children are more secure with their foster mother and able to relate more appropriately to each other, they are open to other treatment approaches that can help them deal directly with their earlier trauma and loss. The Theraplay techniques continue to serve as a catalyst for this other work and as a way of creating the holding environment that helps the children feel secure.

When using Theraplay to promote attachment in children with attachment disorders, the recreation of the healthy interactions seen between very young children and their parents provides a therapeutic environment for cognitive, emotional, behavioral, and interpersonal change. Theraplay promotes a calming of physiological reactivity, emotional change, and eventual cognitive restructuring at a preverbal level through the adult-directed play and caretaking. Theraplay challenges the child's earliest and usually negative experiences. The more healthy view—that the world is a safe place and that adults can and will take care of him—is created by the accepting, caring, and playful Theraplay therapist. Bonds of trust and affection develop between the parent and child, allowing the child to relax his need to be in control of interactions and to engage more fully with others, and allowing caregivers to enjoy and experience success with their caregiving.

Notes

1. We are not focusing on children adopted as newborns and raised by their adoptive families because those children have the opportunity to develop attachments through responsive caregiving just as biological children do, although we acknowledge that they have sustained a loss. Theraplay may be useful for children adopted as newborns if and when later typical issues emerge concerning loss, self-esteem, and identity (Reitz and Watson, 1992).
2. Jarratt (1994, pp. 7–11) discusses helpful ways to talk to children about loss, taking into account the child's stage of thinking.

3. Grabe reports on the conclusions of a survey of adoptive parents and their experience of the therapy process: "The non-directive approach does not work with foster/adoptive issues, nor does an approach that excludes the family, that does not see the family as a resource, or opts for confidentiality. Much of the potential of a therapy session is lost if the family cannot continue to reinforce the issues during the next week" (1990, p. 39).

4. Reitz and Watson, working from a family systems perspective, ask about the family rules concerning the adoption, and how they match other operating rules in the family; they examine the interaction among the family system dynamics of a particular family, its life stages, and adoption; and they encourage the clinician to understand which of four phases of the adoption process (uncertainty, apprehension, accommodation, integration) the family is in and what unfinished business from previous phases may exist (1992, p. 135).

5. Hughes' (1997, p. 30) review of recent research in the areas of attachment, trauma, affect regulation, neurobiology, and developmental attachment sequences illustrates the connection between attachment and development; he states that children with more severe attachment disorders are likely to display a range of problems in relationships, emotional development, behavioral control, and cognitive development.

6. Hughes (1997, p. 2) notes the child's enjoyment of power struggles, feeling of empowerment by repeatedly saying "no", and strong desire to control all situations, "especially the feelings and behaviors of their caregivers." He also describes the child's compulsive need to control teachers and other children (p. 30). Fahlberg (1991, p. 53) describes needing to be in control of all situations as a part of problems in interpersonal interactions, with lack of trust, hostile dependency, impaired social maturity, and demand for affection without depth in relationships. Jarratt (1994, p. 185) notes that children often try to control life by becoming oppositional, overly passive and compliant, anxiously avoidant, or overly competent and self-reliant. James (1994) notes that while children can control through opposition and refusal to cooperate, and so avoid intimacy and feel safe, they also can control through being clingy and demanding. Hughes (1997, p. 30) describes a characteristic poor response to discipline with aggressive or oppositional defiant responses.

7. Symptoms related to engagement and relationship as described by Hughes (1997, pp. 30–31) are: "lack of comfort with eye contact . . . interactions lack mutual enjoyment and spontaneity . . . indiscriminately friendly,

charming . . . poor communication . . . lack of empathy . . . habitual dissociation or habitual hypervigilance."

8. Hopkins-Best advises the adoptive parents of toddlers to meet the child's
needs as quickly as possible and to make the most of the child's overtures,
stating, "Always assume that a request for parental contact and comforting
represents a need for a toddler struggling to develop attachment and meet
that need on demand, day or night. Parents need to reframe their thoughts
about getting up at night with a toddler as a wonderful opportunity to
build attachment rather than a dreaded chore" (1997, p. 198). James, discussing ways to help these children accept parenting and a sense of belonging, talks about the "thousand micro-acts that demonstrate the caregiver
can be trusted. . . . [showing] over and over again that parenting can be
strengthening even if dependence happens. . . . Parents must endlessly
repeat, by words and deeds, 'I won't hurt you. You are safe. You are worthy
and deserving. I like to do this. I am available'" (1994, pp. 83–84).

9. Hughes (1997, p. 32) comments, "The healthy sequence of union, exploration, shame and reunion has been replaced by neglect, self-minimizing,
contempt/rejection, and isolation/splitting."

10. James (1994, p. 18) proposes that puzzling behaviors such as negative
responses to positive events or dangerous/harmful behaviors are not the
result of a poor self-image, but an attempt to deal with overwhelming anxiety by triggering a numbing response; treatment should focus on affect regulation.

11. Lifton, (1994, p. 262) says, "The goal for the adoptee is to feel that he has a
right to exist, and to stake the claims that come with such entitlement."
"The best interests of the adopted child can only be served . . . when the
child is seen as a real person—not a fantasy child, not an idealized child,
not a special child, not a commodity—but a child with his own genetics, his
own talents, and his own identity" (p. 275).

12. James (1994, p. 14) describes an "all or nothing emotional style" with
constricted affect in play mixed with out-of-control affective storms
unrelated to play, flashbacks, and alexithymia (a condition in which a person "is aware only of the physiological aspects of affect . . . and is unable
to name or give symbolic representation to an emotional experience"; she
speaks of the need to work on toleration and modulation of affect, noting
that it is a mistaken belief that helping a child discharge emotions will be
sufficient to rid him of difficult or unpleasant emotions. Hughes (1997, p.
30) notes problems in emotional development as: "limited range of recognition and expression, lability, poor frustration tolerance, habitual
depression, anxiety."

13. The Parent Network for the Post-Institutionalized Child. P.O. Box 613, Meadow Lands, PA 15347.

Voice mail: 724-222-1766
FAX: 770-979-3140
E-mail: PNPIC@aol.com

Theraplay for Adolescents

When we turn our attention from the broad range of troubled younger children to troubled adolescents, the relevance of Theraplay might well be questioned. Can all those babyish techniques—the cuddling, the stroking, the "silly" childish games— appeal to an aggressive, embittered fourteen-year-old? Can an "in-your-face," destructive dropout be restored through well-designed, esteem-enhancing play of the kind we have been recommending?

Anyone who has studied the general problems faced by all adolescents, as described in scores of books by now, might well think Theraplay no longer relevant. Every child moving into the teens faces biological and psychological upheaval: sexual development, changes in physical appearance, changes in relations to parents, blows to self-esteem, exciting but often daunting challenges about "the future." These changes produce characteristics radically different from those we have met in the Theraplay sessions we have seen so far. And the tragic destructive behavior toward self and others that too many adolescents engage in might well lead any therapist to back away from Theraplay: "Let's just leave the troubled ones to other kinds of treatment."

Our experience with Theraplay has demonstrated that though Theraplay must be significantly modified when dealing with adolescents, the experienced Theraplay therapist can reverse threatening behavior, restore child-parent relations, and get the troubled teenager back on the right track.

Theraplay treatment with adolescents is based on the assumption that their attachment needs should be addressed before they can safely move toward autonomy. It is often a weakness in attachment that creates the situation that brings the adolescent into treatment. Typically, adolescents are referred for help because of poor peer relations, poor relationships with authority figures, poor school performance, antisocial behavior, substance abuse, emotional unpredictability, or disengagement. As with younger children, these problem behaviors are often associated with insecure attachment. Thus the underlying issues for many adolescents are related to very early attachment issues.

In this chapter we look at why adolescents are difficult to treat, what Theraplay has to offer, and how it differs from work with younger clients. Next we consider how the Theraplay dimensions can be adapted for adolescents and how the phases of treatment differ. Then we discuss countertransference issues that arise in working with adolescents and, finally, describe how parents can be included in the treatment.

UNDERSTANDING WHY ADOLESCENTS ARE DIFFICULT TO TREAT

Adolescents pose a unique challenge to any psychotherapist. Already mistrustful of adults, the adolescent is resistant to engaging in the treatment process. Too often he comes into treatment because his parents or teachers think he needs help, not because *he* feels a need for it. He sees this as the adults' effort to make him shape up, rather than as an offer of help to deal with his own pain. As a result, the adolescent has a different agenda from that of his therapist or the other adults in his world. Too often his goal is simply to get his parents off his back. Thus right from the beginning he may be resistant and even hostile.

Many adolescents no longer look to adults as authority figures. Those who were unable to benefit from an adult relationship in the past feel that engaging in one now is a waste of time. Those who do relate to adults prefer to treat them as peers rather than as respected authority figures. Thus the therapist can no longer rely on his or her authority, size, verbal ability, life experience, or intellect to take charge of the situation.

Nor, for several reasons, can the therapist assume that the adult style of talking therapy will be effective. Although adolescents love to talk to peers, they are often uncomfortable talking to adults. When the adolescent does verbalize, words can be used to keep the therapist at bay. In an attempt to evade oppressive adult rules and structure, many are masters at manipulation and conning. Finally, the adolescent may not yet have the maturity to understand the complexity of her situation and therefore may find it difficult to admit to confusion when it is felt.

For all of these reasons, therapy of any kind with adolescents can be difficult. As Theraplay therapist, you must understand the adolescent's developmental needs, as well as be alert, creative, and resourceful in order to ensure successful treatment. Theraplay with adolescents is not for the beginner.

UNDERSTANDING WHAT THERAPLAY CAN OFFER

Rather than attempt to adapt adult talking therapy to adolescents, Theraplay offers an alternative method of treatment. It engages the troubled adolescent in an active process, one that is full of fun and surprises. It responds directly to the regressive needs lying behind the adolescent's smokescreen of misbehavior. The Theraplay therapist actively takes charge, providing the clear structure that adolescents so desperately need. The adolescent does not have to talk about his problems, reveal secret fantasies or wishes, or even be motivated to get help. The active, playful nature of Theraplay makes it possible to short-circuit the adolescent's highly developed verbal skills, which he often uses to avoid addressing issues and to control the treatment.

Including parents in Theraplay treatment adds special power to our work with adolescents. By the time a child is in her teens, dysfunctional family patterns of distancing, arguing, and angry fighting are entrenched. Parents, having "tried everything," feel hopeless, angry, hurt, and often ready to give up (as we see in John's case later in this chapter). Structural family therapists recognize, as Theraplay does, the need for parents to regain their leadership role and to provide clear rules and structure at home. Theraplay adds the essential dimension of helping parents understand and respond to their teenager's needs for nurture, for self-esteem enhancing interactions, and for just plain shared fun.

The following case illustrates both how one can shift from one treatment modality to another (with little fanfare) and how Theraplay deals with the adolescent propensity to control through talk.

THERAPLAY IN PRACTICE: *The Adolescent Who Controls Through Talk.* In this case, Theraplay was begun to break the deadlock that had developed after a long attempt to use individual adult-style talking therapy with a troubled adolescent. The therapist, trained in traditional insight therapy, had engaged in twenty-five talking sessions with little effect. Because treatment had begun as individual therapy, the parents were not involved. Aware that a frightened little child cowered inside her talkative, pseudo-sophisticated client, she decided to try the new Theraplay techniques in which she had been receiving training.

June was referred because of her poor relationships with peers and her underachievement at school. A tall, attractive, fourteen-year-old girl with coal-black hair and bright blue eyes, June was clearly of superior intelligence. It was not unusual in her therapy for her to quote poetry in support of her "feelings" and to formulate accurately both her own dynamics and the dynamics of her parents. Through her verbal fluency, catchy phrases, apparent ease with psychological concepts, and ready logic, she had maintained control of her therapy sessions and of the therapeutic relationship at all times. In this way she perpetuated a rigidly defensive posture and kept the only kind of balance with which she felt comfortable.

Despite her poise, however, she had given the impression that were she ever to find herself in a situation that she did not control, she would appear not as the young adult sophisticate, but as an awkward little girl. Had she been permitted to continue resisting another's indulging attentions, she probably never would have been able to form affectively meaningful relationships. Given her unvarying need to "call the shots," her openness to new experiences and to new learning always would have been limited.

The following excerpt is from the record of the first Theraplay session. No introductory remarks were offered with regard to the change in format. Indeed, explaining the new treatment style would have made it impossible for the session to be spontaneous and "fun."

THERAPIST: Hi, June. Here, let me take your coat.

JUNE: (enters the room animatedly, describing an incident with a woman on the bus and explaining that she was late because the bus had broken down) I tell you the lady wore a plunging neckline. It came right about down to here—I swear to God, Marilyn Monroe! *[June, characteristically, is "running the show," keeping her references to events outside the session, focusing on adult sexuality (not inappropriate for a girl of fourteen, yet inappropriate for June, whose developmental level is essentially that of a much younger child).]*

THERAPIST: Oh, my. How cold your hands are! Let me rub them for you. And your cheeks. They're so pink! They make you look so pretty! (taking her hand and guiding her across the room) Let's look in the mirror. Ohh! Just look how beautiful you look with those pink cheeks! *[Takes charge in a direct, firm, physical and caring way. Calls attention to a part of June's body, helping her to identify her physical self as having positive value.]*

JUNE: (looks at herself, obviously pleased; a flicker of a smile crosses her lips) *[Adolescents such as June are often reluctant to admit enjoying the session or feeling engaged with their therapists.]*

THERAPIST: Did you say you had to walk all the way over here? Boy! Your feet must be worn out! Here, let's take off these shoes and look at them. Those are fine shoes, yes indeed! They're absolutely made for all that walking around in school you do. *[The therapist "takes off" on June's stimulus yet not in any way that she could have anticipated or manipulated. The therapist shows empathy for June's sore feet and empathic understanding of June's day. Her parents, incidentally, do not. They attend to June's school achievements only.]*

JUNE: (trying to reclaim her shoes) They're OK. I was going to tell you about my friend Tina. Do you know that just before English she . . . *[A momentary power struggle ensues over the ownership of her shoes, first a physical struggle, then a verbal one ("They're OK"). Then she turns her efforts to directing the session in her typical style, introducing verbal content.]*

THERAPIST: (takes off socks) Oh yes! Just take a look at those calluses. You sure do a lot of walking on these feet, I can see that all right. I think if we . . . oh, let's see how well you can hop on the other foot if I carry this one. (holds one of June's feet, giving her ample time and room for hopping) *[Therapist takes off June's socks in a manner that is warm but matter-of-fact. She attends to a hurt body part with concern and compassion. She has put herself in June's place and has demonstrated both active engagement and the investment of energy that goes with caring. By making her take the difficult hop (challenging) she causes June to be dependent on her (nurturing) while organizing (structuring) an activity that catches June off guard (engaging).]*

JUNE: I can't do that. I'm out of condition. Besides, my feet smell. *[She backs up her refusal with what would appear to be a legitimate excuse and then warns how unpleasant her "real self" may turn out to be if it were discovered.]*

THERAPIST: Here we go.

JUNE: Where are we going? *[She needs to predict what will happen.]*

THERAPIST: It's a surprise. You'll see . . . (they arrive at the sink) Now, some nice warm water to warm your cold foot up a bit. (allowing water from faucet to run over foot while sink is filling)

JUNE: (peers down) *[Intrigued in spite of herself.]*

THERAPIST: Oh, dear, what do I see? This toenail. It needs some special care. Let's soap it up a bit first. *[Like a mother taking care of her infant, she attends to the hurt.]*

JUNE: Oh. That one's OK. Been like that for a long time. *[Again she is saying, "Leave me alone."]*

THERAPIST: And here's the callus from all the walking. Soap on it too.

JUNE: I read that's bad for them. *[The power struggle continues. Outside authorities are introduced in support of her resistance.]*

THERAPIST: Now we'll pat them dry.

JUNE: I can do that. (attempts to reclaim foot) *[Her reluctance to accept caretaking attests to the intensity of the underlying need for it.]*

THERAPIST: And now some nice-smelling lotion. I'll hold it till it's all soaked in. Oh that feels so nice and soft. *[In spite of June's protests the caretaking continues. There are no references to achievement. Positive comments refer only to properties intrinsic to June (for example, "so nice and soft").]*

JUNE: What are we doing anyway? *[Again shows the need to remain "in charge."]*

Several important principles are demonstrated by this excerpt:

- The therapist was in charge at all times and "ran the show." Although what June did, wore, brought, or said may have provided the springboard, her therapist generally did not respond to it in the manner June intended. The therapist never asked questions such as "What would you like to do today?" or "OK?"

- The therapist made no demands on June to talk, to produce, to perform, or even to discuss what was worrying her.

- Just like a mother with her small baby, the therapist kept up a constant, running commentary—a commentary that, requiring no response, conveyed only attention and caring.

- The therapist's conversation was intensely focused on June—her body, her appearance, her lifestyle, and her state of health and well-being.

- The therapist focused on the positive qualities intrinsic to June as a separate person. Her therapist did not focus on June's achievements or on her accomplishments.

- The therapist established body contact at every opportunity.

- The therapist did not attend to June's efforts to direct the conversation.

- Except for responses conveying empathy (for example, "Oh, my! How cold your hands are!"), the therapist made upbeat comments only.

- The therapist moved spontaneously into new activities. She neither announced nor introduced what she and June were about to do.

As June herself said during the appointment she made to see her therapist twelve years later (to introduce her fiancé), "I remember every detail of every active thing you and I *ever* did together. I remember the first time you washed my toes—how startled I was. Nobody had ever done that for me before. And how you oiled my elbows and fed me bananas. And the day we tried on hats. You know, it's funny, I don't remember anything at all about the time when I was coming to see you and we just talked."

UNDERSTANDING HOW ADOLESCENT THERAPLAY DIFFERS FROM THERAPLAY WITH YOUNGER CLIENTS

Although June made relatively little protest during her first Theraplay session, most adolescents show greater resistance than younger children. When you work with adolescents you must have greater perseverance, self-confidence, imagination, and sense of humor. In addition to greater resistance, the adolescent's physical size and sexual and intellectual development must be taken into account.

Dealing with Physical Size

The adolescent's greater height, weight, and strength call for activities in which your control generally does not depend on your being able to "take hold" physically. Rather, your tone of voice, certainty of movements, and commanding attitude must carry the message that you are capable of "running the show" in a safe, playful, and appropriate manner.

To accommodate a large teenager, you will need a somewhat larger room than that for a small child. The large pillows that we recommend for younger children are even more useful for adolescents, and you can use many more of them. They can be used to support the adolescent instead of holding him on your lap, they can be stacked for him to balance on, and they can be made into a huge pile to burrow under.

Taking Sexual Development into Account

The adolescent's heightened sexual awareness precludes many of the Theraplay activities appropriate to younger children. No longer can you engage in such physically intimate activities as rubbing baby powder on tummies, blowing on ears or on eyelids, or holding the young person on your lap while singing lullabies. No longer can you do leg wrestling with a client of the opposite sex. Yet there are still many fun, physical activities that are appropriate and that raise self-esteem and enhance growth.

Although children of any age may be affected by the therapist's sex, at adolescence and beyond it becomes of crucial importance. Just as a seductive eight-year-old boy or a sexually stimulated six-year-old girl should not be assigned opposite-sex therapists, most adolescents should be worked with only by therapists of their own sex. Occasionally there are cases where life experience or sex role confusion may preclude a male treating a male or a female treating a female. Two therapists, perhaps one of each sex, is an ideal arrangement to make everyone comfortable. Two also are helpful for activities that involve holding, swinging, or lifting a large adolescent. If it is impossible to recruit a second therapist, then it is usually satisfactory when the one therapist is the same sex as the adolescent client.

Having two therapists or a same-sex therapist reduces the possibility that the playful, physically intimate Theraplay activities might be sexually stimulating or arouse sexual fantasies in the adolescent client. It also protects you from the possibility that outsiders, aware of the physical nature of Theraplay, might assume that the interaction was sexually provocative or inappropriate, or from the possibility that the young person herself, during an angry or resistant phase, might accuse you of inappropriate intimacy. As a protection against these misperceptions (as we noted earlier), all sessions, especially those with an adolescent, should be videotaped. Having parents and an interpreting therapist observe sessions is an additional safeguard against the false accusation of inappropriate touch.

Responding to Intellectual Development

Because they are older and more intellectually mature, adolescents feel more self-conscious, are more defensive, and are more verbally challenging than younger clients. You need to be prepared to respond to their sophisticated verbal resistance with humor and confidence. To the accusation, "This is dumb," you can answer, "I know. But this is what they taught me in Psych 101 so we have to do it." Patient and therapist thus can share a humorous way of "saving face." The adolescent's protest often seems to be a necessary precondition first of his acceptance and then of his enjoyment. It is as though the adolescent needs to go on record as having renounced such childish carryings-on before he can settle down to participate in them.

ADAPTING THE THERAPLAY DIMENSIONS FOR ADOLESCENTS

As for clients of any age, the Theraplay dimensions of structure, engagement, nurture, and challenge are used to tailor treatment for the needs of each individual adolescent. In the case of adolescents, however, structure and challenge must be emphasized before it is possible to achieve the kind of engagement that can lead to an adolescent's being able to accept nurture. It is very important that all activities be done in a playful, unselfconscious manner. You need to have a good sense of humor and communicate confidence and comfort. Playfulness should be communicated not only in your selection of activities but also in your voice, stance, and gestures.

In the following example from a Theraplay session with Alex, you can see how play helped this angry adolescent experience joy.

THERAPLAY IN PRACTICE: Using Play to Engage an Angry, Withdrawn Adolescent. Alex, a sullen, angry fourteen-year-old boy who was referred for treatment by his adoptive parents because of his angry oppositional behavior entered his third Theraplay session in a very resistant mood. He slouched on the pillows and initially made little response to the playful approaches of Gary, his therapist. Feeling a need to rouse him from his passivity and to bring some lightness to the scene, Gary staged a marshmallow fight. Positioning Alex across the room from his parents, who were observing the action from behind the video equipment, Gary said, "I'll bet you can't throw a marshmallow over the TV and hit Dad on the shoulder." Alex's first efforts were minimal. He barely reached the TV set. "Here, Dad, here's your supply of marshmallows; see whether you and Alex can have a snowball fight." As soon as Dad entered the fray, Alex brightened up and a wild and joyful engagement ensued. The room was soon adrift with marshmallows and Alex's mood had lightened considerably. It was then possible for Alex and his Dad to feed each other marshmallows to the accompaniment of whoops of laughter from Alex and his Dad and cheers from his mother and Gary. This silly, playful activity had roused Alex from his sullen lethargy and made it possible for him and his Dad to share a joyful moment together.

Structuring

All adolescents need clear expectations and firm rules if they are to move successfully toward running their own lives. It is no service to the adolescent (as we also have noted with younger children) to allow him to run the show. Faced with a strong, self-assured therapist, the adolescent can model his own growing sense of self on that strength and self-assurance.

The adolescent from a family where there are few rules, inconsistently enforced, is in great need of structure. The adolescent who is overscheduled and who has too-rigid internal rules, needs spontaneity, flexibility, and fun. The timid adolescent may need to be encouraged to take more initiative.

Structuring activities with adolescents include making life-size body tracings, hand and footprints, hand and foot plaster impressions, and aluminum-foil prints of body parts: hand, foot, ear, elbow, or knee. They include activities in which the adult directs the action, such as where to aim the orange seeds, the water pistol, or the basketball, or which foot to move first in a three-legged walk (the adolescent and the adult tie their adjacent legs together with a bandanna and walk around the room arm in arm). In addition to the activities themselves, structure is provided by giving signals for when to start an activity, stating clearly what the youngster is to do, and making sure that the activity is carried out safely and in an orderly, calm manner.

THERAPLAY IN PRACTICE: *Learning to Follow the Rules.* Erin, an impulsive, defiant, fifteen-year-old girl, has difficulty following the family rules and accepting her parents' legitimate demands for compliance and follow-through on household chores and responsibilities. In the sixth session of her ten-session course of Theraplay treatment, her therapist sets up an activity that will give Erin practice in following her mother's directions and will give her mother practice in clearly defining what she expects Erin to do.

Erin's mother is to give eye signals to indicate which direction they are both to move as they stand facing each other. If she winks her left eye, both she and Erin must move to her left. If she winks her right eye, they must go to her right. Erin says, "That's stupid; anyone can do that." "Wait," her therapist says, "There's one more thing you have to do. Here's a big pillow. I'll put it between the two of you and you must each keep your hands behind your back. Now the only way you can keep the pillow from falling is if you both lean toward each other and watch very carefully when the signal changes." Erin takes up the challenge, and carefully watches for her mother's eye signals. When the activity becomes more complicated—two blinks mean two steps, head back means move back, and so forth—they struggle, and finally, to the accompaniment of joyful laughter, the pillow drops to the floor. In a spirit of challenge and fun, Erin has had an experience of following her mother's clear signals. Because there are no words, there is no opportunity for their typical legalistic arguments and delaying tactics.

Challenging

As you can see from the example, the challenge of supporting a pillow between them while she follows her mother's signals made it possible for Erin to participate. Challenging activities are always a good way of engaging an adolescent and, therefore, we discuss them before turning to the dimension of engagement. In the process of pitting her strength or skill against you or against a standard, the teenager loses her self-consciousness and can enter wholeheartedly into an activity. Challenges should never result in a put-down or a failure, nor should they in any way add to the already overburdened striving teenager. The passive teenager with low self-esteem benefits tremendously from being challenged to succeed in activities that are fun. The essential ingredient is a supportive atmosphere in which she learns to enjoy the feeling of successful competition.

Challenging activities for the adolescent differ little from those for younger children, except that the competition is stiffer. Thumb or arm wrestling becomes a more strenuous exercise for both therapist and client, and contests such as musical chairs require more precision. Challenging activities include tug-of-war, leg wrestling, jumping to see how high he can reach, watermelon-seed-spitting contest, and pillow balancing ("How many can you balance on your head? How high a stack can you balance on?").

THERAPLAY IN PRACTICE: *Challenging the Resistant Adolescent.* Ken, a fifteen-year-old, was referred because of defiant behavior toward his mother. As an introduction to his first session, Ken's therapist challenges him to a wrestling match.

THERAPIST: Hi, Ken! I'm Bill. Let's go downstairs. Boy! Those look like big muscles you have there. (checking his arms) *[Ken's therapist does not ask for permission or announce what they are going to do. Instead, there is immediate physical contact and positive body-image reference.]*

KEN: (pulls away) *[This is an appropriate reaction of a teenage boy toward a stranger who behaves so presumptuously.]*

THERAPIST: Bet you can't push me over. I'm really strong. *[This paradoxical move is designed to turn Ken's negativism into cooperation. It is an assertive self-statement, offering his own self-confidence for identification.]*

KEN: (goes through the motions only) *[Still master of his own destiny. Not an inappropriate stance once it becomes truly his own rather than based, as it now is, on the defiance born of anxiety.]*

THERAPIST: I told you you couldn't do it 'cause I'm so strong. *[The challenge grows.]*

KEN: (begins to push in earnest) *[He can no longer resist the challenge. In addition, his therapist is beginning to look like a fun, appealing person.]*

THERAPIST: Oh, you are strong. *[Therapist praises Ken for the person he is, for his assets. It is clear that his therapist, unlike his mother, has neither a stake in Ken's being cooperative nor a need to be loved by him.]*

BOTH: (tussle vigorously and alternate winning)

This vigorous, challenging tussle begins the process of helping Ken feel better about himself at the same time that it helps to impress on him who this adult is and how involved with him, as a fun-loving person, his therapist has become.

Engaging

Given his resistance to treatment, engaging the adolescent is perhaps the most difficult, as well as the most important, task for the therapist. More than for a younger child, any activity that places the therapist close to the adolescent feels intrusive. For example, just sitting close to a teenager, or touching his hand, makes him uneasy. But the closer you are, the more difficult it is for the teenager to shut you out from awareness. Humor, surprise, and paradox are all useful in disarming, and thus engaging, the resistant adolescent. The goal is to find ways to overcome the adolescent's defensive attempts to keep you at bay, by making him experience your presence intensely and by forging an alliance that will be the basis of a new way of relating and feeling about himself.

The withdrawn, isolated, or obsessive-compulsive adolescent particularly needs to be engaged and intruded upon. Surprises make it difficult for the adolescent to maintain his intellectual distance. The adolescent who comes from an intrusive family, however, needs respect and distance. But this does not preclude surprises or other engaging activities.

Any activity that requires touch and physical closeness serves the function of making the teenager aware of your presence and thus begins the process of engaging him. The structuring activities of body tracing, measuring, weighing, and making aluminum foil body molds all require touch and physical closeness and therefore can be seen as serving to intrude and engage as well as structure. Give-and-take activities, such as hand-clapping games, three-legged races and coordinated two-person juggling acts, also require awareness and serve to foster engagement. Many nurturing activities, such as dressing up with hats and face painting, because they require touch and awareness of the other person, also include an element of intrusion and lead to engagement.

THERAPLAY IN PRACTICE: *Engaging the Reluctant Adolescent.* As an example of how to engage the reluctant adolescent through surprise, humor, and physical touch, we continue with Ken's first session. Immediately following the challenging wrestling match, his therapist takes his hand:

THERAPIST: Those are big hands. Here, let's put some paint on them and see how different we can make your fingers. (grabs Ken's hand and carefully covers it with many colors) *[Identifies and describes body parts in ways that are positive yet not related to performance. Playfulness and caring are expressed through this activity.]*

KEN: (studying the process interestedly) This is dumb. *[Although he continues to save face, he is clearly beginning to enjoy himself.]*

THERAPIST: Wow! That is beautiful. (takes the painted hand and "walks" it up the paper-covered wall) *[Expresses enchantment and excitement like a mother discovering a new characteristic of her baby. Takes charge of an activity that he is certain is fun as well as novel and surprising.]*

KEN: God, this is so dumb! What you doing all this for anyway? *[Still saving face while enjoying it. Shifts again to the man-to-man talk that is obviously his more familiar style, allowing him to keep control.]*

THERAPIST: Oh, I got to do this. They taught it to me in Psych 101 at college. *[With humor and lightness, rather than with a heavy focus on Ken's pathology, his therapist conveys that he takes neither himself nor the "problem" that seriously. He introduces hope and pleasure into a relationship that is nonetheless intense and focused on the patient.]*

THERAPIST: (later, pressing Ken's foot into wet plaster of Paris) This one I learned in Human Behavior 709. *[Another way of making Ken aware of his body boundaries that is positive, yet intensely interpersonal and nurturing. Having established a common bond—reference back to the earlier "Psych 101"—Ken and his therapist reaffirm their "membership in the club."]*

KEN: (laughs, then looks at his therapist with good eye contact) *[Finally lets down his defensive vigilance. Allows himself to interact with his therapist for the first time.]*

Nurturing

Nurturing activities may seem more appropriate for young children than for adolescents, yet everyone of any age needs to feel nurtured and valued. Adolescents, while they may be self-conscious about receiving nurture, are often especially needy. When this need has to be hidden, however, it can become a problem. Evidence that teenagers need nurture can be seen in their poor self-image, their inability to relax, and their development of stress-related illnesses. Terrence Koller (1994, p. 172) writes, "Although not all adolescents need nurture as a primary focus, it is always appropriate for helping the adolescent relax after a more active and lively Theraplay session."

Although adolescents may find it difficult to allow you to lotion their hands or feed them cookies, they often will accept such caretaking combined with another activity or a challenge. Although he protested verbally, Ken made no move to pull his hand away as Bill rubbed paint on it, and he was intrigued when the painted handprints marched up the wall. Both the rubbing of paint on his hands and the washing up were opportunities for gentle touch and caretaking. Feeding can be made part of a challenge such as "doughnut challenge," in which the goal is to see how many bites can be taken before breaking the doughnut ring (poised on the therapist's finger). In seed-spitting contests, each feeds the other a chunk of watermelon and saves the seeds. Then they see who can spit the seeds farthest. A less competitive version of this game is to have one person spit a seed and the other try to get as close to it as possible.

Taking care of hurts, cuts, and bruises by applying lotion or Band-Aids, combing hair, polishing nails, applying lotion to dry hands, feeding, sipping cider through two straws, making powder foot prints, trying on flattering hats, and making crepe paper bow ties, hats, and necklaces are all possible nurturing activities.

In June's first treatment session, we saw an example of several nurturing activities. Her therapist rubbed her cold hands to warm them, attended to her calluses, soaked her feet in warm water, and dried them and put lotion on them, all to the accompaniment of appreciative comments about June. In spite of her surprise and initial discomfort, June accepted these activities, and even twelve years later recalled them vividly.

GUIDING THE ADOLESCENT THROUGH THE PHASES OF TREATMENT

Adolescent treatment does not follow the same sequence of phases described in Chapter Four as typical of the younger child. Instead, it bypasses the initial tentative acceptance phase and jumps right into the resistant phase.

Resistant Phase

There is generally no opportunity for the relationship to evolve slowly from lukewarm acceptance through negative rejection to active participation. When confronted with their painful ambivalence about closeness, adolescents become resistant very quickly. Thus, their "negative phase" starts early and has a strength and a conviction that is likely to catch you off-guard and, if you are inexperienced, even to persuade you to let up.

As we noted, adolescents' highly developed verbal skills make them masters at argument, reasoning, and discussion. Once you get caught in "discussing" the treatment rationale and in "listening" to the patient's resistance against it, much ground has been lost. From then on, you may find treatment interrupted at any point while the client calls for a restatement of the contract or for an explanation of "How's this particular activity going to do me any good?" Only when treatment can proceed without this kind of shifting in and out of playfulness can it be smooth, enjoyable, and free.

Remember June's therapist, who, rather than respond to June's verbal efforts to control the Theraplay session, maintained the focus on physically taking care of June and responding to her needs. You can also avoid getting caught up in the adolescent's resistant maneuvers by planning fast-paced sessions that draw her into intriguing activities in spite of herself.

PREPARING PARENTS. We have said that it is important to prepare parents to handle difficult behavior during a young child's resistant phase. This planning is even more important with adolescents. Their greater capacity for dangerous behavior plus their greater skill at manipulation make preparation especially important. Since the negative stage begins immediately, you must build this warning into the intake process.

Tentative Acceptance Phase

Following an initial strong and often extended period of resistance, there is usually a phase of tentative acceptance comparable to that of the young child. Unable to resist the fun and often still protesting that the activity is ridiculous, the adolescent forgets herself for a moment and laughingly participates in an activity. She may not yet be able to enjoy the pleasure a relationship can bring, but she is becoming curious.

Growing and Trusting Phase

Finally there comes a time when the adolescent interacts with her therapist in a warm, pleasurable way. You will find yourself looking forward to sessions and feeling that they are pure fun. This is your signal that it is time to prepare for termination. Although the relationship may feel much more relaxed, warm, and comfortable, you should not be surprised if the adolescent continues to voice complaints about how silly and meaningless the activities are. Following successful treatment, adolescents often report that they found the activities foolish or "inane" (see John's father's letter at the end of this chapter and June's comment twelve years after treatment) and can see no relationship between the activities and the fact that they are feeling better.

Preparing for Termination

Preparation for termination with adolescents is similar to that with younger children. You point out the adolescent's strengths and tell him that there will be three more sessions including a termination party. The termination phase for adolescents, however, is more difficult than it is for younger children, who are being turned over to the security of their families. Though adolescents also have families, their struggle to achieve independence makes the anticipation of losing the close attachment to their therapist a greater threat. It may throw them into a depression or a regressed state that can be worrisome to you and to the parents. It is important to prepare both the adolescent and her parents for a temporary return to previous behavior. "Adolescents who had academic problems prior to Theraplay may stop doing home-work. Withdrawn, depressed adolescents may retreat to their rooms. Defiant adolescents may temporarily pick fights" (Koller, 1994, p. 174). If parents are well prepared for this eventuality, they can carry on where the therapist left off. This regression does not last long because the adolescent's new pleasure in relating to others in a healthier way will soon take over to help him feel confident about the future.

You must be aware of how difficult termination is for both you and your adolescent client. Koller cautions, "The patient may want to can-cel the last session, claiming that there is nothing left to do, that all problems are resolved. . . . [You] should not allow this retreat from the pain of separation. . . . [You] must be emotionally involved dur-ing this last phase of treatment and seek consultation if [you] experi-ence too much anxiety or depression. [You] must demonstrate the courage to complete the treatment process as planned" (p. 175).

DEALING WITH COUNTERTRANSFERENCE ISSUES IN WORKING WITH ADOLESCENTS

In Chapter Four, we discussed the countertransference challenges that Theraplay presents to the vulnerable therapist, noting that you must be especially aware of your own motivations and must provide your-self with many necessary safeguards. Theraplay with adolescents pre-sents even more challenges.

With a young child it is relatively easy to set limits, challenge and engage him, and assume the role of nurturing caretaker. With an ado-lescent client, there is more temptation to identify with the client's sit-uation and to hold back out of "respect" for his feelings.

Recognizing the Influence of Your Own Adolescence

Based on your own adolescent experience, you may find yourself iden-tifying strongly with your client's rebelliousness and pain. While your empathy can be helpful to the adolescent, your own rebellious feelings may lead you to collude with him against his parents and make it difficult for you to set limits and make challenging demands. On the other hand, if you yourself were a very controlled adolescent and a good, obedient student (as many therapists were), you may not understand how much your client needs to be relieved of the too-heavy demands of his daily life.

If you are a person who has difficulty allowing others to get close to you, you may find it harder to engage the resistant adolescent. If you were not well nurtured, you may find it difficult to nurture an adolescent who, like you, prefers to distance himself from closeness. You will find yourself agreeing (as you would never do with a small child) that she is too old for this baby stuff.

Paying Careful Attention to Your Responses

Perhaps the most challenging aspect of working with adolescents is dealing with their angry, aggressive behavior. To control a small child is one thing; to control a large teenager is quite another. The latter requires an extraordinary amount of self-awareness.

"What can Theraplay do for adolescents whose disturbance takes the form of explosive acting out?" This question is frequently asked by psychiatric, probation, residential care, and education personnel. The answer, "Theraplay can often be helpful," must be carefully qualified. Only the most self-aware, professionally competent, and personally adequate therapists should even attempt to do Theraplay with a belligerent, frightened adolescent who has lost control.

The case of preschool Sam, described in Chapter Six, illustrates this principle. As you recall, his therapist insists that Sam straighten the chairs he has thrown down and in the process she holds the struggling child in her lap and begins to rock and sing a lullaby.

Both the struggle and Sam's experience of feeling safe about "giving in" were necessary prerequisites for meaningful progress. But the bigger and stronger the child, of course, the more difficult the struggle. And herein lies the reason for ensuring an emotionally healthy therapist. A "struggle" with a physically resistant teenager, unlike one with a resistant preschool child, sometimes calls not only for the strength to (more than) match his strength but also for self-protective measures. If the experience is provided in the context of calm confidence and growth-enhancing messages, the patient can feel reassured, cared for, guided, and protected. Carried out in the spirit of derision, threat, and sadism, however, the experience can only be devastating.

Using Teamwork as a Safeguard

Depending upon their own character, therapists working with aggressive adolescents may find it all-too-tempting to respond with sadism or masochism. Obviously no therapist aware of any temptation to cruelty should risk Theraplay with aggressive adolescents. You should watch carefully, for example, for any tendency to administer painful hammerlock holds or, conversely, to suffer broken eyeglasses or torn shirtsleeves. Should this happen to either therapist, it is important that both therapists become aware of it, discuss it between sessions, and plan a strategy in which opportunities for brutality or victimization cannot again present themselves. Some very good teams combine one active, physically strong leader with a supporting partner who is "maternal," soft-spoken, and helpful. Optimum teamwork requires agreement on who will play which role as well as what to do if a planned activity fails to work.

Patients such as the young man whose case is presented next can only be treated effectively with Theraplay, provided his two therapists share a level of comfort that allows them to give each other open feedback. This provides a system of checks and balances that assures the therapists' behavior will not damage the patient's self-esteem—even when physical means are used that might easily lend themselves to "getting even" with a threatening, belligerent, hurting patient. To be effective, Theraplay must move beyond the inhibition of old, destructive behavior to the creation of new, pleasurable experiences.

The following case illustrates the difficulties of working with an angry, aggressive adolescent as well as how two experienced therapists working as a team can overcome such difficulties.

THERAPLAY IN PRACTICE: *The Importance of Teamwork in Working with an Aggressive Adolescent.* Major confrontations played a large part in the early stages of Theraplay with Ralph, an adolescent in the partial-hospitalization adult program of a psychiatric ward. Ralph had set fire to the unit's wastebaskets and had terrorized other patients with his wild shouts and brandishing of billiard cues. He was referred for Theraplay after he had failed to respond to all other treatment forms and was about to be evicted from the program altogether. For obvious reasons, two male therapists, Jeff and Norm (rather than a single therapist or a cross-sex or female team) were assigned to work with him during first once-weekly and then twice-weekly half-hour Theraplay sessions. The following is excerpted from his first Theraplay session.

JEFF: Ralph, today you're coming with Norm and me (guiding him firmly by one arm) *[No questions are asked, no permission is requested. Like a parent leading a child out of danger to safety, Jeff firmly, but not punitively, indicates he knows what is best for Ralph and intends to help him do it.]*

NORM: (guiding the other arm) Right in here, Ralph.

RALPH: I'm not going with nobody! I already told you. I do what I damn well please around here. *[Ralph feels threatened at the outset and announces his intention as though to command. He expresses his expectations that people should obey him (as, of course, they always have). He reiterates who he is and what his rules are.]*

JEFF: Let's sit down right here. *[Ralph's defiant refusals are simply ignored.]*

NORM: I want to see how tough you can arm wrestle. *[Norm has "hooked into" Ralph's facade of toughness. He has made it impossible for Ralph to refuse the challenge and still maintain his tough facade.]*

RALPH: (looks surprised) *[He is not used to being rewarded for his strength. Ordinarily it is his very aggressiveness that leads to rejection.]* I'm not wrestling nobody, I'm getting out of here. *[He recovers himself just as he is about to "give in" to another's invitation. "Getting out of here" is a solution familiar to Ralph. He is quite used to running away when he feels himself "trapped."]*

JEFF: Here, you grab Norm's arm with yours like this. *[The directions are clear, the action is swift, and body contact is accomplished before Ralph can rally his resisting forces. All this, however, is done as "good, clean fun." Nowhere is there a "put-down."]*

NORM: (encircling Ralph's arm with his own) OK, I bet I'm going to win! *[This is a challenge but not a threat. The ease with which the therapist initiates physical contact must convey to Ralph that he is worth getting close to.]*

JEFF: Come on Ralph, come on. I know you can do it. *[He expresses both his confidence and his wish.]*

RALPH: (enters into the contest straining with all his might) *[Ralph has become engaged.]*

NORM: Boy! Ralph, if I'd have known you were this strong . . . *[He praises Ralph again in the very area that has been Ralph's downfall, his physical aggressiveness. This is both surprising and positively valuing of him.]*

RALPH: (struggles hard to push Norm over) *[His negativism has been channeled, while at the same time he remains physically engaged with another person in a way that is safe and fun.]*

JEFF: It's a tie! It's a tie! . . . No, it's not . . . oh, this is close! . . . Come on Ralph! Show him, Ralph! Ah! The winner! The winner, in this corner is . . . Ralph! *[Cheering lends suspense to the engagement. Probably this is one of the very few times in his life that Ralph has ever felt anyone cheering for him. Nor has he often been the winner. For this moment at least, he should feel he has an ally and a fan.]*

NORM: Good work, Ralph! Oh! Am I beat! Jeff, how about cooling the contestants off? *[Praises and thus reassures Ralph. He lets him know that he can have an impact on another person in a way that is playful rather than dangerous. When working in teams like this, therapists often organize the next activity aloud.]*

JEFF: (bringing the damp cloth) Here comes the wet towel now. *[Example to Ralph of cheerfully cooperative teamwork.]* (alternately fans Ralph and Norm with a wet towel)

RALPH: (rejects any effort to cool him off) *[It is probably the very fleeing from his infantile wishes for nurturing that has made Ralph behave as he does.]*

NORM: Those breezes feel so nice and cooling, don't they, Ralph? *[Chatters cheerfully. Clearly he expects no answer.]*

RALPH: Hmm . . . No they don't. *[He is caught off guard for a moment, then recovers his oppositional negativistic stance again.]* You get your filthy hands off me.

NORM: (arm around Ralph's shoulder) You look cooler to me already . . . and handsome . . .

RALPH: (a smile flickers fleetingly across his lips) *[Again he is momentarily disarmed.]*

It is clear that the Theraplay principles illustrated in the session with June described earlier, apply to Ralph as well. But when the resistance is stronger, the therapist's work is restricted to basic confrontations and the settling of power struggles. Thus, whereas with June it was unnecessary to do much more than ignore her efforts to control, with Ralph it was impossible to focus on anything but his unrelenting struggle for power. The more effective the therapy, the greater is the ratio of therapist-initiated activities to those in which the therapist counteracts patient-initiated activities. Except for the wrestling match during this first session, Ralph could receive little in the way of therapist-initiated treatment, so the range of experience was severely limited. There were few surprises, few opportunities for spontaneity or fun. There was only minimal nurturing and not really the range of challenge his therapists knew he would enjoy.

Over the succeeding sessions, however, Ralph allowed himself to participate in a far greater number of experiences (hair combing, foot painting, and so on) and at times was obviously having fun and looking forward to the weekly sessions. After thirty twice-weekly half-hour sessions, he sought Norm out for conversation and pool games and had social telephone contacts with him when he had to miss his sessions. At last report, Ralph had returned to school and was doing well.

INCLUDING PARENTS IN THERAPLAY WITH ADOLESCENTS

Theraplay treatment for young children should always include parents or caretakers if at all possible. For most adolescents we also recommend including parents in the sessions. Many adolescent behavior problems stem from insecure attachment as well as from current problems in the relationship with their parents. Often, by the time a family comes for treatment, the battle lines are drawn and neither side is able to move to a more helpful way of interacting. Parents are angry and stuck in an ineffectual pattern of nagging, complaining, and punishing. The adolescent expects only negative things to come from his parents and therefore shuts them out and distances himself. Many parents have given up trying to establish rules and set limits. Theraplay can give them a chance to practice being clear about what they want their teenager to do and follow through on seeing that they do it.

Helping Parents Understand Their Adolescent

Often parents do not understand the complex mixture of regressive needs and striving for independence that generates the adolescent's confusing behavior. You should help parents understand and find ways to respond to both impulses. Giving parents information about what they can expect during the adolescent years can be helpful. Asking them to recall their own experiences when they were in their teens can give them insight into their child's feelings. Many parents also need guidance in setting appropriate rules and following through. Theraplay provides a model of clear structure, appropriate nurturing experiences, and playful give-and-take that can help parents find an appropriate role during these difficult years. There are many good reasons for including parents in Theraplay with their teenager.

Knowing When to Limit Parent Involvement

In some circumstances, however, Theraplay treatment for adolescents should include parents in only a limited way or should exclude them. Knowing that parents are observing sessions may make the adolescent so self-conscious that he can't allow himself to be involved. With parents observing, he may experience nurturing activities as too babyish to accept. In such cases, it is best to begin Theraplay without parental involvement. It can be explained at the start that parents will join the sessions later when it is time to work out some of the problems that occur between them. When the client is more comfortable, parents can be briefed about what is expected to happen in the session and can be given an opportunity to role-play their part in the interaction before joining the session.

When the adolescent is in residential treatment (as Ralph was), parents are usually unavailable for Theraplay sessions. In that case, the treatment focuses on the relationship between the adolescent and his therapist rather than between him and his parents.

Some adolescents, particularly older ones, need individual Theraplay sessions that do not include their parents. They are at a stage where they need to focus more on developing their own autonomy and on moving toward greater independence. In such cases, including parents in treatment may be inappropriate. Sessions still would aim to meet the regressive needs of the client, but they would place a strong emphasis on supporting his feelings of competence and autonomy.

On the other hand, if the problems are clearly in the parent-child relationship, parents should be included. Following the usual intake interview, a diagnostic session using the Adolescent form of the Marschak Interaction Method can help determine the level of parent involvement. A list of recommended MIM tasks for adolescents is in Appendix B.

In the following case, the focus of treatment was on the relationship between the adolescent boy and his father. Theraplay was able to change a negative father-son relationship by enhancing the teenager's self-esteem and by providing a more playful, positive way of interacting.

THERAPLAY IN PRACTICE: *Including a Father in His Son's Treatment.* John, sixteen, was first referred to the learning disabilities department of his high school. John obviously was highly intelligent, but he was a poor reader, bored by his assignments. Because of his disruptions, he was restricted to the back of his schoolrooms, where he sat throwing pencils at the teachers and tearing up his assignment sheets. John's parents turned to Theraplay after the principal informed them that the staff had done all they could do. If John did not get help right away, he would be expelled from school.

Over the years, his parents had tried in vain to teach him to concentrate, cooperate, and read. His father reported being defiantly rebuffed each time he attempted to help John with his homework. As they knew he was intelligent, both parents could only assume his failure to achieve was deliberate.

ASSESSMENT. During the intake interview, John's father said sadly, "I can't take any more of this. If it keeps on any longer, I know I'm going to get ill from the worry of it. I'm fast reaching the decision that it's either John or me." Since so much conflict seemed to center around John and his father, it was decided to focus treatment around that relationship. Father and son were seen together for a diagnostic MIM, which included the following activities:

1. Adult and child each draw a picture.

2. Adult teaches child something he doesn't know.

3. Adult and child look at each other's hands and read each other's fortunes.

4. Adult and child engage in three rounds of thumb wrestling.

5. Adult asks child, "Tell me about when you're an adult."

Throughout their interaction, his father's message was clear: John should grow up at once; he should become an outstanding business executive; he (as father) would tolerate no regression or error; their relationship (and life itself) was a deadly serious business that allowed no room for play. John's response to his father's lengthy preachments and superior expectations was to "tune him out" or to spill or mess up what he was doing. Rarely was there eye contact between them. Although this sixteen-year-old nearly equaled his father in physical strength, he consistently and meekly lost the thumb-wrestling rounds.

Because of his father's out-of-town business trips, Theraplay was to begin on a schedule of one session every two or three weeks. Sessions were to be geared toward (1) helping John see that it was safe to compete with his father without fear of his father's having a "heart attack"; (2) adding a dimension of fun and frivolity, humor and surprise, to their relationship; (3) encouraging intimacy and trust between them; (4) raising John's self-esteem and raising father's respect for John; and (5) broadening the father's aspirations for John beyond the verbal, intellectual, and cognitive to include the physical.

Because adolescents often begin treatment by resisting strongly, John's parents were told that he might refuse to come and that his behavior at home and at school might get worse before it got better. They were told to warn the teachers of this possibility in order to forbear (but to continue to set appropriate limits) while treatment had a chance to take effect. The parents were told to be matter-of-fact but firm about his coming to sessions. With this forewarning, both the school and his parents weathered the storm of his initial resistance, which in John's case was surprisingly mild.

TREATMENT. With John's knowledge, his father sat with an interpreting therapist behind the one-way mirror. John and his male therapist in the Theraplay room wrestled, matched muscles, dressed each other up in silly hats, painted each other's faces, and drew around John's silhouette. Following John's first four Theraplay sessions, his father joined him for the last half of each of the remaining four sessions. Whenever he did so, the therapist acted as umpire while father and son had wrestling matches and pillow fights, gently combed each other's hair, and, sitting down slowly back to back, competed for the largest area of floor space.

Their interactions throughout were carefully controlled yet were designed to be the most fun possible for both participants. When John was given theatrical makeup and instructed to "make your father look as young as you can," with deft strokes of the greasepaint John gave him cheerful red cheeks, a sprinkling of freckles, and a little boy's straw hat tied under his chin. As they surveyed his masterpiece in the mirror, both father and son giggled in delight, and John appeared obviously relieved.

While he observed his son's first four Theraplay sessions, the father was encouraged to repeat some of the same activities with him at home and to consider what these activities might mean to John. The interpreting therapist pointed out to him, for example, that John seemed to back away from competing with his male therapist, and asked him, "Why do you suppose John does that?" and "Do you see how he really enjoys doing something silly like making handprints on the floor? Can you think of some 'silly' things the two of you could do together at home?" In the process, the father came to see that his own appearance of perfection, coupled with his high expectations of John, had put John in constant awe of him. He began to try at home some of the therapist's techniques for reducing the gap between them.

FATHER'S ASSESSMENT OF TREATMENT. A few months after termina- tion, in a follow-up session, John's father dictated his impressions of the Theraplay experience:

> We have been engaged in Theraplay, attending some eight sessions over a period of several months. Prior to the Theraplay sessions, John indicated that he hated school. Since the Theraplay sessions began, we have noticed a decided change in John's attitude not only toward school but toward other things as well. He seems to be coping with his schoolwork much better and is very happy when he comes home from school and also seems eager to get to school in the morning. He has been doing much better this past term and is not afraid of his homework or his schoolwork. His teachers say that he has even contributed in class without being asked and has taken the initiative in many instances. I'm not positive that the reason for this is the Theraplay except prior to the Theraplay sessions there was no obvious improvement in John's attitude toward school or toward other factors that affected his daily life. I'm referring basically to his relationship with me.
>
> Since the Theraplay sessions (which both he and I think are inane, to say the least), there has been tremendous improvement. He's a much happier boy. He is much more able to cope with his schoolwork. He's doing much better in school, and we're looking forward to a productive academic career.

We have a much freer and easier relationship than we used to have, and I'm hoping that will continue to improve. He is much more talkative than he used to be, and he is making his feelings and his inner thoughts known much more frequently than he used to, particularly with me.

In summary, it would appear that the effectiveness of Theraplay for John and his father was a function of the following:

For John:

1. Building his self-esteem

2. Developing a sense of trust

3. Relieving his anxiety that he would hurt his father if he confronted him or competed with him

4. Helping him view himself as a lovable and "fun" person

5. Teaching him performance (perceptual motor) skills in a light-hearted, playful context

6. Removing the pressure to achieve and showing him that it was legitimate to satisfy regressive needs

7. Helping him feel comfortable when calm

8. Acquainting him with his body boundaries

For John's father:

1. Showing him what a good time he and John can have together

2. Helping him remove the pressure on John to succeed

3. Helping him see John as lovable

4. Building self-confidence in his role as father

5. Teaching him how to take life less seriously himself

6. Helping him show patience with, respect for, and appreciation of his son

The cases in this chapter dramatize how particularly challenging Theraplay is when it is conducted with adolescents. Because Theraplay is based so extensively on the therapist's being "in charge" and because adolescents try so especially hard to tip this balance, Theraplay requires a broader repertoire, a greater sense of humor, and more imagination and spontaneity than does Theraplay with younger children. "Talking" therapy requires adolescents to relate to their therapists as adult-to-adult, verbally, cognitively, and with reference to past and future. Theraplay, on the other hand, is directed to those not-yet-grown-up parts that presumably have remained unfulfilled. Since therapy with adolescents may sometimes be a combination of both talking and Theraplay, a particularly sensitive diagnostic skill and a pronounced therapeutic talent are obvious prerequisites. Therapists for adolescents can often find considerable gratification in conducting well thought-out and well directed, yet spontaneous and fun-filled Theraplay.

CHAPTER TWELVE

Group Theraplay

Phyllis Rubin

———〰———

G roup Theraplay is a logical extension of individual Theraplay. The idea of applying Theraplay to large groups of children originated with school teachers who recognized its value as an individual therapy and wanted *all* of their children to reap the benefits of a Theraplay experience. Group Theraplay was fully described and illustrated by Phyllis Rubin and Jeanine Tregay (1989) in their book, *Play with Them: Theraplay Groups in the Classroom,* but its application has grown significantly in the decade since the book's publication. Not only has it been used in a wider variety of settings with children, but also it has been used with parent groups and even with seniors suffering from depression.

Using Theraplay in groups thus allows its unique approach to relationship building to reach more of those who need it. It is not, however, a substitute for individual treatment when that is also needed. It can be an adjunct to individual treatment, or it can stand alone, offering the experience of spirited, playful, and caring interaction with a group of peers supported by the therapist who acts simultaneously as coach, leader, and participant.

As in individual Theraplay, Group Theraplay aims to enhance self-esteem and to increase trust in others through concrete, personal, and positive experiences. It also strives to increase the sense of family and belonging among group members. It addresses underlying needs that are often disavowed or defended against, rather than those that are manifest. Just as in individual Theraplay, the group will need various degrees or combinations of structuring, engaging, nurturing, and challenging activities.

After summarizing the Group Theraplay approach, we give details about how to plan and structure your group. And finally we describe the diverse groups for whom Theraplay has proved effective.

We begin with a sample Theraplay group session, so that you will have a picture of the process. The session took place in a kindergarten classroom of twenty children. The classroom teacher, Sam, leads the group. His assistant teacher and two parents join him.

GROUP THERAPLAY IN PRACTICE: A Sample Group Session. Sam begins his Theraplay group by saying, "OK, boys and girls, let's all make a line, put your hands on each other's waist and here we go! Choo-choo-choo-choo!" and the line of adults and children chug to the rug, forming a circle as they go. Sam tells them when to stop and when to sit, saying, "Get ready, get set, sit down!" Then, to the tune of "Goodnight Ladies," they sing a welcoming song, naming each participant and giving a handshake as they go: "Hello Mary; hello Paul; hello Natasha; we're glad you're here today!" Then, beginning with Sam, each person "checks" the next person in the circle by lotioning around a hurt or a special spot.

As they go around the circle, Sam notices that Bobby looks sad today and says to him, "Bobby, maybe you have an 'inside hurt.' Tell Suzanne [the child next to him] if you want some lotion or a hug." Bobby says he wants a hug, and after getting one, is able to check and nurture the next person with sensitivity and care. After all the children and adults have attended to and nurtured each other, the fun begins as Sam brings out a cotton ball and says, "I'm going to try to blow this to Mary's nose! Everybody tell me when to blow." The whole group says, "One, two, three, Go!" and Sam blows but gets Mary's shoulder instead of her nose. Everyone laughs, including Sam. "My goodness, I missed that wonderful nose but I got your wonderful shoulder! Now Mary, it's your turn to blow it somewhere on Paul," and the game goes on.

Then, one person is chosen to go under a sheet and guess who is picked from the rest of the group to say "Hi, friend." Next, pairs of children try walking together while balancing a balloon between their stomachs, foreheads, or shoulders. Finally, Sam has everyone sit in a circle once again. One by one, he faces each child with a treat and says something special about each one. "Bobby, I hope your inside hurt feels a little better now. Suzanne, you and Ted balanced that balloon just great between your foreheads."

As Sam acknowledges each child, he feeds them a cracker, looking right at them with a smile on his face and a twinkle in his eyes. After every person in the circle gets a cracker, the children pair up, and, on the count of "One, two, three, go!" they simultaneously feed the treat to each other and quietly listen to themselves all crunching at once. Finally, all join hands to sing, "Twinkle, twinkle little star/What special kids we are/ Nice soft hair and nice warm cheeks/Big sparkly eyes from which we peek/Twinkle, twinkle little star/What special kids we are." Sam tells them to wrap hands around each others' backs, and at the signal, "Get ready, get set, go!," to give each other a gentle squeeze to remember until the next time they play together. The Theraplay Group is over.

UNDERSTANDING THE GROUP THERAPLAY FRAMEWORK

Theraplay groups like the one you have just seen are organized around four group rules and two group rituals that frame the sessions and communicate the Theraplay messages of structure, engagement, nurture, and challenge.

Group Theraplay Rules

Group Theraplay is guided by a simple set of rules that evolved out of the four Theraplay dimensions:

- No hurts.
- Stick together.
- Have fun.
- The adult is in charge (usually unspoken).

As the Theraplay Group leader, you should communicate these rules through both actions and words, but remember that actions always speak louder than words. In contrast to the emphasis of other types of groups, it is what you do, rather than what you say, that creates the therapeutic group atmosphere and contributes both to the healing and enhancement of relationships.

NO HURTS. This rule communicates the nurturing dimension of Theraplay. Your words, your affect, and your actions will converge to communicate that giving and receiving a hurt is unpleasant and undesirable. Regardless of whether a participant insists that he or she was not hurt, that the hurt does not really hurt, or expresses pleasure in or a lack of awareness of getting hurt, you should respond in the same caring manner.

Take all hurts seriously and attend to them by lotioning around them, blowing on them, or responding in any of the myriad ways that a caring parent reacts to a child's pain. Encourage the children to tell you when they are hurt, to alert others if they think someone else is hurt, and to take seriously both "inside" hurt feelings and "outside" injuries. Group members will learn to express the No Hurts rule directly through actions, by lotioning other hurt children, and through words, by expressing their feelings and by verbally asserting their rights. The child who caused the hurt can be encouraged to make restitution by taking care of the hurt child, using lotion or a band-aid, or giving a hug. This may be easy for the child who accidentally caused a hurt. The child who caused the hurt in anger may need time to get over his anger before he is ready to make amends.

Some group leaders lotion the person who purposefully hurt a peer, assuming that the one who did the hurting must have had a hurt in order to give one away. Especially in the case of an accidental hurt, the one who gave the hurt needs nurturing to heal the bad feeling that comes from having hurt another. If we think about the message of community that Theraplay Groups want to convey, there can never be too much nurturing when any hurt is involved. Some groups may even lotion all participants when a hurt happens, because witnessing a hurt is a sad experience for everyone. When we nurture everyone, we are enacting the interconnectedness envisioned in the poem by John Donne: "No man is an *Island*, intire of it selfe; every man is a peece of the *Continent*, a part of the *maine*."

STICK TOGETHER. This rule communicates the structuring and persistently interactive message of Theraplay. Strive in your groups to have all participants engaged together in activities with no one left out for any reason. To this end, you should help children attend to what is happening around the circle and respond to the activity at hand. This develops the children's ability to focus on a joint experience, take turns and wait for each other, delay gratification, and learn vicariously.

In practice, however, this proves difficult in groups that are either too large or whose members are too needy, frightened, or untrusting. Thus, you must be flexible in following this rule. You may sometimes choose to allow a hesitant child to watch peers playing together while you look closely for cues that he might be ready to join in. This will prevent him from depriving others of the group experience, sabotaging the group, or being cast in the role of the problem child.

This flexibility is especially important when you are working with individuals who have been physically or sexually abused. Not only has the child's trust in caring adults been violated, but control (the wrong kind of structure) has been used in an abusive manner. Because these children were unable to protect themselves from the bad things that happened to them, they need to have some sense of control over present experiences. For abused children, the physical closeness and touch that characterize Group Theraplay can be highly charged experiences. While not avoiding matter-of-fact, health-promoting touch (James, 1989), allow abused children to "say no" or to have more space than the typical closeness we create among group members. For example, one group leader acknowledged, "Sometimes people may need more space. If you do, you can tell your closest adult that you need some space, and then you can sit right over there until you are ready to join us again." Later in that session, instead of misbehaving in order to leave the group, children asked a group leader for space, sat out briefly, and returned quickly to the group. This prevented them from acting out in order to get the distance they periodically needed.

HAVE FUN. This rule communicates the stimulation, challenge, and playfulness of Theraplay. Fun engages group members, lifts the burden of excessive or prematurely imposed responsibility, and relieves the pressure for conditional achievement. Group members can let their goal-oriented, competitive drives take a vacation. Leaders enjoy participants, and participants are able to enjoy each other without having to do something to deserve it other than just being themselves. For example, you may send children to hide all over the room, and hear them giggling in anticipation as you look inside desks, backpacks, or pencil cups ("Bet Eddy's in here! No! Now where is he?"). Then you can "find" each child with an ever-increasing group of "found" children helping you. Or you may cover a group of kneeling preschool children with a large sheet (or balance a large piece of cardboard on the heads of older standing children), label them a turtle in its shell, and have them try to move around the room together, keeping the shell on their backs or heads. Or you can see how long the group can keep a beach ball or balloon up in the air. In a society in which goal-directedness and competitiveness are implanted in early childhood, in which children are increasingly stressed and worried, the fun, exuberance, and pure delight experienced in these games are precious and should be cultivated at every opportunity.

THE ADULT IS IN CHARGE. Just as in individual Theraplay, you are always in charge of the group session. This means that you and your co-leaders plan the activities and decide such things as when to start and stop, where participants will sit, and how to handle whatever occurs. When presenting the activities, you should not ask permission: "Do you want to play pass-a-squeeze?" or "How about playing blindfold-walk, OK?" Be positive and clear: "It's time to sing our goodbye song." When a group is well established, it is appropriate to involve children in decisions, as you might in an adolescent or adult group. This is especially the case during the termination phase, when you may ask about favorite games they would like to have repeated.

To coordinate the group's activity, give cues that tell the children when to respond, such as "Ready, get set, go!" You may say, "Bobby, I think you are standing too close to Louie and he needs more space. Stand right here next to me." Taking charge also means that if your group gets overstimulated by an activity, you stop the game, introduce a calming activity, and create a new way to play by adding structure to increase the group's sense of safety.

As with individual Theraplay, you can, of course, take cues for your activities from the behaviors or needs of the children. For example, one group, after checking who was present and absent that day, realized it was an absent child's birthday. The group leader said, "Let's send a great big Happy Birthday to Donna so that she can hear it all the way to her house. On the count of one, two, three, let's yell, Happy Birthday!" and the group practiced three of the loudest Happy Birthday's ever.

Group Theraplay Rituals

Early in the development of Group Theraplay, two rituals emerged as anchors marking the beginning and ending of each group session. They are checkups and food-share, each of which will come to have a powerful meaning to your group members, and thus should never be omitted from your plans.

CHECKUPS. One of the first activities in every session should be a checkup of each child. This allows her to have a "moment in the spotlight" when she is recognized, admired, and cared for without having to ask for it. Many groups use some vehicle for nurturing physically or emotionally hurt group members, such as lotion, cotton balls, hugs, or blowing kisses.

Group leaders have often found that the children whom they would least expect to accept this type of nurturing are the ones who pull up their shirt sleeves and pant's legs and have the leader slather lotion on their arms and legs. Whatever vehicle you use is likely to become a symbol of caring in your group environment, and children will apply it in related situations. If Group Theraplay is provided for a classroom of children, for example, the teacher will find that she needs to keep a bottle of lotion (or container of cotton balls) available in the room so that children can readily nurture peers in distress outside the designated group time. In one class, when Kenny saw two of his classmates accidentally bump into each other, he ran to get the lotion bottle so that he could help take care of their hurts.

FOOD-SHARE. At the end of each group session, a treat is shared by all, regardless of the degree of success of that session or the individual behaviors of group members. Being fed by another person and being able to accept a treat from another—modeled after a parent feeding an infant—is the most basic of nurturing and trusting experiences. Healthy emotional development for every human being depends on being nurtured and on developing trust. During food-share, the group members receiving the treat have the experience of feeling vulnerable and putting their trust in the other to take care of him. The capacity to give away a treat shows that the "giver" trusts that sufficient nurturing is readily available from sources that are either external (nurturing adults) or internal (self-comforting, self-regulating, and self-nourishing behaviors). During the initial stages of the group, the leaders do the feeding. As the group becomes more comfortable with closeness and as trust increases, the children can feed each other.

PLANNING YOUR GROUP

In planning for your group, you need to make a number of decisions. These include how big your group will be and what combinations of children will be included, who will be your co-leaders, how long your sessions will last, and how frequently you will meet.

Designing and Organizing the Group

Group Theraplay is appropriate to many different settings and age groups. Although Rubin and Tregay's (1989) *Play with Them* described Group Theraplay for entire classrooms of children, there are times when you will need to construct smaller groups. One Theraplay therapist, for example, formed a small group chosen from both special education and regular education classrooms in her school. Teachers of small classrooms not only can provide groups for their own children but also can periodically combine their classes for a larger, communal Theraplay experience. Groups can be constructed based on age, issues and behaviors displayed by participants, or on a desired balance among interactional styles. You might, for example, include both overactive and passive-withdrawn individuals in one group to create opportunities for "stretching" the relational styles of participants.

Large classrooms of troubled children demand thoughtful organizing as well as high levels of co-leader cooperation and communication. It may often be necessary to divide such classrooms into smaller groups. The most obvious choice is to have two or three totally separate groups in the same room, each with its own leader and doing the same activities as simultaneously as possible.

Another option is to divide the class into smaller groups that meet separately in a location other than the classroom. This would reduce the amount of distracting and potentially disorganizing stimuli present during the session but would raise problems about how to arrange for group leaders. Would the teacher be able to leave the classroom twice to lead each group? Given that the children in the individual groups improve in self-esteem and social interaction, could the groups merge at some point?

Another alternative is to combine small and large groups. This has been highly successful in preschool classrooms by using three to five co-leaders with fifteen to twenty children. The groups convened as a whole, but check-ups, lotioning, and sharing treats were done in informal "break-out" groups, in which three or four children clustered around their leader. Each adult had a bag that contained lotion, treats, a small mirror, or a prop for the day's planned activity. All the adults were checking, lotioning, or feeding each child in their small group, producing a rather noisy nurturing scene that was nonetheless effective. The greeting activity, at least one mid-session activity, and the ending song were done with the whole group together.

The more distressed, agitated, and emotionally needy the children, the smaller the group should be. Highly defended and chronically traumatized children require as much containment as possible. For them, a large group with children in close proximity can be a threatening experience and exacerbate rather than calm their fears.

Co-Leading

We recommend having a co-leader, particularly if you are working with young children. Having another set of eyes, ears, and hands is indispensable when you have children sitting close together on the floor without the benefit of structuring chairs and desks. You will find more detail about how to plan for and manage co-leading a group in *Play with Them* (Rubin and Tregay, 1989).

Because good teamwork between group leaders is essential, it is crucial that you choose co-leaders carefully. Distressed and troubled children are very sensitive to incompatibility and lack of coordination between group leaders. Distancing, withdrawal, or acting-out of any leader will increase the children's feelings of insecurity and increase tension and anxious behavior within the group. Some leaders may try to distance themselves from the intensity of the children's needs if they feel ill equipped to meet them. In schools or agencies with inadequate resources, leaders may be periodically absent or called out of class to attend to other agency needs. Your group must provide a secure setting to counterbalance the unpredictability in the children's lives. Therefore it is very important to preserve a time to plan, prepare and troubleshoot before the session and to process the session afterward.

Length of Sessions

The length of sessions will depend in part on the group: specifically, the age and attention span of participants, the size of the group, and the severity and type of psychological difficulties exhibited. Sessions generally average thirty to forty-five minutes, but extra time is needed for assembling and dispersing your group. When a group is particularly anxious or having difficulty settling down, you may want to shorten the session.

Frequency of Sessions

Groups can be custom-scheduled and designed for different settings and needs, but to be fully effective, they should meet no less often than once per week. Some leaders schedule their groups two or three times per week. Obviously, the more frequently you meet, the sooner the group will develop cohesion. If you are a teacher you may have more flexibility than a visiting group leader to decide to initiate additional sessions as needed. One teacher we have worked with, routinely gathers her class around any distressed child and uses this "crisis," with the child sitting in her lap, as an opportunity for a caring Group Theraplay experience.

In addition to such crisis-oriented group sessions, a classroom teacher can incorporate Theraplay principles and activities into her everyday schedule. For example, just beginning the school day with a checkup can have very positive results.

PLANNING GROUP SESSIONS

A well-planned single session calls for different types of activities at the beginning, middle, and end. Where you are in the overall course of treatment also dictates the nature of the activities you choose within each session. In the middle phase of treatment, for example, the relational issues your group is dealing with dictate some of the activities you choose.

Planning the Sequence within a Session

The checkup and food-share rituals will anchor the beginning and ending of your session. Begin with one or two activities that welcome the children and acknowledge each child as an individual. The ending allows each child to be given something (food, a hug) and to be nurtured, regardless of how successful the group was or how that child behaved. After food-share comes the ending song that binds the group together in a joyful communal experience.

Nurturing should never be withheld or made contingent on how well the group performed. Such a behavioral perspective is the antithesis of our attachment perspective. In attachment terms, the group is most likely to need nurturing when it is feeling most vulnerable (for example, when things have not gone so well during the session). You should view any "failure" as an opportunity for a caring experience rather than for criticism or unpleasant consequences.

For the middle of each session, choose activities that are lively and engaging and that reflect the stage or the issues of your group. We discuss this part of planning in more detail when we describe the middle phase.

Planning for the Phases Over the Course of Treatment

We think of the group process as falling into three phases: a short beginning get-acquainted phase; a middle phase (the length of which depends on how long your group will be continuing), during which the group can work on special relational issues that need to be dealt with; and a termination phase, during which the group prepares for the ending of sessions.

BEGINNING PHASE. During the beginning phase, which can last the first three to five sessions, activities that help children get to know each other predominate. Group members should be introduced to the rules, rituals, and atmosphere of the Theraplay Group. It is during this stage that they learn how you expect them to "be with" each other. They learn how you will "be with" them when you remain unruffled if the group does not play a game as you or they expected, and when you participate in activities with enthusiasm without worrying whether the group will "get it right." They learn the nonverbal meaning of the No Hurts rule when you stop an activity and lotion a hurt child, of Stick Together when you take the hand of a child who is "doing his own thing" and bring him back into the group, and of Have Fun when you initiate activities that are playful and cooperative rather than competitive.

In addition to learning norms, group members also will be getting to know one another and increasing their comfort with eye contact, touch, and physical closeness. For the beginning phase, simple, well-structured, nonthreatening activities are best. In fact, for your first one or two sessions, you might want simply to sing a hello song, do check-ups, food-share, and sing a goodbye song (without a middle activity). This strategy is particularly advisable if you are yourself learning how to lead a Theraplay Group and this is your first group.

MIDDLE PHASE. Once children have become familiar with the group rules and are more comfortable with each other, you can choose activities that require more trust, self-control, and group cooperation than is possible during the beginning phase. Such activities might include passing a hand squeeze or pat on the back around the circle of children, having a child close his eyes and guess where his neighbor tickled him with a feather or cotton ball, and having the group hold the edges of a blanket and roll a ball to the child whose name is called.[1]

During this phase, in contrast to the nurturing quality of the beginning and ending rituals, you can add other Theraplay dimensions to the mix. Exciting games (moving together while balancing a balloon between tummies or foreheads with no hands) and challenging games (one or two people leave the group while the group forms a tangle; they then try to untangle the group without breaking the hand holds) serve to create a rhythm from low to high arousal and back again. Group members will learn not only that they can be excited together, but also that they can settle down together.

Focusing on Relational Issues. During the middle phase you also can choose activities that address an issue that the group or an individual member is dealing with.

General relational issues around which you might create group activities during the middle phase include, but are not limited to, increasing comfort with eye contact and touch, increasing trust, taking turns, developing cooperation, respecting and appreciating individual differences, managing excitement, and facing challenge. Showing nurturing care of others and having fun together are two issues that should form the basis of activities throughout all sessions. You can also decide to use a session or an activity to meet the needs of one child if, for example, he has just suffered an illness, family disruption, loss, or trauma.

The following are some activities that relate to specific relational themes:

- Eye contact can be promoted through activities like cotton-ball-tickle, magical face painting, and beanbag catch.

- Touch and closeness are fostered by games like pass-a-squeeze, "magnets" (children in a wide, loose circle come closer each time a cue is given), and group massage.[2]

- Trust can be developed by having children guide a blindfolded peer around the room, or eat a treat off safe body parts (for example, elbows, wrists, or shoulders).

- Turn taking: At first you may want to do activities simultaneously ("everybody hold hands and jump together" or "be small or tall with your partners"). Slowly, you will want to add activities that require varying degrees of turn taking. You might divide the group into two teams, each imitating the other's claps, jumps, laughs, and so on, so that each child does not have to wait long to respond. You can gradually build up to activities that go around the circle, one by one.

- Cooperation is promoted through games like blanket-ball (everyone holds onto the edge of the blanket and cooperates to make the ball roll to someone across the circle), stack-of-hands, giant "Row, Row, Row Your Boat," cooperative musical chairs (Orlick, 1978), and partner pull-ups.

- Respecting and appreciating individual differences can be heightened by finding shapes or letters in hands, and by discovering whose noses, hands, or ears are warm and whose are cold.

- Managing excitement: Use less structure, more movement, and more props in games (motor-boat, balloon-balance) to allow children to experience higher levels of excitement or arousal followed by a return to calm.

- Facing challenge: Choose games with a hint of competition, mock aggression, or an academic bent, such as cotton-ball fight, follow-the-leader, blindfold-friend-guess (Rubin and Tregay, 1989), and writing a letter, number, or shape on another person's back.

Deciding Whether to Use Adult-Child, Partner, or Whole-Group Activities. You need to decide whether, during any given game or session, the children will be interacting with the group leader, a partner, or the group as a whole. With young children under age five, with new groups, or with children who are developmentally delayed, it is often best to have the children interact primarily with a group leader until they become comfortable and familiar with the type of directness and intimacy that Theraplay interactions can entail. Gradually, you should support and encourage members to interact with one another. Whole-group activities avoid making individual children feel put "on the spot" and are often useful with older, easily embarrassed children. Whole-group activities, however, tend to be more stimulating and can more easily get out of control.

TERMINATION PHASE. During the termination phase, you will need to gear your activities toward helping participants prepare for and antic-ipate the ending of the group. Just as in individual Theraplay, you should announce in advance that the group will be ending in a cer-tain number of sessions and remind them each time of the remaining number of sessions. During this stage, some groups repeat their favorite games as a way of saying goodbye. You may want to plan time to create tangible memoirs for your group for each member to keep. These might include a group picture, special lists that describe the pos-itive characteristics of each member, and a gift bag for each person containing a small bottle of lotion, cotton balls, stickers, or other meaningful symbols of their Group Theraplay experience.

INFORMING AND INCLUDING PARENTS

Because Group Theraplay is often a new experience for those involved, parents need information about it ahead of time. Not only do they need to be informed about what the Theraplay group will be like, but they should be encouraged to visit or participate in your group and to incorporate Theraplay-like activities into their interactions with their children at home. In these ways, parents can play an important role in integrating the atmosphere of your group into the family.

Orienting Parents to the Theraplay Approach

Offer parents an orientation meeting before you have your first group. At that time, you can tell them about the four group rules, what Group Theraplay is like, and what to expect their children to come home talking about. It is helpful to show a videotape of a group similar to yours. Save time for a live demonstration of Group Theraplay and invite the parents to be the participants. Hand squeezes, feather tickles, cotton-ball blowing, circle shoulder massages, and the usual treats and songs are non-threatening activities that parents enjoy. The orientation meeting provides the opportunity for parents to ask questions and express concerns, and for you to convey your belief in the caring touch that you will model with their children.

Giving Parents Practice

If you decide to include parents in your group, it will be helpful to offer them a few practice sessions before they join their first group. Not only do you want them to be comfortable with touch, play, and nurturing, but you want them to get some of their own needs met before you expect them to be attentive and nurturing with their children. Parents will need to learn how to take charge, nurture, stick together, and have fun. You may want to pair parents so they begin to get the experience of being in charge of someone who represents the child.

Including Parents in Group Theraplay

Parents can be included in groups in several ways. They can be issued an open invitation to observe the group and join as participants when they feel comfortable. Each can be the play partner of his own child, interacting one-on-one with his child and helping his child join whole-group activities when it is appropriate. Or they can first observe their children from behind a one-way mirror while an interpreting therapist helps them understand what is going on in the group and prepares them to join in. The following examples illustrate these three ways of including parents in child groups.

THE OPEN-DOOR APPROACH. This approach invites parents to visit the classroom during group time. They can choose to watch or to join in with their children. If a child finds it difficult to have her parent watch rather than join in, you can encourage the parent to join or allow the child to sit with her parent. When parents do join in, you can make them equal members of the group, having them participate in the fun and receive the same care that you are giving their children. Or you may make each parent the partner of his own child, supporting the child's participation in the group. This arrangement will enable you to identify distressed, poorly attached child-parent pairs for whom treatment should be recommended. When a parent does participate, he should understand clearly that he is responsible for his child only. It would not be appropriate for a parent to be given the responsibility of helping to structure another parent's child.

THE PLAY PARTNER APPROACH. Having parents be the partners of their own children can be used with one parent, one child or with one parent and all the children in her family. (In these two models every child in the group has a parent present.) The following are examples of both.

Adopted Children. In order to enhance the attachments between parents and their children, the one-parent, one-child model was used with a group of families who had adopted children as infants and toddlers from Eastern European orphanages (Bostrom, 1995). Organized as a multifamily group, the focus was on increasing attachment-fostering interactions between parent-child pairs. Each parent simultaneously played games with his or her child while the leader acted as coach to facilitate the emotional connection of each dyad. Meeting with the leader for thirty minutes after each group session, parents shared experiences of the previous week and asked questions, and the leader and parents exchanged observations of positive changes in the children.

In sessions, parents formed the containing outer circle of the group. Their children, forming an inner ring, were seated on pillows facing their parents. During initial sessions, the leader called out directions for each activity, and each dyad took a turn playing the game while the others watched. As everyone became more comfortable and capable, all the pairs did the activities simultaneously. The leader then acted as coach to further facilitate the emotional connection between each parent-child pair. Sessions began with parents lotioning, making handprints, and rocking their children. They ended with children cradled in their parents' arms for the "Twinkle Song." Not only did the children develop new language skills, but they also were more connected to their parents through increased eye contact and "touchability." Their parents were more relaxed, were more comfortable with "silliness," and felt more competent.

With this group of adopted children, all activities remained between the dyads so as not to dilute the familial attachment that was being nurtured. If you use this model with other populations, you could bring everyone together for a whole-group play time after the initial parent-child play time. You might even use the same activity that they did as pairs and modify it so that the all group members can do it together. Such a format would allow families to join together, children to pair up, or children to group together while their parents watched and supported only as needed.

Mothers and Their Children in a Shelter for Homeless Families. This group consisted of mothers and their children living in a two-year residential housing facility. Because homeless women often have had painful and traumatic attachment histories and feel undermined as mothers by shelter-living (Rubin, 1996), the goal of this Theraplay group was to strengthen the sense of family and to build opportunities for nurturing the mothers and their children. Both mothers and children were included in the group from the beginning, and the mothers became the focal point for play with their own children. The leader developed the activities and facilitated interaction between mothers and children. For mothers who had more than one child (most of them), the leader played with children awaiting their turn with their mothers or encouraged play between waiting children so that their feeling of deprivation and sibling resentment would be minimal. In addition to emphasizing the family unit, the group format thus allowed a focus on sibling and peer interaction.

Sessions were kept simple and laid-back because the mothers had significant trouble trusting others. They tended to be depressed, angry, or were dominating and oppositional. The opening "Hello Song" was sung not to an individual child but to the whole family. For example, while Tessa and her children hid under a blanket, everyone would sing, "Where is Tessa's family?" When it was time to respond, Tessa and her children would pop out, singing, "Here we are!" Each mother was given her own small bottle of lotion to use for interactive lotioning with her children. At the end of each session, the mothers got a bag of bite-sized treats to share with their children. Mid-session activities involved inexpensive, homemade "toys" (for example, toilet paper tubes for making eye contact, and pompon "warm fuzzies" for gentle touches) that the children could keep for play with family or friends. Mothers made hand- or footprints of themselves and their children on construction paper to mount on their refrigerators. At Christmas time, mothers decorated their children with ribbon, tinsel, stickers, and coffee filter "hats" and each family posed for Polaroid pictures that they took as mementos to their small apartments within the shelter housing facility. Involving the mothers in this way helped them learn that playing with their children was not just acceptable but enjoyable. The group format also allowed the children to play with each other in games like boat-ride in a plastic laundry basket and ring-around-the-rosie. As the children played, the mothers could relax. Mothers were grateful for some respite while simultaneously having the opportunity to see their children interacting positively with peers.

THE OBSERVATIONAL APPROACH. Being able to observe their children in a Theraplay group gives parents the opportunity to learn more about how their children interact as well as about how the group works before joining in. A school-based parent-child assessment and treatment model was developed for teen mothers and their children (Talen and Warfield, 1997). The parent-child component was part of a comprehensive "family health and wellness" program that provided primary health and mental health care to preschool children both within their community and among the children and their caregivers.

The teenaged parents used their study hall breaks for fifteen- to twenty-minute observations of their children, who were participating in a "healthy self-esteem group" within the Head Start program located in their parents' high school. To prepare for these visits, the children had had a few weeks of Group Theraplay before parents began visiting. Across three different observation times, the interpreting therapist pointed out each child's positive characteristics, normalized age-appropriate behaviors, and modeled positive interactions. The parents readily joined in the group with their children for the final session. The group leaders describe a joyful, caring atmosphere with children sitting comfortably in the laps of their parents. One mother spontaneously created a rap song to end the session. This, and the laughter and smiles that accompanied the games, attest to the success of this model.

USING GROUP THERAPLAY INFORMALLY

Finally, we describe ways of including Group Theraplay ideas in settings where it is not possible to organize a regular group.

Recently, a Group Theraplay training class was provided for teachers in a school district serving kindergarten through eighth-grade children. The class consisted of elementary and junior high school teachers, including physical education teachers, an art teacher, a speech/language pathologist, and a liaison to the school from a residential treatment center for abused children. Not all participants were in a setting where they could assemble and lead a Theraplay group. Those who could not created "Theraplay Moments" that incorporated the Theraplay atmosphere into the school day. One physical education teacher planned a cooperative game with the goal of the children working together, verbalizing feelings, and demonstrating concern for one another—all of which was a focus very different from her typical activities geared to competition and physical mastery. The art teacher made an outline of each child's head. The outlines were passed around the class so that each child could add a special "likable" feature to the picture. At the end, each child had a picture that contained contributions from the entire class.

One teacher (Wiedow, 1997), who co-taught two classes of first and second graders with a colleague, found an innovative way of providing a small Group Theraplay experience. Because of the numbers of children involved and scarcity of time for a formal group, she offered the children the opportunity to be in a "Best Friends Group" instead of going to recess. Up to five children could choose to stay in for Group, and the teacher was surprised always to have volunteers. Thus, all the children in her class were able to have a Group Theraplay experience.

Most noteworthy, however, was how this teacher and her colleague integrated checkups into the regular education setting. After lunch, when the children were often stirred up, they checked each child before beginning the afternoon lessons. As the children entered the room and sat at their desks, the two teachers, with bottles of lotion in hand, went from child to child, asking how they were feeling and if they had any hurts. By lotioning hurts and addressing any conflicts between children, the teachers helped the class settle down. Checkups provided a perfect transitional activity during which they took the time to attend to each child before expecting the children to attend to their school agenda.

Such an integration of "Theraplayful" interactions occurs frequently in special education classrooms. This application in a regular education classroom shows that such experiences do not have to be limited to the Theraplay group or to the Theraplay facilitator. This example communicates an important message. Kids—who are emotionally needier than they have ever been—not only welcome but *need* nurturing attention in order to achieve the state of mind conducive to learning. It would serve society well for schools and other goal-oriented institutions to find more ways to make time for such emotionally nourishing moments for those in their care.

Notes

1. For more ideas on group activities, and explanations of activities mentioned here, refer to the following books: *Play with Them* (Rubin and Tregay, 1989), *Messy Activities and More* (Morin, 1993), the two *Cooperative Sports and Games* books (Orlick, 1978, 1982), and *Baby Games* (Martin, 1998).
2. Participants stand in a circle, turned toward the right. All place their hands on the shoulders of the person in front of them and simultaneously copy the leader who begins the group massage. On cue, the group turns to the left and participants massage the person now in front of them.

Appendix A: Procedures for Obtaining Certification as a Theraplay Therapist

Candidates must be qualified, registered professionals in a field that prepares them to work with children and families (thus professionally accountable for the well-being of the client) or have on-site supervisors who are qualified in their respective fields (thus able to take ultimate responsibility for each case). This requirement generally means that candidates have at least a bachelor of arts or a master's degree and have completed any further training necessary to qualify in their field of specialization. Upon successful completion of the requirements, a candidate can describe himself as a Certified Theraplay Therapist. Candidates who have experience working with children and families but have not yet completed their professional training (for example, those with diplomas in early childhood education or in child and youth work) may be admitted into Theraplay training and, upon completion of the requirements for certification, will be certified as Associate Theraplay Therapists. Associate Theraplay Therapists must arrange to have ongoing Theraplay supervision once a month with their certification supervisor. When professional requirements are completed, the Associate's status will be changed to Certified Theraplay Therapist.

STEP I: COURSES

A. Satisfactory completion of the introductory course in Theraplay
B. Satisfactory completion of the intermediate course in Theraplay

It is recommended that candidates begin their practicum as soon as possible after completing the introductory course and that they have

---

at least three to six months experience before taking the intermediate course, so that it can build on and refine their developing skills.

STEP II: APPLICATION FOR PRACTICUM

A. Submit the following written materials:
- • Future autobiography
- • Personal history
- • Self-description
- • Description of relevant experience

B. Demonstration:
- • Theraplay with one withdrawn child
- • Theraplay with one overactive, aggressive child

The demonstration requirements can be met by presenting video-tapes of a full session with each type of child.

STEP III: PRACTICUM

A. Required number of service hours and cases:

A minimum of 200 half-hour Theraplay sessions with at least ten cases. The minimum time for completing the practicum is one year. (*Note:* cases should be selected so that they represent as broad a range of client problems as possible; that is, some should be overactive/aggressive, some withdrawn, and so on.)

B. Required number of sessions to be supervised

Each candidate must receive supervision on fifty-eight sessions. This includes:

- • Fifty-two Theraplay sessions
- • Four complete Marschak Interaction Method (MIM) sessions with full written reports
- • Two full sessions to serve as mid-term and final exams

The fifty-two supervisory sessions must be spread out over all ten cases so that each case has at least five supervisory sessions.

C. Supervision options

    1. Group supervision.

When a group of at least three but no more than four candidates is organized, fifty-six two-hour supervisory sessions will be conducted. Candidates present videotapes of ongoing sessions at each meeting. Supervision of each individual's fifty-eight sessions is required. This option has the advantage of sharing information and learning from other candidates.

    2. Individual supervision.

The candidate brings videotapes of Theraplay sessions to the supervisor, or the supervisor visits the candidate on-site and observes him or her doing Theraplay there. This option has the advantage of providing individual attention from the supervisor, but it is more costly.

    Sometimes it is possible for a candidate to participate in a case with a supervisor. When the supervisor is observing each session, as in the case of a candidate working with the child and the supervisor working with the parents, the planning and review of each session is part of the supervision. This option provides intensive training and ongoing feedback, and is to the advantage of the candidate, but it may not always be available.

    3. Long-distance supervision.

Supervision by videotape is available for candidates who work at a distance from a training facility. Candidates submit videotaped segments of their sessions, which are returned with audiotaped or written comments. Following the first submission of tapes, a telephone conference is held to allow personal feedback. In order to reduce the cost of supervision to candidates, supervisors look at ten-minute segments of each session rather than full sessions.

    Candidates have the option of (a) editing tapes and submitting a ten-minute segment, (b) identifying a particular segment of a tape, which they want the supervisor to look at, or (c) having the supervisor choose a segment at random. It greatly facilitates identification of the session and the segment being supervised if the date and time can be indicated on the video screen. Although every effort will be made to review tapes immediately upon receipt, candidates should not expect to receive comments before they see the child for the next session. If immediate feedback is needed, telephone consultation is available.

D. Equipment

The Theraplay Institute owns equipment for recording and playing back of audiotape cassettes (standard size), half-inch VHS video-tape cassettes, and 8 mm videotape cassettes.

E. Material to be submitted
   1. Beginning cases. The following material should be submitted at the beginning of each new case:
       • Background or intake information on the child and family. Delete family name in order to give some measure of confidentiality.
       • A tape of an MIM session with one or both parents, along with a brief summary of the interaction and recommendations for treatment. Four of these MIM's should be accompanied by finished written reports (for supervision of report writing) and will be counted toward the total of fifty-eight sessions.
       • A copy of a form signed by the parent(s) of the child giving permission to videotape and permission to share the tapes and information about the family with the candidate's supervisor.
   2. Ongoing sessions. Written reports about each supervised session should be made, including
       • Plan of activities and goals for the session
       • Comments on the child's response to the session
       • Candidate's assessment of the session
       • Report on work with parent(s)
       • Plan for next session

- Transference and countertransference issues
- Questions for the supervisor

Since long-distance candidates will be sending random samples of their work, issues may arise that are not on the submitted video-tapes. Candidates should bring these issues to the supervisor's attention by describing them in written notes accompanying the videotape. Enclose a blank audiotape with each videotape, if you want audiotaped feedback.

3. Accounting for supervision hours. Each candidate should keep a record of supervision received, including:
   - Name of child
   - Date of session
   - Date mailed or date supervised
   - Payment made
   - Date of receipt of supervisory comments

The Theraplay Institute will keep a similar record. Forms are available for the record keeping.

In order to document the completion of the required 200 hours of Theraplay sessions, a list of first names of clients seen and dates of sessions should be submitted at the time of the mid-term and final exams.

4. Payment.

Payment for group or individual supervision should be made at the time of each supervision session. For long-distance supervision, each videotape should be accompanied by a check covering the number of segments enclosed. Be sure to indicate clearly the number of segments for which you expect to receive credit.

STEP IV: EVALUATION

At the middle and at the end of the practicum, candidates submit full half-hour sessions for evaluation. They should also submit a list of the families seen, the number of supervised sessions for each family, and the total number of sessions conducted up to this point. A Theraplay trainer/supervisor who has not been the candidate's regular supervisor does the evaluation. Candidates whose supervisor is not at the Theraplay Institute in Chicago must submit mid-term and final sessions to the Theraplay Institute in Chicago for evaluation. Evaluators rate the candidate's performance as pass, fail, or probationary pass. A probationary pass would be accompanied by a request for further work on the part of the candidate.

STEP V: CERTIFICATION

Certification entitles the therapists to identify themselves as Certified Theraplay Therapists and to identify the treatment provided as Theraplay®. (*Note:* the Certified Theraplay Therapist may wish ongoing supervision if he or she is working in isolation. Post-graduate supervisory groups are available through Theraplay training facilities.)

It is necessary to complete certification and practice as a Theraplay therapist for two years before pursuing Theraplay Trainer/Supervisor status.

PRACTICUM FEES

Information about fees for training and supervision is available from the Theraplay Institute, 1137 Central Avenue, Wilmette, IL 60091. Phone (847) 256–7334

Appendix B: Marshak Interaction Method–Recommended Basic Lists of Tasks

When two activities are listed, for example, lotioning and combing, use one for each parent.

One to Three Years
1. Adult and child each take one squeaky animal. Make the two animals play together.
2. Adult teaches child something child doesn't know.
3. Play patty-cake with the child.
4. Hold child's hands still for the count of twenty.
5. Rub lotion on child.
6. Adult leaves room for one minute without child.
7. Adult tells child about when child was a baby, beginning, "When you were a little baby . . ."
8. Ring bell where child cannot see it.
9. Adult builds a simple structure with blocks and encourages child to copy it.
10. Adult and child feed each other (raisins, candy, crackers, etc.).

Three Years and Older
1. Adult and child each take one squeaky animal. Make the two animals play together.
2. Adult teaches child something child doesn't know.
3. Adult and child each take one bottle. Apply lotion to each other. Adult combs child's hair and asks child to comb adult's hair.

Reproduced with permission of the Theraplay Institute, 1137 Central Ave., Wilmette, IL 60091.

4. Adult tells child about when child was a baby, beginning, "When you were a little baby. . . ." For an adopted child: Adult tells child about when child first came to live with her/him.

5. Adult leaves the room for one minute without child.

6. Play a game that is familiar to both of you.

7. Adult and child each take paper and pencil. Adult draws a quick picture, encourages child to copy.
   Adult takes one set of five (eight) blocks. Hands other set to child. Adult builds a structure with own blocks. Then says to child, "Build one just like mine with your blocks."

8. Adult and child put hats on each other.

9. Adult and child feed each other (raisins, candy, crackers, etc.).

Adolescent

1. Adult and child each take one squeaky animal. Make the two animals play together.

2. Adult teaches child something child doesn't know.

3. Adult and child look at each other's hands and read each other's fortune.

4. Adult and child each take one bottle. Apply lotion to each other. Adult combs child's hair and asks child to comb adult's hair.

5. Play a game that is familiar to both of you.

6. Adult leaves the room for one minute without child.

7. Adult and child engage in three rounds of thumb wrestling.

8. Adult asks child to describe a day in child's life ten years from now.

9. Adult and child put hats on each other.

10. Adult and child feed each other (raisins, candy, crackers, etc.).

Appendix C: Theraplay Activities by Dimension

Activities are listed alphabetically under each dimension. A few activities at the end of each list are especially suitable for use when parents enter the session or when more than one adult is present. Depending on how an activity is carried out, it may fit more than one dimension. Other games enjoyed by young children also can be adapted and used in sessions. To encourage give and take and extend the child's attention span, you can take turns with the child and vary the activity whenever possible. We have not attempted to indicate the age level for activities, since many activities can be used across a wide range of ages. Activities for very young children must be within their physical ability and must make sense to them. Simple activities can be adapted to make them more challenging or more interesting to older children.

STRUCTURE

Purpose of Activity

The idea is to relieve the child of the burden of maintaining control of interactions. The adult sets limits, defines body boundaries, keeps the child safe, and helps to complete sequences of activities.

BEAN BAG GAME. Place beanbag or soft toy on your own head, give a signal and drop the beanbag into child's hands by tilting your head toward the child. Take turns.

COTTON BALL HOCKEY. Lie on the floor on your stomachs (or sit with a pillow between you). Blow cotton balls back and forth, trying to get the cotton ball past your partner's defense. You can increase the complexity by saying how many blows can be used to get the ball across the pillow, or by both trying to blow at the same time to keep the ball in the middle.

DRAWING AROUND HANDS, FEET, OR BODIES. Make a picture of the child's hand or foot by drawing it on a piece of paper. Full-body drawings require the child to lie still for some time and are therefore more challenging. Be sure to maintain verbal contact with the child as you draw, for example, "I'm coming to your ankle, I'm coming to the tickle spot under your arm."

EYE SIGNALS. Hold hands and stand facing each other. Use eye signals to indicate direction and number of steps to take; for example, when you wink your left eye two times, both you and the child take two side steps to your left. For older children, you can add signals for forward and backward movement as well (head back for backward, head forward for forward). You can hold a balloon or a pillow between you by leaning close to each other as you move.

MEASURING. Measure the child's height, length of arms, legs, feet, hands, and so forth. Keep a record for later comparisons. Measure surprising things, such as the child's smile, the length of his ears, how high he can jump, and so forth. You can use fruit tape for measuring, then tear off the length and feed it to the child. "This is just the size of your smile." You thus combine structure with nurture.

PATTY-CAKE. Hold child's hands and lead her through "patty-cake." "Patty cake, patty cake, Baker's man/Bake me a cake as fast as you can/Roll it and pat it and mark it with a [child's initial]/ And toss it in the oven for [child's name] and me!" You can use feet as well.

PEANUT BUTTER AND JELLY. Say "peanut butter" and have child say "jelly" in just the same way. Repeat five to ten times, varying loudness and intonation.

POP THE BUBBLE. Blow a bubble and catch it on the wand. Have child pop the bubble with a particular body part, for example, finger, toe, elbow, shoulder, or ear. This is a structured way of playing with bubbles. Bubbles readily capture the interest of young children and can be used as an engaging activity either in this structured form or in a manner that invites more spontaneity (for example, by having the child pop all the bubbles as quickly as she can).

RED LIGHT, GREEN LIGHT. Ask child to do something, for example, run, jump, move arms. Green light means go, red light means stop. For a more challenging version, stand across the room facing away from the other participants. When you say "green light," the child and parents or co-therapist creep toward you as quietly as they can. When you say "red light," turn quickly to see whether anyone is still moving. Anyone caught moving must return to the beginning. The goal is to creep up and touch the person whose back is turned.

STACK OF HANDS. Put your hand palm down in front of child, guide child to put his hand on top. Alternate hands to make a stack. Take turns moving the hand on the bottom to the top. You can also move top to bottom. This can be made more complicated by going fast or in slow motion. Lotioning hands first makes for a slippery stack and adds an element of nurture.

TOILET-PAPER-BUST-OUT. Wrap child's legs, arms, or whole body with toilet paper or crepe-paper streamers. To let a hesitant child know what is in store, have her hold her arms together in front of her body and wrap them first. On a signal, have child break out of wrapping.

THREE-LEGGED WALK. Stand beside the child. Tie your two adjacent legs together with a scarf or ribbon. With arms around each other's waist, walk across the room. You should be responsible for coordinating the movement. For example, you can say "inside, outside" to indicate which foot to use. You can add obstacles (pillows, chairs) to make this more challenging.

WEIGHING. Weigh the child on a simple bathroom scale. Stand in front of child. Have the child make himself heavier by pulling up on your hands or lighter by pushing down on your hands. Depending on the size of the child, you may need to stoop down to make this work.

When Parents Enter, or with Two Adults

FOLLOW THE LEADER TRAIN. All participants stand and form a line holding onto the waist of person in front of them. The first person moves in a particular way and all others copy. The leader goes to the back of the line and the new leader demonstrates a new way to move around the room. This can be done sitting in a circle and moving only arms, head, and shoulders.

FUNNY WAYS TO CROSS THE ROOM. One adult and child stand at one end of mat (or play space), another adult stands at other end of the mat. The second adult directs the child to come toward her in a certain way; for example, hopping, tiptoeing, crawling, or walking backward. Child is greeted on arrival, then called back to first adult in a specified way. Adult and child can come across the mat together if the child cannot manage alone. With older children, each participant can come up with a funny way to cross the room that everyone must try; for example, crab walk, elephant walk, or scooting.

HIDE SOMETHING ON CHILD AND FIND IT. One adult hides and the other finds something on the child. The hidden object can be a note directing the finder to do something with the child ("Pop Sara's cheeks"; or a cotton ball that can be used to give a soft touch or food that can be fed to the child).

HOKEY POKEY. Everyone stands in a circle and sings: "You put your right foot in/You put your right foot out/You put your right foot in/And you shake it all about/You do the Hokey Pokey/And you turn yourself around/That's what it's all about/Hokey Pokey!" Arms, heads, whole bodies can be put in to the middle of the circle and shaken. When you do the Hokey Pokey, you dance in whatever way you like, arms in air, with playful, energetic gestures.

MOTOR-BOAT. Holding hands, everyone walks around in a circle, chanting "Motor boat, motor boat, go so slow/Motor boat, motor boat, step on the gas/Motor boat, motor boat, go so fast!" Gradually increase the speed until it is very fast. Suddenly stop and start over with the slow tempo. This can also be done with the child and therapist alone.

"MOTHER, MAY I?" Parent gives instructions to the child to do something, for example, "Take three giant steps toward me." Child must say "Mother, may I?" before responding to the command. If the child forgets, she must return to the starting line. The goal is to have the child come to her parent and get a hug on arrival.

RING-AROUND-THE-ROSY. Hold hands and walk around in a circle chanting, "Ring around a rosy/A pocket full of posies/Ashes, ashes, we all fall down." All fall down at the end.

ZOOM-ERK. Sitting in a circle, the word "zoom" is passed around the circle quickly. When one person stops the action by saying "erk," the "zoom" reverses and is sent back the way it came.

ENGAGEMENT

Purpose of Activity

The idea is to establish and maintain a connection with the child, to focus on the child in an intense way, and to surprise and entice the child into enjoying new experiences.

BEEP AND HONK. Press child's nose and say "beep!" then press chin and say "honk!" Guide child to touch your nose and chin. Make appropriate beeps and honks as you are touched. Child may be able to supply noises also.

COTTON BALL HIDE. Hide cotton ball (candy, a touch of lotion, or powder) somewhere on the child. An older child can hide the cotton ball on himself. If a parent or another adult is available, she can find the cotton ball; if not, you can find it.

BLOWING OVER. Sit facing the child and holding hands (or cradle the child in your lap), have child "blow you over." Fall back as the child blows. Once the child understands the game, you can blow her over.

CHECKUPS. Check body parts, such as nose, chin, ears, cheeks, fingers, toes, knees to see whether they are warm/cold, hard/soft, wiggly/quiet, and so on. Count freckles, toes, fingers, and knuckles.

FOIL PRINTS. Using aluminum foil, shape a piece of foil around the child's elbow, hand, foot, face, ear, and so forth. It helps to place a pillow under the foil and have the child press her hand or foot into the soft surface to get impressions of the fingers and toes. A parent may be called in to guess which print goes with which body part. This is also structuring, since it defines body shapes and boundaries.

HAND-CLAPPING GAMES. Older children enjoy these games very much. They can be simple (patty-cake) or complex (elaborate rhythmic clapping patterns) and can have a variety of chants; for example, "Miss Mary Mack" or "The Sailor Went to Sea."

KNOCK ON THE DOOR. This is a simple baby activity. "Knock on the door" (tap on the child's forehead) "Peep in" (peek at child's eyes), "Lift up the latch," (gently push the child's nose up), and "Walk in!" (pretend to walk fingers into child's open mouth or pop a piece of food in).

MIRRORING. Face the child, move your arms, face, or other body parts and ask child to move in the same way. For a very active child you can use slow motion or vary the tempo. Take turns being the leader.

PIGGY-BACK/HORSEY-BACK RIDE. Help the child get onto your back. Jog around the room with the child on your back. Child can give signals, "Whoa!" and Giddy-up!"

PEEK-A-BOO. Hold child's hands (or feet) up together in front of your face. Peek around or separate the hands (or feet) to "find" the child.

POPCORN TOES. As you take the child's shoes off, ask whether she has popcorn, peanuts, grapes, and so forth, inside her shoe. Then pull off the shoe and discover wonderful toes.

POP CHEEKS. Inflate your cheeks with air and help the child pop them with his hands or feet. The child inflates his cheeks and you pop them in turn.

STICKY NOSE. Put a colorful sticker on your own nose. Ask child to take it off. Or stick a cotton ball on your nose with lotion. Have child blow it off.

PUSH-ME-OVER, LAND-ON-MY KNEES. Kneel in front of standing child (so that child comes to your eye level) or sit in front of sitting child. Hold child's hands. On a signal, have child push you. As you fall back, pull child onto your knees and bounce child up and down.

PUSH-ME-OVER, PULL-ME-UP. Sit on the floor in front of the child. Place child's palms against yours, or put child's feet against your shoulders. On a signal, have child push you over. Fall back in an exaggerated way. Stretch out your hands so that the child can pull you back up.

ROW, ROW, ROW YOUR BOAT. Sing the familiar song, adding the child's name at the end ("Erin's such a dream"). Small children can be held in your lap. Older children can sit facing you. If another adult is available, seat the child between you as though in a boat as you row back and forth.

SPECIAL HANDSHAKE. Make up a special handshake together, taking turns adding new gestures; for example, high five, clasp hands, wiggle fingers, and so on. This can be cumulative over several sessions and can be your beginning or ending ritual.

THIS IS THE WAY THE BABY RIDES. Adult holds child on knees and bounces the child, varying the pace as she moves from baby, to lady, to gentleman, to farmer.

THIS LITTLE PIG. Wiggle each toe as you chant, "This little pig went to market/This little pig stayed home/This little pig had roast beef/This little pig had none/This little pig cried 'Wee, wee, wee,' all the way home." Change details to fit the particular child. As you say "all the way home," walk your fingers up the child's arm or leg in a playful way.

When Parents Enter, or with Two Adults

HIDE AND SEEK. Hide with the child under a blanket or under pillows and ask parents or other adult to find you both. Parents should be coached to make appreciative comments about their child as they look for him and to find him quickly if he is very young and impatient. A big hug is in order once the child is found.

PROGRESSIVE PASS AROUND. Sitting in a circle, one person passes a gentle touch to the next person (such as a nose beep, or pat on the back). The second person passes that touch to the third person plus one of her own. Each person adds a new touch. Everyone helps each other recall the sequence of touches.

FREE-THROW. Divide into two teams. Using cotton balls, marshmallows, or newspaper balls, each team throws the balls at the other, trying to get rid of all balls on their side. Players may set up a "shield" with pillows and throw from behind the shield.

NURTURE

Purpose of Activity

The idea is to reinforce the message that the child is worthy of care and that adults will provide care without the child having to ask.

CARING FOR HURTS. Check hands, feet, face, and so forth, for scratches, bruises, hurts, or "boo-boos." Put lotion on or around the hurt, touch with cotton ball, or blow a kiss. Check for healing in the next session.

COTTON BALL TOUCH. Have child close eyes. Touch child gently with cotton ball. Have child open eyes and indicate where she was touched.

DECORATE CHILD. Make rings, necklaces, bracelets with play-doh, crazy foam, crepe-paper streamers, or aluminum foil.

DOUGHNUT/PRETZEL CHALLENGE. Put a doughnut or pretzel on your finger. See how many bites the child can take before breaking the circle.

FACE PAINTING. Paint flowers and hearts on cheeks, or make the child up like a princess. Mustaches and beards are interesting for boys and their fathers. A variation on this is to use a soft dry brush and pretend to paint the child's face, describing her wonderful cheeks, her lovely eyebrows, and so forth as you gently brush each part.

FEEDING. Have a small snack and drink available for all sessions. Take the child on your lap or face her as she sits propped on pillows. Feed the child, listening for crunches, noticing whether the child likes the snack and when the child is ready for more. Encourage eye contact.

LOTION OR POWDER PRINTS. Apply lotion or powder to the child's hand or foot and make a print on paper, the floor mat, a pillow, your dark clothing, or a mirror. If you make a lotion print on dark construction paper, you can shake powder on it and then blow or shake it off to enhance the picture (take care to keep the powder away from the child's face).

LOTIONING/POWDERING. Lotion or powder child's arms/hands, legs/feet. You can sing a personalized song as you do this, "Oh lotion, oh lotion on Sarah's feet/It feels so good, it feels so sweet. Oh lotion, oh lotion on Sarah's hands/It feels so good, it feels so grand."

LULLABY. Cradle the child in your arms in such a way that eye contact can be maintained. Sing your favorite lullaby or any quiet, soothing song. Add details about the particular child to the traditional words.

MANICURE. Soak the child's feet or hands in warm water. Using lotion, massage the feet or hands. Paint the child's toes or fingernails using a variety of colors or letting the child choose the color he wants. Make sure that the child is comfortable having the nail polish remain when he leaves the room. If not, take it off.

PAINT PRINTS. Rub paint on child's hand or foot, using one color or creating a pattern with several colors. Press the painted hand or foot onto paper to make a print. After prints are made with paint, gently wash, dry, and powder the hand or foot.

SLIPPERY, SLIPPERY, SLIP. This is a lotioning activity with an added element of surprise (as well as giving an opportunity to apply firm pressure to the child's body). First rub lotion on the child's arm or leg. Then, holding firmly, say "slippery, slippery, slip" and pull toward you, falling backward with an exaggerated motion as the slippery arm or leg escapes.

SOFT AND FLOPPY. Have the child lie on the floor and help him get "all soft and floppy." Gently jiggle each arm and leg and let it flop to the floor. If the child has difficulty getting floppy, have him get "stiff like a board" and then let go. Once the child is relaxed, ask him to wiggle just one part of his body: his tummy, his tongue, his big toe, and so forth.

TWINKLE SONG. Adapt the words of "Twinkle, twinkle, little star," to the special characteristics of the child. "What a special boy you are/Dark brown hair, and soft, soft cheeks/ Bright brown eyes from which you peek/Twinkle, twinkle little star/What a special boy you are." Hold the child in your arms and touch the parts you refer to as you sing.

When Parents Enter, or with Two Adults

BLANKET SWING. Spread a blanket on the floor and have the child lie down in the middle. The adults gather up the corners and give a gentle swing while singing a song. At the end bring him down for a "soft landing." Position parents so that they can see the child's face. If the child is fearful of being lifted off the floor, rock him gently back and forth while he remains in contact with the floor.

FANNING. After a vigorous activity, one adult or both parents rest with child in their arms; one adult fans everyone with a large pillow, fan, or newspaper. Watch how everyone's hair blows.

LOTION OR POWDER PASS. Pass a dab of lotion or a powder touch from person to person in a circle.

SHOE AND SOCK RACE. Adults race to put kisses on feet and then put child's shoes back on before the kiss flies away. Ask parents to see whether the kisses are still there and add new ones when the child goes to bed at night.

SPECIAL KISSES. *Butterfly kiss:* Have parent place her cheek against the child's cheek and flutter her eyelashes so that the child feels the brush of her eyelashes. *Elephant kiss:* You or a parent hold both fists in front of your mouth (like a pretend trumpet); keep one fist by your mouth as you make a kissing noise. Move your outer fist toward the child's cheek, completing the kissing noise with a flourish as you touch the child's cheek.

CHALLENGE

Purpose of Activity

The idea is to help the child feel more competent and confident by encouraging the child to take a slight risk and to accomplish an activity with adult help.

BALANCING ACTIVITIES. Child lies on back on the floor with feet up in the air. Place one pillow on child's feet and help child balance it. Add additional pillows one at a time as long as the child is successful. Balance books, pillows, or hats on the child's head and have her walk across room.

BALANCE ON PILLOWS, JUMP OFF. Help child balance on pillows, starting with one and increasing as long as the child can easily manage. Once the child is balanced, tell him to "jump into my arms (or down to the floor) when I give the signal."

BALLOON BETWEEN TWO BODIES.   Hold a balloon between you and the child (such as between foreheads, shoulders, elbows) and move across the mat without dropping or popping the balloon. See whether you can do this without using hands.

BALLOON TENNIS. Keep balloon in air by using specific body parts: heads, hands, no hands, shoulders, and so forth. If you choose feet, everyone lies on the floor and keeps the balloon in the air by kicking it gently.

BUBBLE TENNIS. Blow bubbles high in the air between you and the child. Choose a bubble and blow it to the child. The child blows it back. Continue until balloon pops.

COOPERATIVE COTTON BALL RACE. You and the child get on hands and knees at one end of room. Take turns blowing a cotton ball (or a ping-pong ball) to the other side of the room. You can try to better your time on repeated trials. A competitive version would be for each to have his own cotton ball and see who can get it across the room first.

COTTON BALL OR FEATHER GUESS. Have the child close her eyes and tell where you have touched her and whether you did it with a cotton ball or a feather. This adds challenge to a nurturing activity.

CRAWLING RACE. You and the child crawl on your knees as fast as you can around a stack of pillows. Try to catch the other's feet. Switch direction.

FEATHER BLOW. You and the child each hold a small pillow in front of you. Blow a feather from your pillow toward the child's pillow. Child must catch it on her pillow and blow it back.

NEWSPAPER PUNCH, BASKET TOSS. Stretch a single sheet of newspaper tautly in front of child. Have child punch through the sheet when given a signal. You must hold the newspaper so firmly that it makes a satisfying pop when the child punches it. To extend the activity, you can add a second or third sheet of paper, have child use the other hand, and vary the signals. For the basket toss, crush the torn newspaper into balls. Have child toss a ball into the basket you make with your arms.

PARTNER PULL-UP. Sit on the floor holding hands and facing each other with toes together. On a signal, pull each other up to a standing position.

PICK UP SOMETHING WITH TOES. Have child pick up a cotton ball with his toes (shoes and socks off). You can make this more challenging by having the child hop around the room with the cotton ball between his toes.

PILLOW PUSH. Place a large pillow between you and the child. Have child push against pillow to try to push you over.

SEED-SPITTING CONTEST. Feed the child chunks of watermelon or orange or tangerine with seeds. You should eat some too. Both save your seeds. Have the child spit her seed as far as she can. Try to spit your seed as close to it as possible.

STRAIGHT FACE CHALLENGE. Child has to keep a straight face while you try to make him laugh either by gently touching him (avoid sensitive spots or prolonged tickling) or by making funny faces.

THUMB, ARM, OR LEG WRESTLING. Adult guides activity, giving starting signals and insuring safety.

WHEELBARROW. Have child put her hands on floor. Stand behind her and clasp her firmly by the ankles or just above the knees. Child "walks" on her hands. This is hard work for the child, so you must stop as soon as it becomes too tiring.

MUSICAL CHAIRS. Have each participant sit on a pillow (or a chair) in a circle. As the music plays (or you sing a song) everyone stands up and walks around the circle. When the music stops, everyone sits on a pillow. Remove one pillow each time you stop. Participants must sit on each other's laps as the number of places diminishes.

When Parents Enter, or with Two Adults

TANGLE. Standing in a circle, all cross their arms in front of themselves and take the hands of two others in the circle, deliberately creating a tangle of hands. Participants then untangle without breaking the handholds. It is OK to slide hands around in the grip or to face different ways when untangled. It adds to the fun to put lotion on everyone's hands first.

TUG-OF-WAR. Divide into teams, for example, child and parents versus therapists. With each team holding onto the ends of a scarf, a blanket, or a soft rope, pull the other team to your side. Make sure that the child has a good grip and that there is nothing to bump into if one team falls.

TUNNELS. Child crawls through a tunnel made of pillows or of kneeling adults to meet you or his parent at the end.

WIGGLE IN AND OUT. Child wiggles out of one adult's encircling arms and into the other's arms. This is best with small children and is useful when the child is already wiggling and wanting to get out of your arms.

References

Ainsworth, M. "Object Relations, Dependency and Attachment: A Theoretical Review of the Infant-Mother Relationship." *Child Development,* 1969, *40,* 969–1,025.

American Psychiatric Association. *Diagnostic and Statistical Manual of Mental Disorders* (4th ed.). Washington, D.C.: American Psychiatric Association, 1994.

Ames, E. *The Development of Romanian Orphanage Children Adopted to Canada: Final Report.* Canada: National Welfare Grants Program Human Resources Development Canada, 1997.

Ayers, A. J. *Sensory Integration and the Child.* Los Angeles, Calif.: Western Psychological Services, 1979.

Barnard, K. E., and Brazelton, T. B. *Touch: The Foundation of Experience.* Madison, Conn.: International Universities Press, 1990.

Behen, M., and Chugani, H. T. "Update on Research on the Functional Neuroimaging and Neuropsychological Correlates of Early Severe Deprivation." *The POST. The Parent Network for the Post-Institutionalized Child,* May/June, 1997, 1–2.

Belsky, J., and Nezworski, T. *Clinical Implications of Attachment.* Hillside, N.J.: Erlbaum, 1988.

Bennett, S. "Infant-Caretaker Interactions." *Journal of the American Academy of Child Psychiatry,* 1971, *10*(2), 321–335.

Booth, P. B., and Koller, T. J. "Training Parents of Failure-to-Attach Children." In J. M. Briesmeister and C. E. Schaefer (eds.), *Handbook of Parent Training: Training Parents as Co-Therapists for Children's Behavior Problems* (2nd ed.). New York: Wiley, 1998.

Bostrom, J. "Fostering Attachment in Post-Institutionalized Adopted Children Using Group Theraplay." *The Theraplay Institute Newsletter,* Fall 1995, 7–8.

Bowlby, J. *Maternal Care and Mental Health.* New York: Columbia University Press, 1951.

Bowlby, J. *Attachment and Loss.* Vol. 1: *Attachment.* New York: Basic Books, 1969.

Bowlby, J. *Attachment and Loss.* Vol. 2: *Separation Anxiety and Anger.* London: Hogarth Press, 1973.

Brazelton, T. B. "Touch as a Touchstone: Summary of the Round Table." In K. E. Barnard and T. B. Brazelton (eds.), *Touch: The Foundation of Experience.* Madison: International Universities Press, 1990.

Brody, V. A. "Developmental Play: A Relationship-Focused Program for Children." *Journal of Child Welfare,* 1978, *57*(9), 591–599.

Brody, V. A. *The Dialogue of Touch: Developmental Play Therapy.* Treasure Island, Fla.: Developmental Play Training Associates, 1993.

Brodzinsky, D. M., Schecter, M. D., and Henig, R. M. *Being Adopted: The Lifelong Search for Self.* New York: Anchor Books, 1992.

Bruner, J. "Vygotsky's Zone of Proximal Development: The Hidden Agenda." In B. Rogoff and J. Wertsch (eds.), *Children's Learning and the Zone of Proximal Development.* San Francisco, Calif.: Jossey-Bass, 1984.

Campbell, R. *How to Really Love Your Child.* Wheaton, Ill.: Victor Books, 1978.

Cermak, S. "The Relationship Between Attention Deficit Disorder and Sensory Integration Disorders." Part I: "Theory." Part II: "Treatment." *Sensory Integration Special Interest Section Newsletter,* 1988, *11*(2), 1–4; *11*(3), 3–4.

Clancy, H., and McBride, G. "The Autistic Process and Its Treatment." *Journal of Child Psychology and Psychiatry,* 1969, *10,* 233–244.

Copeland, J. *For the Love of Ann.* London: Arrow Books, 1973.

DeGangi, G. A. "Assessment of Sensory, Emotional, and Attentional Problems in Regulatory Disordered Infants: Part 1." *Infants and Young Children,* 1991, *3*(3), 1–8.

Des Lauriers, A. *The Experience of Reality in Childhood Schizophrenia.* Monograph Series on Schizophrenia, No. 6. New York: International Universities Press, 1962.

Des Lauriers, A., and Carlson, C. F. *Your Child is Asleep—Early Infantile Autism: Etiology, Treatment, and Parental Influence.* Homewood, Ill.: Dorsey, 1969.

Elson, M. *Self Psychology and Clinical Social Work.* New York: Norton, 1986.

Erikson, E. *Identity and the Life Cycle.* Psychological Issues, Vol. 1, No. 1. New York: International Universities Press, Inc. 1959.

Fahlberg, V. I. *A Child's Journey Through Placement.* Indianapolis: Perspectives Press, 1991.

Fanslow, C. A. "Touch and the Elderly." In K. E. Barnard and T. B. Brazelton (eds.), *Touch: The Foundation of Experience.* Madison, Conn.: International Universities Press, 1990.

Federici, R. S. "Commentary on Neuropsychological Evaluation of Post-Institutionalized Children." *The POST. The Parent Network for the Post-Institutionalized Child,* Fall/Winter 1995, 2–3.

Federici, R. S. "Institutional Autism." *The POST: The Parent Network for the Post-Institutionalized Child,* Nov./Dec. 1997, 1–4.

Field, T. "Infant Massage Therapy." In Field, T. (ed.), *Touch in Early Development.* Mahwah, N.J.: Erlbaum, 1995.

Finnie, N. *Handling the Young Cerebral-Palsied Child at Home.* New York: Dutton, 1975.

Fraiberg, S. *Every Child's Birthright: In Defense of Mothering.* New York: Basic Books, 1977a.

Fraiberg, S. *Insights from the Blind.* New York: Basic Books, 1977b.

Fuller, W. S. "Theraplay as a Treatment for Autism in a School-Based Day Treatment Setting." *Developments in Ambulatory Mental Health Care: Continuum: The Journal of the American Association for Partial Hospitalization,* 1995, *2*(2), 89–93.

Fuller, W. S., and Booth, P. B. "Touch with Abused Children." *The Theraplay Institute Newsletter,* Fall 1997, 4–7.

Gil, E. *The Healing Power of Play: Working with Abused Children.* New York: Guilford Press, 1991.

Gil, E. *Play in Family Therapy.* New York: Guilford Press, 1994.

Grabe, P. V. "The Therapy." In P. V. Grabe (ed.), *Adoption Resources for Mental Health Professionals.* New Brunswick: Transaction Publishers, 1990.

Grandin, T. *Thinking in Pictures and Other Reports from My Life with Autism.* New York: Vintage Books, 1995.

Grandin, T., and Scariano, M. *Emergence: Labeled Autistic.* Novato, Calif.: Arena, 1986.

Greenberg, J. R., and Mitchell, S. A. *Object Relations in Psychoanalytic Theory.* Cambridge, Mass.: Harvard University Press, 1983.

Greenspan, S. I. *Infancy and Early Childhood: The Practice of Clinical Assessment and Intervention with Emotional and Developmental Challenges.* Madison, Conn.: International Universities Press, Inc., 1992a.

Greenspan, S. I. "Reconsidering the Diagnosis and Treatment of Very Young Children with Autistic Spectrum or Pervasive Developmental Disorder." *Zero to Three,* 1992b, *13*(2), 1–9.

Greenspan, S. I., and Wieder, S. "An Integrated Developmental Approach to Interventions for Young Children with Severe Difficulties in Relating and Communicating." *Zero to Three,* 1997, *17*(5), 5–18.

Greenspan, S. I., and Wieder, S. *The Child with Special Needs: Encouraging Intellectual and Emotional Growth.* Reading, Mass.: A Merloyd Lawrence Book, Addison-Wesley, 1998.

Groze, V. K. *Successful Adoptive Families: A Longitudinal Study of Special Needs Adoption.* Westport, Conn.: Praeger, 1996.

Guerney, L. "Filial Therapy." In K. O'Connor and L. Braverman (eds.), *Play Therapy Theory and Practice: A Comparative Presentation*. New York: Wiley, 1997.

Gunnar, M. "The Impact of Orphanage Rearing on Emotional Behavior and Stress Hormone Production." Paper presented at the Parent Network for the Post-Institutionalized Child and Uniting Families Foundation Conference, Itasca, Ill., Feb. 1997.

Gunnar, M., Brodersen, L., Krueger, K., and Rigatuso, J. "Dampening of Adrenocortisol Responses During Infancy: Normative Changes and Individual Differences." *Child Development*, 1996, *67*, 877–889.

Haley, J. *Uncommon Therapy: The Psychiatric Techniques of Milton H. Erickson, M.D.* New York: Norton, 1973.

Haley, J. *Problem-Solving Therapy: New Strategies for Effective Family Therapy*. San Francisco: Jossey-Bass, 1976.

Harlow, H. F. "The Nature of Love." *American Psychologist*, 1958, *13*, 673–685.

Harlow, H. F., Harlow, M. K., and Hansen, E. W. "The Maternal Affectional System in Rhesus Monkeys." In H. L. Rheingold (ed.), *Maternal Behavior in Mammals*. New York: Wiley, 1963.

Haslip, G. R. "ADD/ADHD: Statement of Drug Enforcement Administration." Concluding Remarks at the Conference on Stimulant Use in the Treatment of ADHD, San Antonio, Texas, Dec. 10–12, 1996.

Hertsgaard, L., Gunnar, M., Erickson, M., and Nachmias, M. "Adrenocortical Responses to the Strange Situation in Infants with Disorganized/Disoriented Attachment Relationships." *Child Development*, 1995, *66*, 1,100–1,106.

Hopkins-Best, M. *Toddler Adoption: The Weaver's Craft*. Indianapolis, Ind.: Perspectives Press, 1997.

Hughes, D. *Facilitating Developmental Attachment: The Road to Emotional Recovery and Behavioral Change in Foster and Adopted Children*. Northvale, N.J.: Jason Aronson, 1997.

James, B. *Treating Traumatized Children: New Insights and Creative Interventions*. Lexington, Mass.: Lexington Books, 1989.

James, B. *Handbook for Treatment of Attachment-Trauma Problems in Children*. New York: Lexington Books, 1994.

Jarratt, C. J. *Helping Children Cope with Separation and Loss*. Boston: The Harvard Common Press, 1994.

Jernberg, A. M., "Combining Theraplay with Sensory Integration for Children with Sensory Motor Dysfunction." Paper presented at the Annual Meeting of the American Psychological Association, Los Angeles, Aug. 1981.

Jernberg, A. M. "Training Parents of Failure-to-Attach Children." In C. E. Schaefer and J. M. Briesmeister (eds.), *Handbook of Parent Training: Parents as Co-Therapists for Children's Behavior Problems.* New York: Wiley, 1989.

Jernberg, A. M. "Attachment Enhancing for Adopted Children." In P. V. Grabe (ed.), *Adoption Resources for Mental Health Professionals.* New Brunswick, N.J.: Transaction Publishers, 1990.

Jernberg, A., Hurst, T., and Lyman, C. *Here I Am,* 1969. 16 mm film. Available on videotape from the Theraplay Institute, 1137 Central Ave., Wilmette, Ill., 60091.

Jernberg, A., Hurst, T., and Lyman, C. *There He Goes,* 1975. 16 mm film. Available from the Theraplay Institute, 1137 Central Ave., Wilmette, Ill., 60091.

Karen, R. "Becoming Attached." *Atlantic Monthly,* Feb. 1990, pp. 35–70.

Karen, R. *Becoming Attached: Unfolding the Mystery of the Infant-Mother Bond and Its Impact on Later Life.* New York: Warner, 1994.

Kaufman, B. N. *Son-Rise.* New York: Harper & Row, 1975.

Klaus, M. H., Kennell, J. H., Plumb, N., and Zuehlke, S. "Human Maternal Behavior at the First Contact with Her Young." *Pediatrics,* 1970, *46,* 187–192.

Klein, M. *The Psychoanalysis of Children.* London: Hogarth Press, 1932.

Kohut, H. *The Analysis of the Self.* New York: International Universities Press, 1971.

Kohut, H. *The Restoration of the Self.* New York: International Universities Press, 1977.

Kohut, H. *How Does Analysis Cure?* A. Goldberg (ed.). Chicago: University of Chicago Press, 1984.

Koller, T. J. "Older Child Adoptions: A New Developmental Intervention Program." Paper presented at the Annual Meeting of the American Psychological Association, Los Angeles, Aug. 1981.

Koller, T. J. "Adolescent Theraplay." In K. J. O'Connor and C. E. Schaefer (eds.), *Handbook of Play Therapy,* Vol. 2: *Advances and Innovations.* New York: Wiley, 1994.

Koller, T. J., and Booth, P. "Fostering Attachment Through Family Theraplay." In K. J. O'Connor and L. M. Braverman (eds.), *Play Therapy Theory and Practice: A Comparative Presentation.* New York: Wiley, 1997.

Landreth, G. L., and Sweeney, D. S. "Child-Centered Play Therapy." In K. J. O'Connor and L. M. Braverman (eds.), *Play Therapy Theory and Practice: A Comparative Presentation.* New York: Wiley, 1997.

Lee, A. C. "Psychoanalytic Play Therapy." In K. J. O'Connor and L. M. Braverman (eds.), *Play Therapy Theory and Practice: A Comparative Presentation.* New York: Wiley, 1997.

Leslie, E., and Mignon, N. "Group Theraplay for Parents in a Public Housing Program." *The Theraplay Institute Newsletter,* Fall 1995, 6–7.

Lifton, B. J. *Journey of the Adopted Self.* New York: Basic Books, 1994.

Lovaas, O. I. *The Autistic Child: Language Development Through Behavior Modification.* New York: Irvington/Halsted/Wiley, 1977.

Main, M. "Parental Aversion to Infant-Initiated Contact Is Correlated with the Parent's Own Rejection During Childhood: The Effects of Experience on Signals of Security with Respect to Attachment." In K. E. Barnard and T. B. Brazelton (eds.), *Touch: the Foundation of Experience.* Madison, Conn.: International Universities Press, 1990.

Main, M., and Goldwin, R. "Predicting Rejection of Her Infant from Mother's Representation of Her Own Experience: Implications for the Abused-Abusing Intergenerational Cycle." *Journal of Child Abuse and Neglect,* 1984, *8*(2), 203–217.

Main, M., and Hesse, E. "Parents' Unresolved Traumatic Experiences Are Related to Infant Disorganized Attachment Status: Is Frightened and/or Frightening Parental Behavior the Linking Mechanism?" In M. T. Greenberg, D. Cicchetti, and E. M. Cummings (eds.), *Attachment in the Preschool Years: Theory, Research, and Intervention.* Chicago: University of Chicago Press, 1990.

Main, M., Kaplan, N., and Cassidy, J. "Security in Infancy, Childhood, and Adulthood: A Move to the Level of Representation." In I. Bretherton and E. Waters (eds.), *Growing Points in Attachment Theory and Research.* Monographs of the Society for Research in Child Development, *50* (1–2, Serial No. 209), 1985.

Marschak, M. "A Method for Evaluating Child-Parent Interaction Under Controlled Conditions." *Journal of Genetic Psychology,* 1960, *97,* 3–22.

Marschak, M. "Imitation and Participation in Normal and Disturbed Young Boys in Interaction with Their Parents." *Journal of Clinical Psychology,* 1967, *23*(4), 421–427.

Marschak, M., and Call, J. "Observing the Disturbed Child and His Parents: Class Demonstrations for Medical Students. *Journal of the American Academy of Child Psychiatry,* 1966, *5,* 686–692.

Martin, E. *Baby Games.* Philadelphia: Running Press, 1998.

Maurice, C. *Let Me Hear Your Voice: A Family's Triumph Over Autism.* New York: Knopf, 1993.

Maurice, C. (ed.), *Behavioral Intervention for Young Children with Autism.* Austin: Pro-Ed, 1996.

Middlemore, M. *The Nursing Couple.* London: Hamilton, 1941.

Minuchin, S. *Families and Family Therapy.* Cambridge, Mass.: Harvard University Press, 1974.

Montagu, A. *Touching: The Human Significance of the Skin.* New York: Columbia University Press, 1971.

Morin, V. *Messy Activities and More.* Chicago: Chicago Review Press, 1993.

Moustakas, C. *Psychotherapy with Children: The Living Relationship.* New York, Harper & Row, 1959.

Myrow, D. L. "In Touch with Theraplay." *The Theraplay Institute Newsletter,* No. 9, Fall 1997, 1–4.

Nachmias, M., Gunnar, M., Mangelsdorf, S., Parritz, R. H., and Buss, K. "Behavioral Inhibition and Stress Reactivity: The Moderating Role of Attachment Security." *Child Development,* 1996, *67,* 508–522.

Nichtern, S. *Helping the Retarded Child.* New York: Grosset & Dunlap, 1974.

Orlick, T. *The Cooperative Sports and Games Book.* New York: Pantheon Books, 1978.

Orlick, T. *The Second Cooperative Sports and Games Book.* New York: Pantheon Books, 1982.

Pederson, E., Faucher, T. A., and Eaton, W. W. "A New Perspective on the Effects of First-Grade Teachers on Children's Subsequent Adult Status." *Harvard Educational Review,* February 1978, *48*(1), 1–31.

Perry, B. D. "Medicine and Psychotherapy: Neurodevelopment and the Neurophysiology of Trauma." *The Advisor,* 1993, *6,* 1–18.

Perry, B. D. "The Effects of Traumatic Events on Children: Material for Parents." CIVITAS Child Trauma Programs, Department of Psychiatry and Behavioral Sciences, Baylor College of Medicine, Houston, Tx. [http://www.bcm.tmc.edu/civitas/publicat/effect.html]. 1994a.

Perry, B. D. "Neurobiological Sequelae of Childhood Trauma: PTSD in Children." In M. Murburg (ed.), *Catecholamines in PTSD.* Washington, D.C.: American Psychiatric Press, 1994b.

Porges, S. W. "The Infant's Sixth Sense: Awareness and Regulation of Bodily Processes." *Zero to Three, 14(2),* 1993, 12–16.

Prizant, B., and Wetherby, A. "Enhancing Communication: From Theory to Practice. In G. Dawson (ed.), *Autism: New Perspectives on Diagnosis, Nature, and Treatment.* New York: Guilford Press, 1989.

Racker, H. *Transference and Countertransference.* New York: International Universities Press, 1968.

Reitz, M., and Watson, K. W. *Adoption and the Family System.* New York: Guilford Press, 1992.

Rieff, M. "Theraplay with Developmentally-Disabled Infants and Toddlers." *The Theraplay Institute Newsletter,* Fall 1991, 4–5.

Richards, M.P.M. "The Development of Psychological Communication in the First Year of Life." In K. Connolly and J. Bruner (eds.), *The Growth of Competence.* New York: Academic Press, 1974.

Robertiello, R. C. *Hold Them Very Close, Then Let Them Go.* New York: Dial Press, 1975.

Robertson, J. *A Two-Year-Old Goes to Hospital.* London: Tavistock Child Development Research Unit, 1952. Film. Available from University Park, Penn.: Penn State Audiovisual Services.

Robertson, J., and Robertson, J. *Young Children in Brief Separation,* 1967–1973: "John, Aged Seventeen Months, for Nine Days in a Residential Nursery." 1969. Film series. Available from University Park, Penn.: Penn State Audiovisual Services.

Rosen, J. *Direct Analysis.* New York: Grune & Stratton, 1953.

Rosen, M. "Origin of Mind: The Secret Brain; Learning Before Birth." *Harper's,* Apr. 1978, 46–47.

Rubin, P. "Understanding Homeless Mothers: The Dynamics of Adjusting to a Long-Term Shelter." Unpublished doctoral dissertation, Illinois School of Professional Psychology, Chicago, 1996.

Rubin, P., and Tregay, J. *Play with Them—Theraplay Groups in the Classroom: A Technique for Professionals Who Work with Children.* Springfield, Ill.: Charles C. Thomas, 1989.

Sacks, O. "An Anthropologist on Mars." *New Yorker,* Dec. 27, 1993/ Jan. 3, 1994, 106–125.

Shahmoon-Shanok, R. "Giving Back Future's Promise: Working Resourcefully with Parents of Children Who Have Severe Disorders of Relating and Communicating." *Zero To Three,* 1997, *17*(5), 37–48.

Shapiro, J. P. (with Friedman, D., Meyer, M., and Loftus, M.). "The Biology of Soul Murder." *U.S. News and World Report,* Nov. 11, 1996, 71–73.

Spangler, G., and Grossman, K. E. "Biobehavioral Organization in Securely and Insecurely Attached Infants." *Child Development,* 1993, *64,* 1,439–1,450.

Spitz, R. A. "Hospitalism: An Inquiry into the Genesis of Psychiatric Conditions in Early Childhood." *Psychoanalytic Study of the Child,* 1945, *1,* 53–74.

Spitz, R. A. *Grief: A Peril in Infancy.* 1947. Film. Available from University Park, Penn.: Penn State Audiovisual Services.

Spitz, R. A. "The Effect of Personality Disturbances in the Mother on the Well-Being of Her Infant." In J. E. Anthony and T. Benedek (eds.), *Parenthood.* Boston: Little, Brown, 1970.

Sroufe, L. A. "A Developmental Perspective on Day Care." *Early Research Quarterly,* 1988, *3,* 283–291.

Stern, D. N. "The Goal and Structure of Mother-Infant Play." *Journal of the American Academy of Child Psychiatry,* 1974, *13*(3), 402–421.

Stern, D. N. "A Microanalysis of Mother-Infant Interaction." In E. Rexford, L. Sander, and T. Shapiro (eds.), *Infant Psychiatry.* New Haven, Conn.: Yale University Press, 1976.

Stern, D. N. *The Interpersonal World of the Infant: A View from Psycho-analysis and Developmental Psychology.* New York: Basic Books, 1985.

Stern, D. N. *The Motherhood Constellation: A Unified View of Parent-Infant Psychotherapy.* New York: Basic Books, 1995.

Stringer, L. *The Sense of Self: A Guide to How We Mature.* Philadelphia: Temple, 1971.

Talen, M. R., and Warfield, J. R. "Guidelines for Family Wellness Checkups in Primary Health Care Services." In L. VandeCreek, S. Knapp, and T. L. Jackson (eds.), *Innovations in Clinical Practice: A Source Book,* Vol.15. Sarasota, Fla.: Professional Resource Exchange, 1997.

Tepper, T. "A Message from Thais Tepper." *The POST: The Parent Network for the Post-Institutionalized Child,* Sept.-Oct. 1997, 1–2.

Thomas, A., and Chess, S. *Temperament and Development.* New York, Brunner/Mazel, 1977.

Thomas, J. "Traumatic Stress Disorder Presents as Hyperactivity and Disruptive Behavior: Case Presentations, Diagnoses, and Treatment." *Infant Mental Health Journal,* 1995, *16*(4), 306–317.

Tronick, E. Z. "Touch in Mother-Infant Interaction." In Field, T. (ed.), *Touch in Early Development.* Mahwah, N.J.: Erlbaum, 1995.

Tronick, E. Z., Als, H., Adamson, L., Wise, S., and Brazelton, T. B. "The Infant's Response to Entrapment Between Contradictory Messages in Face-to-Face Interaction." *Journal of the American Academy of Child Psychiatry,* 1978, *17*(1), 1–13.

van den Boom, D. C. "Do First Year Intervention Effects Endure?: Follow-Up During Toddlerhood of a Sample of Dutch Irritable Infants." *Child Development,* 1995, *66,* 1,798–1,816.

van der Kolk, B. A. "The Compulsion to Repeat the Trauma: Re-enactment, Re-victimization, and Masochism." *Psychiatric Clinics of North America,* 1989, *12*(2), 389–406.

Weiss, S. J. "Parental Touching: Correlates of a Child's Body Concept and Body Sentiment." In K. E. Barnard and T. B. Brazelton (eds.), *Touch: the Foundation of Experience.* Madison, Conn.: International Universities Press, 1990.

Weitzman, E. "The Hanen Program for Early Childhood Educators: Inservice Training for Child Care Providers on How to Facilitate Children's Social, Language, and Literacy Development." *Infant-Toddler Intervention: The Transdisciplinary Journal,* 1994, *4*(3), 173–202.

Wieder, S. "Creating Connections: Intervention Guidelines for Increasing Interaction with Children with Multisystem Developmental Disorder (MSDD)." *Zero To Three,* 1997, *17*(5), 19–27.

Wiedow, K. Personal communication, December, 1997.

Wilbarger, P. "Planning an Adequate 'Sensory Diet.' Application of Sensory Processing Theory During the First Year of Life." *Zero To Three,* 1984, *5*(1), 7–12.

Williams, D. *Autism—An Inside-Out Approach: An Innovative Look at the Mechanics of 'Autism' and Its Developmental 'Cousins.'* Bristol, Penn.: Kingsley, 1988.

Williams, D. *Nobody, Nowhere: The Extraordinary Autobiography of an Autistic.* New York: Random House, 1993.

Williamson, G. G., and Anzalone, M. "Sensory Integration: A Key Component of the Evaluation and Treatment of Young Children with Severe Difficulties in Relating and Communicating." *Zero to Three,* 1997, *17*(5), 29–36.

Winnicott, D. W. *Collected Papers: Through Paediatrics to Psychoanalysis.* London: Tavistock, 1958.

Winnicott, D. W. *The Maturational Processes and the Facilitating Environment: Studies in the Theory of Emotional Development.* London: Hogarth Press, 1965.

Winnicott, D. W. *Playing and Reality.* London: Tavistock, 1971.

Zuckerman, B., and Bresnahan, K. "Developmental and Behavioral Consequences of Prenatal Drug and Alcohol Exposure." In J. Blackman (ed.), *Development and Behavior: The Very Young Child,* 1991, *38*(6), 1,387–1,406. Monograph series published by Pediatric Clinics of North America.

Publications About Theraplay and the Marschak Interaction Method (MIM)

The following is a comprehensive list of publications about Theraplay and the MIM that were available at the time of printing. (Note that *The Theraplay Institute Newsletter* is published twice a year by the Theraplay Institute in Chicago; the *Theraplay Journal* is published twice a year by U. Franke in Heidelberg, Germany.)

Adamitis, C. "Theraplay with the Elderly: A Case Study." *The Theraplay Institute Newsletter,* Spring 1982, 1–3.

Adamitis, C. "Theraplay with an Older Adult: Marge." *The Theraplay Institute Newsletter,* Winter 1985–86, 2–4.

Allert, A. "Temperament and Early Parent-Child Interactions: Changes from Infancy to Toddlerhood." Unpublished doctoral dissertation, Illinois Institute of Technology, 1982.

Ammen, S., and York, L. *The Many Measures of Attachment.* Unpublished manuscript, California School for Professional Psychology-Fresno, 1994.

Azoulay, D., Ali, J., Lawrence, H., and Munns, E. "Strengthening the Bond Between a Mother and Her Child: A Case Study of Family Therapy." *Playground,* Spring 1994, 5–11.

Bekker, Y. C. "Family Theraplay for Toddlers: An Educational Psychological Perspective." Unpublished masters thesis, University of Pretoria, South Africa, 1993.

Bernt, C. "Theraplay as Intervention for Failure-to-Thrive Infants and Their Parents." Unpublished doctoral dissertation, The Chicago School of Professional Psychology, 1990.

Bernt, C. "Theraplay with Failure-to-Thrive Children and Their Mothers." *The Theraplay Institute Newsletter,* Fall 1992, 1–3.

Bligh, S. B. "Theraplay: Facilitating Communication in Language-Delayed Children." In J. Andrews and M. Burns (eds.), *Selected Papers in Language and Phonology,* Vol. 2: *Language Remediation.* Evanston, Ill.:

Institute for Continuing Education, 1977.

Booth, P. B., and Koller, T. J. "Training Parents of Failure-to-Attach Children." In J. M. Briesmeister and C. E. Schaefer (eds.), *Handbook of Parent Training: Parents as Co-Therapists for Children's Behavior Problems* (2nd ed.). New York: Wiley, 1998.

Bostrom, J. "A Preschool Curriculum Based on Theraplay." *The Theraplay Institute Newsletter,* Fall 1995a, 3–4.

Bostrom, J. "Fostering Attachment in Post-Institutionalized Adopted Children Using Group Theraplay." *The Theraplay Institute Newsletter,* Fall 1995b, 7–8.

Breuer, J., and Munns, E. "Theraplay with a Toddler and His Parents." *Playground,* Spring 1994, 7–8.

Bundy-Myrow, S. "Group Theraplay for Children with PDD." *The Theraplay Institute Newsletter,* Spring 1994, 9.

Burger, U. "Daniel hat sein eigenes Tempo: Theraplay bei einem entwicklungsverzögerten Kind ["Daniel Has His Own Tempo: Theraplay with a Developmentally Delayed Child"]. *Theraplay Journal,* 1997, *14,* 14–20.

Call, J., and Marschak, M. "Styles and Games in Infancy." *Journal of the American Academy of Child Psychiatry,* 1966, *5*(2), 193–210.

Chambers, C. L. "Group Theraplay with Children Impacted by HIV." *The Theraplay Institute Newsletter,* Fall 1995, 5–6.

Clark, P. A. "The Theraplay Preschool Assessment and Treatment Manual: Preparing Mental Health Professionals to Use Structured Play to Remediate Experience-Derived Relationship Disturbances in Three-to Five-Year-Old Children and Their Caregivers." Unpublished doctoral dissertation, Adler School of Professional Psychology, 1997.

Coetzee, A. M. "'Theraplay' Founded Within the Orthopedagogical Context." Unpublished master's thesis, University of Pretoria, South Africa, 1987.

Crume, J. "Theraplay: Skills for the Timid Adoptive Parent to Deal with Her Very Active Three Year Old." *The Theraplay Institute Newsletter,* Fall 1996, 2–4.

De Wet, W. "Theraplay with the Deaf Child." Unpublished doctoral dissertation, University of Pretoria, South Africa, 1993.

Des Lauriers, A. "Play, Symbols, and the Development of Language." In M. Rutter and E. Schopler (eds.), *Autism.* New York: Plenum, 1978.

Dunn, N. "The Usability of Theraplay as a Technique for Therapy with Children with Enuresis." Unpublished masters thesis, University of Pretoria, South Africa, 1987.

Finnell, N. "Adoption and Attachment." *The Theraplay Institute Newsletter,* Fall 1996, 1–2.

Fitzka, K. "Ich falle aufwärts: Theraplay am Anfang" ["My Mistakes Help Me Move Forward: Theraplay in the Beginning."] *Theraplay Journal,* 1995, *11,* 26–27.

Fitzka, K. "Theraplay mit einem sexuell missbrauchten Mädchen" ["Theraplay with a Sexually Abused Girl"]. *Theraplay Journal,* 1997, *14,* 4–10.

Franke, U. "Theraplay: eine direktive kommunikative Spieltherapie" ["Theraplay: A Directive Communicative Playtherapy"]. *Praxis der Kinderpsychologie und Kinderpsychiatrie [Practice of Child Psychology and Child Psychiatry],* 1990a, *39,* 12–17.

Franke, U. "Theraplay und seine Wirkung auf das Kommunikationsverhalten" ["Theraplay and Its Effect on Communication"]. In G. Grohnfeldt (Hrsg.), *Handbuch der Sprachtherapie [Handbook of Speech Therapy],* Band 2. Berlin: Edition Marhold, 1990b.

Franke, U. "Theraplay." *Gesellschaft zur Förderung des Festhaltens (Hsg): I. Internationaler Kongress "Festhalten" in Regensburg [Society for the Advancement of Holding Therapy: The First International Congress of Holding Therapy],* 1991a, 427–440.

Franke, U. "Die Theraplay Ko-Therapeutin" ["The Theraplay Co-Therapist"]. *Theraplay Journal,* 1991b, *3,* 15–17.

Franke, U. "Die sensorische Wahrnehmung" ["Sensory Perception"]. *Theraplay Journal,* 1991c, *6,* 4–7.

Franke, U. "Aufmerksamkeit" ["Attention: An Aim in Theraplay Sessions"]. *Theraplay Journal,* 1992a, *6,* 20–25.

Franke, U. "Naschraten" ["Guessing the Taste"]. *Theraplay Journal,* 1992b, *6,* 8–14.

Franke, U. "Warum wirkt Theraplay?" ["Why Does Theraplay Work?"] *Theraplay Journal,* 1992c, *6,* 14–15.

Franke, U. "Theraplay: eine Hilfe für schwierige Kinder und ihre Eltern" ["Theraplay: Help for Difficult Children and Their Parents"]. In W. Leixnering und F. Wurst (Hrsg.), *Krise als Chance.* Wien: Tagungsband, 1993a.

Franke, U. "Unterschiede zwischen Theraplay in den USA und in Deutschland" ["Differences between Theraplay in the United States and Germany"]. *Theraplay Journal,* 1993b, *7,* 4–8.

Franke, U. "Theraplay bei spracherwerbsgestörten Kindern" ["Theraplay with Language Disordered Children"]. In H.Grimm, und F. Weinert (Hrsg.), *Intervention bei sprachgestörten Kindern [Intervention with Language Disordered Children].* Stuttgart: G. Fischer, 1994a.

Franke, U. "Zehn Grundannahmen und die therapeutischen Schlussfolgerungen" ["Ten Basic Hypotheses About Theraplay and Their Therapeutic Conclusions"]. *Theraplay Journal*, 1994b, *8*, 6–15.

Franke, U. "Ergotherapie und Theraplay" ["Occupational Therapy and Theraplay"]. *Theraplay Journal*, 1995, *11*, 16–21.

Franke, U. "Alexander der grosse Schweiger: Theraplay bei Mutismus" ["Alexander the Great Mute: Theraplay with Mutism"]. *L.O.G.O.S. interdisziplinär*, 1996a, *4*(1), 20–29.

Franke, U. "Magdalena, ein nichtsprechendes wahrnehmungsgestörtes Kind" ["Magdalena, a Non-Speaking Perceptually Handicapped Child"]. *Theraplay Journal*, 1996b, *12*, 4–15.

Franke, U. "Theraplay Handlungsanalysen" ["Micro-Analysis of Some Procedures in Theraplay Sessions"]. *Theraplay Journal*, 1998a, *15*, 20–24.

Franke, U. "Theraplay: Welche Rolle spielen die Eltern?" ["Theraplay: What Role Do Parents Play?"]. *Theraplay Journal*, 1998b, *15*, 4–13.

Fuller, W. S. "Theraplay as a Treatment for Autism in a School-Based Day Treatment Setting." *Continuum, the Journal of the American Association for Partial Hospitalization*, 1995, *2*(2), 89–93.

Fuller, W. S., and Booth, P. "Touch with Abused Children." *The Theraplay Institute Newsletter*, No. 9, Fall 1997, 4–7.

Fux, G. "Die Anwendungsmöglichkeiten und die Grenzen des Theraplay Konzeptes in der Logopädie" ["The Possibilities and Limits of Using Theraplay for Speech-Language Pathology"]. Unpublished thesis for the Heilpädagogiches Seminar, Institut Freiburg, 1991.

Golden, B. R. "How Theraplay Facilitates Healthy Narcissism." *Journal of Child and Adolescent Psychotherapy*, 1986, *3*(2), 99–104.

González, C. M. "La Actividad Lúdica Como Instrumento de Intervención en el Autismo Infantil. La Técnica Theraplay" ["Active Play as an Instrument of Intervention with an Autistic Child: The Theraplay Technique"]. *Revista de Educación Especial [Review of Special Education]* Salamanca, Spain, 1988, *3* (July–Dec.).

Händel-Rüdinger, M. "Isabell." *Theraplay Journal*, 1992, *5*, 12–13.

Händel-Rüdinger, M. "Verena: Theraplay mit einem Kleinkind" ["Verena: Theraplay with a Young Child"]. *Theraplay Journal*, 1995, *11*, 22–25.

Händel-Rüdinger, M., und Franke, U. "Was lernt Jens wie in der Therapie?" ["What Did Jens Learn in Therapy?"]. *L.O.G.O.S. interdisziplinär*, 1993, *1*(2), 97–101.

Hölzel, L. "Entwicklung eines Auswertungsverfahrens im Rahmen der Diagnostik von Eltern-Kind-Interaktionen" ["Development of a Method

of Analysis for the Assessment of Parent-Child Interactions"].
Unpublished master's thesis, Technische Universität, Berlin, 1993.

Imperiale, N. "Professor Preaches the Power of Positive Discipline." *Chicago Tribune*, May 3, 1994, Tempo, p. 3.

Jernberg, A. M. "Psychosomatic Similarities in Adoptive Mothers and Their Infants." *Human Development Bulletin*, Paper presented at 9th Annual Symposium, Chicago, March 1, 1958.

Jernberg, A. M. "Theraplay Technique." In C. E. Schaefer (ed.), *Therapeutic Use of Child's Play*. New York: Jason Aronson, 1976.

Jernberg, A. M. *Theraplay: A New Treatment Using Structured Play for Problem Children and Their Families*. San Francisco: Jossey-Bass, 1979.

Jernberg, A. M. "Combining Theraplay with Sensory Integration for Children with Sensory Motor Dysfunction." Paper presented at the Annual Meeting of the American Psychological Association, Los Angeles, Aug. 1981.

Jernberg, A. M. "Theraplay: History and Method." In E. Nickerson and K. O'Laughlin (eds.), *Helping Through Action-Oriented Therapies*. Amherst, Mass.: Human Resource Development Press, 1982a.

Jernberg, A. M. "Theraplay: The Initial Stages of Treatment." *Association for Play Therapy Newsletter*, 1982b, *1*(1), 3–5.

Jernberg, A. M. "Theraplay: The Nursery Revisited." In L. E. Abt and I. R. Stuart, (eds.), *The Newer Therapies: A Sourcebook*. New York: Van Nostrand Reinhold, 1982c.

Jernberg, A. M. "Therapeutic Use of Sensory-Motor Play." In C. E. Schaefer, and K. J. O'Connor, (eds.), *Handbook of Play Therapy*. New York: John Wiley & Sons, Inc., 1983.

Jernberg, A. M. "Theraplay: Child Therapy for Attachment Fostering. *Psychotherapy*, 1984, *21*(1), 39–47.

Jernberg, A. M. "The Theraplay Technique for Children." In P. A. Keller and L. G. Ritt (eds.), *Innovations in Clinical Practice: A Source Book*, Vol. 5. Sarasota, Fla.: Professional Resource Exchange, 1986.

Jernberg, A. M. "Helping Foster or Late-Adopted Children to Make It in the Classroom." *Stepping Stones*. Illinois Council on Adopted Children, Inc., July/August 1987a, 9–11.

Jernberg, A. M. "Theraplay für das aggressive Kind" ["Theraplay for the Aggressive Child"]. *Forum des Zentralverbandes für Logopädie [Forum of the Central Union for Speech and Language Pathology]*, 1987b, *4*, 1–3.

Jernberg, A. M. "Untersuchung und Therapie der pränatalen Mutter-Kind-Beziehung" ["Evaluation and Treatment of the Mother-Child Relationship"]. (U. Franke, trans.) In B. G. Fedor-Freybergh (ed.), *Pränatale und Perinatale Psychologie und Medizin: Begegnung mit dem Ungeborenen [Prenatal and Perinatal Psychology and Medicine: Encounter with the Unborn]*. Sweden: Saphir, 1987c.

Jernberg, A. M. *Theraplay: eine direktive Spieltherapie.* Deutsche Übersetzung und bearbeitung nach der amerikanischen 1. Auflage von U. Franke [Theraplay: A Directive Play Therapy. Translated and revised from the first American edition by U. Franke]. Stuttgart: G. Fischer, 1987d.

Jernberg, A. M. "Promoting Prenatal and Perinatal Mother-Child Bonding: A Psychotherapeutic Assessment of Parental Attitudes." In P. G. Fedor-Freybergh and M.L.V. Vogel, (eds.), *Prenatal and Perinatal Psychology and Medicine: Encounter with the Unborn.*. Park Ridge, N.J.: Parthenon Publishing Group, 1988a.

Jernberg, A. M. "The Theraplay Approach to the Self-Contained Patient." In E. M. Stern (ed.), *Psychotherapy and the Self-Contained Patient.* Special Issue of *The Psychotherapy Patient,* 1988b, 4(3/4), 85–93.

Jernberg, A. M. "Theraplay als eine Ergänzung der sensomotorischen Integrationstherapie" ["Theraplay as a Compliment to Sensory Integration Therapy"]. *Praxis Ergotherapie [Sensory Integration Practice],* 1988c, *1,* 292–304.

Jernberg, A. M. "Theraplay for the Elderly Tyrant." *Clinical Gerontologist,* 1988d, 8(1), 76–79.

Jernberg, A. M. "Training Parents of Failure-to-Attach Children." In C. E. Schaefer and J. M. Briesmeister (eds.), *Handbook of Parent Training: Parents as Co-Therapists for Children's Behavior Problems.* New York: Wiley, 1989.

Jernberg, A. M. "Attachment Enhancing for Adopted Children." In P. V. Grabe (ed.), *Adoption Resources for Mental Health Professionals.* New Brunswick: Transaction Publishers, 1990a.

Jernberg, A. M. "Bindungsförderung für adoptierte Kinder" ["Attachment Enhancing for Adopted Children"]. *Kindeswohl: Zeitschrift fur Pflegekinder-und Adoptionswesen [Journal for Foster Children and the Practice of Adoption],* 1990b, *4,* 25–28.

Jernberg, A. M. "Helping Children Cope with War." *The Theraplay Institute Newsletter,* Winter 1990–1991, 4–5.

Jernberg, A. M. "Assessing Parent-Child Interactions with the Marshak Interaction Method (MIM)." In C. E. Schaefer, K. Gitlin, and A. Sandgrund (eds.), *Play Diagnosis and Assessment.* New York: John Wiley & Sons, 1991.

Jernberg, A. M. "The Marital Marschak Interaction Method (MMIM): A Technique for Structured Observation and Clinical Intervention in Helping Troubled Marriages." *The Theraplay Institute Newsletter,* Winter 1992a, 1–2.

Jernberg, A. M. "The Older Sibling." *The Theraplay Institute Newsletter,* Fall 1992b, 4–5.

Jernberg, A. M. "The Prenatal Marschak Interaction Method (PMIM): A Tool for Bonding." *The Theraplay Institute Newsletter,* Winter 1992c, 4–5.

Jernberg, A. M. "Attachment Formation." In C. E. Schaefer (ed.), *The Therapeutic Powers of Play.* Northvale, N.J.: Jason Aronson, Inc., 1993.

Jernberg, A. M. "Theraplay für das aggressive Kind" ["Theraplay for the Aggressive Child"]. In U. Franke (ed.), *Therapie aggressiver und hyperaktiver Kinder [Therapy for Aggressive and Hyperactive Children]* (2nd ed.). Stuttgart: Gustav Fischer Verlag, 1995.

Jernberg, A. M., Allert, A., Koller, T. J., and Booth, P. *Reciprocity in Parent-Infant Relationships.* Chicago, Ill.: The Theraplay Institute, 1983.

Jernberg, A. M., and Booth, P. B. "Theraplay and the James Method of Treatment for Traumatized Children." *The Theraplay Institute Newsletter,* Winter 1990–1991, 1.

Jernberg, A. M., Booth, P., Koller, T. J., and Allert, A. *Preschoolers and School Age Children in Interaction with Their Parents: Manual for Using the Marschak Interaction Method (MIM).* Chicago, Ill.: The Theraplay Institute, 1982.

Jernberg, A. M., and Des Lauriers, A. "Some Contributions of Three Pre-School Children to Behavior Changes in Their Mothers." Paper presented to the Research Seminar, Psychosomatic and Psychiatric Institute, Michael Reese Hospital, Chicago, June 1962.

Jernberg, A. M., Hurst, T., and Lyman, C. *Here I Am,* 1969. 16 mm film. Available on videotape from the Theraplay Institute, 1137 Central Ave., Wilmette, Ill., 60091.

Jernberg, A. M., Hurst, T., and Lyman, C. *There He Goes,* 1975. 16 mm film. Available on videotape from the Theraplay Institute, 1137 Central Ave., Wilmette, Ill., 60091.

Jernberg, A. M., and Jernberg, E. "Family Theraplay for the Family Tyrant." In T. Kottman and C. E. Schaefer (eds.), *Play Therapy in Action: A Casebook for Practitioners.* Northvale, N.J.: Jason Aronson, Inc., 1993.

Jernberg, A. M., Thomas, E., and Wickersham, M. *Mothers' Behaviors and Attitudes Toward Their Unborn Infants.* Chicago: The Theraplay Institute, 1985.

Koller, T. J. "The Relationship of Infant Temperament to Mother-Infant and Father-Infant Interaction." Unpublished doctoral dissertation, Illinois Institute of Technology, Chicago, 1980.

Koller, T. J. "New Family Bonding." *The Theraplay Institute Newsletter,* Summer 1981, 3–6.

Koller, T. J. "Stealing in the Adopted Child in School." *Stepping Stones.* Illinois Council on Adopted Children, Inc., July/August 1987, 11–15.

Koller, T. J. "Adolescent Theraplay." In K. J. O'Connor and C. E. Schaefer (eds.), *Handbook of Play Therapy,* Vol. 2: *Advances and Innovations.* New York: Wiley, 1994.

Koller, T. J., and Booth, P. "Fostering Attachment through Family Theraplay." In K. J. O'Connor and L. M. Braverman (eds.), *Play Therapy: Theory and Practice.* New York: Wiley, 1997.

Kupperman, P., Bligh, S., and Goodban, M. "Activating Articulation Skills through Theraplay." *Journal of Speech and Hearing Disorders,* 1980a, *45,* 540–545.

Kupperman, P., Bligh, S., and Goodban, M. "Use of Theraplay in Speech Impairment." *Journal of Speech and Hearing Disorders,* 1980b, *45,* 545–548.

Leslie, E., and Mignon, N. "Group Theraplay for Parents in a Public Housing Program." *The Theraplay Institute Newsletter,* Fall 1995, 6–7.

Lindaman, S. "Theraplay for Adopted Children." *Adoption Therapist,* 1996, *7*(1), 5–8.

Lindaman, S., and Haldeman, D. "Geriatric Theraplay." In C. E. Schaefer and K. J. O'Connor (eds.), *Handbook of Play Therapy,* Vol. 2: *Advances and Innovations.* New York: Wiley, 1994.

Lleras, B. "Veränderungen bei Müttern hinter der Scheibe" ["Changes of Mothers Behind the Two-Way Mirror"]. *Theraplay Journal,* 1992, *5,* 22–23.

Lovejoy, T. "Theraplay in a Preschool Mental Health Program." *The Theraplay Institute Newsletter,* Fall 1995, 8.

McKay, J. M., Pickens, J., and Stewart, A. "Inventoried and Observed Stress in Parent-Child Interactions." *Current Psychology: Developmental, Learning, Personality, Social,* 1996, *15*(3), 223–234.

Marschak, M. *A Comparison of Polish and Italian Fathers in Interaction with Their Pre-school Sons.* New Haven: Yale Child Study Center, 1960a.

Marschak, M. "A Method for Evaluating Child-Parent Interactions under Controlled Conditions." *The Journal of Genetic Psychology,* 1960b, *97,* 3–22.

Marschak, M. "Child-Parent Tie in Present Day Japan." *Child and Family,* 1967a, *6*(Summer/Fall), 72–79, 80–88.

Marschak, M. "Imitation and Participation in Normal and Disturbed Young Boys in Interaction with Their Parents." *Journal of Clinical Psychology,* 1967b, *23*(4), 421–427.

Marschak, M. *Nursery School Child/Mother Interaction,* 1967c. Film. Available from New York University Film Library, 26 Washington Place, New York, N.Y., 10003.

Marschak, M. "The Obstinate Checklist." *Journal of the American Academy of Child Psychiatry,* 1969, *8,* 456–464.

Marschak, M. *Two Climates of Israel,* 1975. Film. Available from New York University Film Library, 26 Washington Place, New York, N.Y., 10003.

Marschak, M. *Parent-Child Interaction and Youth Rebellion.* New York: Gardner Press, 1980.

Marschak, M., and Call, J. D. "Exposure to Child-Parent Interaction as a Teaching Device." *Journal of Medical Education,* 1964, *39,* 879–880.

Marschak, M., and Call, J. D. "A Comparison of Normal and Disturbed Three-Year Old Boys in Interaction with Their Parents." *American Journal of Orthopsychiatry,* 1965, *35,* 247–249.

Marschak, M., and Call, J. D. "Observing the Disturbed Child and His Parents: Class Demonstrations for Medical Students." *Journal of the American Academy of Child Psychiatry,* 1966, *5,* 686–692.

Martin, D. "Applications of Theraplay in Early Childhood Classrooms." *The Theraplay Institute Newsletter,* Fall 1995, 4.

Miller, P. "Therapeutic Touch with Sensory Defensive Children." *The Theraplay Institute Newsletter,* No. 9, Fall 1997, 7–9.

Morgan, C. E. "Theraplay: An Evaluation of the Effect of Short-Term Structured Play on Self-Confidence, Self-Esteem, Trust, and Self-Control." Unpublished Research, The York Centre for Children, Youth and Families, Richmond Hill, Ontario, Canada, 1989.

Morin, V. *Messy Activities and More.* Chicago: Chicago Review Press, 1993.

Moser, K. "Gruppentheraplay in einem Integrationskindergarten" ["Group Theraplay in an Integrated Kindergarten"]. *Theraplay Journal,* 1993, *7,* 15.

Moser, K. "Gruppentheraplay mit erwachsenen geistig Behinderten?" ["Group Theraplay with Mentally Retarded Adults?"]. *Theraplay Journal,* 1997, *14,* 26–28.

Moyer, M. "Group Theraplay in a Special Needs Day School." *The Theraplay Institute Newsletter,* Fall 1995, 8–9.

Munns, E. "Theraplay." *Playground,* Spring 1994, 3–4.

Munns, E. "Theraplay at Blue Hills Play Therapy Services." *The Theraplay Institute Newsletter,* Fall 1995, 7.

Munns, E. "Theraplay." In B. Bedard-Bidwell, and M. Sippel (eds.), *Hand in Hand.* London, Ontario: Thames River Publishing, 1997.

Munns, E., Jenkins, D., and Berger, L. "Theraplay and the Reduction of Aggression." Unpublished research, Blue Hills Child and Family Services, Aurora, Ontario, Canada, 1997.

Myrow, D. L. "In Touch with Theraplay." *The Theraplay Institute Newsletter* No. 9, Fall 1997, 1–4.

O'Connor, K. J. *The Play Therapy Primer: An Integration of Theories and Techniques.* New York: Wiley, 1991.

O'Connor, K. J., and Ammen, S. *Play Therapy Treatment Planning and Interventions: The Ecosystemic Model and Workbook.* San Diego, Calif.: Academic Press, 1997.

Ogintz, E. "Kid Burnout: Work Stress Trickles Down to the Playground." *Chicago Tribune,* Apr. 6, 1989, Tempo, p. 1.

Preto, V. M., and Munns, E. "Nurturing the Aggressive Child, Theraplay: A Case Study." *Playground,* Spring 1994, 9–10.

Putka, G. "Tense Tots: Some Schools Press So Hard Kids Become Stressed and Fearful—Flashcards, Computers, Tests All Day Long Take a Toll on Fast-Track Students—Burning Out by the Age of 10." *Wall Street Journal,* July 6, 1988, p. 1.

Rantala, K. "Terapeuttin leikka sairaan lapsen hoitona—kokemuksia Theraplay-Työskentelytavasta" ["Therapeutic Play as Treatment for a Sick Child: Using the Theraplay Method"]. In E. Saarinen (ed.), *Sairaan ja vammaisen lapsen hyvä elämä [The Good Life of the Sick and Disabled Child].* Helsinki: Oy Edita Ab, 1998.

Reeves, K. "Achieving Therapeutic Goals Through Group Theraplay—and Having Fun with It!" *The Theraplay Institute Newsletter,* Fall 1990, 2–3.

Reeves, K., and Munns, E. "Group Theraplay in a Playschool Setting." *Playground,* Spring 1994, 12–13.

Rieff, M. L. "Theraplay with Developmentally-Disabled Infants and Toddlers." *The Theraplay Institute Newsletter,* Fall 1991, 4–5.

Rieff, M. L. "Revisiting the Theraplay Dimensions with Post-Institutionalized Children." *The Theraplay Institute Newsletter,* Fall 1996, 4–5.

Rieff, M. L., and Booth, P. "Theraplay for Children with PDD/Autism." *The Theraplay Institute Newsletter,* Spring 1994, 1–7.

Ritterfeld, U. "Evaluation einer psychotherapeutischen Interventionsmethode, Theraplay, bei sprachgestörten Vorschulkindern" ["Evaluation of a Psychotherapeutic Intervention Method, Theraplay, with Language Disordered Preschool Children"]. Unpublished study qualifying for the Diplomat in Psychology, Universität Heidelberg, 1989.

Ritterfeld, U. "Theraplay auf dem Prüfstand. Bewertung des Therapieerfolgs am Beispiel sprachauffälliger Vorschulkinder" ["Putting Theraplay to the Test: Evaluation of Therapeutic Outcome with Language Delayed Preschool Children"]. *Theraplay Journal,* 1990, *2,* 22–25.

Ritterfeld, U. "Das Rätsel Paul. Möglichkeiten einer systematischen Beobachtung der Eltern-Kind-Interaktion" ["Paul, the Problem: Possibilities of a Systematic Observation of Parent-Child Interaction"]. *L.O.G.O.S. interdisziplinär,* 1993, *1*(1), 18–25.

Ritterfeld, U. "Welchen Stellenwert kann Theraplay in der logopädischen Behandlung haben?" [What Importance Can Theraplay Have in Language Therapy?"]. In H. Grimm und F. Weinert (Hrsg.), *Intervention bei sprachgestörten Kindern [Intervention with Language Disordered Children].* Stuttgart: Fischer, 1994.

Ritterfeld, U., and Franke, U. *Die Heidelberger Marschak-Interaktionsmethode [The Heidelberg Marschak Interaction Method].* Stuttgart: G. Fischer, 1994.

Robbins, J. "Nurturing Play with Parents." *Nurturing Today,* Summer 1987, 6.

Rotenberk, L. "Touching." *Chicago Sun-Times,* Aug. 17, 1986, Living Section, p. 8–9.

Rubin, P. "Speech Theraplay in the Public Schools: Opening the Doors to Communication." *The Theraplay Institute Newsletter,* Summer/Fall 1982, 3–7.

Rubin, P. "Theraplay: Schlüssel zur Kommunikation [Theraplay: Key to Communication]." *Theraplay Journal,* 1990, *2,* 3–8.

Rubin, P. "Multi-Family Theraplay in a Shelter for the Homeless." *The Theraplay Institute Newletter,* Fall 1995, 5.

Rubin, P. "Understanding Homeless Mothers: The Dynamics of Adjusting to a Long-Term Shelter." Unpublished doctoral dissertation, Illinois School of Professional Psychology, Chicago, 1996.

Rubin, P. B., and Tregay, J. *Play with Them—Theraplay Groups in the Classroom: A Technique for Professionals Who Work with Children.* Springfield, Ill.: Thomas, 1989.

Rubin, P., and Tregay J. "Die fünf Theraplay-Elemente [The Five Theraplay Dimensions]." *Theraplay Journal,* 1990, *1,* 4–9.

Safarjan, P. T. "Use of the Marschak Interaction Method (MIM) in Forensic Evaluation." *The Theraplay Institute Newsletter,* Winter 1992, 3.

Searcy, K. "The Mercy Aproach to Theraplay." In M. Burns and J. Andrews (eds.), *Selected Papers: Current Trends in the Treatment of Language Disorders.* Evanston, Ill.: Institute for Continuing Education, 1981.

Simons, L. *Interplay Groups: Group Sessions to Develop Social Interaction Skills.* Bellevue, Wash.: Family Interplay Associates, 1995.

Sjölund, M. "Framgäng för ny form av lekterapi I Chicagos slum" (Success of a New Form of Play Therapy in Chicago's Slums). *Psyklognytt [Psychology]* (Stockholm), 1980, 28.

Talen, M. R. "Community-Based Primary Health Care: A New Role for Theraplay." *The Theraplay Institute Newsletter,* Fall 1995, 1–3.

Talen, M. R., and Warfield, J. "Guidelines for Family Wellness Checkups in Primary Health Care Services." In L. VandeCreek, S. Knapp, and T. L. Jackson, (eds.), *Innovations in Clinical Practice: A Source Book,* Vol.15. Sarasota, Fla.: Professional Resource Exchange, 1997.

Vorster, C. M. "The Parent's Experience of Theraplay." Unpublished masters thesis, University of Pretoria, South Africa, 1994.

Wilson, P. "Review of *Here I Am.*" *Hospital and Community Psychiatry,* 1973, *24,* 347–348.

Winkler, B. "Bedeutung der Nicht-Direktivität und der Direktivität in der nicht-direktiven und direktiven Spieltherapie" ["The Significance of Non-Directive and Directive in Non-Directive and Directive Play Therapy"]. Unpublished master's thesis, Würzburg, 1994.

Witten [Whitten (sic)], M. R. "Assessment of Attachment in Traumatized Children." In B. James (ed.), *Handbook for Treatment of Attachment-Trauma Problems in Children.* New York: Lexington Books, 1994.

Index